HTML5 and C Masterclass

In-depth Web Design Training with Geolocation, the HTML5 Canvas, 2D and 3D CSS Transformations, Flexbox, CSS Grid, and More

Robin Nixon

www.bpbonline.com

Group Product Manager: Marianne Conor
Publishing Product Manager: Eva Brawn
Senior Editor: Connell
Content Development Editor: Melissa Monroe
Technical Editor: Anne Stokes
Copy Editor: Joe Austin
Language Support Editor: Justin Baldwin
Project Coordinator: Tyler Horan
Proofreader: Khloe Styles
Indexer: V. Krishnamurthy
Production Designer: Malcolm D'Souza
Marketing Coordinator: Kristen Kramer

First published: 2023

Published by BPB Online
WeWork, 119 Marylebone Road
London NW1 5PU

UK | UAE | INDIA | SINGAPORE

ISBN 978-93-55511-218

www.bpbonline.com

Dedicated to

My family and extended family for their continuing support, and all my loyal readers who continuously encourage me to keep on writing more books about web development.

About the Author

- **Robin Nixon** is a web developer and educator who has been writing software since the 1980s. He has previously been a computer magazine editor, director of several software development companies and more recently author of a variety of top-selling books on computers and technology published by O'reilly. Robin's areas of interest are front-end development with HTML, CSS and JavaScript, and back-end management with PHP and MySQL. He is also a keen researcher into machine intelligence.

Acknowledgement

○ To all the hard working people at BPB who have toiled through numerous revisions, edits and technical reviews to ensure this book is as comprehensive, accurate and up-to-date as is possible.

Preface

This book is intended for anyone with an interest in enhancing their web design knowledge and skills, whether as a hobbyist, an existing developer, or with the intention of building a web design career.

The tools available to web developers are constantly evolving due to the demands of bigger, better and more powerful and interactive web properties from existing developers. In the past most enhancements had to be created using JavaScript code, but nowadays there are so many new technologies ready-built into web browsers, that web designers can make really fantastic pages and sites.

The only problem is that you need to know what's available, and how to use it. That's where this book comes in, because it brings you right up-to-date with all the latest enhancements to both HTML5 and CSS3, and explains and teaches you how to use them in simple, easy-to-digest language.

This book is packed with working examples and figures illustrating what is being taught at every step of the way. Plus each chapter begins with an outline explaining what you are about to learn, and sets an objective that you should be able to complete by the time you finish the chapter.

Once you have worked through this book, you will have truly mastered all there is to know about the best of the enhancements to HTML5 and CSS3. You will be ready to proceed on your web development journey, certain in the knowledge that you are capable of building whatever type of site you make be called upon to create, as follows:

- In **Chapter 1** you will learn about the features that are now available in both HTML5 and CSS3, and understand why they were added and what they have to offer you.

- **Chapter 2** takes you through installing a Web Server on your computer so that you can work on and test your designs locally, with no need to upload them to a development server.

- In **Chapter 3** you will learn about probably the best free code editor available, Visual Studio Code, and will understand why it's so powerful, as well as how to install and use it.

- **Chapter 4** teaches you all about the Developer Consoles that are built into all modern browsers and with which you can test and debug your projects.

- Starting in **Chapter 5** you will begin to learn the basics of the newest HTML5 features and what they can do for you.

- **Chapter 6** introduces the HTML5 Canvas, with which you can write and draw directly in a web browser to create any manner of images and effects.

- Starting with **Chapter 7** you will begin looking in detail at the various Canvas features and how to use them, beginning with rectangles and fills.

- In **Chapter 8** you will learn all about writing text onto the Canvas, in a variety of different way, sizes and fonts.

- **Chapter 9** then takes you onto how to draw on the Canvas using simple and logical JavaScript commands.

- In **Chapter 10** you will start to master the Canvas by directly manipulating the color and transparency data in it.

- **Chapter 11** then takes you onto the most advanced Canvas features you could need, providing access to every remaining option you might require.

- In **Chapter 12** you will learn all about Geolocation for use with mapping and helping users to reach locations of interest.

- **Chapter 13** reveals several new and very handy form handling features that now come built into HTML5.

- In **Chapter 14** you will learn how you can improve on using cookies by replacing them with accessing local storage.

- **Chapter 15** introduces HTML5 Audio and Video, and shows you how to drop these media directly into your web pages.

- Starting at **Chapter 16** you will turn your attention to CSS3 and the new features this technology now has to offer.

- In **Chapter 17** you will learn all about the new CSS3 attribute selectors and how to make the best use of them.

- In **Chapter 18** you will start creating backgrounds that were not possible before the advent of CSS3.

- **Chapter 19** introduces the new borders features that have been incorporated in CSS3 and shows several ways of using them.

- In **Chapter 20** you will learn all about the new CSS3 box and text properties that you can use to significantly add impact to your designs.

- **Chapter 21** shows you all the new color and opacity features now available to you courtesy of CSS3.

- In **Chapter 22** you will discover how you can easily add a variety of effects to your text and even access thousands of free web fonts.

- **Chapter 23** shows you how you can transform any web elements in two dimensions by stretching, rotating and more.

- In **Chapter 24** these transformations are taken to the next level by manipulating objects in three dimensions, and also animating them.

- **Chapter 25** introduces the massively powerful Flexbox layout which makes it easier than ever to create pages that look good on any size of device.

- In **Chapter 26** you will learn about the alternative to Flexbox with even greater flexibility, namely CSS Grid.

- **Chapter 27** introduces you to Sass, which is an extension to CSS that will absolutely take your designs to a higher level.

- In **Chapter 28** you will learn how you can even use variables and control the logical flow of instructions in Sass.

- Finally in **Chapter 29** you will complete your journey of discovery by mastering various advanced Sass techniques.

Code Bundle and Coloured Images

Please follow the link to download the
Code Bundle and the *Coloured Images* of the book:

https://rebrand.ly/li50tj8

The code bundle for the book is also hosted on GitHub at **https://github.com/bpbpublications/HTML5-and-CSS3-Masterclass**. In case there's an update to the code, it will be updated on the existing GitHub repository.

We have code bundles from our rich catalogue of books and videos available at **https://github.com/bpbpublications**. Check them out!

Errata

We take immense pride in our work at BPB Publications and follow best practices to ensure the accuracy of our content to provide with an indulging reading experience to our subscribers. Our readers are our mirrors, and we use their inputs to reflect and improve upon human errors, if any, that may have occurred during the publishing processes involved. To let us maintain the quality and help us reach out to any readers who might be having difficulties due to any unforeseen errors, please write to us at :

errata@bpbonline.com

Your support, suggestions and feedbacks are highly appreciated by the BPB Publications' Family.

Did you know that BPB offers eBook versions of every book published, with PDF and ePub files available? You can upgrade to the eBook version at www.bpbonline.com and as a print book customer, you are entitled to a discount on the eBook copy. Get in touch with us at :

business@bpbonline.com for more details.

At **www.bpbonline.com**, you can also read a collection of free technical articles, sign up for a range of free newsletters, and receive exclusive discounts and offers on BPB books and eBooks.

Piracy

If you come across any illegal copies of our works in any form on the internet, we would be grateful if you would provide us with the location address or website name. Please contact us at **business@bpbonline.com** with a link to the material.

If you are interested in becoming an author

If there is a topic that you have expertise in, and you are interested in either writing or contributing to a book, please visit **www.bpbonline.com**. We have worked with thousands of developers and tech professionals, just like you, to help them share their insights with the global tech community. You can make a general application, apply for a specific hot topic that we are recruiting an author for, or submit your own idea.

Reviews

Please leave a review. Once you have read and used this book, why not leave a review on the site that you purchased it from? Potential readers can then see and use your unbiased opinion to make purchase decisions. We at BPB can understand what you think about our products, and our authors can see your feedback on their book. Thank you!

For more information about BPB, please visit **www.bpbonline.com**.

Table of Contents

1. **About HTML5 and CSS3** 1

   Introduction 1

   Structure 3

   Objectives 3

   Introducing HTTP and HTML 3

      HTML tags *3*

      Tag attributes *5*

      The style attribute *5*

   Introducing CSS 6

      *Using **span** and **div** elements* *6*

      Using id and class attributes *7*

      Using stylesheets *8*

   The need for HTML5 and CSS3 10

   Conclusion 11

2. **Installing a Web Server** 13

   Introduction 13

   Structure 13

   Objectives 14

   Explaining WAMPs, MAMPs, and LAMPs 14

   Installing on Windows 14

      Working with the document root *18*

   Installing on MacOS 20

      Working with the document root *22*

   Installing on Linux 24

      Working with the document root *25*

   Conclusion 25

3. **Visual Studio Code** 27

   Introduction 27

Structure...27

Objectives...28

The popularity of VS Code..28

    Installing VS Code on Windows 29

    Installing VS Code on MacOS 31

    Installing VS Code on Linux...33

Getting Started with VS Code...34

Conclusion..36

4. The Developer Console...37

Introduction..37

Structure...37

Objectives...38

Accessing the developer console...38

Useful things you can do..43

    Autocompletion...43

    Inspecting elements 46

Conclusion..47

5. Introduction to HTML5..49

Introduction..49

Structure...50

Objectives...50

HTML5 is more than HTML4 + 1...50

    The `<canvas>` *element* 50

    Geolocation 52

    Forms 55

    Local storage and session storage 57

    Microdata...58

        Other semantic tags 58

    Web workers and applications 58

        Web applications 59

Audio and video 59

Using audio *60*

Using video *60*

SVG and MathML 62

Conclusion 62

6. The HTML5 Canvas **63**

Introduction 63

Structure 64

Objectives 64

A crash course in JavaScript 64

Code within the `<script>` tags *64*

Code in a separate file *67*

The `getElementByID()` function *70*

Converting a canvas to an image *71*

Conclusion 74

7. Rectangles and Fills **75**

Introduction 75

Structure 75

Objectives 76

About the canvas examples 76

Drawing rectangles 78

Using variables *78*

Applying drawing styles *79*

Changing the line width *80*

Clearing a rectangle *81*

Applying gradient fills *82*

Multicolored gradient fills *85*

Using pattern fills *88*

Conclusion 93

8. Writing on the Canvas **95**

Introduction 95

Structure 96

Objectives 96

Writing text 96

Changing how text displays 96

    Aligning text 98

    Changing stroke width 100

    Writing filled text 103

       Using a pattern for a text fill 105

Conclusion 107

9. Drawing on the Canvas **109**

Introduction 109

Structure 109

Objectives 110

Drawing lines with paths 110

Applying fills 115

Clipping canvas areas 115

Drawing curved lines 118

    Selecting direction 119

    Drawing an arc to a location 123

    Using attractors 125

    Capping and joining lines 127

Conclusion 131

10. Manipulating the Canvas **133**

Introduction 133

Structure 134

Objectives 134

Drawing with an image 134

    Extracting image parts 136

    Using the canvas as a source image 138

Attaching shadows 139

    More than just images 141

Editing pixels directly 142

How the color data is stored... 145

Looping through the data... 145

Processing the image data.. 146

Averaging the color data... 146

Other effects 147

Creating your own image data 150

Conclusion 150

11. Advanced Canvas Features... **151**

Introduction.. 151

Structure.. 151

Objectives.. 152

Compositing and transparency 152

Using a loop... 155

Drawing the image 156

Changing transparency 157

Applying transformations 157

Using rotations 160

Applying translations.. 160

Applying multiple transformations............................... 161

Conclusion 161

12. Using Geolocation... **163**

Introduction.. 163

Structure.. 164

Objectives.. 164

Explaining GPS 164

Alternatives to GPS 164

Testing whether geolocation is available....................... 165

Using the developer console.. 167

Redirecting users 169

Obtaining a user's location 170

Named functions..173

When permission is granted 173

Conclusion 175

13. Form Handling..**177**

Introduction..177

Structure...177

Objectives...178

HTML5 form attributes..178

The autofocus attribute 178

The autocomplete attribute 180

The form attribute 182

The formaction attribute 184

Other form overrides 185

The multiple attribute 186

The novalidate attribute..186

The width and height attributes 186

The list attribute and `<datalist>` *and* `<option>` *tags*............................187

The min, max, and step attributes 189

Other date and time input types 190

The pattern attribute...191

The placeholder attribute 192

The required attribute 193

The color input type..194

Numbers and ranges...195

The search input type..198

Conclusion 198

14. Local Storage and More...**199**

Introduction..199

Structure...199

Objectives...200

Using local storage 200

Storing and retrieving local data 200

Removing and clearing local data 203

Using session storage instead 204

Microdata 205

Web workers 208

Offline web applications 211

How offline web apps work 211

Drag and drop 213

Cross document messaging 213

Conclusion 214

15. Audio and Video 215

Introduction 215

Structure 215

Objectives 216

HTML5 audio 216

Audio codecs 216

Playing audio 217

HTML5 video 220

Video codecs 221

Playing video 221

Conclusion 227

16. Introduction to CSS3 229

Introduction 229

Structure 229

Objectives 230

CSS3 is still in development 230

New in CSS3 231

Attribute selectors 231

Backgrounds 233

Borders 234

Box shadows 237

Columns and overflow 238

Colors and transparency 239

Text effects and fonts 241

Transitions and transformations 244

Flexbox layout 245

Flexbox is a module 245

CSS grid 248

Conclusion 251

17. CSS3 Attribute Selectors **253**

Introduction 253

Structure 253

Objective 254

CSS attribute selectors 254

Name selector 255

Value selector 256

Word list selector 257

Hyphen selector 258

Start selector 259

End selector 260

Global selector 262

Case-insensitive flag 263

Case-sensitive flag 264

Conclusion 265

18. Creating Backgrounds **267**

Introduction 267

Structure 268

Objectives 268

Background clip and origin 268

Template literals 268

Using the background-clip property 271

Using the background-origin property 271

Background clip and origin together 272

The JavaScript section 275

Background size 277

Using gradients 280

Color stops 282

Stop distances and repeating 282

Radial and conic gradients 283

Conclusion 284

19. Building Borders 285

Introduction 285

Structure 285

Objectives 286

Border radius 286

Border colors 289

Gradient borders 290

Multiple backgrounds 292

Using a single image 294

Conclusion 297

20. Box and Text Properties 299

Introduction 299

Structure 299

Objectives 300

Adding shadows 300

Element overflow 302

Multi column layout 304

Conclusion 310

21. Colors and Opacity 311

Introduction 311

Structure 311

Objectives 312

RGB colors 312

    Using a color wheel 315

    RGBA colors 317

HSL colors 320

Applying transparency 323

Conclusion 324

22. Text Effects and Fonts **325**

Introduction 325

Structure 326

Objectives 326

Box sizing 326

Text overflow 328

Wrapping long words 330

User resizing of elements 332

Outlining focus 334

Text shadows 335

Web fonts 337

Conclusion 340

23. 2D Transformations **341**

Introduction 341

Structure 342

Objectives 342

Transformations 342

Transitions 344

Translation 347

    Coming soon – A translate property 348

Scaling 348

Rotation 350

Skewing 351

Using matrixes 353

Conclusion 355

24. 3D and Animation..**357**

    Introduction..357

    Structure...357

    Objectives...358

    3D transformations..358

    Setting a perspective 361

        Two ways to change perspective 363

        Setting the transform style 365

        Changing the transform origin...366

    Working in 3D space 367

        Controlling the cube 369

    3D translation...370

    3D scaling...370

    3D rotation...371

    Back face visibility 372

    Conclusion 373

25. Flexbox Layout..**375**

    Introduction..375

    Structure...375

    Objectives...376

    About Flexbox 376

        Making a Flexbox playground..376

        How the example works 380

        Using the example 382

    Flex direction...383

    Wrapping flex items 385

    Content justification 385

    Aligning items..387

    Aligning the content..389

    Other properties...391

    Conclusion 392

26. CSS Grid **393**

    Introduction.. 393

    Structure.. 393

    Objectives... 394

    About CSS Grid... 394

        How the example works 398

        Using the example 399

        Grid flow 401

        Justifying content 402

        Aligning items 404

        Setting gaps 406

    Changing locations and dimensions... 407

    Conclusion 410

27. Introducing Sass **411**

    Introduction.. 411

    Structure.. 412

    Objectives... 412

    Sass is the answer 412

    About Sass 412

    Different versions of Sass 413

    Installing on Windows... 413

        Other Windows installers.. 416

    Installing on MacOS... 417

    Installing on Linux 419

        Alternative Linux installations 420

    Pre-processing to CSS.. 421

    Conclusion 422

28. Sass Variables and Flow **423**

    Introduction.. 423

    Structure.. 423

    Objectives... 424

Variables in CSS 424

Variables in Sass 427

   Default variable values 428

   Variable scope 429

      Forcing global scope 430

Flow control 431

   Sass operators 431

   Sass expressions (Sass Script) 432

   @if ... @else 433

      @each ... in 436

      @for ... from ... through 437

      @for ... from ... to 439

      @while 440

Conclusion 441

29. Advanced Sass **443**

Introduction 443

Structure 444

Objectives 444

Nesting in Sass 444

   Nested properties 447

Inheritance in Sass 447

Using mixins 450

   Sass modules 451

Future versions 452

Conclusion 452

Index **455-462**

CHAPTER 1
About HTML5 and CSS3

Introduction

In the beginning was Web 1.0, as created by *Sir Tim Berners-Lee* in 1990, when he developed the world's first web browser and matching web server. Working at CERN (the European Organization for Nuclear Research), he built a system called ENQUIRE based around hypertext, which is text containing links to other text in the same or other documents.

At the time CERN was the largest node on the Internet due to the vast amount of data it was creating and needing to share, and *Berners-Lee* realized that this was a great opportunity to combine hypertext with the Internet. And that, as they say, is how it all started.

But pretty soon, smart as the concept initially was, its limitations were becoming plain. HTML was restricted to simple text and images, and web pages were static documents with no user interactivity. And so, the dynamic web needed inventing, namely, Web 2.0, which started enabling users to interact with each other on web pages that did not require reloading each time there was any user input because that was taken care of behind the scenes with **Asynchronous JavaScript And XML (AJAX)**, which was a means of sending and fetching data on demand, without the user having to think about it or do anything.

Web 2.0 led to the advent of social networking and products such as *Facebook*, *Gmail*, and a new type of publishing called **Web Logs** (**Blogs**), mainly through platforms like *WordPress*. Perhaps the name Web 2.0 is more of a semantic than a major change from Web 1.0, but what *was* developing was a far cry from the very first HTML pages, and so Web 2.0 stuck as a moniker.

The most significant thing about Web 2.0 (compared with Web 1.0) is that the user is invited to contribute to a site's content by commenting, or creating an account and matching profile, enabling the ability to add content to the site. The result is dynamically changing, user-generated content (such as with *Wikipedia*), and scalability using cloud platforms like **Amazon Web Services** (**AWS**).

However, enabling as it has been, Web 2.0 on its own was simply not enough to satisfy the growing demands of web developers, who needed significantly more power if they were to bring the quality of the web page and web app experience up to that of software programs that had been (until then) written specifically for an operating system.

Thus, two technologies were enhanced, more or less in parallel with each other, to bring a range of new interactive, dynamic, and animated features, and these were HTML5 and CSS3. Using them, developers were now able to add audio and video to their projects. They could use geolocation to provide mapping services. There was a **canvas** element added to the HTML specification with a tremendous range of associated drawing tools. It became possible to store a large amount of data on a user's local PC (rather than the very limiting (and short) cookies that were all that was previously available), and ways of offloading processor-intensive code to separate processes was provided with web workers, plus a number of other new and innovative features.

Meanwhile, CSS was rapidly advancing too. You see, CSS2 was a single specification defining a number of features, but greater control and features were needed; some of which the developers had not yet even imagined. So, they created CSS3 in such a way that separate modules could add new capabilities as necessary but (importantly) in a backwardly compatible way so that existing web sites would not break. These new features included better background handling, an extension to the Box Model, improved cascade management, text effects, transformations, animations, and much more.

Note: There is, on the horizon, a Web 3.0, which will see a massive change-over to highly distributed content, spread all around the world, rather than being centralized on individual sites and cloud platforms, with a blockchain (a digital ledger of transactions that is duplicated and distributed across the entire network of computer systems), being used to verify the authenticity of all the data on the various nodes. It will also offer support for new technologies such as cryptocurrencies and NFTs (Non Fungible Tokens – or proofs of ownership of

digital products). But all this (at least initially) will be more of a back-end change, rather than an update to the user experience. However, a discussion of Web 3.0 would require a whole book in itself and it is not relevant to understanding HTML5 and CSS3.

Structure

In this chapter, you will:

- Learn about (or refresh your knowledge of) HTML and CSS

- Understand the need to separate styling from content

- Learn some of the new features in HTML5 and CSS3

- Become ready to start learning how to use the technologies

Objectives

After you complete reading this chapter, you will have a basic understanding of HTML and CSS (if you didn't already), what it is that HTML5 and CSS3 bring to the table, and why you need to thoroughly understand these technologies and incorporate them in your web development toolkit.

Introducing HTTP and HTML

This book assumes that you already have a basic understanding of HTML, but just to get you started, or if you are a little rusty, here is a very short recap of the HTTP communication standard and the HTML language. You may skip this (and possibly the following) sections if you feel up to speed already.

Hyper Text Transfer Protocol (**HTTP**) is the method by which a web browser communicates with a web server. The web server's job is to accept a request from a client and then reply to it in some meaningful way, usually by returning an HTML document (or perhaps an error message such as **404 Not Found**).

HTML tags

HTML documents are simply text files within which special commands are embedded using angle brackets, like this: **<body>**, which denotes the start of the main body of a document. Many tags come with matching closing tags such as **</body>**, which ends the document's body section.

Not all tags have matching closers, though, because some can close themselves. For example, a tag to display an image might look like this: **<img src='myimage.**

jpg' />. The final **/>** self-closes the tag. For a period, this form of self-closing was required by the HTML standard but because it was considered obvious that certain tags must close themselves, it was eventually decided to make the **/>** optional, so that you could simply close such tags with just **>**, which is the style used in this book, although both are accepted by all browsers.

> **Note: The data-handling version of HTML called XML is much stricter and, whenever you are using it, for example, in an Really Simple Syndication (RSS) feed, you must properly self-close tags by inserting the preceding slash before the closing angle bracket.**

Let's take a look at a standard HTML5 template document, as shown in *Example 1.1*.

Example 1.1:

```
 1. <!DOCTYPE html>
 2. <html lang="en">
 3.   <head>
 4.     <meta charset="utf-8">
 5.     <title>My Webpage</title>
 6.   </head>
 7.   <body>
 8.     My Content
 9.   </body>
10. </html>
```

Here, you can see a set of various tags used to create the absolute bare bones of an HTML document. The **<!DOCTYPE html>** tells your web browser that this is an HTML5 document – yes, that's all you have to do to start using HTML5. In fact, if you leave it out, the web browser will interpret the document using HTML4 rules.

You will see that **!DOCTYPE** is a self-closing tag (as there is no accompanying **</!DOCTYPE>**), and therefore the line following it is not indented. Although indents are not a requirement of HTML, using them makes your documents much easier to create and update, and for others to understand. So, in this book indentation is used judiciously throughout (in all the HTML, CSS, and JavaScript examples).

Next, you will see **<html lang="en">**, which denotes the start of the HTML section of the document, and also notifies the browser that it will use the English language. Then, underneath, indented and within a pair of **<head>** ... **</head>** tags (which denotes a part of the document known as the head), follows the type of character set the browser should be using, which is **utf-8**, and the title of the web page is within a pair of **<title>** … **</title>** tags. Other tags might also be used here for other purposes such as sharing keywords and descriptions for search engines to make use of, and so on.

Next, comes the document's body, which is located inside a pair of **<body>** … **</body>** tags, within which is some text, that is the content of the web page, and which may (and most certainly will) contain many separate sections and different types of tags. Finally, the HTML section is closed with a **</html>** tag.

This will be plain enough to most readers, but should you be a newcomer, you now know pretty much all there is to understand about creating HTML documents, except (of course) that there are also a number of other tags you will need to learn in order to make great web pages, but they will be mostly obvious in their use when you come across them. If not, a quick web search is all you need.

Tag attributes

Clearly, there's a lot more to HTML than just inserting a bunch of tags and text because you also need to provide attributes to many tags. Remember the **img** tag just mentioned. As well as being a self-closing tag, it is an example of one that accepts an attribute. In this case, it's **src**, or the file location from which to fetch the image to be displayed. For example, **<img src='myimage.jpg'>** tells the web server to fetch the **myimage.jpg** file from the current folder and, when received, the web browser then inserts it at the correct location in the web document.

Or, a link to the *Google* website might look like: **<a href='http://google.com'>click me</a>**. Here, the **href** attribute is provided a URL (**Universal Resource Locator** (**URL**), or web link) indicating the destination to which the web browser should be pointed, if the contents between the **<a>** and **</a>** is clicked.

The style attribute

Each HTML tag can support a wide array of possible attributes, according to the tag type, but pretty much all of them support the **style** attribute. This is one way of styling the textual (or other) output. For example, **<p style='font-weight:bold'>bold text</p>** defines a section of text known as a paragraph to be displayed in bold.

This isn't the best way to apply styling because it's hardwired into your document, the opposite of what CSS sets out to offer, which is the separation of text and styling. But it serves to illustrate another type of attribute and introduces the concept of styling.

However, this is purely one way you can modify the output. For example, you can simply place text within a pair of **** … **** tags to achieve the same effect, but this also hardwires the styling, which is not always the best approach, especially if you wish your document's output to be re-styleable.

So, now that we've looked at a couple of instances of using attributes, and after realizing that HTML offers many different ways to achieve the same result, let's move onto what exactly CSS is all about in the following section:

Introducing CSS

The term **Cascading Style Sheet** (**CSS**) and the concept behind it is all about separating the style of a web page from its content. But why would you want to do that? Well, consider the case of someone with limited vision who needs better contrasting colors and, perhaps, larger, easier to read fonts.

Without CSS, you might only be able to cater to such a person by creating alternate web pages. And how about preparing a page for print? Often printing out a web page without modifying it will not look right, and you may prefer to re-arrange parts of the page, change colors, and more to make it fit the paper better. And what about presenting your page differently to desktop/laptop and mobile browsers, and to different screen sizes of tablets and phones too? Well, with CSS all you need to do is load in a different set of styling commands to achieve this, leaving your web page untouched – you have to admit that this is sensible and powerful too.

In an earlier example, I broke this disconnect between style and content by applying a direct style attribute to an HTML element. But this was just to show you what is possible, and how HTML and CSS offer many different ways to achieve similar results. But it doesn't mean you *should* embed styles in web pages. In fact, I recommend you never do this mainly because there are some much better ways to achieve styling, as follows.

Using `span` and `div` elements

Two elements were added to HTML to make CSS more efficient, and these were **span** and **div**. They both serve to distinguish a section of HTML from the rest of a document, but work in different ways.

A **span** is generally used in-line with text to modify the styling of letters, numbers, and characters. It, like text, wraps from line to line, flowing with the text, and you use it like this: `<span>This is a section of text in a span element</span>`. You can include images and other non-textual elements in a **span** if you wish, and they will do their best to flow along with the text, although results are not always what you expect, especially when these elements have very different dimensions to the font in use.

On the other hand, a **div** has a broader purpose; it will block out a section within a document. Unlike a **span,** it does not flow with the text and wrap around because a **div** is rectangular, and everything within it flows and fits within its boundaries. A **div** element might look like this: `<div>This is a section of text in a div element</div>`.

You don't see very much difference between the two new element types until you use and style them, which you could do by providing a **style** attribute, as in this manner: `<span style='font-weight:bold'>Some bold text</span>`, but you would still not have the desired disconnect between style and content, and that's where we meet the other main parts of CSS, as follows:

Using id and class attributes

In order to provide a way to apply any styles to wither individual or elements or groups of elements, the next step needed is to give them either uniquely identifying names, or group names. In CSS, these are called **id** and **class** attributes. For example, if you have the main heading on a page, and you want to be able to uniquely apply styles to it, you could use the **id** attribute, like this: `<h1 id='mainhead'>Welcome to my page</h1>`.

Here, the name **mainhead** has been supplied as a value to the **id** attribute. Shortly you will see how identified elements can be accessed from CSS, but let's first look at using a **class**. Suppose you have a lot of notes in a document and you wish to style them all in a similar manner. This is where applying a **class** to each comes in, like this: `<span class='note'>This is a note</note>`.

Having done this, each note you write can now be modified as a group using a single CSS command. But before howing you how, let's return to how HTML and CSS allow you to approach web development in many different ways because instead of using the **h1** HTML heading tag, I could have used a **span**, and instead of using the **span** tag for the note, the text could have been inside an **h1** or **h2**, or any other two part HTML tag, and so on.

This brings up the concept of readability. When you build a website using HTML and CSS, because there are so many ways to achieve your desired results, it becomes clear that you need to adopt certain rules as your projects get bigger and more expansive. This is so that you can easily return to parts you worked on some time ago and instantly understand what you had in mind, and it also helps anyone else who has to work on your creations too.

Therefore, it's best to stick to using the elements provided by HTML, wherever possible. If reating a level one heading, put it within an **h1** tag. Or, if creating something like a note, for which there is not a tag, I put it in a **span** (or, if warranted, a **div**) and provide a clearly descriptive name value to its **class** or **id** attribute. The idea is to keep it simple, logical, and to use descriptive attribute values.

Using stylesheets

That's all well and good, you might say, but how can the styles be assigned to the various elements in a document, if they aren't applied directly to them? The answer is that you use a stylesheet, which is a set of instructions that you can include either in the same document, or in separate documents that are loaded in as required.

Let's start by reminding ourselves how to include styles within a document, by assuming that we wish all level one headings to appear in **24pt bold**, all regular text in **14pt** using a **serif** font, and all notes to be in **italic** using a **sans-serif** font. In which case, the standard HTML5 template from *Example 1.1* might be updated to look like *Example 1.2*.

Example 1.2:

```
1.  <!DOCTYPE html>
2.  <html lang="en">
3.    <head>
4.      <meta charset="utf-8">
5.      <title>My Webpage</title>
6.    <style>
7.      body {
8.        font-size   : 14pt;
9.        font-family : serif;
10.     }
11.     h1 {
12.        font-size   : 24pt;
13.        font-weight : bold;
14.     }
15.     .note {
16.        font-style  : italic;
17.        font-family : sans-serif;
18.     }
19.   </style>
```

```
20.  </head>
21.  <body>
22.    <h1>My Content</h1>
23.    <p>This is some text</p>
24.    <span class='note'>And this is a note</span>
25.  </body>
26. </html>
```

Here, you can see that the default styling for the document body has been set within a pair of **<style>** ... **</style>** tags, by applying styles to the **body** element. Then, all **h1** elements have been given their styling, followed by all classes with the name **note** being assigned their styles.

Note: Remember that in a stylesheet, a period before an attribute name denotes that the rule applies to a class. To make the rule apply to an ID of that name, you can preface the name with a # sign instead. And, as you have seen, without either a period or a #, the rule applies to an element of that name.

Alternatively, the stylesheet can be saved in the current folder (or elsewhere); perhaps, using the name **styles.css**. In which case, it can be saved separately and might look like *Example 1.3*.

Example 1.3:

```
1.  body {
2.    font-size   : 14pt;
3.    font-family : serif;
4.  }
5.  h1 {
6.    font-size   : 24pt;
7.    font-weight : bold;
8.  }
9.  .note {
10.   font-style  : italic;
11.   font-family : sans-serif;
12. }
```

And now the HTML file can be shortened back to look like as shown in *Example 1.4*.

Example 1.4:

```
1.  <!DOCTYPE html>
2.  <html lang="en">
3.    <head>
4.      <meta charset="utf-8">
5.      <title>My Webpage</title>
6.      <link rel="stylesheet" href="styles.css">
7.    </head>
8.    <body>
9.      <h1>My Content</h1>
10.     <p>This is some text</p>
11.     <span class='note'>And this is a note</span>
12.   </body>
13. </html>
```

All that's different between this and *Example 1.1* is that the following line has been inserted inside the head of the document:

```
<link rel="stylesheet" href="styles.css">
```

This tells the web browser to request the web server to return the stylesheet saved in **styles.css** back to it, and then the browser uses the instructions in that file to re-style the current document as required.

> **Note: I won't go into it at this point, but now you see how stylesheets can be loaded in, you will understand that there are also ways to decide between loading in from a choice of multiple different pre-saved stylesheets according to needs, such as the screen dimensions and computer type on which the browser is running. This is indeed powerful, especially considering that the main HTML document needs no further modification in order to be displayed in an infinite variety of styles.**

The need for HTML5 and CSS3

So far, in this chapter, you have simply refreshed your memory of basic HTML and CSS (or introduced you to these technologies, hopefully with enough detail so that you can work with this book). It should all look pretty straightforward. So what's all the fuss about HTML5 and CSS3?

Well, the answer is that your users will nowadays expect to see and use all the bells and whistles that modern web browsers have to offer. But not only that, the latest developments in these two technologies also make your life as a developer a great deal simpler by making features that were a real headache to implement in the past (if they were even possible) become a breeze, using short and simple instructions.

You can insert audio or a video with a couple of lines of HTML5. You can make your text transform or animate with a line or two of CSS3, and you can create the most incredible web apps and games in the **canvas** element that previously would have required intricate coding in *Flash* or *ActiveX* embedded elements. This was extremely time-consuming and often bug-ridden and rife with security issues.

Conclusion

HTML5 and CSS3 are no-longer the goodies, or extensions added to the web experience that only a few daring developers would choose to use. They are now fully tested, debugged, and mainstream, and if you are to be any type of a web developer worth your salt, you *need* to fully understand and master these technologies, and use them often and skillfully in all your projects.

And that's what this book is all about. Whatever your current skill level, this book will take you through using all these fabulous new technologies until they become everyday tools that you don't even have to think twice about using them. By the time you have finished reading this book, and played with the accompanying example files (and hopefully, created many of your own), you will have mastered everything you need to know to make the most dynamic and exiting websites and web apps around – and your abilities will surely be in high demand.

But, let's begin at the beginning, as they say, starting with the following chapter, in which we will show you how to install your own web development back and front end stack, and associated tools, totally free and very easily, so that you can immediately work through this book and test the examples (and your own projects), just as if they were uploaded to a real-world development server.

CHAPTER 2
Installing a Web Server

Introduction

A lot of HTML and CSS web development can be managed using a simple file system and a basic notepad-like text editor. You can, but do you really want to limit yourself, when there is a wealth of free development tools available? Also, some more advance features of websites such as **Asynchronous JavaScript And XML (AJAX)**, or local storage and cookies, insist on being run from a web server, and will fail if you attempt to use them by just loading files into a web browser from a folder.

Therefore, before we can get started on the nitty-gritty of using all the goodies in HTML5 and CSS3, we need to get a PC, Mac, or Linux machine equipped with a reasonable set of development tools. In this chapter, we will install a web server for testing our projects, and in the following one, we'll set up an integrated development environment with Visual Studio Code.

Don't worry, the tools recommended are totally free to use and easy to install and use, so they won't cost you in either money or time.

Structure

In this chapter, you will:

- Understand what a WAMP, MAMP, or LAMP is

- Learn how to install one on Windows, MacOS, or Linux

- Find out what a document root is and how to access it

- Discover how to store pages for web serving

Objectives

After studying this chapter, you will be able to install a local web server on your computer capable of serving HTML with accompanying CSS (including HTML5 and CSS3), and also supporting PHP for back-end processing tasks, which you will need for some examples later in this book.

Explaining WAMPs, MAMPs, and LAMPs

A web server that is any good at all usually offers a lot more than just being a simple server. It will incorporate all of a server, a database, and a back-end programming language. Such an integrated solution is commonly known as **Windows, Apache, MySQL, and PHP, or sometimes Python or Perl (WAMP)**. On a *Mac*, it will be called a **MAMP**, and on *Linux*, it's called a **LAMP**. The product recommended in this book is simply called MAMP, and you can download it from **mamp.info**. There are versions for *Windows*, and also *Intel* or *M1 MacOS* computers. For Linux, there are instructions on what you may need to set up a LAMP later in this chapter, as you may already have everything pre-installed.

> **Note: Please bear in mind that books can have a long lifespan, and that if the MAMP website or product changes substantially, or even if it becomes no-longer available, there will always be many other alternatives that you can search for with the keywords WAMP, MAMP, or LAMP. You will just have to follow their installation instructions instead of those set out here, but you will find out that they will all provide the same features, even if you use them in slightly different ways.**

Installing on Windows

The MAMP program comes in two versions: basic and pro. The basic version is free, and you can upgrade to the pro version later if you choose. To download MAMP for Windows, just go to **mamp.info** and you will be redirected to the Windows section of the website, where you need to click on the download link called **Free MAMP download**, and on the page that comes up, select **MAMP & MAP PRO** for Windows. At the time of writing, the current version is *5.0.5*, but you may see a newer version.

When you click on the download link you may see a pop-up window offering you to download "*NAMO DBS App*". You should ignore this by clicking outside the pop-up to make it disappear. Then, if you are prompted whether or not to keep the file, choose "*Keep*". Your download will then proceed, and for version *5.0.5*, it will be 682MB in size.

Once it is downloaded, you must run the installer, and if you don't have the .Net runtime, you will be asked to install it. If so, click on **OK** and a window similar to *Figure 2.1* will be displayed.

Figure 2.1: *Installing the .Net runtime*

Select **Install** and allow the installation to proceed. Once done, you will move on to the Mamp installation screen itself, as shown in *Figure 2.2*. Just click on **Next** to commence installing MAMP.

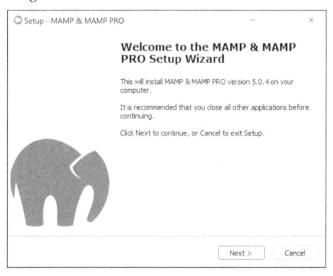

Figure 2.2: *The MAMP installation window*

When prompted whether to install Mamp Pro and/or Bonjour, as shown in *Figure 2.3*, it is recommended that you ensure both boxes are left unchecked as you don't need either of these at this point, and you can always add them later if you wish.

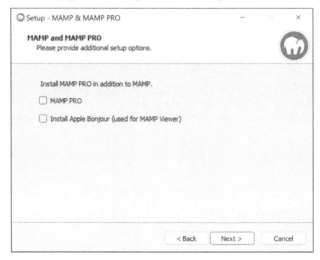

Figure 2.3: *It's recommended not to install the extras at this point*

Once you click on **Next**, there will be a couple more windows asking you to agree to the license (click on **Next**), and asking in which folder you wish to install MAMP (it's recommended to accept the default of **C:\MAMP** and click on **Next**), the name of the startup folder (you are recommended to keep the default of **MAMP** and click on **Next**), and whether to create a desktop icon (you're recommended to check this box and then click on **Next**). Finally, you will reach the screen, as shown in *Figure 2.4*, at which point you are ready to click on the **Install** button. Once the installation is complete, you can click on **Finish** to exit from the installer.

Figure 2.4: *MAMP is now ready to install*

Now, you are ready to run the program; however, even though you are not asked to do so, it seems that some PCs will work better if you now reboot. So before proceeding, you should reboot your computer. After rebooting, you should be ready to click on the MAMP icon which should now appear on your desktop. The first time you do so you may encounter one or more pop-up windows as shown in *Figure 2.5*. These are sent by your firewall asking for permission to allow either *Apache* and/or *MySQL* to operate.

Figure 2.5: *Allow your firewall to give access to MySQL and/or Apache*

You will need to click on **Allow Access** in either case in order for MAMP to operate correctly. After you have allowed access through your firewall, MAMP should now be running as shown in *Figure 2.6*, where you will see a green light next to both "*Apache Server*" and "*MySQL Server*". You do not need to use the cloud functions being advertised to you at the bottom of the window.

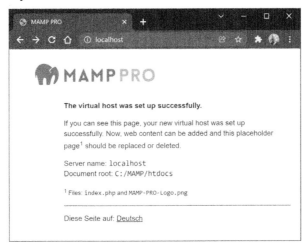

Figure 2.6: *Displaying the default index.php file*

Working with the document root

On a Windows file system, there is always a root directory or folder. For example, this is almost always **C:**. The root folder of other drives is **D:**, **E:**, and so on. A web browser has a similar root called the document root. This does not have to be the very root of a drive (and actually should not be for security reasons). This is the highest level of files that the server will offer access to, and it is in different places for different web servers (and even different installations of the same brand of web server).

In the case of MAMP, assuming that you accepted the default offered during installation, the document root can be found at **C:\MAMP\htdocs** (if you prefer to use forward slashes like this: **C:/MAMP/htdocs**, or you can even use all lowercase too, such as: **c:\mamp\htdocs**, or even **c:/mamp/htdocs**).

By default, after the first installation, the document root will contain two files: **index.php** and **MAMP-PRO-Logo.png**. This location can be accessed through the file system, and files in it can loaded locally from your web browser by entering **http://localhost** into its address bar (or even just **localhost**). The result of which, by default, will look like *Figure 2.7*.

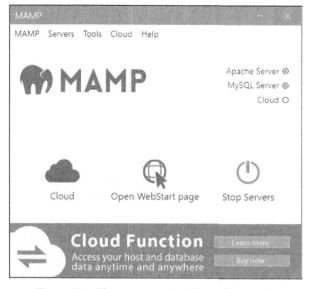

Figure 2.7: *Allow access to MySQL and/or Apache*

If you prefer, or have a particular reason to do so, you may also use the IP numbers reserved for localhost on computers, which is: **http://127.0.0.1**, or just enter: **127.0.0.1**.

If you see the display, as shown in *Figure 2.7*, then MAMP has been correctly installed and all of PHP, MySQL, and the Apache web server should be running. So, now that we have tested the installation, you're recommended to delete the two files in the document root and place your own various HTML and other files in that folder (and any subfolders you require) for them to instantly become viewable by refreshing your browser or pointing it to the localhost.

So, let's test everything now by deleting **index.php** and **MAMP-PRO-Logo.png**, saving the following example in this folder (using the filename **index.html**), and then typing **localhost** in the address bar of your browser.

Example 2.1

```
1.  <html lang="en">
2.    <head>
3.      <meta charset="utf-8">
4.      <title>My Webpage</title>
5.    </head>
6.    <body>
7.      <h1>Hey, it works!</h1>
8.    </body>
9.  </html>
```

Assuming all is well, the result that you see in your browser should look like *Figure 2.8.* And, if so, congratulations, you have now installed MAMP on your computer. If not, carefully go through the instructions in this chapter once more, and check the MAMP website for further information.

Figure 2.8: *The new HTML document has displayed*

Or, if you have chosen to use a different WAMP stack, follow the advice given in that project's instruction on where to find its document root, and how to ensure its Apache web server is up and running.

Otherwise, you are now ready to move onto the next chapter, where we'll install the second part of our development environment, Microsoft's *Visual Studio Code*.

Installing on MacOS

Hi Mac users! Yes, your computer is equally as powerful as a PC at running a web server, and you can use the same program recommended for Windows: MAMP. It comes in two versions, basic and pro. The basic version is free and you can upgrade to the pro version later if you choose.

To download MAMP for MacOS, just go to **mamp.info**, and you should be redirected to the MacOS section of the website, where you should click on the download link called **Free MAMP download**, and on the page that comes up, select **MAMP & MAP PRO** for whichever version of Mac you have (*Intel* for *MacOS 12.12* and higher, or *M1* for *MacOS 11* and above). At the time of writing the current version is 6.6, but you may see a newer version.

When you click on the download link, you may see a pop-up window offering you to download "*NAMO DBS App*". You are recommended to ignore this by clicking on outside the pop-up to make it disappear. This is not needed for our purposes, and you can always get it later if you decide you need it.

Once you have downloaded the file, you will need to install the **.pkg** file by clicking on it, which should result in a window as shown in *Figure 2.9* (which will look slightly different if you are installing the Intel version).

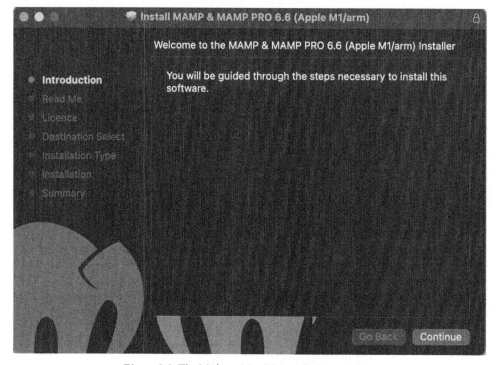

Figure 2.9: The M1/arm MacOS installation window

Just click on **Continue** to start and you will see another window pop up asking you to agree to the terms, to which you must click on **Agree** in order to proceed. Once done, you will probably see a window as shown in *Figure 2.10*. If so, you will have to use the touch ID, or your password to enable the installation to continue.

Figure 2.10: Verifying your credentials in order to proceed

When the installation is done, you can now navigate to your **Applications** folder where you will find a newly-installed icon labelled **MAMP**, which you can now click on to run. This will probably result in the window as shown in *Figure 2.11*, in which you must enter your password to be able to start and stop servers and other functions.

Figure 2.11: Enter your password to start the helper tool

After the helper tool has been set up, you will see the MAMP main window, where the first thing you must do is select the **Preferences** option near the top left, and then click on the **Ports** tab, where you need to change the Apache Port number to **80**, as shown in *Figure 2.12*.

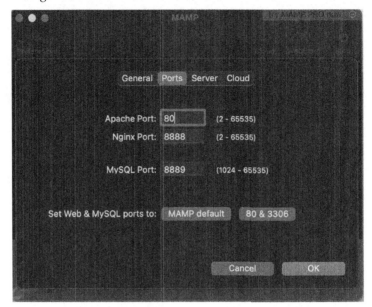

Figure 2.12: *Changing the Apache Port to 80*

The reason for this is that the default port used when you type the word **localhost** into a web browser is port **80**, so that is the one you should enter by preference in order not to need entering port numbers every time you call up a local web page.

Working with the document root

On a MacOS file system there is always a root directory or folder, normally accessible with just a forward slash, like this **/**. A web browser has a similar root called the **document root**. This does not have to be the root (or bottom) level folder of a drive (and actually should not be for security reasons). This is the highest level of files that the server will offer access to, and it is in different places for different web servers (and even different installations of the same brand of web server).

In the case of MAMP, assuming that you accepted the default offered during the installation, the document root can be found at: **/Applications/MAMP/htdocs**.

By default, after the first installation, the document root will contain a file called: **index.php**. This location can be accessed through the file system, and files in it can be loaded locally from your web browser by entering **http://localhost** in its address bar (or even just **localhost**). The result of which, by default, will look like *Figure 2.13*.

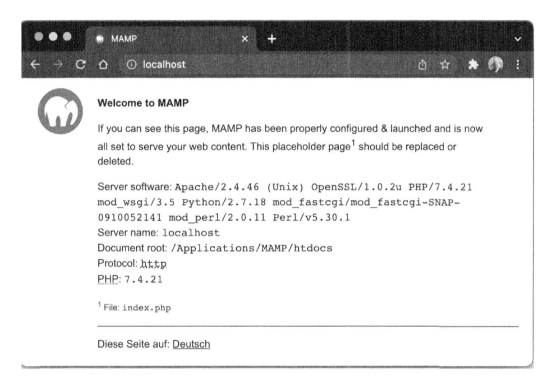

Figure 2.13: *Displaying the default index.php file*

If you prefer, or have a particular reason to do so, you may also use the IP numbers reserved for the localhost on computers, which is: **http://127.0.0.1**, or just enter: **127.0.0.1**.

If you see the display as shown earlier in *Figure 2.7*, then MAMP has been correctly installed and all of PHP, MySQL and the Apache web server should be running. So, now that we have tested the installation, you are recommended to delete the file in the document root and then place your own various HTML and other files in that folder (and any subfolders you require) for them to instantly become viewable by refreshing your browser or pointing it to the localhost.

So, let's test everything now by deleting **index.php**, save *Example 2.1* (from the *Installing on Windows* section a little earlier) in this folder (using the filename **index.**

html), and then type **localhost** in the address bar of your browser. Assuming all is well, the result you will see in your browser should look like *Figure 2.14*.

Figure 2.14: *The new HTML document has displayed*

And, if so, congratulations, you have now installed MAMP on your computer. If not, carefully go through the instructions in this chapter once more, and check the MAMP website for further information.

Or, if you have chosen to use a different MAMP stack, follow the advice given in that project's instruction on where to find its document root, and how to ensure its Apache web server is up and running.

Otherwise, you are now ready to move onto the next chapter, where we'll install the second part of our development environment, Microsoft's *Visual Studio Code*.

Installing on Linux

If you use Linux, hi! As you know, things are a little different for you, and you're probably used to installing all the software you need. However, just in case you don't have a LAMP stack set up on your computer, you may need to allow an installer to do the work for you, as there are so many differing versions of the operating system. Therefore, since it supports all of *Debian, RedHat, CentOS, Ubuntu, Fedora, Gentoo, Arch, SUSE* and many others, you are recommended to go with *Xampp*.

So, go to **apachefriends.org** and download the Linux installer of your choice for (mainly depending on the version of PHP you desire, or if in doubt go for 64-bit version *8.1.6* or similar). Each installer is about 150MB and has the file extension **.run**. Here's how you can run such files from Ubuntu (other Linuxes will be very similar), assuming you are installing 64-bit version *8.1.6*:

Open a Terminal window and navigate to the directory where the file has been saved, and enter the following (or similar, according to the downloaded filename), to ensure the file is executable:

```
chmod +x xampp-linux-x64-8.1.6-0-installer.run
```

Finally, to run the installer, enter the following code:

```
run xampp-linux-x64-8.1.6-0-installer.run
```

Working with the document root

On a Linux file system, there is always a root directory or folder, normally accessible with just a forward slash, like this **/**. A web browser has a similar root called the document root. This does not have to be the very root of a drive (and actually should not be for security reasons). This is the highest level of files that the server will offer access to, and it is in different places for different web servers (and even different installations of the same brand of web server).

In the case of Xampp, the document root can normally be found at **/opt/lampp/htdocs/**. However, since this may only be writable as root, you may wish to create a symbolic link to a folder where you already have write access such as; for example, one you might create called **/home/web/**, as follows:

```
ln -s /home/web /opt/lampp/htdocs/web
```

This will now enable you to save your files in your **/home/web** folder, but access them in your web browser from **localhost/web**. This is not the best solution, and if you don't want to have to use the **/web** subdomain off **localhost**, you may wish to research how to create a new virtual server, or how to change your document root. However, this is not a book on using Linux, and it is assumed that as a Linux, you are up to the task of ensuring you can set up your web server appropriately. These are only guidelines to help you get started, in case you need it.

Conclusion

Well done! Having reached this point, the hardest part is over. You now have a working web server that will enable you to run and test all the examples in this book, without needing to upload them to a production server. It will be fast, secure, and easy to use. Now, we just need to get you a decent program editor in the following chapter, and you'll be all set to become a true master of HTML5 and CSS3.

CHAPTER 3
Visual Studio Code

Introduction

Of course, being largely text-based, all you really need to create web pages is a bare-bones text editor to build even the most dynamic and attractive websites. But that's like saying all you need is Microsoft Paint to create fantastic digital art. It might be technically *possible* given an inordinate amount of time, but would you really *want* to?

That's where Microsoft's totally free *Visual Studio Code* comes in. Microsoft's programming languages have generally been highly powerful and well-respected, and Visual Studio Code (let's call it VS Code from now on) is also powerful and very easy and intuitive to use. So much so, in fact, that VS Code seems to be becoming almost a de-facto standard for programming and web development.

Structure

In this chapter, you will:

- Understand the power that VS Code provides
- Learn how to install VS Code on your computer
- See how to load and edit a file in VS Code

- Access VS Code's interactive editor playground

Objectives

By the time you complete studying this chapter, you will have installed and learned to use the powerful VS Code program editor, which will make your web development much easier and more efficient than using a plain text editor.

The popularity of VS Code

Why is VS Code so popular? Well, it's fast, clearly designed, highly customizable, offers handy features like multi-cursor editing, smart parameter recognition, clear code formatting, and a lot more. Using it will speed up the development cycle of almost everyone who uses it, especially when it recognizes the language you are using (even if it's HTML or CSS) and helpfully suggests what to enter as you type. Once you are up to speed it's like a magical helper, always a step ahead of you. Just take a look at VS Code running on Windows in *Figure 3.1* (below) to see what's in store. Here, a dark theme is used as that can be easier on the eyes for long sessions, but you can choose whatever theme you desire.

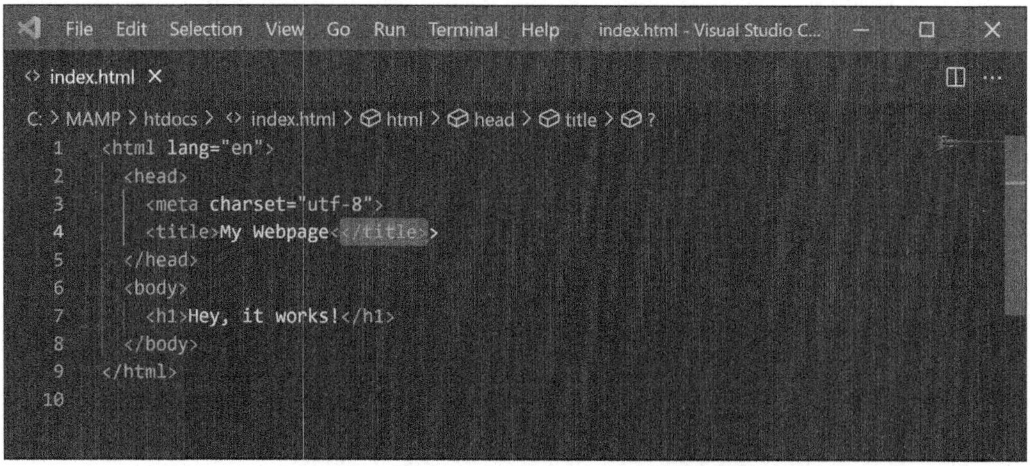

Figure 3.1: Editing an HTML file in VS Code

Note how on line 4, after the title text, you will see a **<** left angle bracket and then the forward slash **/** has been typed, and VS Code has supplied a closing **>** angle bracket which clearly needs adding, and then make a best guess as to what should appear within the two, and it is indeed correct that it was intended to enter **/title**.

All that's now needed is to press *Tab* or *Enter*, or move the cursor to where you want to edit next, and the automatic insert is accepted. Also, just above the HTML, you can see that VS Code has analyzed where the cursor is in the document and shows the level of nesting at that point. Isn't that smart and time saving?

Even better, VS Code is available for all Windows, MacOS, and Linux. So, let's see how to download and install it for each of the operating systems.

Installing VS Code on Windows

Go to **code.visualstudio.com**, click on the **Download** link, and then select the Windows version for download. The download should commence automatically, and at the same time, a helpful Getting Started page will be displayed in the browser so that you can acquaint yourself with its features while you wait. If your browser asks you whether to *keep* or *discard* the download, you need to select **Keep**.

Once it is downloaded, click on the installer to start the installation and accept the license agreement by checking the correct box, as shown in *Figure 3.2*, and then click on **Next**.

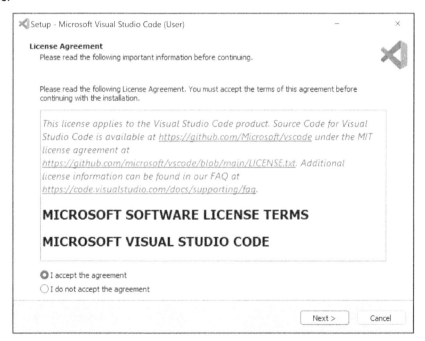

Figure 3.2: Accept the agreement to continue

You will then be given the options to create a desktop icon, and whether to add **Open with Code** to the File Explorer menu, as well, as supporting certain file types and setting up a PATH, as shown in *Figure 3.3*, where you can see the options recommended to choose (basically, accept all the options except the PATH, which would require a restart and probably won't affect you, at least not initially).

Figure 3.3: *Check the boxes you wish to include*

Click on **Next** to continue, and you'll be taken to the main installation window, where you need to click on **Install** to start the installation. In a short while, the installation should be done and you can click on **Finish** to exit, which will launch the program if the checkbox suggesting this is ticked. The first thing you should do is select **Help**, followed by **Editor Playground** as shown in *Figure 3.4*.

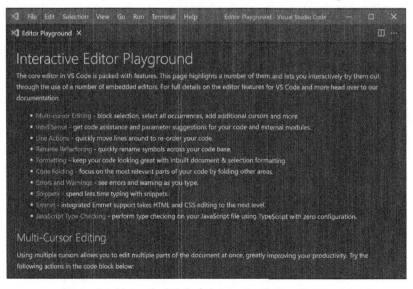

Figure 3.4: *Using the VS Code Interactive Editor Playground*

This is a sort of interactive document that you can work with to learn all the 10 main areas of using VS Code. Once you feel acquainted with VS Code and its capabilities, you can type in *Example 3.1,* or if you have downloaded the companion set of example files, use the **File** menu to load, or simply drag and drop Example 3.1 onto VS Code to start editing it, as follows:

Example 3.1

```
1.  <html lang="en">
2.    <head>
3.      <meta charset="utf-8">
4.      <title>My Webpage</title>
5.    </head>
6.    <body>
7.      <h1>Hey, it works!</h1>
8.    </body>
9.  </html>
```

Installing VS Code on MacOS

Installing VS Code on MacOS is extremely easy. Just go to **code.visualstudio.com**, click on the **Download** link, and then select the Mac version for download. The download should commence automatically, and at the same time, a helpful Getting Started page will be displayed in the browser so that you can acquaint yourself with its features while you wait.

The downloaded file will have the extension **.zip**. To unzip it, just find the location that you need to download it to, which normally will be in your **Downloads** folder. You can get to this by using Finder and then select **Go** followed by **Downloads**. Now, run the **.zip** file as if it is a program and it will extract the files into a program file called Visual Studio Code, as shown in *Figure 3.5*.

Figure 3.5: *The downloaded ,zip file has been extracted*

You can run VS Code from where it is, but it's probably better that you open up another explorer window by choosing **File** from the menu bar followed by *New Finder Window*. Now, choose **Go** followed by **Applications** to change the new window to your **Applications** folder, and drag and drop the Visual Studio Code file from the **Downloads** folder into the **Applications** folder.

You now have the program saved in the appropriate place, and you can run it as normal by clicking on it; the result of which may look like *Figure 3.6*, which is a warning about running programs downloaded from the Internet. If so, just click on **Open** to proceed and VS Code will now be up and running.

Figure 3.6: *You may see a warning about running VS Code*

The first thing you should now do is select **Help** from the Menu bar, followed by **Editor Playground** as shown in *Figure 3.7*. This is a sort of an interactive document that you can work with to learn all the 10 main areas of using VS Code.

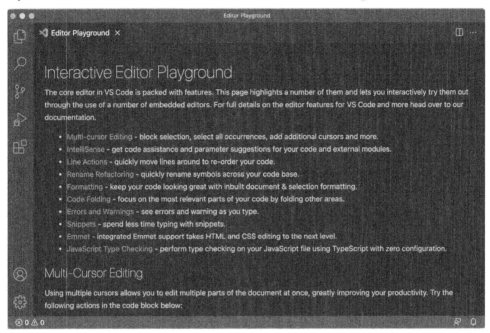

Figure 3.7: *Using the VS Code Interactive Editor Playground*

Once you feel acquainted with VS Code and its capabilities, you can type in *Example 3.1* (from the previous section on *Installing VS Code on Windows*) or, if you have downloaded the companion set of example files, use the **File** menu to load, or simply drag and drop *Example 3.1* into VS Code to start editing it, as shown in *Figure 3.1* (at the start of this chapter) which, although it is the Windows versions, is almost exactly what you will see on a Mac.

Installing VS Code on Linux

VS Code is also great on a Linux PC and is supported by all of *Debian*, *Ubuntu*, *Red Hat*, *Fedora* and *SUSE* (and potentially many others too). Now, as with installing a LAMP, the mere fact that you are using Linux means you must already be quite used to command line installing a variety of software.

VS Code is as easy as any software to install and comes in both **.deb** and **.rpm** installer versions and for various chipsets too. In case you are new to Linux, though, under Debian style Linux distributions, the way to install a **.deb** file is to type the following (changing the filename according to that of the downloaded file):

```
sudo dpkg -i code_1.71.0-1662018389_amd64.deb
```

If you are running a distribution that uses **.rpm** files, you will normally type the following (changing the filename according to that of the downloaded file):

```
rpm -ivh code-1.71.0-1662018467.el7.x86_64.rpm
```

These are just suggestions of what you normally would do, and you can also use your graphical interface too. If in doubt, refer to the instructions for your version of Linux.

Once you have installed VS Code, the first thing you should now do is select **Help** followed by **Editor Playground** as shown in *Figure 3.7* (in the *Installing VS Code on MacOS* section). This is a sort of an interactive document that you can work with to learn all the 10 main areas of using VS Code.

Once you feel acquainted with VS Code and its capabilities, you can type in *Example 3.1* (from the earlier section on *Installing VS Code on Windows*) or, if you have downloaded the companion set of example files, load in, or simply drag and drop *Example 3.1* onto VS Code to start editing it, as shown in *Figure 3.1* (at the start of this chapter) which, although it is the Windows versions, is almost exactly what you will see on Linux too.

> **Note: For the sake of simplicity only a single operating system has been chosen for taking the screen grabs in this book, so after this chapter, they will usually be from Windows because this is the OS used by the majority of developers, but it really makes very little difference either way.**

Getting Started with VS Code

OK. So, now you've installed VS Code on your computer and operating system. Let's take a look a little more closely at how to use it and some of the things we can do with it. For this, you are recommended to download the free companion archive of example files, and then store the unpacked directory tree directly within your document root folder.

If you recall from *Chapter 2, Installing a Web Server*, where it was suggested you install MAMP, by default on Windows your document root will be: **C:/MAMP/htdocs**. On MacOS, it will be **/Applications/MAMP/htdocs**, and if you installed Xampp on Linux, it will usually be: **/opt/lampp/htdocs/**, or a symbolic link you were suggested to make for it at: **/home/web**.

Once you have copied all the example files to the correct location, you should have a sub-folder called **Examples**, within which will be the various sections and chapters of this book, and the example files will be within subfolders of these. To test this, if your web server is running, you should just be able to type **localhost** in your browser's address bar and navigate through all the examples.

You can then use this document root as your home directory in VS Code by selecting **File** from the menu, followed by **Add Folder to Workspace…** (as shown on Windows in *Figure 3.8*), and then choose the document root folder in the file selector dialog box that is provided. You may be prompted with a question asking whether you trust the authors of the files in that folder, to which you should answer Yes.

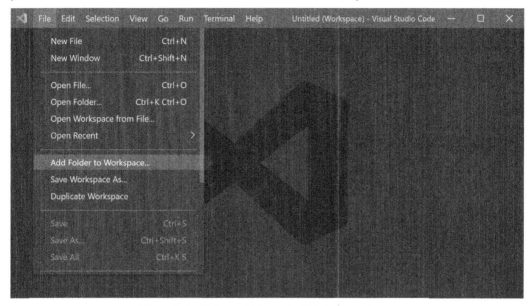

Figure 3.8: Adding a folder to the VX Code workspace

You are now ready to load in and work on the examples. So, select the **File** menu again and load in **example_01.html** from the **Section_1/03** folder. The result should look like *Figure 3.9*.

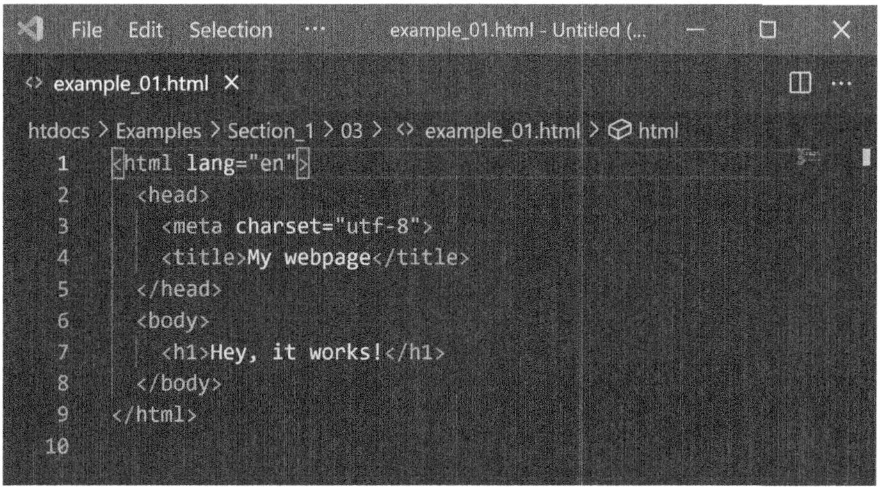

Figure 3.9: Editing the example from this chapter

You are now ready to work on what is basically just a shell of a web document. So, let's go to line 8 of the file and add a little more HTML, just for practice, inserting something along the following lines:

```
8. <p>Here is a paragraph of additional text just to practice using
   VS Code for editing documents. </p>
```

Even without saving the file, you can now load the document into your browser in the debug mode by pressing *F5*. Or if you just want to load the document in without debugging, then *Ctrl + F5* will do the trick. Or you can select either of these options from the run menu.

Try it and if you have more than one browser installed (for example, both *Chrome* and *Edge* on Windows), the first time you may be prompted which browser you prefer to use. After that, the one you select should stay as the default.

You are now ready to use VS Code as your editor and debugger all at the same time, and you will find working with the examples in this book as easy as possibly could be. You will also be able to edit the example sand play with them, which is a great way to fully absorb the features you are learning.

Of course, VS Code is a fully-fledged program with multiple features, offering tremendous power at your fingertips (and mouse), but you now have enough information now to already get started and making very good use of it.

For full documentation on everything you can do with VS Code, please visit the following URL, which will tell you everything else you need to know:

code.visualstudio.com/docs

Conclusion

Congratulations! You have now installed a WAMP, MAMP, or LAMP in the previous chapter, and the Visual Studio Code editor in this chapter, so you are now almost ready to start playing with all the examples to come. But there is just one more step needed to go through in the following chapter, which is to learn how to use your web browser's in-built development console, so that you can easily inspect and debug your code.

CHAPTER 4
The Developer Console

Introduction

In the past, when developing for the web, especially when you are applying styling with CSS (or the advanced CSS3 features), or perhaps incorporating some JavaScript, or inserting HTML5 features, you might have difficulty inspecting exactly what was going on when tracking down weird results or unusual bugs. This is why the developer console was created. With it, you can zoom down through all the elements of the HTML/CSS box model in the finest detail, and even send information to the console while a page is loading or JavaScript is running.

In this chapter, we'll take a look at how to invoke the developer console in various browsers, and look at some of the neat things you can do with it. Then, once you have mastered it, you'll be all set to begin your journey to learn HTML5 and CSS3.

Structure

In this chapter, you will:

- Learn about the developer console and its purpose
- Discover the difference between developer consoles
- Understand how to call up the console on your browser
- Become ready to debug your projects using the console

Objectives

After studying this chapter, you will have learned how to use your browser's built-in developer console to help you perfect your web documents and CSS styling, and use it to create dynamic and bug free website and web apps.

Accessing the developer console

Some years ago, there were various different approaches to help you to debug your programs from within the browser (initially, just through simple calls to the `document.write()` function to display various variable values), but nowadays, things have become a lot simpler and more standardized, especially since Google's Chrome web browser (already, the world leader) now has its core source code incorporated in many other browsers too, including *Microsoft Edge* and the *Opera* browser.

This leaves just two other main competing web browsers, which are *Mozilla Firefox* and Apple's *Safari*. Different monitoring organizations give different figures for browser popularity, but if you average them out it seems that *Google Chrome* has about 60%, of the market, *Safari* 20%, *Edge* 4%, *Firefox* 4%, *Samsung's* Internet browser 3%, *Opera* 2%, and about 7% for all others combined.

In light of this and because Google Chrome is available on almost all platforms, it is the default in this book, but *Table 4.1* shows how to bring up the developer Console in most popular browsers. You can also bring up the developer Console from most browsers' menus if you prefer. As you can see, on a PC it's usually the same key press combination, while there are generally two different ways to bring up the console on MacOS, according to the browser used, as in *Table 4.1*.

Browser / OS	Windows / Linux	Apple MacOS
Google Chrome	Shift + Ctrl + I	Option + ⌘ + I
Apple Safari	*(Does not apply)*	Option + ⌘ + C
Microsoft Edge	Shift + Ctrl + I	Option + ⌘ + I
Firefox	Shift + Ctrl + I	Shift + ⌘ + I
Opera	Shift + Ctrl + I	Option + ⌘ + I

Table 4.1: Developer console keyboard shortcuts

Developer consoles are powerful tools with many features, but this chapter will introduce you to the main ones you need. So, showing you how to bring them up and alert you to what they offer is the main task here. Once you really start developing with HTML5 and CSS3, and if you don't already do so, you will come to rely on the developer console as a constant programming companion.

For example, just take a look at *Figure 4.1*. This is a screen grab taken using Chrome on Windows, in which the very simple and short web document in *Example 4.1* uses the HTML5 canvas feature to draw the Mandelbrot set in color.

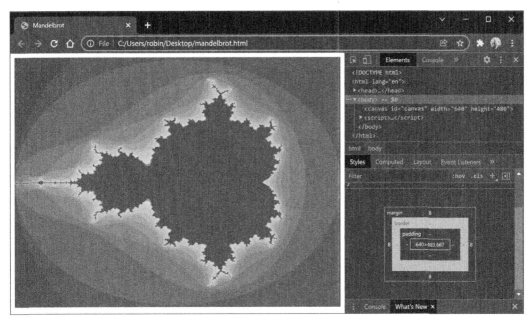

Figure 4.1: The Chrome developer console is open displaying information about the document

To the right, you can see the developer console, with the document source at the top right-hand corner, and a representation of the current box model below it. As you pass the mouse over the different elements, they are automatically highlighted in all the three windows, giving you a detailed, at-a-glance information on the structure of your document.

Note: Surprisingly (to some, perhaps), Microsoft used to have the number one browser, in the form of Internet Explorer, yet it allowed this fantastic lead to be eroded away by not keeping up with the latest Internet developments, and opting to implement features in its own, non-standard ways. The end result was that Microsoft has in recent years been forced to give up on its own browser code base, and now uses the open-source base for Chrome, so that Edge and Chrome are now very similar browsers indeed. And even then, because users have such long memories, almost all of them download a different browser to Edge when they buy a new computer, even though Edge should theoretically offer all that Chrome does. Thankfully, we don't have to worry about this anymore, anyway, because Edge and Chrome are the same to all the intents and purposes of this book. And, for similar reasons, so also is Opera, which also runs on the same code base.

Example 4.1

```
1.  <!DOCTYPE html>
2.  <html lang="en">
3.    <head>
4.      <meta charset="utf-8">
5.      <title>Mandelbrot</title>
6.    </head>
7.    <body>
8.      <canvas id='canvas'></canvas>
9.      <script>
10.       canvas          = document.getElementById('canvas')
11.       context         = canvas.getContext('2d')
12.       w               = 640
13.       h               = 480
14.       canvas.width  = w
15.       canvas.height = h
16.
17.       z  =  16
18.       y  =  0
19.       rm = -2
20.       rx =  1
21.       ix =  1.35
22.       im = -ix
23.
24.       for (i = im ; i <= ix ; i += (ix - im) / h, ++y)
25.       {
26.         for (x = 0, r = rm ; r <= rx ; r += (rx - rm) / w)
27.         {
28.           for (x1 = r, y1 = i, j = 0 ; j < z ; ++j)
29.           {
30.             xsq = x1 * x1; ysq = y1 * y1
```

```
31.              if (xsq + ysq > 4.0) break
32.
33.              y1 = 2 * x1 *  y1 + i ; x1 = xsq - ysq + r
34.            }
35.
36.            context.fillStyle =           '#' +
37.              ( j      % 16).toString(16) +
38.              ((j + 2) % 16).toString(16) +
39.              ((j + 7) % 16).toString(16)
40.            context.fillRect(x++, y, 1, 1)
41.          }
42.        }
43.    </script>
44.  </body>
45. </html>
```

This is not the place to explain what a Mandelbrot is or how you create it, but by looking at lines 10–15 and 36–40, you can see the few JavaScript commands needed to draw on the HTML5 canvas element, all of which are explained in *Section 2* of this book.

You can click on the vertical triple-dot settings icon displayed just before the console's close button to dock the console to any side of the browser you choose, or even pop it into its own window.

If you choose to use the *Firefox* browser, instead, things will look a little different, as shown in *Figure 4.2*, again grabbed using a Windows PC. Here, you can see that the console occupies the bottom of the screen, which is the default, but if you click on the horizontal triple-dot settings icon just to the left of the close console button, you can choose to dock it to any side you like, or even give it its own window.

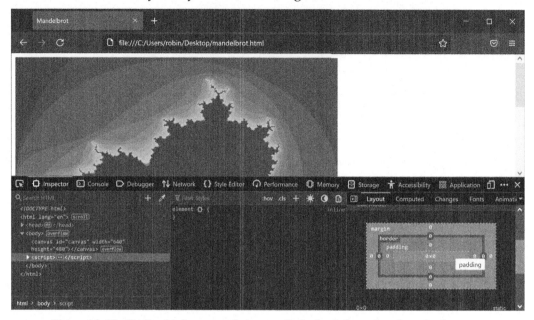

Figure 4.2: *The Firefox developer console is open displaying information about the document*

Similar though they may be, different consoles work in slightly different ways to each other and their menus are in different orders, with different names and list items. So, now this point has been illustrated, it's not really necessary to show you all the other consoles in different browsers on different operating systems because you will expect them to have differences.

Therefore, it's now down to you to choose the browser you wish to develop with, although you are highly recommended to have access to all browsers on multiple operating systems when you get close to deployment of a new project (or even during development if you can), in order to ensure your web pages look great on all of them.

Once you've selected you favorite development browser (and Chrome is recommended here, simply due to its massive popularity among both users and developers), you will need to acquaint yourself with the developer console it provides, so *Table 4.2* provides a list of the various documentation URLs, which you really should at least browse through to get started:

Browser(s)	Documentation Website
Chrome / Edge / Opera	**developer.chrome.com/docs/devtools**
Firefox	**firefox-source-docs.mozilla.org/devtools-user**
Safari	**support.apple.com/en-in/guide/safari-developer**

Table 4.2: *Various browser developer console documentation websites*

Useful things you can do

The developer console is so vast and powerful that you might at first wonder what on earth you would do with all its features. To give you some ideas of ways you can use it as a creativity and bug testing tool while developing websites, here are a few suggestions.

Firstly, have you ever visited a web page and been struck with how well it has been put together? And then maybe wondered what it would do if you changed just one little thing? Normally, when you have an idea for improving a web page you just let it slide because you'd have to copy it and all its content to somewhere local and then make the modifications.

In the good old days of the web this is how many developers learned how to create their own web pages by copying the existing ones and playing with them. But now you can make the whole web page editable and see what happens right there and then by opening up the developer console and typing the following:

```
document.body.contentEditable=true
```

Now, you can edit any of the content on the currently loaded web page to see what effect it has. That means this tool is great for testing out new headlines and other layouts in place. Of course, you won't be actually modifying the web page on the website, just the local copy in your web browser. Having said that, it's a fantastic tool for when you stumble across a website that catches your attention and you want to see what it would look like if modified in certain ways, perhaps to see whether And should be you'd like to implement some effect or feature you saw on your own web page.

When you've finished and want to try out your changes, just enter the following into the console, by first calling up the console in the way specified in *Table 4.1* for your computer, then typing the following:

```
document.body.contentEditable=false
```

Autocompletion

Ok, that first idea was just a bit of fun more than anything to get you using the console. But now, let's get a little more serious and look up a value using *Example 4.1*, which you should first load into your browser (ideally, using the freely downloadable companion archive of examples, to save you typing it in).

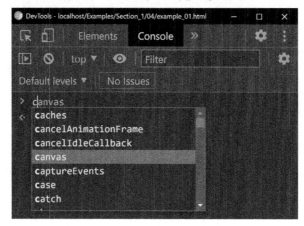

Figure 4.3: The word canvas is in the pop-down menu

This example contains a few HTML elements such as the **<html>** section, the **<head>**, a **<title>**, the **<body>** a **<canvas>**, and a **<script>** section. As you progress through this book, anything here that you don't understand will be explained. But suppose you wish to know the width of the canvas element without already having access to the source listing, and also if you don't wish to plough through lines of code to find out, but you *do* know it has the id of **canvas**.

Well, just start typing that ID into the console, and as soon as you enter the first letter **c,** a pop-up menu of potential options will be displayed, as shown in *Figure 4.3*. You can now directly select the word **canvas** from this list and the canvas in the web page will be highlighted too, then type a **.** (period) character, followed by the first two letters of **width**, that is **wi**, and you'll see the pop-up menu shown in *Figure 4.4*.

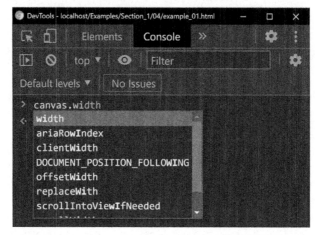

Figure 4.4: After a couple of key presses the canvas width property has been found

Just select the word **width** from the menu and presto, the console now tells you that the width of the canvas is 640 pixels, as shown in *Figure 4.5*, even without you pressing *Enter*. Isn't that really convenient and quick?

Figure 4.5: The width of the canvas is now displayed

While you're at it, you can append an assignment to this value to change the width of the canvas. Let's see what happens if we change a CSS style of the canvas using the following instruction:

```
canvas.style.opacity = .5
```

If you enter this command, you should immediately see the image in the canvas become half transparent, as shown in *Figure 4.6*.

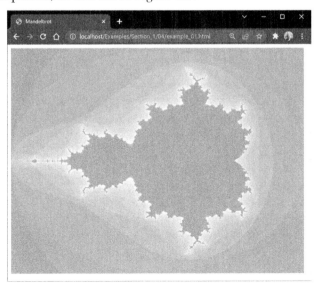

Figure 4.6: The opacity of the canvas is set to half

What you are learning here is how to access CSS styles on elements from within the console. First, specify the element **id** name, followed by a period, then the word **style** and a period to select it's CSS style properties, then enter the property name followed by the = symbol, and finally, enter a value to assign to that property.

In cases where a CSS property uses a hyphen to split the property name into two words, remove the hyphen and set the first letter of the second word to upper case. This is because the hyphen is a minus sign in JavaScript, so a different way to access CSS properties has been chosen. So, for example, to set the **margin-top** property of the canvas to 50 pixels you can enter the following instruction:

```
canvas.style.marginTop = '50px'
```

When you do this a blank, 50 pixel margin is immediately placed above the canvas.

Inspecting elements

Another great way to get information about elements is to inspect them. You can do this by pointing and clicking on the various elements shown in different parts of the console, or you can issue a textual command to drill right down to any element of interest. Let's do that with the canvas using the **inspect()** function, as follows:

```
inspect($('canvas'))
```

Here, the **inspect** function has been called and it is passed a value of **$('canvas')** which is an instruction to the browser to get the element by its **id**, the **$** being shorthand for the much longer named JavaScript call **getElementById()**. The result is that the **Elements** tab of the console will now display, as shown in *Figure 4.7*.

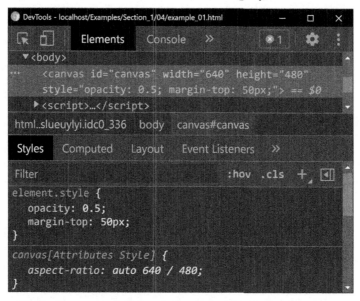

Figure 4.7: *The Elements and Styles tabs list various details about the canvas element*

At the top of the console, you can see a copy of the web document's source, with the canvas element highlighted. Then, below that in the **Styles** tab, you can see the two styles that we have just applied to the canvas, and under that, the aspect ratio the canvas has of 640 x 480 pixels is reported. At a glance, all the details you might need to know about an element are in clear view, just from entering a single **inspect()** instruction.

As you might imagine, there's a great deal more you can do with the development console, but at least you now have a flavor for some of the possibilities. For comprehensive details on the development console as explained by the *Google Chrome* developers, check out the following URL (the features described should be similar, if not identical, in all consoles):

tinyurl.com/devcons

Conclusion

We are still not quite in the age where all web browsers work identically, but we are a lot closer than we ever have been. Thankfully for the users we develop for, browsers are very close to each other indeed on how they perform and display, but as developers, we must still live with the different quirks lurking behind the scenes. Having said that, they all do offer the same powerful features; it's just that you may need to access them in slightly different ways on different browsers and operating systems.

As you progress through this book, when asked to check something out with the developer console (such as inspecting logged output), you will now know what that means and how to achieve the task.

And now you are ready to get your teeth stuck right into HTML5 web developing starting in *Section 2* (and then CSS3 in *Section 3*), and should be looking forward to this because you are surely going to be amazed at how easy it is to add an incredible range of new features and interactivity to your web projects.

CHAPTER 5
Introduction to HTML5

Introduction

Although, it may seem by its name that HTML5 is simply the next release of HTML, it's not quite that, and yet it's more than that. To explain this, you need to realize that web development has sort of merged and converged, and that while we may talk of HTML5 and CSS3, they are in a way intertwined and interconnected with JavaScript too.

So, when we try to separate out HTML5, it's not really possible to do fully because much of the HTML5 specification relies on the use of both CSS3 and JavaScript, but we will do our best to distinguish between them wherever possible, and then point out where the lines become blurred.

For example, one of the most important features in HTML5 is the new `<canvas>` element, but you can only use it by issuing JavaScript commands. On the other hand, some of the graphical effects you see in a canvas can also be achieved using CSS3 transformations. Because of this, it is often best to think of the triad of HTML5, CSS3 and JavaScript, and you will learn about how they all integrate with each other in this book.

But don't worry, if you're not a programmer, you're not going to have to learn JavaScript programming in its entirety because the HTML5 canvas and other HTML features can be accessed using a very simple subset of JavaScript commands, which you'll be able to easily learn, as they are used more like an extension to HTML than anything.

The point is, though, don't just assume you'll be learning new HTML tags and attributes, because HTML5 is more than that. Having said this, let's start by looking at what HTML5 brings to the programmer's toolkit, mainly in the form of new elements.

Structure

In this chapter, you will:

- Learn a the new features in HTML5

- Understand the basics of what these features do

- Work through a few examples for yourself

- Get to grips with the specifics of using HTML5

Objectives

In this chapter, you'll be introduced to all the main technologies and features that comprise HTML5. By the time you finish it, you'll know exactly what new tools are available in HTML5, and you'll be ready to start learning how to leverage them into creating the best results for your projects by following the information provided in the remaining chapters in the section.

HTML5 is more than HTML4 + 1

As discussed in the introduction of this chapter, HTML5 is a lot more than simply the next version of HTML. But let's approach our investigation into what it actually is carefully by examining the parts of HTML5 that are simply new HTML features.

Once we've done that, we'll then take a look at the parts of the HTML5 specification that start blurring boundaries with other technologies. So, having already discussed the new canvas element, let's begin there.

The <canvas> element

One of the main things that was lacking in HTML for a very long time was the ability to draw and manipulate graphics. Initially, this was corrected with the use of *Microsoft ActiveX* controls, and then by the *Adobe Flash* plug-in. But these proved to be buggy and offered too many security vulnerabilities. Besides, they required installing and a built-in solution is what was truly needed.

Note: The issues with these plug-ins, and Flash in particular, were so huge that the author of this book published an article back in 2015, entitled, HTML5 is the new Flash, detailing all the main problems with it, and how HTML5 was the obvious solution. If you are interested, you can still read the complete article here: ics.ie/news/view/1675, which will explain what the landscape was like at the time.

The main answer to Flash was the **<canvas>** element (alongside the addition of audio and video features), which was first supported by the *MacOS WebKit* component back in 2004, powering the *Dashboard* and *Safari* browser. In 2006, *Firefox* and *Opera* added support, before the **Web Hypertext Application Technology Working Group** (**WHATWG**) added it as a standard, and browsers such as *Google Chrome* incorporated it in 2010.

This is one example of how web standards have developed over time, and a reminder of the days when you needed to write conditional code to detect the browser running in order to determine which features were available. It was a nightmare for developers, which thankfully is now only the remainder of a bad dream, because the HTML5 specification is now considered mature. Although, new web technologies are always likely to come along and will probably take a while to filter into all browsers and look and work the same way.

Anyhow, we now have a fantastically powerful means of drawing right within the browser, as long as we set up the canvas element correctly in the HTML, and use a few JavaScript commands. All will become clear in the following chapter, but for now, *Figure 5.1* shows a canvas element in which a rectangle has been drawn, with a filled in color gradient, using the simple commands in the following example:

Figure 5.1: *A color gradient filled rectangle on an HTML5 canvas element*

Example 5.1

```
1.  <!DOCTYPE html>
2.  <html lang="en">
3.    <head>
4.      <meta charset="utf-8">
5.      <title>Gradient Example</title>
6.    </head>
7.    <body>
8.    <canvas id='canvas'></canvas>
9.      <script>
10.        canvas       = document.getElementById('canvas')
11.        context      = canvas.getContext('2d')
12.        w            = 640
13.        h            = 320
14.        canvas.width = w
15.        canvas.height = h
16.        gradient     = context.createLinearGradient(0, 0, w, 0)
17.
18.        gradient.addColorStop("0",   "magenta")
19.        gradient.addColorStop(".25", "blue")
20.        gradient.addColorStop(".50", "green")
21.        gradient.addColorStop(".75", "yellow")
22.        gradient.addColorStop("1.0", "red")
23.
24.        context.fillStyle = gradient
25.        context.fillRect(0,0,640,320)
26.      </script>
27.    </body>
28. </html>
```

Geolocation

One of the biggest new features needed for mobile browsing was geolocation. Using it, you can call up a map of your locality if you're lost, or search for nearby gas stations or other facilities. Unfortunately, for non-programmers, you will need a little knowledge of JavaScript to make full use of the geolocation, but actually, this can sometimes consist of just some lines of code that you can cut and paste.

For example, *Figure 5.2* shows a map that has been displayed as a result of looking up the location at which the web browser is being used (the south-east of England, in this case). The document used to create this screen grab can be seen in *Example 5.2*. We won't discuss how it works just yet, as there's much greater detail in *Chapter 12, Using Geolocation*, but for now just note line 8, which mentions two functions: **granted** and **denied**. This is because it's up to the user whether or not to reveal their location to the browser as there are potential security implications.

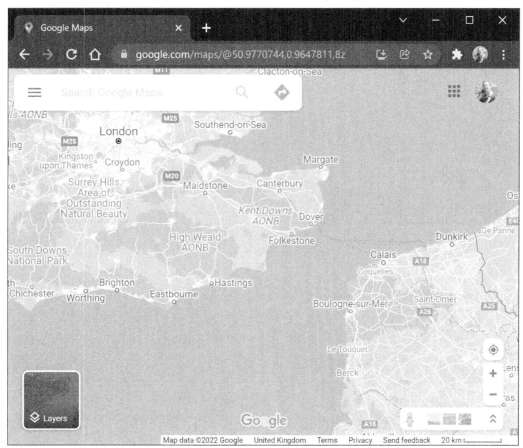

Figure 5.2: A map displayed as the result of a geolocation lookup

Example 5.2

```
1. <!DOCTYPE html>
2. <html lang="en">
3.    <head>
```

```
4.      <title>Geolocation Example</title>
5.    </head>
6.    <body>
7.     <script>
8.       navigator.geolocation.getCurrentPosition(granted, denied)
9.
10.       function granted(position)
11.       {
12.         var lat = position.coords.latitude
13.         var lon = position.coords.longitude
14.
15.         alert("Permission Granted. You are at location:\n\n"
16.           + lat + ", " + lon + "\n\nClick 'OK' to load "
17.           + "Google Maps with your location")
18.
19.         window.location.replace("https://www.google.com/maps/@"
20.           + lat + "," + lon + ",8z")
21.       }
22.
23.       function denied(error)
24.       {
25.         var message
26.
27.         switch(error.code)
28.         {
29.           case 1: message = 'Permission Denied';     break;
30.           case 2: message = 'Position Unavailable'; break;
31.           case 3: message = 'Operation Timed Out';   break;
32.           case 4: message = 'Unknown Error';         break;
33.         }
34.
35.         alert("Geolocation Error: " + message)
```

```
36.        }
37.     </script>
38.   </body>
39. </html>
```

If the user agrees, the function named **granted** is called at line 10, otherwise the one called **denied** is run at line 23. In the former case, the coordinates are looked up and passed to a Google map to be displayed; otherwise, the reason why the map could not be displayed is given. Of course, a production website will give more than just a terse error message, but this code is just there for explanation of what's going on. And, as previously said, don't worry if the example makes little sense to you right now; it will surely become clear as you work through the book.

Forms

There are a number of new enhancements of how you can use forms in HTML5. For example, you can now place **<input> tags outside** of **<form>** and **</form>** tags as long as the new **form attribute** is used to identify the form to which the input refers. Similarly, you can change the method (either **GET** or **POST**) of a form with the new **formmethod** attribute.

There are also several new enhancements that allow you to change the **encoding type** of a **form**, create or even **override** a new **novalidate attribute**. You can also use the **formaction** attribute to change the **action** (otherwise known as the **destination**) of a form, and you can use **formtarget** to change the **target** to a **frame**, **tab** or **window**. At the same **time** you can now change the **height** and **width** of the **image** type of the **<input>** tag using **height** and **width attributes**.

There are a couple of particularly handy new attributes that you can see in action every day at the Google search engine, as shown in *Figure 5.3*. These are **autocomplete**, which allows pre-filled values for a field to be offered as suggested values, and **autofocus**, which makes the browser, focus on a form field automatically.

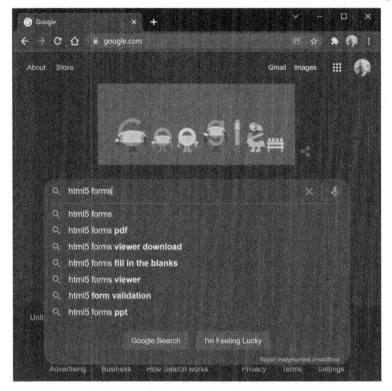

Figure 5.3: *The Google search engine offering a choice of inputs*

The figure shows what it thinks are the most likely searches you mean as a set of pre-filled inputs you can choose to select from HTML5 forms also bring new **min**, **max,** and **step** attributes so that you have better control of the input of data such as numbers or dates, and you can also make use of a new **multiple** attribute, which you can use in conjunction with an **<input>** tag to allow the submission of more than one value at a time.

You can now match patterns in forms using the **pattern** attribute and the new **placeholder** attribute makes it possible for you to display a hint within an input field to help guide the user what to enter. Also, the **type** attribute supports a number of new values, including **color**, **date**, **month**, **time**, **week**, **number**, **range**, **Tel**, **url**, and **email**. With these, you can ensure that the correct values are entered into your forms and make doing so a lot easier for the user.

There are several other important enhancements to forms not yet mentioned, all of which are explained in *Chapter 13, Form Handling*.

Local storage and session storage

Once you really start producing interactive and dynamic web pages, there comes a time when the use of cookies is simply not powerful enough to provide the speediest environment. More than that, many countries have strict rules on the use of cookies, which means you often need to add warnings and ask for their acceptance. What's more cookies are limited in their size to just 4KB of data.

But there is a better way, which is to use local storage to allow users to navigate through websites quickly and easily, by retaining information about their surfing session in local storage. Local storage offers up to 5MB per website, easily accessed in key/data pairs. It has an additional advantage in that unlike cookies which may support accessing by numerous different websites (and therefore be used to track surfing behavior); only the site that saves to local storage can access the data that it stores. It stays private between the user and the website.

The reason you would want to do store anything on a user's computer is to save having to keep on sending the same data to a user over and again. If you just store cookies with a username/password pair (for example), you can fully personalize a site to a user's needs, sending the correct details to the user for each web page they surf to. For example, you can keep the contents of a user's shopping cart (or anything else you need to keep track of) in their local storage.

And with local storage, you can enhance the natural caching of web pages your browser might manage (where it saves the contents of documents to bring up from memory if you return to a previously visited page, saving download time and data), by also storing data that would otherwise not be cached on the user's system.

Having access to 5MB of data in the form of key/data pairs is like having a mini database of sorts available on the user's computer, and this means you can also create local web apps that store no data on a remote server, and therefore are able to run fully stand-alone. It just adds a lot more flexibility and choice when it comes down to your choosing how you will store and manage a user's data, and in *Chapter 14, Local Storage and More*, you'll learn a few simple JavaScript lines of code you can enter to access local storage.

Session storage is the same as local storage, with the exception that the data it stores is wiped when the browser is closed or restarted, making it a better solution for security conscious websites and apps, where long term storage should not be an option. It is also covered in *Chapter 14, Local Storage and More*.

Note: There is another type of local storage called IndexedDB, which offers storage of a gigabyte or more depending on the browser (and if the user grants it) and, as its name suggests, with it you can use indexes to access the data, making it a great deal more powerful than the standard local storage. However, it is not covered in this book because its use requires prior knowledge of how indexed databases work, and a fair understanding of using JavaScript. If you'd like to learn more, though, the following website is a good place to start, where you will also learn about libraries you can use to make the programming task a little simpler: tinyurl.com/using-indexdb

Microdata

One aspect of HTML5 that is particularly useful for promoting your site to search engines is the use of microdata. This is a new set of tags you can use to precisely explain the data represented within some HTML. For example, you can let an engine like Google know which words are names of people, which are job titles, which parts of an address are the name, number street, town and so forth, which strings of text are affiliations to organizations a person may have, which items of texts are names of qualifications, and so forth.

Supplied with all this clarifying data, search engines can understand a document far better, and then make better matches with the right people searching for what the content of your page is about. In *Chapter 14, Local Storage and More*, you will learn all the available microdata tags and attributes, which will be a highly worthwhile exercise if you are ever tasked with **Search Engine Optimization (SEO)**, as this will add a powerful set of strings to your development bow.

Other semantic tags

Many new syntactic features have also been included in HTML5 which aren't considered microdata, but do serve to further explain to search engines (or text to speech readers for blind people, for example) the content of a web page. There are the new `<summary>` and `<details>` tags, plus new page structure elements, including `<main>`, `<section>`, `<article>`, `<header>`, `<footer>`, `<aside>`, `<nav>`, and `<figure>`, all of which are explained in *Chapter 14, Local Storage and More*.

Web workers and applications

A couple of other features came from what was called the **Web Apps Working Group (WAWG)** and were then sort of absorbed into HTML5 when they were transferred to the **Web Platform Working Group (WPWG)** in 2015. So, although not originally planned as such, they have become thought of as part of HTML5 by pretty much everyone.

The first of these is web workers, which are a way to offload heavy processing tasks to a separate document containing JavaScript instructions. The idea is to allow these to run in the background at maximum speed, exchanging messages with the foreground task as necessary. Web workers cannot be interrupted by clicks or other user interactions and therefore are fast and powerful. They also can run away with themselves if you leave a bug, so you must be careful.

Normally, to achieve background processing in JavaScript, you need to set up a timer that is constantly called, supplying slices of processor time to one or more functions, and these functions must then quickly do a small piece of work and return, in order to not slow down the browser and make it seem sluggish.

Web workers require knowledge of JavaScript, but don't worry if you are not a programmer, you can either copy and paste from the code supplied in *Chapter 14, Local Storage and More*, or simply not concern yourself with web workers, as they are more of a niche technology.

Web applications

Along with web workers came the concept of web applications, which are groups of web pages that you can download and treat as a separate application. This is how some mobile websites make themselves look and work offline, very much as if they are apps downloaded from an app store. Again, these are more advanced features of HTML5 and if you are not a programmer, or you don't currently see a need for them, you can safely skip the section about them in *Chapter 14, Local Storage and More.*

Audio and video

Possibly, the most popular addition to the HTML specification was the inclusion of multimedia, such as audio and video. Finally, there are now ways to play most of the major media types without needing plug-ins and spaghetti code, and at high quality and low bandwidth too thanks to powerful and fast compression and decompression routines (called CODECs).

That's right. Gone forever are the days of needing to own a copy of Flash in order to play the animations you make, or show home videos in your blog. Now, all you need to do insert a pair of **<audio>** and **</audio>** or **<video>** and **</video>** tags, provide a link to a media file (whether on your server or elsewhere), and you're done.

Using audio

This is not the place to visit the process in detail, but to illustrate the ease of adding audio to a web page. Take a look at *Example 5.3*, which will display as *Figure 5.4*.

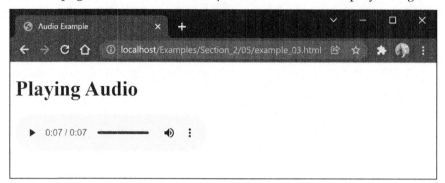

Figure 5.4: Playing a short MP3 audio file

As you can see, all the work is done by lines 8–10, in which the **<audio>** tag is used with user controls enabled, and the audio source is **example.mp3** located in the current folder.

Example 5.3

```
1. <!DOCTYPE html>
2. <html lang="en">
3.   <head>
4.     <title>Audio Example</title>
5.   </head>
6.   <body>
7.     <h1>Playing Audio</h1>
8.     <audio controls>
9.       <source src='example.mp3'>
10.    </audio>
11.  </body>
12. </html>
```

Using video

It's equally easy to include a video on a web page, as shown in *Example 5.4*, which displays as *Figure 5.5*, in which lines 8–10 use a **<video>** tag to insert a short movie with dimensions of 640 by 360 pixels, and with user controls displayed. The video is stored in the local folder as **example.mp4**.

Figure 5.5: *Playing a short MP4 video file (by Ruitong Yu from pixabay.com)*

Example 5.4

```
1.  <!DOCTYPE html>
2.  <html lang="en">
3.    <head>
4.      <title>Video Example</title>
5.    </head>
6.    <body>
7.      <h1>Playing Video</h1>
8.      <video controls width='640' height=>'360'>
9.        <source src='example.mp4'>
10.     </video>
11.   </body>
12. </html>
```

Isn't it amazing how easily you can incorporate multimedia in your web pages? And, as you will learn in *Chapter 15, Audio and Video*, there are other features you can also use to further improve the way they display and play.

SVG and MathML

HTML5 also brought support for two amazingly powerful technologies, SVG and MathML. They are both ways of drawing graphically on a web page without using the canvas. **Scalable Vector Graphics** (**SVG**), and with it, you can draw two-dimensional vector graphics right on a web page. You can use it to draw images on the fly, scale them as you see fit without any loss of quality (something impossible with bitmapped images such as PNG, GIF, or JPG), and you can even create animations with it, all via plain XML text files, or there are some graphical tools you can use to make life simpler.

MathML, on the other hand, is aimed at mathematicians and scientists who need the ability to display complicated formulae and equations, which is not a feature offered by normal HTML or ASCII. What's more, MathML preserves the meaning of a formula, so that it can be expressed in different forms, perhaps by printing and even through text to speech.

Unfortunately, these two technologies are far too extensive for covering in this book, as they would each require an entire book in order to fully teach them. But at least you are now aware that these are available to you, and if they have captured your imagination, you can explore them further for yourself at the following URLs:

- tinyurl.com/using-svg
- tinyurl.com/using-mathml

Conclusion

You now have a basic understanding of what HTML5 is, why it was a necessary evolution of HTML, and what its features can do to help you create the best web documents possible. You know how easy it is to add audio and video to your web pages, how to find out where a user is located (if they agree), how to draw on a canvas, and the use of semantic and syntactic elements to make your web documents make more sense to search engines, and also to apps that need to understand them such as screen readers for blind people.

In the following chapter, you will really begin to get stuck into the hows and wherefores of creating impressive web graphics, by learning to use the `<canvas>` element.

CHAPTER 6
The HTML5
Canvas

Introduction

This book devotes a lot of pages to the HTML5 `<canvas>` tag because it's one of the most powerful and significant new additions to HTML. It has enabled almost all the features that plugins such as Flash previously provided, but in a highly secure and easy-to-use manner.

You will need to learn a little JavaScript to make use of the canvas, but really all you will do is learn a few drawing commands that are not much harder to pick up than either HTML or even CSS. As a bonus, if you choose to ever add the JavaScript language to your web development toolkit, you'll already be well on your way, just from what you learn here.

But don't worry, I promise that this type of programming is little more than creating shopping lists based on the order that items appear in your local supermarket. It's simply a matter of issuing a few commands in the right order. And you are effectively programming or, in the case of the HTML5 canvas, you will be drawing.

Structure

In this chapter, you will:

- Learn what the HTML5 canvas is and how to access it

- Understand how to pass element IDs to JavaScript

- Learn how to use a context to control drawing on the canvas

- Convert canvases to images

Objectives

In this chapter, you will get a thorough introduction to the HTML5 canvas element. You will also learn some elemental JavaScript, with which you'll be able to draw rectangles of different colors, and even convert canvases to images. This will prepare you for delving into more advanced drawing techniques in the following chapters.

A crash course in JavaScript

You're going to need to learn a little JavaScript if you're to make the best use of all the goodies provided by HTML5. As there's no time like the present, let's jump in at the deep end and start programming right away.

You need to incorporate JavaScript within HTML documents by inserting it within a pair of `<script>` … `</script>` statements. Often, these will be placed within the head section of a document to ensure the code runs early on during a page's loading, but you will also see JavaScript sections of code elsewhere, such as in a document's body.

There are two ways on inserting the code. The first is to type it between the two tags, and the second is to save it in a separate document and load that in. The first is more often used for very short code snippets, while the latter is best suited for longer programs. Let's take a look at both of them.

Code within the `<script>` tags

Take a look at *Example 6.1*, in which you see a typical HTML5 document, into which some JavaScript programming code has been inserted between lines 15 and 25. You have already seen code similar to this in the previous chapter, in which the canvas element was introduced by drawing a gradient filled rectangle.

Example 6.1

```
1.  <!DOCTYPE html>
2.  <html lang="en">
3.    <head>
4.      <meta charset="utf-8">
5.      <title>Using script tags 1</title>
6.      <style>
7.        #canvas {
8.          background-color : cyan;
9.          border           : 1px solid black;
10.       }
11.     </style>
12.   </head>
13.   <body>
14.     <canvas id='canvas'></canvas>
15.     <script>
16.       canvas         = document.getElementById('canvas')
17.       context        = canvas.getContext('2d')
18.       canvas.width   = 640
19.       canvas.height  = 320
20.
21.       context.beginPath()
22.       context.strokeStyle = 'green'
23.       context.rect(20, 20, 600, 280)
24.       context.stroke()
25.     </script>
26.   </body>
27. </html>
```

This example, however, just draws a plain rectangle without any fill, keeping the code as simple as possible, as shown in *Figure 6.1*:

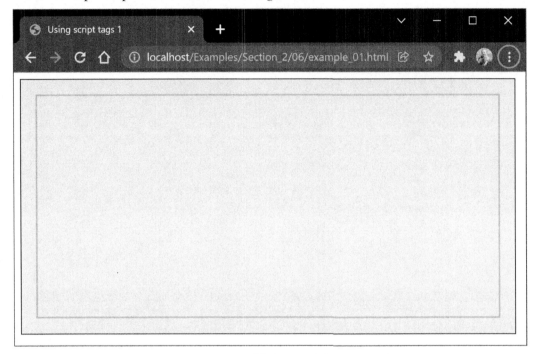

***Figure 6.1**: Drawing an unfilled rectangle in a canvas element*

There are a few things to note here. Firstly, there's a **<style>** section between lines 6 and 11 in which the object called **canvas** is given a black border and a cyan background, so that it stands out from the default white background of the web page. Secondly, at line 14, the canvas is given the ID of **canvas** so that it can be referenced by both the CSS styling and also the programming code that follows.

Having pointed these two things out, let's take a look at the JavaScript code itself. On line 16, a thing called a JavaScript object is created with the name **canvas**. This is followed by connecting this object to the canvas we previously created using a complicated looking JavaScript command. All this is doing is looking up the HTML element that has the ID of **canvas** and then creating an object that JavaScript can understand, which is also called **canvas**.

Note: The naming here of the IDs and the objects being all called the same name serves to make it as clear as possible just what is happening. But in the real world, where you might have multiple canvases and objects, you would need different names to tell them apart, so you would probably name them something like canvas1, canvas2 and so on, or perhaps mapcanvas, for example, if you were drawing a map.

Then, having put the **<canvas>** element into the JavaScript object named **canvas**, on line 17 a thing called a 2D context is created based on this object. Now, you don't need to feel confused here or really understand what's going on, other than to know that the context (which has been given the obvious name of **context**), is like a reference we will use to access the canvas from now on for all future drawing commands on that canvas. Effectively, in this book, you can just copy and paste lines 16 and 17 wherever you intend to access a canvas, as long as the canvas has the ID of **canvas**.

On lines 18 and 19, the width and height of the canvas are set. This has been done in JavaScript here, but it could equally have occurred when the canvas was created, as follows:

```
<canvas id='canvas' with='640' height='320'></canvas>
```

However, you *cannot* set the width and height of the canvas in the CSS section, as follows, as this would only scale the canvas from whatever its default dimensions happen to be. You must remember to set a canvases dimensions either in the HTML or within JavaScript.

```
Width :640px; // CSS such as this will not
height:320px; // work as you might think
```

There just remains four lines of code to explain. When drawing lines on a canvas, you generally need to define the start of a path and then draw along that path. So line 21 says, "*Let's start a path on this context*", by calling the **beginPath()** function on the current context. Following that, the color green is chosen to draw with, so line 22 assigns the color green to the attribute **strokeStyle** of the current context. This is like attaching a green pen to the drawing head of a plotter.

And now, we are set to do some drawing at line 23, which simply tells the browser to move the pen to the location 20 pixels in and 20 pixels down the canvas, and then draw an unfilled rectangle of dimensions 600 by 280 pixels using the current styles that have been set, which in this case is simply the color green.

However, the rectangle has not yet been drawn because we are in the middle of following a path. In order to close off the path and place the drawing on the canvas, a final command is required on line 24, which calls the **stroke()** function on the current context, which is like telling JavaScript, "*OK, you have your instructions, now draw that path as described.*"

Code in a separate file

Now that you've seen the code running within a web document and understood how it works, let's look at how you can tuck it away in a separate file, as shown in *Example 6.2*, which is a pure JavaScript file, which normally would be saved with an extension of **.js**. In this case, it's saved as **canvas.js**.

Example 6.2

```
1.  canvas        = document.getElementById('canvas')
2.  context       = canvas.getContext('2d')
3.  canvas.width  = 640
4.  canvas.height = 320
5.
6.  context.beginPath()
7.  context.strokeStyle = 'green'
8.  context.rect(20, 20, 600, 280)
9.  context.stroke()
```

As you can see, this file contains just the JavaScript itself, and it hasn't required so much white space to indent it because there's no surrounding HTML. Nothing about the code has changed other than removing the unnecessary white space and saving the file as **canvas.js**.

Now, let's modify *Example 6.1* to *Example 6.3*, and see what pulling in an external JavaScript file looks like.

Example 6.3

```
1.  <!DOCTYPE html>
2.  <html lang="en">
3.    <head>
4.      <meta charset="utf-8">
5.      <title>Using script tags 2</title>
6.      <style>
7.        #canvas {
8.          background-color : cyan;
9.          border           : 1px solid black;
10.       }
11.     </style>
12.   </head>
13.   <body>
14.     <canvas id='canvas'></canvas>
15.     <script src='canvas.js'></script>
```

```
16.  </body>
17. </html>
```

Take a look at line 15, which is now all that remains of the JavaScript in this HTML document. All the previous code has been replaced with a simple assignment to the **src** attribute, telling it where to fetch a JavaScript file from (in this case, it's the local file **canvas.js** that we just saved), rather than looking for the code within the tags to run.

See how it keeps your HTML uncluttered, while you can load your JavaScript code into a separate file and work on it on its own. And in an editor, such as VS Code, you can have multiple tabs open at a time, making this kind of multi-tasking development super easy, as shown in *Figure 6.2*, where you should also note the cute little color box the editor places before the color names for your convenience.

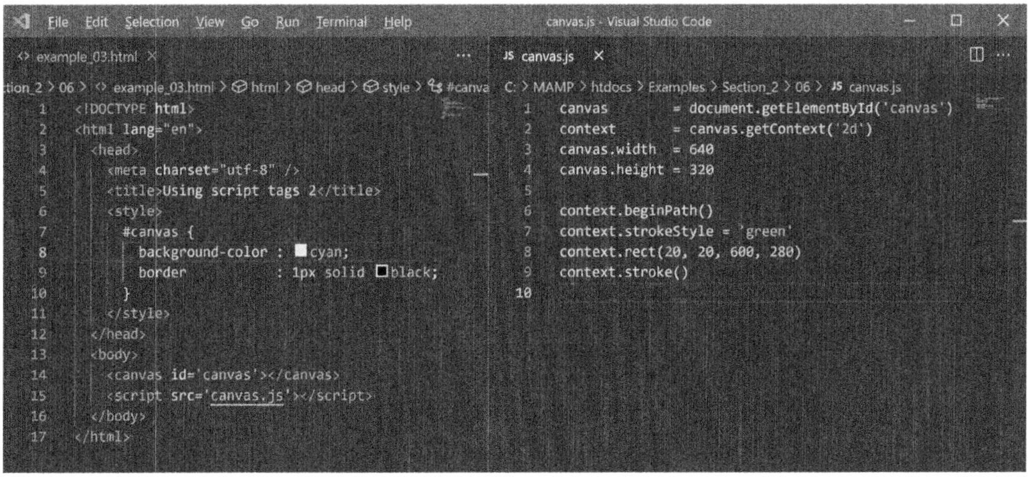

Figure 6.2: Editing two files at a time in VS Code

These hint boxes are especially helpful when you are using color numbers instead of names. Try passing your mouse over them and you'll see a color selector window pop up (as shown in F*igure 6.3*), from which you can change the colors with just a click – very handy.

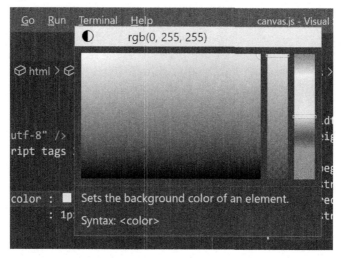

Figure 6.3: VS Code offering a color selection pop-up

Of course, there's a great deal more to JavaScript programming than the small amount you have seen here. However, you are off to an excellent start and as and when additional features become necessary to be included in this book, they are explained at the time.

> **Note: A note about JavaScript and semicolons. In many programming languages such as PHP, C or even plain old CSS, you must place a semicolon at the end of every completed line. And, indeed, you can also do so in JavaScript, and you will very often see the code where this is the case. However, in JavaScript such semicolons are optional, so a simple view is that if it's not needed, why use it? (the same way that this book doesn't recommend you should use the optional forward slash to self-close certain tags). There are, admittedly, a couple of very unusual edge cases in which you do need to use a semicolon, but you will almost certainly be an advanced programmer if that's the case and will know when to do so. If you wish, you can use semicolons to separate multiple JavaScript statements on a single line. But as a beginner, this is not a recommended practice.**

The getElementByID() function

We already saw **getElementByID()** being used to get the ID of an element as follows:

```
canvas = document.getElementById('canvas')
```

And it's important to remind you that this is a very common instruction that is used wherever you need to allow access to an element from JavaScript. You will see it frequently in the third-party code, and some developers use it so much that they write a new function (or use a framework such as jQuery) to reduce the amount they have to type (saving 22 characters each time), as follows:

```
canvas = $('canvas')
```

So, if you ever see the code that uses a **$** symbol in this manner, it's almost certainly passing the element's ID to a JavaScript object. But whatever name is used for this feature, the result is that the object is now able to access that HTML element and all its CSS properties, all from within JavaScript. So, it's almost the case that if you can style with CSS, you can also style in JavaScript.

Note: In case you are wondering whether using JavaScript for styling can mess with the separation of content and styling, then the answer is yes it can. Wherever possible you should try to style everything using CSS. But the fact is, you need to know how you can also do so in JavaScript, for those cases when you need features unmodifiable by CSS, such as video, audio and, as per this chapter, the canvas.

As you progress through this book, you will see many examples of element IDs being passed to JavaScript – you now are ready for that and will know what is happening.

Converting a canvas to an image

One downside to the **<canvas>** element (or it could be an upside too), is that it is not an image that can be dragged and dropped or saved. However, as a developer you might wish to use the canvas to create a graphic that you wish to share, without having to include all the associated JavaScript code (which you might want to keep proprietary).

Thankfully, there's a relatively easy way you can convert your canvases to standard web images, and that's by means of what's known as a data URL. This is a URL string that doesn't point to a link on your server, or anywhere on the web. Rather it contains all the data to construct the image right within the URL.

To achieve this, you must first create an empty image element in your HTML and then from the JavaScript, you will copy the canvas data to the **src** attribute of that image, thus giving it a data URL. At that point, the image will display and you can drag, drop, or save it as you wish!

Take a look at *Example 6.4*. This is a document that incorporates the JavaScript within itself, to keep the example all in one place, with which it draws on the canvas and saves it to the (previously) empty image on line 15. The result looks like *Figure 6.4*.

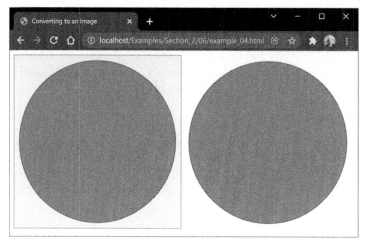

Figure 6.4: The image on the right has been created from the canvas on the left

If you now try to drag and drop both the canvas and the image on your desktop, you'll discover that the canvas will not respond, while the image will happily allow this. Go on, give it a go.

Example 6.4

```
1.  <!DOCTYPE html>
2.  <html lang="en">
3.    <head>
4.      <meta charset="utf-8">
5.      <title>Converting to an Image</title>
6.      <style>
7.        #canvas {
8.          background-color : yellow;
9.          border           : 1px solid red;
10.       }
11.     </style>
12.   </head>
13.   <body>
14.     <canvas id='canvas' width='320' height='320'></canvas>
```

```
15.    <img id='image'>
16.    <script>
17.      canvas  = document.getElementById('canvas')
18.      context = canvas.getContext('2d')
19.
20.      context.beginPath()
21.      context.arc(160, 160, 150, 0, 2 * Math.PI)
22.      context.fillStyle    = 'green'
23.      context.strokeStyle = 'blue'
24.      context.fill()
25.      context.stroke()
26.      document.getElementById('image').src = canvas.toDataURL()
27.    </script>
28.  </body>
29.</html>
```

Just for the sake of mixing things up a little, this example draws a green circle with a blue border. In the following chapter, you'll learn how this is done (if you haven't worked it out for yourself already), and then the magic happens on line 26, where the **src** attribute of the image is provided with a data URL of the canvas, and the image is then immediately displayed alongside the canvas.

Note, however, that the yellow background and red border of the canvas are *not* present in the newly created image because they are CSS attributes of the canvas and do not comprise part of the actual canvas. If you wanted those to appear in the new image, they would need to be drawn on the canvas, not applied as CSS styling.

If you do drag the image to the desktop, it will most likely be saved using a filename such as **download.png**. From there, you can do what you like with the image, which will be a standard **.png** file.

> **Note: Some recent browsers may allow you to right click on a canvas and then save it as an image, but that's just from the user's point of view. As a developer, you sometimes need to create images on the fly on an off-screen canvas and then load them as actual images in the correct places in your web documents, and converting a canvas to an image is how you would achieve this.**

Conclusion

Now that you've completed this chapter, you know a great deal about the HTML5 canvas, including how to set one up, how to style it in both CSS and JavaScript, how to draw on a canvas with simple JavaScript commands, and also how to convert a canvas to a regular image. In the next chapter, we'll start digging deeper into some more advanced drawing features.

CHAPTER 7
Rectangles and Fills

Introduction

By now, you will be quite familiar with the HTML5 canvas and also with using JavaScript to draw on it. So now, we'll start looking much more deeply into the various drawing tools to offer you as a developer.

As we proceed through this chapter, you will inevitably come across many JavaScript features. This is unavoidable because that's the only way you can use the canvas, but think about it like this. You are learning some of the fundamentals of JavaScript as a free bonus for reading this book.

Even if you consider yourself lacking in artistic skills, you will still find many uses for all these features, from being able to design charts and graphs, to making your own icons and illustrations. And because it's all instruction-driven, you'll find that for most simple designs, the precision this gives you is so much easier than attempting to draw with a mouse or pen using a graphics editor.

Structure

In this chapter, you will:

- Learn how to draw rectangles on the HTML5 canvas

- Understand how to enhance rectangles with fills, gradients, and patterns

- Discover how to load and manipulate images in JavaScript

- Learn to save, translate, and restore a canvas context

Objectives

By the time you finish reading this chapter, you will have a full set of rectangle drawing skills added to your web development toolkit. Not only that, but you will along the way have picked up some basic but very handy JavaScript techniques applicable to other canvas and HTML features, as well as for drawing rectangles.

About the canvas examples

To keep things clear and simple, from now on in this section of the book, when providing examples for using the canvas element, the surrounding HTML will be omitted, leaving just the JavaScript. You should assume that a **<canvas>** element with the ID **canvas** has already been created in the document (generally, with a width of 640 and height of 320 pixels), and also assume that the first two lines of JavaScript that create a context for writing to the canvas (lines 16 and 17 of *Example 7.1*) have already been issued.

Example 7.1 shows you the full HTML document you should assume is there in all the canvas examples. You may recognize it as the familiar unfilled green rectangle code from *Chapter 6, The HTML5 Canvas*. In future, however, only the code within the two comments (lines 19 and 24) will be shown (and many additional lines will be inserted there as we progress through the chapter). However, the companion archive of example files does include all the surrounding HTML, so that you can run the examples straightaway for yourself, without typing in anything extra.

Example 7.1

```
1.   <!DOCTYPE html>
2.   <html lang="en">
3.     <head>
4.       <meta charset="utf-8">
5.       <title>Example Document</title>
6.       <style>
7.         #canvas {
8.           background-color : cyan;
9.           border           : 1px solid black;
```

```
10.          }
11.       </style>
12.    </head>
13.    <body>
14.       <canvas id='canvas' width='640' height='320'></canvas>
15.       <script>
16.          canvas  = document.getElementById('canvas')
17.          context = canvas.getContext('2d')
18.
19.          // The examples will start here
20.          context.beginPath()
21.          context.strokeStyle = 'green'
22.          context.rect(20, 20, 600, 280)
23.          context.stroke()
24.          // The examples will end here
25.       </script>
26.    </body>
27. </html>
```

This example also serves to show you how to comment code in JavaScript. Comments are text you enter to remind you (and other developers who may need to update your code) exactly what was intended when you wrote it. Comments are a very good practice to include as you write because they will be fresh in your mind and will help you later with debugging, or if it's been a while since you last looked at the code, and may not remember all the details.

To create a comment, you enter two forward slashes like this **//**, anywhere you like, and all the text following on that line will be ignored and not treated as JavaScript instructions.

The following code lists the only part of each example that will be shown in this book (unless the surrounding document has to be different for a particular example). You must therefore assume that all the remainder of the document is already in place for each example, so that we can simply concentrate on just the commands being discussed, such as these.

```
context.beginPath()
context.strokeStyle = 'green'
context.rect(20, 20, 600, 280)
context.stroke()
```

You have already seen these commands and how they work in the previous chapter, and here it has been assumed that the canvas is already created and of an appropriate size, and that it has been styled as necessary, and also that the context has been created from the canvas ID of **canvas**. So, with that explained, let's get onto more drawing examples.

Drawing rectangles

Rectangles are one of the easiest shapes to draw on the HTML5 canvas. You can draw them filled or outlined, using various styles that you set up separately on the current context, or if you don't set any styles, the basic defaults.

The first type of rectangle you've already seen, which is an unfilled one with simple styling, which you can create with a command such as this:

```
context.strokeRect(20, 30, 50, 70)
```

This will draw a rectangle with its top-left corner starting at a location 20 pixels in and 30 pixels down, and with a width of 50 pixels and a depth of 70 pixels. The basic thing to remember with drawing rectangles is the arguments that you pass should be (in order), the left, right, width and height desired, and you might also call the function as shown in the following line of code. But what does it mean?

```
context.strokeRect(r_left, r_top, r_width, r_height)
```

Using variables

Well, in JavaScript, like all programming languages, there are things called variables. These are named **containers** that hold values, which can be digits, numbers, strings of text, and so on. In this case, we just want regular umbers, and if the preceding code were to be made to work, we would first have to assign values to the variables, which would look like this:

```
r_left   = 10
r_top    = 20
r_width  = 400
r_height = 200
```

The **r_** before the words stands for a rectangle and is to ensure that these are unique variable names because some words such as **top**, **left,** and so on may be reserved words in JavaScript, used for purposes beyond the scope of this book.

Anyway, these lines placed before the rectangle drawing command result in a rectangle being drawn that is 400 by 200 pixels in dimension, with its top-left corner 10 pixels in and 20 pixels down.

Remember, though, that we must first start a path. Let's pull all these lines together into some working code, as shown in *Example 7.2* (remembering that all the surrounding HTML and some other parts have been omitted), the result of which is displayed in *Figure 7.1*.

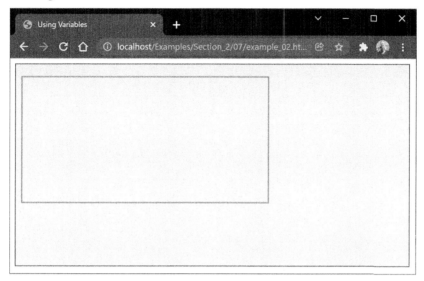

Figure 7.1: Variables have been used for drawing an unfilled rectangle

Example 7.2

```
r_left   = 10
r_top    = 20
r_width  = 400
r_height = 200


context.beginPath()
context.strokeRect(r_left, r_top, r_width, r_height)
context.stroke()
```

If you have never programmed before, see how you just picked up a bit more about programming JavaScript, simply as part of learning to draw a rectangle. You may be surprised yourself with what you have learned by the end of this book!

Applying drawing styles

Now, you can draw rectangles, let's see ways in which we can make these rectangles a little more interesting, by modifying the way they are drawn, starting with filling them in. As you may remember from *Chapter 5, Introduction to HTML5*, you don't have to content yourself with only unfilled rectangles. More often than not, you'll want them filled in, and there are many different effects that you can use when doing so, starting off with a plain fill (as created with *Example 7.3*), in which a filled yellow rectangle is drawn with a blue border, as shown in *Figure 7.2*.

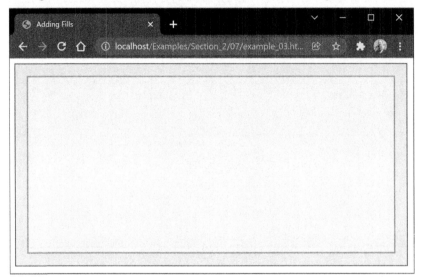

Figure 7.2: A filled yellow rectangle with a blue outline

Example 7.3

```
context.strokeStyle = 'blue'
context.fillStyle   = 'yellow'

context.beginPath()
context.fillRect   (20, 20, 600, 280)
context.strokeRect(20, 20, 600, 280)
context.stroke()
```

It should be clear to you by now that what is going on in this code. Firstly, the outline border of the rectangle is set to the color blue and the inside fill to yellow, then a path is started, the rectangle is filled, the outline is drawn, and finally the path is closed.

Changing the line width

Now, let's take a look what happens in *Figure 7.3* when we change a new property of the context, its **lineWidth**, by adding another command as shown in *Example 7.4*, which is simply *Example 7.3* with one extra instruction added at the start of the drawing commands (remember that in the accompanying archive of files, the examples are complete).

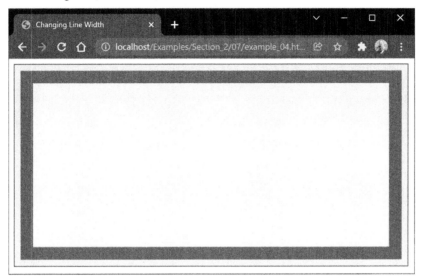

Figure 7.3: *The outline line width is increased*

Example 7.4

```
context.lineWidth = 20
```

See how easy it is to choose the width of the lines you draw. And also, note that the width extends out on either side of the line, so it has extended both outwards and inwards. Sometimes, you might expect it to be one or the other, but just remember that it's both when you design your shapes, which means that as a result of the line width change, the new rectangle (including its outline) now occupies greater space than the specified 600 × 280 pixel rectangle.

This is just the start of what you can do with lines and you will learn much more about modifying the lines you draw on the canvas in *Chapter 9, Drawing on the Canvas*. But now let's turn to other things you can do with rectangles, including clearing them and enhancing the fills with gradients.

Clearing a rectangle

Along with drawing rectangles, you can also clear areas of the canvas back to their default values, which means removing all red, green, and blue pixel values, along with their alpha values too. The alpha value, when used as a term in graphics, refers to the transparency of a pixel, which can be fully opaque, fully transparent, or somewhere in-between. When you clear a rectangle, the alpha values in it will be returned to zero, which means no transparency, and the colors will all be set to zero too.

Let's take *Example 7.4* and then clear a section of the canvas inside the rectangle it draws, by adding one further command, to create *Example 7.5*. This is shown in *Figure 7.4*, in which you can see that a rectangle in the middle of the one just drawn has now been restored back to the canvases default values, and so appears cyan, which is the default color that has been applied in the style section of the document (to differentiate from the surrounding white of the document).

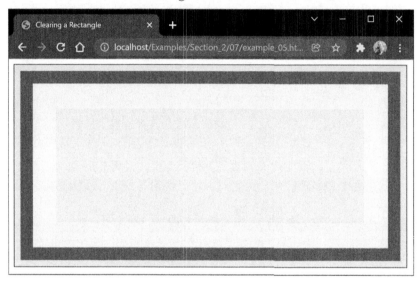

Figure 7.4: A rectangular section of the canvas has been cleared

Example 7.5

```
context.clearRect(70, 70, 500, 180)
```

Having learned how to set the all the **strokeStyle**, **fillStyle**, **lineWidth**, **fillRect**, **strokeRect,** and **clearRect** attributes, let's now really start to have some fun with gradient fills.

Applying gradient fills

You saw a very simple gradient effect in *Chapter 5, Introduction to HTML5*. Let's now take a look into how that can be achieved using **fillRect()** for rectangles (or plain **fill()** as detailed in *Chapter 9, Drawing on the Canvas*), combined with the **createLinearGradient()** function. The arguments this function takes are simply two pairs of X,Y coordinates for the start and the end of the gradient on the canvas.

The way you draw a gradient on the canvas is to specify a group of colors and the positions in the gradient at which they should appear. This gives you very precise control over gradients so that they do not just graduate from one color to another, but can (if you choose) go through many colors at a time. The simplest type of gradient is the one with a single start and single end color.

So, let's take draw four different black and white gradients using *Example 7.6*, in which the first three gradients are linear and the final one is a radial gradient. Note first, though, that lines 1 and 2 use variables (as described earlier in this chapter), which are **color1** and **color2**, to make assigning colors easier to edit by just modifying the first two lines.

Example 7.6

```
1.   color1 = '#FFF'
2.   color2 = '#000'
3.
4.   gradient = context.createLinearGradient(55, 10, 55, 160)
5.   gradient.addColorStop(0, color1)
6.   gradient.addColorStop(1, color2)
7.   context.fillStyle = gradient
8.   context.fillRect(10, 10, 90, 150)
9.
10.  gradient = context.createLinearGradient(110, 85, 200, 85)
11.  gradient.addColorStop(0, color1)
12.  gradient.addColorStop(1, color2)
13.  context.fillStyle = gradient
14.  context.fillRect(110, 10, 90, 150)
15.
16.  gradient = context.createLinearGradient(210, 10, 300, 160)
17.  gradient.addColorStop(0, color1)
18.  gradient.addColorStop(1, color2)
19.  context.fillStyle = gradient
20.  context.fillRect(210, 10, 90, 150)
21.
22.  gradient = context.createRadialGradient(355, 85, 0, 355, 85, 100)
23.  gradient.addColorStop(0, color1)
24.  gradient.addColorStop(1, color2)
25.  context.fillStyle = gradient
26.  context.fillRect(310, 10, 90, 150)
```

Looking at the first gradient fill, in line 4, the start location for the gradient is set to the location **55,10** and the end point is at **55,160**. The reason for this is that you must specify gradients based on absolute canvas coordinates, not positions relative to any shapes you wish to fill.

Therefore, because the first gradient fill (shown at line 8) has a width of **90** and height of **150** pixels, and its top-left corner starts at location **10,10**, the location **55,10** is therefore halfway along the top edge of the fill area, and **55,160** is halfway along the bottom. This means that the gradient will commence at the top of the area to fill (right in the center, but spread out horizontally), and will then flow top-to-bottom, down to the center of the bottom edge.

Lines 5 and 6 set the start location to begin with a color of white (from the variable called **color1**, which is set to **'#FFF'** in line 1), and the bottom to black (from the variable **color2**, which is set to **'#000'** in line 2), such that the gradient will flow evenly between these two colors. Line 7 applies the gradient details that were just set up, to the **fillStyle** property of the context. After which, line 8 calls the **fillRect()** function to draw the fill. The result of which is the left-hand rectangle shown in *Figure 7.5* where, for the sake of code brevity (and therefore simplicity), only the fills have been drawn without outlining the rectangles, as we have done in some earlier examples.

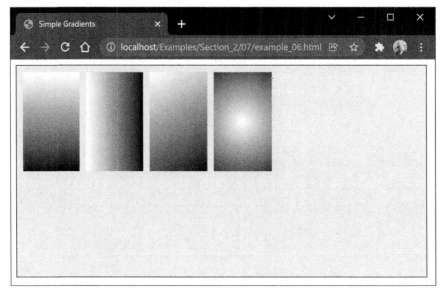

Figure 7.5: A selection of 4 different gradient fills

From this, you should be able to see what is happening in the following two area fills, in which the second one has its gradient flowing left-to-right from halfway down the left-hand side to halfway down the right of the rectangle, as specified by the values in line 10 (from coordinate **110,85** to location **200,85**). Likewise, the third rectangle has the gradient flowing diagonally from its top-left corner, down to the bottom-right of the rectangle (from coordinate **210,10** to location **300,160**).

Applying a radial gradient

The fourth fill is somewhat different because it shows a radial gradient flowing from the center to the outside of the rectangle. What's going on becomes clear once you realize that the first three arguments are the X,Y coordinate and radius of the start color, and the latter three arguments are the end point X,Y and radius, namely, from location **355,85** with a radius of **0**, to the same position (**355,85**) but with a radius of **100** pixels.

The radius value of **100** was chosen for the second circle because that places its diameter outside of much of the rectangular area. Otherwise, if it were limited (for example) just to the width of the rectangle (perhaps using a value of **45** for the radius as the rectangle width is 90 pixels), then the top and bottom of the rectangle would be all black, with only its center displaying the fill. But at **100** pixels, a gradient is visible all the way to the corners of the rectangle.

So, to recap, the start position is a zero size point rather than a circle (due to having zero radius), and the end circle has its center in the same place as the start circle, but it has a wider radius. The reason why you provide the details for two circles (rather than a single X,Y center point and two radii) is to provide flexibility in your designs, allowing you to create radial fills that are not just circular, but can expand across the fill area as you choose.

So, that's how to create monochromatic fills. Let's now move on to filling in using different and more colors.

Multicolored gradient fills

At this point in the chapter, the easiest way to show you a change of color is to swap all the black and white colors in *Example 7.6* for different colors. If you were to do that by, for example, changing lines 1 and 2 as follows, then *Figure 7.5* would now display in various shades of yellow, through oranges, and then finally to reds. Why not try this for yourself as a simple exercise, using various different pairs of colors?

```
1. color1 = 'yellow'
2. color2 = 'red'
```

But why stop there, when we can create multicolored rainbow effects? Let's do this with *Example 7.6*, by adding three more colors to the mix at the start (and inserting references to them at each of the four rectangle fills), to create *Example 7.7*, where you will see that the orders of the colors chosen are re-arranged for rectangles 2 to 4, just to mix things up a bit.

Example 7.7

```
1.   color1 = 'yellow'
2.   color2 = 'green'
3.   color3 = 'red'
4.   color4 = 'violet'
5.   color5 = 'blue'
6.
7.   gradient = context.createLinearGradient(55, 10, 55, 160)
8.   gradient.addColorStop(0.0, color1)
9.   gradient.addColorStop(0.2, color2)
10.  gradient.addColorStop(0.5, color3)
11.  gradient.addColorStop(0.8, color4)
12.  gradient.addColorStop(1.0, color5)
13.  context.fillStyle = gradient
14.  context.fillRect(10, 10, 90, 150)
15.
16.  gradient = context.createLinearGradient(110, 85, 200, 85)
17.  gradient.addColorStop(0.0, color1)
18.  gradient.addColorStop(0.2, color3)
19.  gradient.addColorStop(0.5, color5)
20.  gradient.addColorStop(0.8, color2)
21.  gradient.addColorStop(1.0, color4)
22.  context.fillStyle = gradient
23.  context.fillRect(110, 10, 90, 150)
24.
25.  gradient = context.createLinearGradient(210, 10, 300, 160)
26.  gradient.addColorStop(0.0, color3)
27.  gradient.addColorStop(0.2, color4)
28.  gradient.addColorStop(0.5, color1)
29.  gradient.addColorStop(0.8, color5)
30.  gradient.addColorStop(1.0, color2)
```

```
31. context.fillStyle = gradient
32. context.fillRect(210, 10, 90, 150)
33.
34. gradient = context.createRadialGradient(355, 85, 0, 355, 85, 100)
35. gradient.addColorStop(0.0, color4)
36. gradient.addColorStop(0.2, color2)
37. gradient.addColorStop(0.5, color1)
38. gradient.addColorStop(0.8, color5)
39. gradient.addColorStop(1.0, color3)
40. context.fillStyle = gradient
41. context.fillRect(310, 10, 90, 150)
```

The result of loading *Example 7.7* into a browser can be seen in *Figure 7.6*, where you'll notice there's a great deal of difference from the previous monochrome fills.

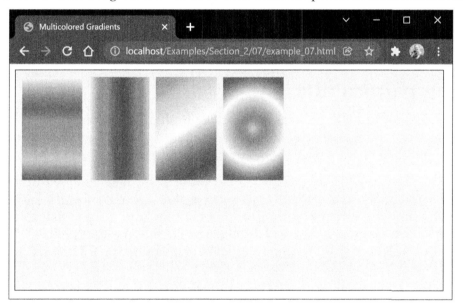

Figure 7.6: *Four different multicolored gradient fills*

As you may have noticed, the way you add more colors is to slot them in as additional calls to the **addColorStop()** function, with values for the first parameter that are between **0** and **1**. For example, when there were just two colors for the gradient, this parameter was either a **0** for the first color or a **1** for the second one, but take a look at lines 8 to 12 of *Example 7.7* and you'll see that the five colors have been added using floating point arguments between **0.0** and **1.0** for this parameter.

The way this works is that you should imagine the entire gradient fill as occupying a floating point space between the values **0.0** and **1.0**. Now, if you would like a certain color to appear in the gradient at a location 25% along, then you would set its **addColorStop()** initial distance parameter to **0.25**, likewise you would use the value **0.33** for a color that must appear after a third of the gradient has been displayed.

In the example, you'll see that the color values chosen are 0%, 20%, 50%, 80%, and 100% along the gradient because the distance arguments provided for the five colors are **0.0**, **0.2**, **0.5**, **0.8**, and **1.0**. You can be as precise as you like with this positioning; for example, you can choose a distance **0.3145927** from the start for a color if you like.

Once again, because the color names are defined in the first five lines of this example, you are encouraged to change these names to other names (or CSS-style **#** color value strings), and to modify the orders used in the four rectangles, as well as the distances each color appears along each gradient, to see what other affects you can create. In fact, you can add as few or as many colors as you like to a gradient, so have fun playing with the example.

Once you are finished with the example, and with gradients under our belt, let's now take a look at filling areas using patterns.

Using pattern fills

You are certainly not limited to plain or gradient fills because you can also choose to fill areas of a canvas using a pre-defined pattern, and you can choose between varieties of different ways of applying the pattern fill too.

You can do this using a function called **createPattern()** passing it two arguments, which are the image to use and the type of repeat to apply for the fill. *Example 7.8* shows the previous example with an additional few lines of code that fill a fifth, larger rectangle. Be prepared to read through the example a couple of times, though, because you will need to understand a little more JavaScript in order to see how this works.

Example 7.8

```
43.  image     = new Image()
44.  image.src = 'tile.png'
45.
46.  image.onload = function()
47.  {
48.    pattern = context.createPattern(image, 'repeat')
```

```
49.    context.fillStyle = pattern
50.    context.fillRect(410, 10, 220, 300)
51. }
```

As you can see by the numbering, these lines are a continuation of *Example 7.6.* Let's look at what they do. Firstly, line 43 creates a new JavaScript object from an empty, non-existent image. An object is like a variable, but it can hold a wider variety of data types (in this instance, it's an image). Once the object is created, the **src** attribute (just the same as **src** in HTML) is given the filename **tile.png**, which tells JavaScript to start fetching the image and placing it into the image object. At this point the image object in JavaScript is very similar to an image element in HTML or CSS.

But there's sometimes a problem when you do this because JavaScript, being mostly pure text, often loads in far more quickly than other page elements that may be larger, such as images. And if an attempt is made to use such an element before it has been loaded then nothing happens, and the code fails in its task. Therefore, an additional piece of JavaScript is required which will only allow the instructions to execute once the object has loaded. This is achieved by attaching what is known as an anonymous function (a function that has not been given a name) to the **onload** event of the **image** object.

In JavaScript, there are many different events that can be responded to, such as when a key is pressed, or if the mouse is moved. In this case, we only want to know when the image has been loaded into memory, and so on line 46, the anonymous function is attached to the **onload** event, along with matching opening **{** and closing **}** braces. These tell JavaScript where to find the instructions to execute once the image has loaded. Only those instructions within the braces will be run at that time.

And within the braces, there are just three lines of code. Line 48 creates a pattern object by calling the **createPattern()** function on the context, giving it the name of the image to use and the type of repeat required. In this case, the image is the one just loaded into the **image** object, and the repeat value of **repeat** is set to tile both in the X and the Y directions (across and down).

The image to be loaded can be seen in *Figure 7.7,* and the result of adding all this code to the example is shown in *Figure 7.8.*

Figure 7.7: The tile.png file

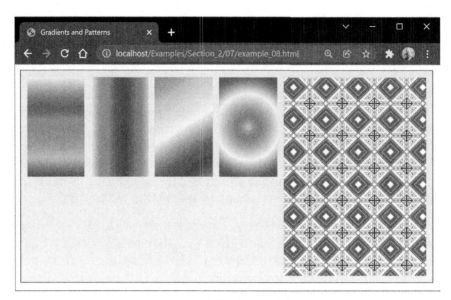

Figure 7.8: A pattern fill has been added to the canvas

Using translation

At line 48 of *Example 7.8*, the repeat type given is simply **repeat**, which means to repeat in both the X and Y directions. The repeat type could also be omitted to achieve the same result by default. But you can also choose to repeat only in the X horizontal direction, or the Y vertical direction.

However, there's a potential snag with using either of these because pattern fills commence exactly at the **0,0** coordinate at the top-left of a canvas. And, while you will only see the fill within the area specified by the fill instruction, the pattern is still drawn invisibly behind. When you draw a pattern fill in a defined area, it's as if you open up a window to a section of a full canvas of the tiled pattern.

So, looking first at the Y axis, you will realize that tiling down the canvas from the top-left, we can specify a fill anywhere along that edge and you will see some of the tiling, as drawn by the code in *Example 7.9*, which is a continuation of *Example 7.8*, placed after the first three lines of code in the anonymous function that drew the right-hand rectangle in *Figure 7.8*.

Example 7.9

```
53.  pattern = context.createPattern(image, 'repeat-y')

54.  context.fillStyle = pattern

55.  context.fillRect(10, 170, 190, 140)
```

The only things that are different in these lines of code are that a repeat value of **repeat-y** is set on line 53, and line 55 draws a rectangle at the bottom-left of the canvas, as shown in *Figure 7.9*.

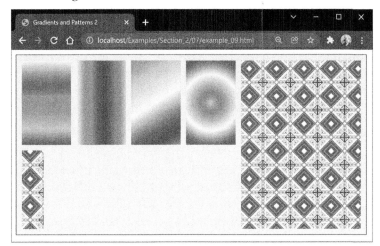

Figure 7.9: A vertical pattern fill applied to the bottom left of the canvas

Even then this is not a perfect solution if you wanted the left-hand edge of the first tile in each row to not be cut off. Also, what happens if we wish to use a repeat value of **repeat-x** and not to also tile the pattern in the Y direction? Well, that would work fine, but only for fills made at the top of the screen, and you still might not see all of the tile if the area to fill is offset down from the top by any amount.

In order to fix these issues, and to apply the fill starting at the top-left corner of a fill area, you can perform an action called a *translation* on the canvas, to temporarily move the origin, or top-left drawing start location, to the exact start position you require. You then draw the tiled background and afterwards translate the canvas back to its proper position at the top-left of the canvas. Don't worry, it's a lot simpler than it may sound, as shown in *Example 7.10*:

Example 7.10

```
57.  context.save()
58.  context.translate(210, 170)
59.  pattern = context.createPattern(image, 'repeat-x')
60.  context.fillStyle = pattern
61.  context.fillRect(0, 0, 190, 140)
62.  context.restore()
```

Translating a context from its original location can cause confusion if you later forget what you've done, so a **save()** function is available in JavaScript to save all the details about a context to a safe part of memory, along with a matching **restore()** function, which brings the previous settings back again. So that's what we have done in lines 57 and 62 – we've saved and then later restored the state of the context, so that we can do as we wish between those lines.

Line 58 translates the top-left corner of the canvas to the position where we want the top-left of the fill area to be, at location **210,70**. In other words, it leaves the canvas where it is, but all future commands will be translated to apply in locations offset from the new location by the translation amounts. This translation of coordinates now applies until the code ends, another translation occurs, or the previous state of the context is restored.

On lines 59 and 60, the pattern is created using a repeat value of **repeat-x**. Then, on line 61, since the area to fill has its top-left corner already at the translation location, we simply provide values for this corner of **0,0**, along with a width and height of **190 x 140** pixels. Because the canvas is temporarily translated to **210,170**, then the **0,0** at the top-left of the fill area is actually at the **210,170** location we originally desired.

Finally, by issuing the call to **restore()** on line 61, everything is returned to normal and the result is shown in *Figure 7.10* which, if you examine it carefully, you'll see that only the latest pattern fill has the top-left corner of the first tile match the top-left corner of the fill area.

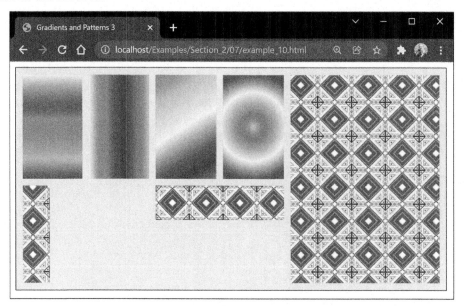

Figure 7.10: A horizontal fill has been drawn at a translated location

In comparison, the fully tiled fill and the vertical fill of the two previous examples are both missing parts of either or both of the left- and top-most tiles. Perhaps, you might like to use the translation technique yourself as an exercise to fix those pattern fills to fit better, like the most recent example.

Oh! By the way, there is also a **no-repeat** option for pattern fills, where the image does not tile. This is best-suited for larger backgrounds that will completely fill an area and are not wanted to tile. It could be argued that in such cases, often you might prefer to draw the pattern there in the regular way, and not worry about translations, as described in *Chapter 10, Manipulating the Canvas*.

Conclusion

With this, you've covered a massive amount of ground in this chapter. From filled and unfilled rectangles, outline stroke widths, monochrome, and multicolored gradients (both linear and radial), to various types of pattern fills.

Along the way, you've learned more JavaScript too, including how to load images in directly from code without using HTML, and you even learned how to wait until an image is loaded before you access it. What's more, you now learned how to translate the context of a canvas to different locations in order to achieve the desired effects, and also saw how to save and restore the state of the context.

That is indeed a great deal of new knowledge. But hopefully this chapter has helped you to pick everything up as you learned more about manipulating the HTML5 canvas in quite detailed ways. In the following chapter, we'll take a look at all the different methods you can use to write text on the canvas.

CHAPTER 8

Writing on the Canvas

Introduction

In this chapter, you'll learn all about the different ways in which you can write text to the HTML5 canvas, using different styles, colors, font families, and more. You'll also see how the various fills, gradients, and patterns discussed in the previous chapter can be applied to writing as well.

Of course, the text part of **HyperText Markup Language** (**HTML**) is there because its roots are as a vehicle for creating textual web pages, as there have been ways of incorporating different fonts, weights, colors and styles, right from the start. And CSS takes what you can do a great deal further.

But while you can overlay text on a canvas using HTML and CSS, you can't write it into the pixels of a canvas image. Neither can you get all the fantastic gradient and fill effects that the canvas offers. Therefore, there are very good reasons for wanting to create textual effects using a canvas, and this chapter is where you'll learn all you need to know to create some stunning effects.

Structure

In this chapter, you will:

- Learn a variety of ways of writing text to the HTML5 canvas
- Become familiar with text alignment and base lines
- Understand how to either outline or fill your text in different ways
- Know how to use any fonts and even apply patterns as text fills

Objectives

By the time you finish this chapter, you will be able to write any text you like to the HTML5 canvas using a wide range of fonts, colors, and styles, including linear and radial gradients in color or monochrome, single color fills or outline strokes, and you will also know how to load in images to use as pattern fills for the text.

Writing text

One way to write fonts to the canvas is to use the **strokeText()** function. It takes three arguments, which are the text to write and the X,Y coordinates of the bottom-left corner location at which to start writing. You might do so with a command like this:

```
context.strokeText('To be, or not to be...', 50, 50)
```

By default, however, without altering any other attributes of the context, the result will probably be smaller than you intend, and may not be in a font you would choose, so before continuing we need to look at how we can get the text at the right size and in the right font, and also in a color of our choice with a line width we like, among other attributes.

Changing how text displays

The first thing you may want to choose when deciding to display some text is the font you wish to use, and this is easily achieved by assigning values to the **font** property of the context. What's more, you can also choose the size of font you require at the same time, and do so using measurements you are used to using with CSS. For example, all of the following statements are valid:

```
context.font = '3em Helvetica'
context.font = '16px Impact'
context.font = '150% Courier'
```

```
context.font = '10mm Times'

context.font = '50pt Arial'
```

So, let's take some of these and use them to write text on the canvas, as shown in *Example 8.1*, in which we have saved on needing to repeat the output text by assigning a string to the variable **output**, which is then displayed five times using different font names and sizes, always starting 10 pixels in horizontally, but fairly evenly distributed in the vertical axis, accounting for the differing font heights, as shown in *Figure 8.1*.

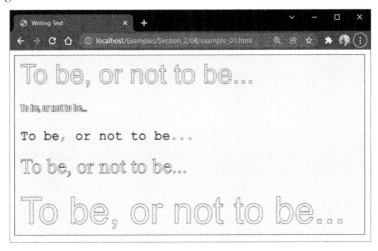

Figure 8.1: *A variety of different fonts and sizes*

Example 8.1

```
1.  output = 'To be, or not to be...'

2.

3.  context.font = '3em Helvetica'

4.  context.strokeText(output, 10,  50)

5.

6.  context.font = '16px Impact'

7.  context.strokeText(output, 10, 100)

8.

9.  context.font = '150% Courier'

10. context.strokeText(output, 10, 150)

11.

12. context.font = '10mm Times'
```

```
13. context.strokeText(output, 10, 210)
14.
15. context.font = '50pt Arial'
16. context.strokeText(output, 10, 300)
```

We haven't created any paths for this example because each string of text displayed using the **strokeText()** function acts like its own path, with its own opening and closing of the various paths used within its drawing.

Aligning text

Often, as is the case with word processing for example, you want your text to align to the right or the center instead of the left, and you can do this using the **textAlign** property of the context, which actually supports five values: **start**, **end**, **left** (the default), **right,** and **center**.

However, to all intents and purposes, **left** and **start** are fairly similar to each other, as are **right** and **end**, except that with **start** the output is left-aligned for left-to-right locales, and right-aligned for right-to-left locales. On the other hand, **end** is right-aligned for left-to-right locales, and left-aligned for right-to-left locales. These give support for languages that read from right to left, but are best ignored as a beginner due to the confusion that may ensue (see the Note below for more details).

Anyway, let's see how throwing some of these alignments into the mix of *Example 8.1* will change things, as has been done with *Example 8.2*, in which a new **textAlign** property assignment has been added to each of the five instruction pairs, as you can see in *Figure 8.2*.

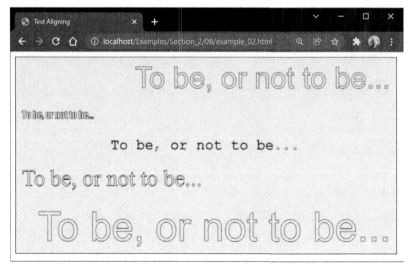

Figure 8.2: The text has been aligned according to the five supported properties

Example 8.2

```
1.  output = 'To be, or not to be...'
2.
3.  context.font      = '3em Helvetica'
4.  context.textAlign = 'right'
5.  context.strokeText(output, 630,  50)
6.
7.  context.textAlign = 'left'
8.  context.font      = '16px Impact'
9.  context.strokeText(output, 10, 100)
10.
11. context.textAlign = 'center'
12. context.font      = '150% Courier'
13. context.strokeText(output, 320, 150)
14.
15. context.textAlign = 'start'
16. context.font      = '10mm Times'
17. context.strokeText(output, 10, 210)
18.
19. context.textAlign = 'end'
20. context.font      = '50pt Arial'
21. context.strokeText(output, 630, 300)
```

Once again, the variable **output** is used to store the string to display. After that, the five sections have been modified to align in order to the **right**, **left**, **center**, **start,** and **end**. To support this, the horizontal offset from the left edge of the canvas has been moved all the way to just 10 pixels before the right edge for the first and fifth group of instruction, which are aligned to the **right** and **end**. And the **center** aligned text in the third group has a horizontal offset exactly in the center of the canvas because the text will center around whatever coordinate is provided, and we want the text exactly in the middle.

Note: Because the start and end properties have been used in the final two groups of instructions, if you were to change the language direction to right-to-left by adding the attribute assignment dir="rtl" to the <HTML> tag of Example 8.2, the result would look a mess, with most of the text flowing off the canvas. Try doing this to see what result you get, and then try to correct the display to how it ought to look, by altering the horizontal offset values of those two groups of instructions. If you do this, you'll quickly see why it's advised not to use these properties as a beginner, as there are many potential pitfalls.

Changing stroke width

Just as we were able to change the width of the stroke used to draw rectangles in *Chapter 7, Rectangles and Fills*, we can also do the same with text drawn using the **strokeFont()** function. So let's modify the previous example to *Example 8.3* and see what effects can be created. Since these examples are getting longer as we go, just the new lines added at the start of each of the five groups is shown, and therefore no line numbers are provided (remember that the full example *is* included in the accompanying archive).

Example 8.3

```
context.lineWidth = 2
context.lineWidth = .5
context.lineWidth = .8
context.lineWidth = .25
context.lineWidth = 7
```

What this example does is specifies the line width of **2**, **.5**, **.8**, **.25,** and **7** in order to the five groups of instructions. The result of this is shown in *Figure 8.3*, in which you can see that you can choose between very fine and light text, through to overly emboldened, and quite ugly results in the final one, where the line width is 7 pixels.

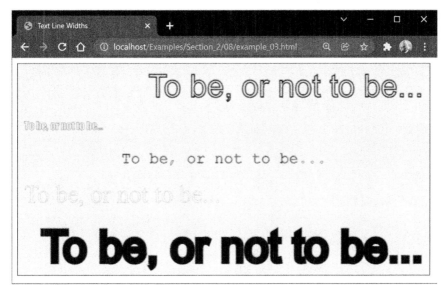

Figure 8.3: *The result of applying a variety of line widths*

So you see how you are not limited to integer numbers of these values. Beware of using a value of **0**, though, because that seems to be ignored (and what would the point of a zero width line be anyway?), and whatever the previously assigned **lineWidth** setting was just remains in place.

If you actually wanted filled in text (and for it to look good), there is a better way, which is given in detail later in the section *Writing Filled Text*, but before that, there's one more property we need to examine, which is the **textBaseline** property, used to specify a horizontal line about which the text will align in certain ways.

You have four choices of how you can align the base of your text, between **top**, **middle**, **alphabetic** (the default), and **bottom**. To show what these terms mean, *Example 8.4* writes these five terms as text on-top of a horizontal guide line, showing exactly where the text will appear relative to the line for each applied term.

Example 8.4

```
1. context.strokeStyle = "blue"

2. context.moveTo(0,    160)

3. context.lineTo(640, 160)

4. context.stroke()

5. context.strokeStyle = "red"

6. context.lineWidth    = 2

7. context.font         = '26pt Helvetica'
```

```
8.
9.  context.textBaseline = 'top'
10. context.strokeText('Top', 20, 160)
11.
12. context.textBaseline = 'middle'
13. context.strokeText('Middle', 150, 160)
14.
15. context.textBaseline = 'bottom'
16. context.strokeText('Bottom', 300, 160)
17.
18. context.textBaseline = 'alphabetic'
19. context.strokeText('Alphabetic', 450, 160)
```

In this example, lines 1 through 4 give our first instance of drawing a single line. After having drawn many rectangles, it should be clear to you by now how it works. Line 1 sets the drawing color to blue, line 2 moves to a location on the left of the canvas halfway down, line 3 defines a horizontal line across to the right-hand side, and then line 4 draws the line specified by the previous instructions.

Then, lines 5 to 7 change the color to red, set the line width to 2 pixels, and select the font size and name. Then, follows four pairs of instructions, each of which sets the **textBaseline** property and then writes some text based on that property. The result of this can be seen in *Figure 8.4*, where the only item you may find confusing is the third one, which appears to float above the base line.

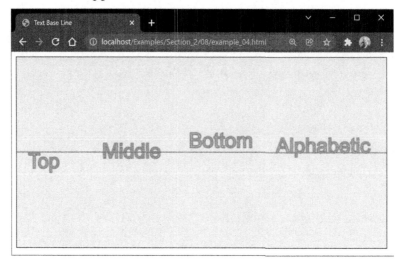

Figure 8.4: How the different base line properties are applied

But it doesn't really because there are no descending lower-case characters. But if there were a letter y or g in the word (for example), it would sit right on the base line. There are two other property values you can apply to the **textBaseline** property: **hanging** (similar to **top**) for Tibetan and other Indic scripts, and **ideographic** (similar to **bottom**) for Chinese, Japanese, and Korean scripts. A web search will explain their use.

Writing filled text

Just as with rectangles, you can apply all the fills, gradients, and patterns to your text as well. Let's take a look at some of the results you can achieve, beginning with *Example 8.5*, in which the word ART is written in very large text using the font Impact, filling most of the canvas.

Example 8.5

```
1. context.font = '290pt Impact'
2. context.fillText('ART', 30, 312)
```

The default color of any fill is black, as shown in *Figure 8.5*.

Figure 8.5: *A word has been written to fill the canvas*

But let's play with this now by changing the fill to a gradient, as in *Example 8.6*, in which a simple gradient from white to black has been applied, as shown in *Figure 8.6*:

Figure 8.6: *The fill is now a gradient, and an outline has been added*

Example 8.6

```
1. context.font = '290pt Impact'
2. gradient     = context.createLinearGradient(320, 0, 320, 320)
3. gradient.addColorStop(0, 'white')
4. gradient.addColorStop(1, 'black')
5. context.fillStyle = gradient
6. context.fillText   ('ART', 30, 312)
7. context.strokeText('ART', 30, 312)
```

As before, line 1 sets the font size and face. But then line 2 sets up a gradient effect from halfway along the top of the canvas vertically down to the canvas bottom. Two color stops are then applied in lines 3 and 4, then the **fillStyle** property of the context is set to this gradient, and the **fillText()** function is called to display the text on line 6. In order to make it stand out a little better, a call to **strokeText()** is also made in line 7 to give the writing an outline.

This is already starting to look a lot better, but now let's transform the writing by going straight to a radial gradient in rainbow colors and make the word **ART** really arty. *Example 8.7* illustrates one way of doing this by remembering the acronym of ROYGBIV for the colors of a rainbow: red, orange, yellow, green, blue, indigo, and violet, all of which are equally spread out across the gradient at intervals of just over 0.16, or about $1/6^{th}$ of the gradient between them.

Example 8.7

```
1.  context.font = '290pt Impact'
2.  gradient    = context.createRadialGradient(320, 320,  30,
3.                                              320, 320, 400)
4.  gradient.addColorStop(0.00, 'red')
5.  gradient.addColorStop(0.16, 'orange')
6.  gradient.addColorStop(0.33, 'yellow')
7.  gradient.addColorStop(0.50, 'green')
8.  gradient.addColorStop(0.66, 'blue')
9.  gradient.addColorStop(0.83, 'indigo')
10. gradient.addColorStop(1.00, 'violet')
11. context.fillStyle = gradient
```

```
12.  context.fillText   ('ART', 30, 312)

13.  context.strokeText('ART', 30, 312)
```

Other than the seven color stops in place of the previous two, the only other difference is the gradient being radial, and set to start with a circle of 30 pixels radius centered at the bottom-middle of the canvas, spreading out to a circle of 400 pixels radius, using the same center. The result is the rather magnificent rainbow fill shown in *Figure 8.7*.

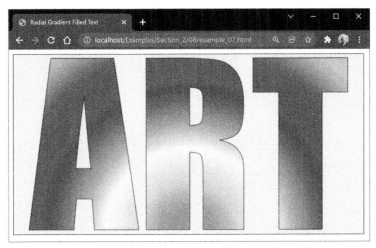

Figure 8.7: *The writing has been filled with a rainbow radial gradient effect*

Using a pattern for a text fill

Not only can you perform single color, monochrome, gradient color, and radial gradient fills in your text, but you can also fill your text with any pattern of your choosing. If the pattern is large enough it can simply appear in its completeness inside the text, or you can have the pattern tile as much as is necessary to fill up the text.

Example 8.8 shows the pattern we used in *Chapter 7, Rectangles and Fills*, being repurposed as a fill for the word ART, as shown in in *Figure 8.8*.

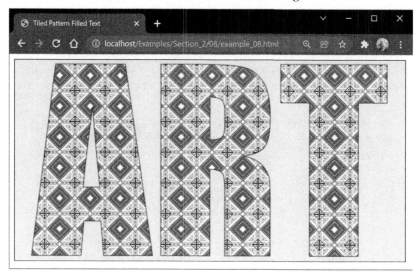

Figure 8.8: The word is filled with a tiled pattern

You may recognize the code from the chapter in lines 2 to 5 for loading in the **tile. png** image and then waiting until the browser is ready before using the image. Then, within the braces of the anonymous function, a pattern object is created and assigned to the **fillStyle** property of the context, with lines 9 and 10 being the same as the final lines in the previous example, drawing the filled and outlined word on the canvas.

Example 8.8

```
1.  context.font = '290pt Impact'
2.  image        = new Image()
3.  image.src    = 'tile.png'
4.
5.  image.onload = function()
6.  {
7.    pattern = context.createPattern(image, 'repeat')
8.    context.fillStyle = pattern
9.    context.fillText   ('ART', 30, 312)
10.   context.strokeText('ART', 30, 312)
11. }
```

And there you have it, you can now work with text on the HTML5 canvas in pretty much the same way you have learned how to use rectangles.

Conclusion

As you will have realized, learning how to write text was not really a great deal different to drawing rectangles, and that's one of the benefits of working through this book in order. Each new chapter is generally based on the knowledge gained in previous ones, and as you learn more, then more of what you need to learn becomes obvious because you've already used similar techniques.

So, with text and rectangles now mastered, in the upcoming chapter, we'll start to draw more fine and precise details using lines and curves based on creating paths.

CHAPTER 9

Drawing on the Canvas

Introduction

You are now a little over halfway through your journey into learning how to draw and write on the HTML5 canvas. In this chapter, most of the remaining fine drawing details will be revealed, and you'll also start to learn a little about when you can actually ignore some commands because they can be implicit in many circumstances.

If you have forgotten it, you'll also be refreshed with a little geometry when you look at different ways of drawing and filling in arcs, curves, and circles. And you'll also learn how you can mask out areas of the canvas to preserve areas outside when drawing inside a clipped area.

You'll also learn that you can draw arcs in both a clockwise and counter-clockwise direction, and understand when and why this difference can be important.

Structure

In this chapter, you will:

- Learn the remaining line drawing functions
- Know how to draw all manner of different arcs and curves

- Discover how to make a mask using the `clip()` function

- Become comfortable working with lines, paths, end caps, and joins

Objectives

By the time you finish this chapter, you will have acquainted yourself with all the main line, fill, curve, arc and text drawing techniques covered in this and the previous chapters. This will give you most of the tools you need for drawing on the HTML5 canvas, leaving only the manipulation of images, transparency, and other advanced techniques to absorb in the following two chapters.

Drawing lines with paths

The HTML5 canvas relies a great deal on the use of paths for drawing. The main reason is that you can create all sorts of paths in advance and then quickly draw the entire path with a single command, making for extremely fast drawing that could even be used for animation.

But it's sort of quirky because you can sometimes seem to get away without first creating a path, as we managed in the previous chapter when drawing the horizontal line to illustrate the use of base lines with text. That example worked because there was nothing else being drawn, and so no stray lines or errors would occur.

However, when you start drawing closed shapes of any kind that you might wish to fill in one way or another, you will soon run into strange and unexpected results unless you properly open and close paths in the right places. Therefore, it is recommended that as a beginner you should always open and close paths each time you draw anything that could be considered a stand-alone shape, or which you may wish to later treat as a single shape.

Let's look into this a little deeper with *Example 9.1*, which draws a sequence of lines forming an outlined plus sign sort of shape, overlaid with a diamond shape, as shown in *Figure 9.1*.

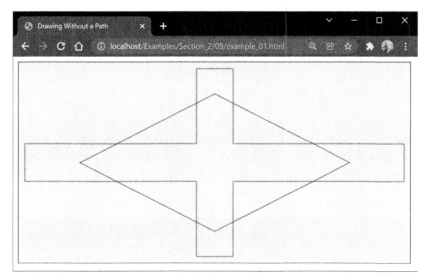

Figure 9.1*: A pair of shapes drawn on the canvas*

Example 9.1

```
1.    context.moveTo( 10, 130)
2.    context.lineTo( 10, 190)
3.    context.lineTo(290, 190)
4.    context.lineTo(290, 310)
5.    context.lineTo(350, 310)
6.    context.lineTo(350, 190)
7.    context.lineTo(630, 190)
8.    context.lineTo(630, 130)
9.    context.lineTo(350, 130)
10.   context.lineTo(350,  10)
11.   context.lineTo(290,  10)
12.   context.lineTo(290, 130)
13.   context.lineTo(10,  130)
14.
15.   context.moveTo(100, 160)
16.   context.lineTo(320,  50)
17.   context.lineTo(540, 160)
```

```
18. context.lineTo(320, 270)

19. context.lineTo(100, 160)

20.

21. context.stroke()
```

All looks well and good! You might think. But now let's see why all may not be as it seems at the first glance, by adding just a single extra instruction after the call to the **stroke()** function on line 21, as follows, and then look at what happens in *Figure 9.2*.

```
22. context.fill()
```

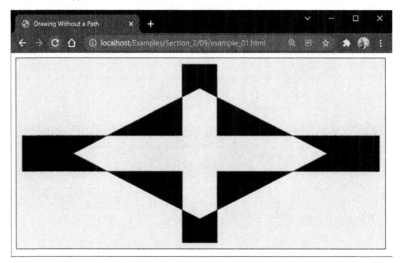

Figure 9.2: A fill has been applied with unexpected results

We will now examine the **fill()** command in more detail very shortly, but what can be done to get a result more like what we might have expected? Well, the answer is to split the two shapes apart by separating them into individual paths, as in *Example 9.2*, where you can see there are now two separate and independent sections, with the result of this code a shown in *Figure 9.3*, much more like what we were probably planning to create.

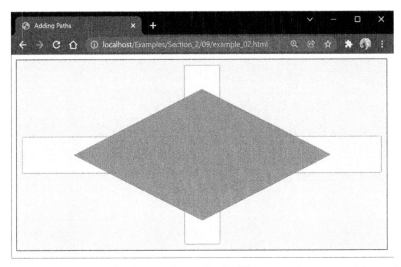

Figure 9.3*: By separating the shapes using paths the fills now work as expected Example 9.2*

Example 9.2

```
1.   context.beginPath()
2.   context.moveTo( 10, 130)
3.   context.lineTo( 10, 190)
4.   context.lineTo(290, 190)
5.   context.lineTo(290, 310)
6.   context.lineTo(350, 310)
7.   context.lineTo(350, 190)
8.   context.lineTo(630, 190)
9.   context.lineTo(630, 130)
10.  context.lineTo(350, 130)
11.  context.lineTo(350,  10)
12.  context.lineTo(290,  10)
13.  context.lineTo(290, 130)
14.  context.lineTo(10,  130)
15.  context.closePath()
16.
17.  context.stroke()
18.  context.fillStyle = 'yellow'
19.  context.fill()
```

```
20.
21. context.beginPath()
22. context.moveTo(100, 160)
23. context.lineTo(320,  50)
24. context.lineTo(540, 160)
25. context.lineTo(320, 270)
26. context.lineTo(100, 160)
27. context.closePath()
28.
29. context.stroke()
30. context.fillStyle = 'red'
31. context.fill()
```

Let's take a look at why this works. Firstly, lines 1 to 15 create the plus shape, placing it within its own path. Then, lines 17 to 19 apply a stroked outline, select a fill color of yellow, and apply the fill. In the second part of the example, in lines 21 to 28, the diamond shape is created within its own path. Then, lines 29 to 31 apply the stroked outline, select a fill color of red, and then apply the fill, a shown in *Figure 9.4*.

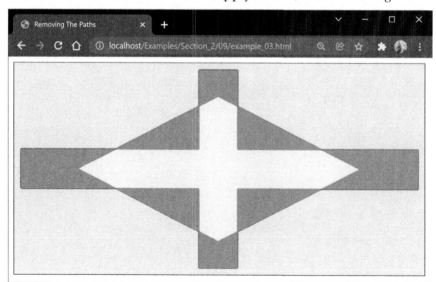

Figure 9.4: Without the paths the fills are again unpredictable

There are two distinct filled shapes, with the newer one overlaying the earlier one – all very much as we would expect. Now, just for fun, let's comment out the path instruction lines 1, 15, 21, and 27 (so that they will not be executed) by placing pairs of forward slashes (**//**) before the instructions, as shown in *Example 9.4* (in which only the changed lines are shown to save on space). Then, check out the result in *Figure 9.4*, which is back to being not what was intended.

Example 9.3 (just the commented lines):

```
1.  // context.beginPath()

15. // context.closePath()

21. // context.beginPath()

27. // context.closePath()
```

Of course, the effect in *Figure 9.4* is actually quite interesting. But if it's not what you wanted then, it's of no use to you. So, let this serve as a very clear lesson as to why you are probably better off enclosing all the shapes you draw on a canvas within their own paths; at least until you are very experienced at drawing on the canvas.

Applying fills

We've seen the **fill()** function used a couple of times already in this chapter, so now let's find out exactly how it works and is used. You should find this short section very easy because it's very similar to using the **fillRect()** instruction, which we examined in detail in the previous chapter.

The main thing **fill()** has in common with **fillRect()** is that whatever the **fillStyle** properties you have selected will be applied in either case. The difference between the two is that **fill()** applies to the most recent path. Each time you start a new path, **fill()** will apply only to the new one and any previous path is as good as forgotten.

Knowing this, which means you now know how to draw any shape you desire that can be made using straight lines, and you can then fill it with any solid color, linear or radial gradient, or any pattern image of your choice. All the details on these types of fill are discussed in *Chapter 8, Writing on the Canvas*.

Clipping canvas areas

Sometimes, when drawing using an art program, it is useful to set up a mask such that only the area within the mask will get drawn. You can achieve a similar effect when drawing on the canvas by selecting a clipped subsection, within which future drawing or fills will work (until a new clip path is created), but outside which nothing will happen.

To illustrate this, let's compare simply drawing a shape on a canvas, with first setting a clipping area and then drawing, using *Example 9.4* (where the lines intentionally start at line 12 to leave space for some code coming up), in which first a filled green diamond is drawn, over which is placed a single-lined diagonal cross, a shown in *Figure 9.5.*

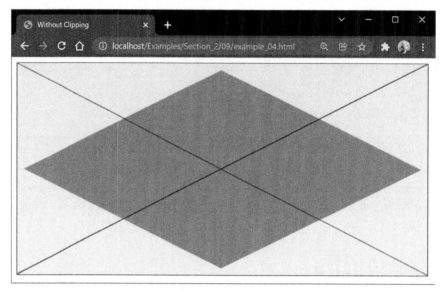

***Figure 9.5**: A couple of shapes drawn onto the canvas*

Example 9.4

```
12.  context.beginPath()
13.  context.moveTo(320,  10)
14.  context.lineTo(630, 160)
15.  context.lineTo(320, 310)
16.  context.lineTo( 10, 160)
17.  context.lineTo(320,  10)
18.  context.closePath()
19.
20.  context.fillStyle = 'green'
21.  context.fill()
22.
23.  context.beginPath()
24.  context.moveTo(0,      0)
25.  context.lineTo(639, 319)
26.  context.moveTo(0,    319)
27.  context.lineTo(639,   0)
```

```
28.  context.closePath()

29.

30.  context.stroke()
```

This should all look very clear to you; in that there are two sections of code: the first of which sets up a path for a diamond shape, then filles it in with the color green, while the second section of code draws a simple, single-lined diagonal cross on top of that.

Now, let's see what happens if the code in *Example 9.5* is inserted *before Example 9.4* to first create a clipped area of the canvas in the form of a rectangle. On line 9, an additional call to **stroke()** is made because the boundary of a clipped area is invisible, but by calling **stroke(),** you can see it. Whether or not you add a call to **stroke()** for a clipped area is up to your intent with each drawing.

Example 9.5:

```
1.   context.beginPath()

2.   context.moveTo(170,  10)

3.   context.lineTo(470,  10)

4.   context.lineTo(470, 310)

5.   context.lineTo(170, 310)

6.   context.lineTo(170,  10)

7.   context.closePath()

8.   context.lineWidth = 1

9.   context.stroke()

10.  context.clip()
```

The result of setting up this clipping area first is that the display now looks like *Figure 9.6*, which shows a hexagonal shape with two diagonal lines. As you can see everything drawn outside the clipped area has been ignored, whether drawn with the **stroke()** function, or using a call to **fill()**.

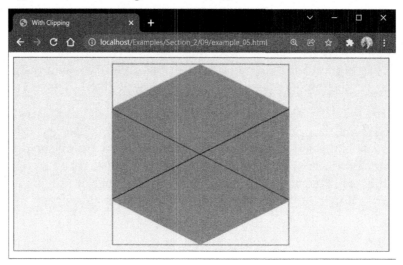

Figure 9.6: All drawing outside the clipped area is ignored

The most important thing you need to remember when you set up a clipped area of the canvas is that it will stay effective until either you set up a new clipped area, or the end of the instructions is reached.

Therefore, once you've finished using a clipped area, you may wish to reset the clipping mask back to the whole canvas (or to a new area if that's what is required) or, much more easily, do you recall how we used the **save()** and **restore()** functions on the context in *Chapter 7, Rectangles and Fills*, when translating a canvas' coordinates?

Well, these two functions save *everything* about the current context, so when using clipping, it's often a good idea to first issue the instruction **context.save()**. And when you've finished with the clipping mask, you can restore whatever settings were in place on the context beforehand with a quick call to **context.restore()**.

Now, you don't need to recall the size of the canvas to reset the clipping mask back to its full dimensions. In fact, it makes good sense to get used to using **save()** and **restore()** wherever you make big changes to the context, as they are the simplest and easiest way to return to previous values.

Drawing curved lines

When you want to draw a circle or any form of curved line, your first avenue is to use the **arc()** function, but you do need to understand a little geometry to do so effectively as the function takes a number of different arguments. The first two arguments are the X and Y horizontal and vertical coordinate at the arc's center. These are followed by the radius of the arc and the start and end angles.

This is where your geometry comes in because the start and end angles are specified in radians, which are angular units of measure based around the constant PI. As you may remember, PI has a value of approximately 3.1416, and the circumference of a circle is 2 times PI, or about 6.2832. You will also remember that there are 360 degrees in a circles.

Now, imagine that you have to walk all the way around a large circle. To do so, you will require to travel through 360 degrees or 6.2823 radians. However, because 360 degrees is a large number when all you are using are half or quarter circles, and so would have to apply values of 180 or 90 degrees, and also because 6.2823 is a slightly unwieldy floating point number to use, the value of radian was devised, such that 1 radian is the same as 180 degrees divided by PI, or roughly 57 degrees.

If this seems to you harder to use than degrees, it's actually not because now, when you want to draw an arc of half a circle in diameter, you can just say you want it to be PI radians. Or, for a full circle, you need 2 times PI radians, while a quarter circle in radians is PI divided by 2. What this means is that you don't normally use radians on their own. Rather you use them in conjunction with PI as well. Just remember that a full circle is 2 times PI radians and you're all set.

Selecting direction

There's one final (optional) argument you can provide to the **arc()** function, which is whether to draw in a clockwise or a counter-clockwise direction. The default value is **false** for a clockwise direction, or you can supply a value of **true** to draw in a counter-clockwise direction.

Let's look at how these six arguments come together by drawing a set of four arcs, using *Example 9.6*, in which each set of instructions draws ¼, ½, ¾, and finally a full circle in turn. The result of loading this example into a browser can be seen in *Figure 9.7*.

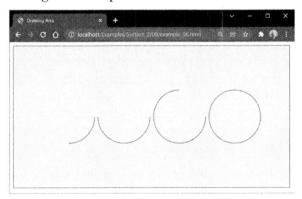

Figure 9.7: Four different arcs

Example 9.6:

```
1.   context.beginPath()
2.   context.arc(128, 160, 60, 0, Math.PI / 2)
3.   context.stroke()
4.
5.   context.beginPath()
6.   context.arc(256, 160, 60, 0, Math.PI)
7.   context.stroke()
8.
9.   context.beginPath()
10.  context.arc(384, 160, 60, 0, Math.PI / 2 * 3)
11.  context.stroke()
12.
13.  context.beginPath()
14.  context.arc(512, 160, 60, 0, Math.PI * 2)
15.  context.stroke()
```

Note: **Did you notice something interesting about the paths in Example 9.6? Well, this code takes advantage of the fact that every time you start a new path, the previous path is automatically closed, so there was no need to issue any closePath() function calls because none of these shapes have been filled, and therefore, closePath() is not required to close the paths back to their starting points. In fact, if you are happy for your start and end points to automatically connect to each other, or you manually issue a moveTo() or lineTo() call to close a shape yourself, you still don't always need to close a path. But, should you ever see results you don't expect and haven't closed a path that is likely to be your problem.**

If you compare lines 2, 6, 10, and 14, which draw the arcs, you'll see that in line 2, the final argument giving a value of PI (referenced in JavaScript with the name `Math.PI`) is divided by 2, which tells the `arc()` function to draw just a quarter circle. Then, line 6 just uses PI on its own for a half circle, while line 10 first obtains the value of PI / 2 to get the value for a quarter circle, then multiplies this by 3 to arrive at the value needed for three-quarters of a circle. Finally, line 10 uses PI multiplied by 2 to achieve a full circle.

The radius of each of these arcs is 60 pixels, but did you notice how all the arcs begin at the 3 O'clock position, 90 degrees around from the top of a circle? That's because the start value provided in each case was 0, which will always begin at the right-most point on a circle's circumference, or at 3 O'clock.

Also, because no sixth argument was supplied for the direction of drawing, all the arcs go around in a clockwise direction. If, instead, a value of **true** were supplied for each of these lines, as shown in *Example 9.7* (where only the modified lines are shown to save space), the result displayed would look like *Figure 9.8*, which should serve to make clear the importance of choosing the correct direction of drawing when using the **arc()** function, as all but the full circle are now inverted.

Figure 9.8: The drawing direction has been reversed to counter-clockwise

Example 9.7 (modified lines from Example 9.6 only):

```
2.   context.arc(128, 160, 60, 0, Math.PI / 2,     true)

6.   context.arc(256, 160, 60, 0, Math.PI,         true)

10.  context.arc(384, 160, 60, 0, Math.PI / 2 * 3, true)

14.  context.arc(512, 160, 60, 0, Math.PI * 2,     true)
```

Now, let's take a look at filling in these paths, but not from the start to end points, as that wouldn't be very neat, but using the center point of each arc, so that the arcs will look either like a whole cake, or a cake with slices removed, as in *Example 9.8*, in which a **moveTo()** call is issued before each **arc()** call, in order to establish the center of each arc for the **fill()** calls, as shown in *Figure 9.9*.

Figure 9.9: *The arcs have now been filled like segments of cake*

Example 9.8:

```
1.   context.beginPath()
2.   context.moveTo(128,160)
3.   context.arc(   128, 160, 60, 0, Math.PI / 2)
4.   context.fill()
5.
6.   context.beginPath()
7.   context.moveTo(256,160)
8.   context.arc(   256, 160, 60, 0, Math.PI)
9.   context.fill()
10.
11.  context.beginPath()
12.  context.moveTo(384,160)
13.  context.arc(   384, 160, 60, 0, Math.PI / 2 * 3)
14.  context.fill()
15.
16.  context.beginPath()
```

```
17. context.moveTo(512,160)
18. context.arc(   512, 160, 60, 0, Math.PI * 2)
19. context.fill()
```

Note: Once again, in Example 9.8, there was no need to close the paths because a start point was previously selected for each arc using the moveTo() calls, such that when the fill() function is called, it automatically closes the path back to the start point, just as we intended.

Drawing an arc to a location

So far we've looked at drawing arcs based around a set center point, but there are other ways you can draw an arc on the HTML5 canvas, one of which is with the **arcTo()** function. With it, you draw an arc based on the current path location and a pair of imaginary tangent lines touching the perimeter of the arc, as if it were a full circle.

In effect, what you should imagine is two lines that meet at a point, with a single location along each line representing the outside edge of the arc. Now, imagine an arc being drawn between these two points, with the arc circumference facing into the imaginary corner.

Example 9.9 sets the scene by drawing two such imaginary lines so that you can see them, with a circle drawn around the start and subsequent two locations, all in red. It then uses the **arcTo()** function to draw the arc represented by the start point and two way points in blue, as shown in *Figure 9.10*.

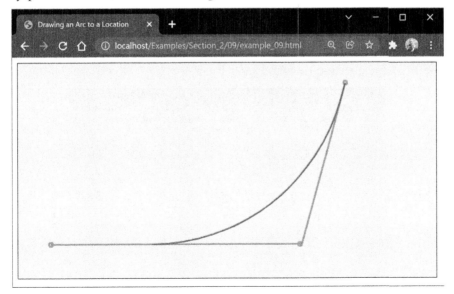

Figure 9.10: Drawing an arc to a location

Example 9.9:

```
1.   context.strokeStyle = 'red'
2.   context.lineWidth   = 2
3.
4.   context.beginPath()
5.   context.arc(   500,  30, 3, 0, Math.PI * 2)
6.   context.moveTo(500,  30)
7.   context.arc(   430, 270, 3, 0, Math.PI * 2)
8.   context.lineTo(430, 270)
9.   context.arc(    50, 270, 3, 0, Math.PI * 2)
10.  context.lineTo(50,  270)
11.  context.stroke()
12.
13.  context.beginPath()
14.  context.strokeStyle = 'blue'
15.  context.moveTo(500,  30)
16.  context.arcTo( 430, 270, 50, 270, 300)
17.  context.stroke()
```

Here, lines 1 and 2 set up the color and line width ready to draw the imaginary lines and the circles around the three points. Then, lines 4 to 11 draw the two red lines, with the start point at the top-right and end point at the bottom-left. Finally, lines 13 to 17 move to the start location at **500,30**, and then draw a blue arc using that start location through the next two pints at **430,270,** and **50,270**, at a radius of **300** pixels. Without these guide lines in place, the result looks like *Figure 9.11*.

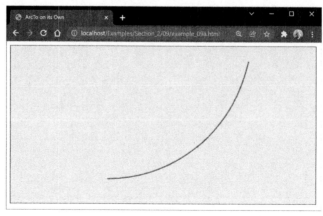

***Figure 9.11**: The arc is shown without the imaginary guidelines*

Using attractors

Lastly, in the set of curved line functions is the ability to draw any type of curve you can imagine using quadratic and Bezier curves. These work like the **arcTo()** function in some ways, but are more like having a gravitational attractor nearby that pulls the curve towards it. A quadratic curve has one attractor, while a Bezier curve uses two.

Let's start off with a single attractor and the **quadraticCurveTo()** function. This takes two sets of arguments; the first of which is the location of an imaginary attractor, while the other two are the final points on the arc. Before calling the function, though, you need to move the current path to when you wish the curve to begin. The attractor can even be located somewhere off the canvas to really pull on a curve, or anywhere inside the canvas for smaller effects.

Example 9.10 draws an imaginary base line and a circle at an imaginary attractor point, both in red. Then, it draws the quadratic curve of this setting in blue, as shown in *Figure 9.12*.

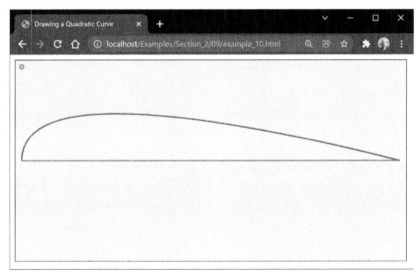

Figure 9.12: A quadratic curve pulled by an imaginary attractor

Example 9.10:

```
1.   context.strokeStyle = 'red'
2.   context.lineWidth   = 2
3.
4.   context.beginPath()
5.   context.moveTo( 10, 160)
```

```
6.   context.lineTo(630, 160)
7.   context.stroke()
8.   context.beginPath()
9.   context.arc(10, 10, 3, 0, Math.PI * 2)
10.  context.stroke()
11.
12.  context.strokeStyle = 'blue'
13.  context.beginPath()
14.  context.moveTo(10, 160)
15.  context.quadraticCurveTo(10, 10, 630, 160)
16.  context.stroke()
```

Lines 1 and 2 of *Example 9.10* set the color and width of the imaginary line and attractor. Then, lines 4 to 10 draw this line horizontally across the center of the canvas, and a circle around the attractor point at the top-left.

Lines 12 to 16 then move to the left-hand side of the imaginary line and then draw the quadratic curve in blue across to the right-hand side of the line, but with the attractor exerting its pull on the curve:

As previously mentioned, a Bezier curve gives you a second attractor, as drawn by *Example 9.11*, which is almost the same as *Example 9.10*, with the addition of a second attractor point at location **630,310**. The result is the fetching double curve as shown in *Figure 9.13*.

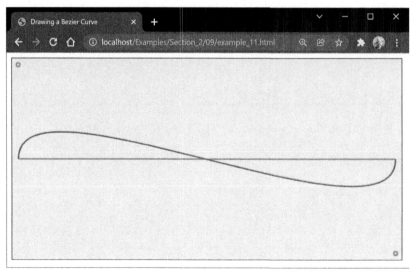

Figure 9.13: *A Bezier curve featuring two imaginary attractors*

Example 9.11:

```
1.   context.strokeStyle = 'red'
2.   context.lineWidth   = 2
3.
4.   context.beginPath()
5.   context.moveTo( 10, 160)
6.   context.lineTo(630, 160)
7.   context.stroke()
8.   context.beginPath()
9.   context.arc(10, 10, 3, 0, Math.PI * 2)
10.  context.stroke()
11.  context.beginPath()
12.  context.arc(630, 310, 3, 0, Math.PI * 2)
13.  context.stroke()
14.
15.  context.strokeStyle = 'blue'
16.  context.beginPath()
17.  context.moveTo(10, 160)
18.  context.bezierCurveTo(10, 10, 630, 310, 630, 160)
19.  context.stroke()
```

Similar to the previous example, *Example 9.11* starts in lines 1 and 2 by setting the color to red and line width to 2 for the imaginary line and attractors. Then lines 4 to 13 draw the horizontal line and two circles for the attractors at the top-left and bottom-right of the screen. Finally, lines 15 to 19 move to location **10,160** and then draw a blue curved line to location **630,160**. On the way, it is pulled first up and to the left by the attractor at **10,10**, and later pulled down by the attractor at **630,310**.

Of course, all these recent curves have been drawn using the **stroke()** function, but you can equally use any of the supported fill methods too if you desire.

Capping and joining lines

There is one final piece remaining to the line drawing puzzle, which is the question of what to do when two lines meet. Should there be a flat edge to the join? Should it be rounded? Or is pointed better? Also, how should a single line end? Should it be square edged, pointed or round?

Thankfully, these choices are down to you and can be made using the **lineCap** property, which offers all three options in the form of supplying an argument of **butt**, **round,** or **square** to it, and the **lineJoin** property, which supports values of **round**, **bevel**, and **miter**.

Let's take a look at how these can be employed in *Example 9.12*, where lines 1 to 7 create a pair of reference lines in red, indicating the bottom and top of the lines to be drawn. Then, in lines 9 to 11, the line drawing properties are increased from the default to 20 pixels and to use the color blue. This is so that we can easily see the different effects of these properties, as shown in *Figure 9.14*.

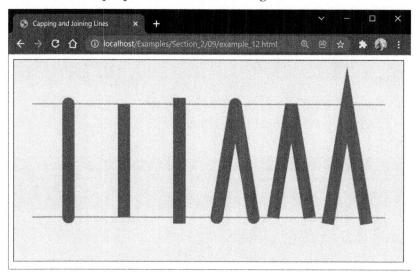

Figure 9.14: A selection of line caps and joins

Example 9.12:

```
1.    context.strokeStyle = 'red'
2.    context.beginPath()
3.    context.moveTo(30,   70)
4.    context.lineTo(610,  70)
5.    context.moveTo(30,  250)
6.    context.lineTo(610, 250)
7.    context.stroke()
8.
9.    context.beginPath()
10.  context.lineWidth    = 20
11.  context.strokeStyle = 'blue'
```

```
12.
13. context.beginPath()
14. context.lineCap = 'round'
15. context.moveTo( 91, 250)
16. context.lineTo( 91,  70)
17. context.stroke()
18.
19. context.beginPath()
20. context.lineCap = 'butt'
21. context.moveTo(183, 250)
22. context.lineTo(183,  70)
23. context.stroke()
24.
25. context.beginPath()
26. context.lineCap = 'square'
27. context.moveTo(274, 250)
28. context.lineTo(274,  70)
29. context.stroke()
30.
31. context.beginPath()
32. context.lineCap  = 'round'
33. context.lineJoin = 'round'
34. context.moveTo(335, 250)
35. context.lineTo(365,  70)
36. context.lineTo(395, 250)
37. context.stroke()
38.
39. context.beginPath()
40. context.lineCap  = 'butt'
41. context.lineJoin = 'bevel'
42. context.moveTo(427, 250)
43. context.lineTo(457,  70)
44. context.lineTo(487, 250)
```

```
45.  context.stroke()

46.

47.  context.beginPath()

48.  context.lineCap  = 'square'

49.  context.lineJoin = 'miter'

50.  context.moveTo(518, 250)

51.  context.lineTo(548,  70)

52.  context.lineTo(578, 250)

53.  context.stroke()
```

The first three sets of instructions in lines 13 to 17, lines 19 to 23, and lines 25 to 29 each draw a line with ends that, in turn, use the **lineCap** properties of **round, butt,** and **square**. As you can see from *Figure 9.14*, the rounded line ends exceed the bounds of the guideline, as do the squared ends. However, the butted ends do as you might expect and butt right up to the guidelines.

The three sets of code following in line 31 to 37, lines 39 to 45, and lines 47 to 53, repeat the same **lineCap** properties on the end points of each pair of lines, but also apply the **lineJoin** properties where they join **round, bevel,** and **miter** in turn. Again, you will see how the rounded and mitered joins exceed the bounds of the guideline, with the miter having to go a long way out to achieve the correct pointed effect. The butted join, however, again butts right up to the guideline.

Hopefully this is all quite clear, but you may be wondering just how far a mitered join might extend, especially with very thick lines combined with quite acute angles. Well, the answer is very far, but you can modify this with another property called **miterLimit**, to which you can apply a limiting value in pixels. What this does is allow all miters that might extend up to a set number of pixels, but if it would extend any further, then the miter is forced back into using a bevel instead.

So, let's try adding the following line just before the final call to **stroke()** on line 53, like this:

```
context.miterLimit = 6
```

This will enable us to see how the miter is now limited to extend by 6 pixels only, and because the actual extent is at least 7 pixels, a bevel is forced, as shown in *Figure 9.15*.

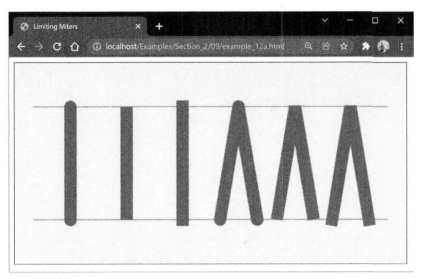

Figure 9.15: *The right-hand mitered join has been forced into a bevel*

Conclusion

This chapter now completes all your learning over the recent few chapters of how to draw straight and curved lines, their types of joins and end caps, filled in shapes, writing text on the canvas, and using all manners of gradients and patterns. In the next chapter, we'll begin exploring manipulating images in greater detail, as well as adding shadows, and learning more about transformations.

CHAPTER 10
Manipulating the Canvas

Introduction

You've reached a milestone in this book. You've learned almost all the drawing features of the HTML5 canvas, and along the way you should have become fairly familiar with writing basic JavaScript code, a sort of bonus you get for learning the canvas.

Now, though, you're ready to move onto the few remaining, but slightly more complex canvas manipulation operations, including things such as drawing images directly to the canvas, something you've already seen done for creating tiled fills, but now you'll see how you can resize images to your preference, or even create new images from parts of the canvas, and use transparency and shadows to provide more professional results.

You'll even look at how canvas image data is stored so that you can directly modify it, perhaps by altering an image's colors, lightening an image, or making it greyscale. Of course, that means learning a little more JavaScript, but you're more than ready for that by now, and all will make sense as you work through it.

Structure

In this chapter, you will:

- Learn many different ways to draw on a canvas with images

- Discover how to extract parts of images and also enlarge and resize them

- Be able to attach shadows to all types of canvas drawing

- Master manipulating canvas data itself directly

Objectives

In this chapter, you will finish off learning the main features of the HTML5 canvas, before moving onto the final canvas chapter following, which will take your advanced skills up to the level of mastery.

Drawing with an image

The HTML canvas has the ability to load an image into JavaScript and then place it on the canvas in a variety of different ways using the **drawImage()** function, which normally takes three arguments such as the name of an image object and the coordinates of the top left-hand corner where it should be pasted into the canvas. You can, if you wish, also provide a couple of additional arguments to specify a new width and height to use.

You will recall from earlier chapters that the loading and manipulating of images with JavaScript requires special handling because images are much larger than scripts, and therefore, may not be loaded in by the time a script starts execution. To overcome this, we use the **onload** event of an image object to only execute these instructions once we are sure an image has been fully loaded into memory.

Example 10.1 shows a new (empty) image object being created. Then, an image name to load in is applied to the **src** property of that object to start the image loading. Immediately after there is an anonymous function (one not given a name), where the code to run once the image is ready is placed between the curly braces for the function. The result is shown in *Figure 10.1*.

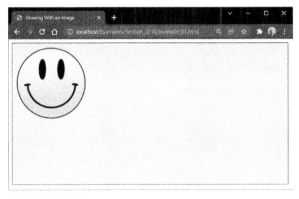

Figure 10.1: *Drawing with an image*

Example 10.1:

```
1. image    = new Image()
2. image.src = 'smiley.png'
3.
4. image.onload = function()
5. {
6.    context.drawImage(image, 10, 10)
7. }
```

The image **smiley.png** has dimensions of 160×160 pixels, and it uses transparency for all pixels outside the image area. It is loaded onto the canvas with its top left-hand corner at location **10,10**. But let's see what happens if two extra arguments are added, with a further three calls to the **drawImage()** function, one larger, and two other smaller ones, with one even smaller than the first, using the code in *Example 10.2*, as shown in *Figure 10.2*.

Figure 10.2: *Drawing the image at various sizes*

Example 10.2:

```
1.  image     = new Image()
2.  image.src = 'smiley.png'
3.
4.  image.onload = function()
5.  {
6.    context.drawImage(image, 10,  10)
7.    context.drawImage(image, 200, 10, 240, 240)
8.    context.drawImage(image, 460, 10,  80,  80)
9.    context.drawImage(image, 560, 10,  40,  40)
10. }
```

If you look closely at *Figure 10.2* you'll notice one of the downsides of resizing images in this way, which is that if you enlarge them a great deal, they can become a little blurry, and if you shrink them too much, they start to look speckly where there should be solid lines.

Nevertheless, as long as you start with an image fairly close to the size at which you intend using it, you can generally get away with small changes in size with little noticeable effects. When you do need major size differences, though, your best bet is to use a graphic program to create the variously sized images, saving them with different filenames.

Extracting image parts

When drawing an image on the canvas, you can also decide whether to use the whole image, or just a part of it. But this requires you to re-think when passing arguments to the **drawImage()** function because, rather than adding yet more arguments to those passed, you must insert the arguments between the image object name and the coordinates and dimensions for drawing the image.

This may seem confusing and you may ask, "*How does JavaScript know what you intend?*". The answer is that it is looking for one of two, four, or eight arguments after the image. If there are two, the image is placed at that top left-hand location without change. If there are four, the image is still placed at that location, but resized to the dimensions given in the final two arguments.

But if there are eight arguments, then the first two are taken to represent the location within the image at which to extract a rectangular portion, and the next two are the width and height of the area to extract. Finally, the four remaining arguments are a pair of coordinates defining where to place the top-left of the extracted area, and the final two specify the width and height to resize this portion to. You may not enter just six arguments thinking the selected area will be drawn at its extracted size, so you *must* specify the width and height to use.

Bearing this in mind, *Example 10.3* once again draws the image at its original size on the top left-hand corner of the canvas. Line 7 draws a version extracted from around the eyes at the same 160 × 160 dimensions of the original complete image, while line 8 does the similar thing but enlarges the drawing.

Example 10.3:

```
1.  image      = new Image()
2.  image.src = 'smiley.png'
3.
4.  image.onload = function()
5.  {
6.      context.drawImage(image, 10,  10)
7.      context.drawImage(image, 43, 12, 75, 75, 200, 10, 160, 160)
8.      context.drawImage(image, 43, 12, 75, 75, 380, 10, 240, 240)
9.
10.     context.strokeStyle = 'blue'
11.     context.strokeRect(10 + 43, 10 + 12, 75, 75)
12.     stroke()
13. }
```

In *Example 10.3*, lines 10 to 12 have been added just to draw a rectangle over the original image in blue, showing the section that is being extracted, offset by 10 pixels horizontally and vertically to compensate for the image being offset by that amount from the top-left corner. The result of all this can be seen in *Figure 10.3*.

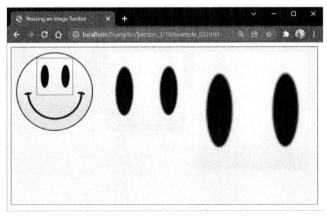

Figure 10.3: *A subsection of the image is resized*

Using the canvas as a source image

You can even use the canvas itself as your source image, and then draw with that, as in *Example 10.4*, which grabs the canvas and draws it back to the canvas resized at the bottom left-hand corner.

Example 10.4:

```
1.   image     = new Image()
2.   image.src = 'smiley.png'
3.
4.   image.onload = function()
5.   {
6.     context.drawImage(image, 10,  10)
7.     context.drawImage(image, 43, 12, 75, 75, 200, 10, 160, 160)
8.     context.drawImage(image, 43, 12, 75, 75, 380, 10, 240, 240)
9.
10.    context.drawImage(canvas, 10, 10, 620, 300, 10, 200, 270, 130)
11.  }
```

Effectively, *Example 10.4* comprises the first section of *Example 10.3*, followed by a final instruction on line 10, on which an area of the canvas beginning at location **10,10**, and with a width and height of **620 × 300**, is grabbed, and then redrawn back to the canvas starting at location **10,200**, and with dimensions of **270 × 130** pixels, as shown in *Figure 10.4*.

Figure 10.4: *The canvas itself is used as a source image*

As you can imagine, this power gives you the ability to repeatedly grab the canvas and draw it back again, creating effects such as when you hold the faces of two mirrors towards each other and an infinite tunnel seems to appear.

Attaching shadows

There is a reason that an image containing transparency was used in these examples, and that's to show you how you can add shadow effects to images. Of course, shadows added to rectangular shapes such as photographs can look great, but if you have an image that's not rectangular, you will want any shadow to apply to the main content of the image, not the whole picture.

So let's take a look at what happens if we apply values to some properties that enable the creation of shadows, of which there are four, namely, **shadowOffsetX**, **shdowOffsetY**, **shadowBlur**, and **shadowColor**. As you'd imagine the first two represent the number of pixels horizontally and vertically that the shadow should be offset from the main image, and the other two define the amount of blurring and color to apply to the shadow.

Without any blurring, a shadow could well look far too sharp to be real, also if the shadow is purely black (or grey) it may be a little boring, and adding just a hint of color from the image can make it look better.

In *Example 10.5*, these four shadow properties are set up, and then the familiar smiley face image is drawn on the canvas, along with a shadow. To illustrate the different types of effects that you can achieve, there are four sets of instructions, each with a slightly more offset, more blurred, and more yellowy shadow, as shown in *Figure 10.5*.

***Figure 10.5**: Attaching shadows to images*

Example 10.5:

```
1.   image       = new Image()
2.   image.src = 'smiley.png'
3.
4.   image.onload = function()
5.   {
6.      context.shadowOffsetX = 4
7.      context.shadowOffsetY = 4
8.      context.shadowBlur    = 4
9.      context.shadowColor   = '#000'
10.     context.drawImage(image, 10, 10, 140, 140)
11.
12.     context.shadowOffsetX = 6
13.     context.shadowOffsetY = 6
14.     context.shadowBlur    = 6
15.     context.shadowColor   = '#220'
16.     context.drawImage(image, 160, 10, 140, 140)
17.
18.     context.shadowOffsetX = 8
19.     context.shadowOffsetY = 8
20.     context.shadowBlur    = 8
21.     context.shadowColor   = '#440'
22.     context.drawImage(image, 310, 10, 140, 140)
23.
24.     context.shadowOffsetX = 10
25.     context.shadowOffsetY = 10
26.     context.shadowBlur    = 10
27.     context.shadowColor   = '#660'
28.     context.drawImage(image, 460, 10, 140, 140)
29.  }
```

In this example, let's take a look at lines 6 to 10 first. Here, you can see all four of the shadow properties have been set to quite low values, and then the image is drawn on line 10 using these settings. As you progress through each set of instructions, the values are increased a little. You will probably agree that the best settings are probably somewhere around the middle two images. In other words, an average of about 6 to 8 pixels of shadow offset tends to work well, and just a very slight tint towards one of the main colors either in the offset, or from any background that may be behind it will help the shadow appear more realistic. But that's a matter of your design choice because you can choose absolutely any settings you like now that you know how to add shadows.

More than just images

You can actually attach an object to almost anything you draw on the canvas, and are not limited to only images. For example, take a look at *Example 10.6*, which draws a shadowed rectangle with a shadow that is not offset (as shown in *Figure 10.6*), and then writes three lines of text with attached shadows of varying offsets.

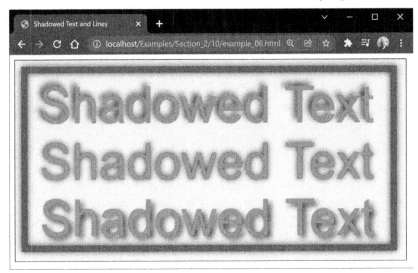

Figure 10.6: Attaching shadows to text and lines using different offsets

Example 10.6:

```
1. context.shadowOffsetX = 0
2. context.shadowOffsetY = 0
3. context.shadowBlur    = 10
4. context.shadowColor   = '#000'
5. context.strokeStyle   = 'blue'
6. context.lineWidth     = 10
7. context.strokeRect(15, 15, 605, 285)
```

```
8.
9.  context.fillStyle      = 'red'
10. context.font           = '60pt Arial'
11.
12. context.fillText('Shadowed Text', 40, 190)
13.
14. context.shadowOffsetX = -5
15. context.shadowOffsetY = -5
16. context.fillText('Shadowed Text', 40, 100)
17.
18. context.shadowOffsetX = 5
19. context.shadowOffsetY = 5
20. context.fillText('Shadowed Text', 40, 280)
```

The first section of instructions should now be familiar. All the shadow properties are set, followed by the line width and color, and then a large rectangle is drawn along with a shadow that is not offset. And in the other three sections, different shadows are applied to lines of text, first offset up and to the left, then centered, and finally offset down and to the right.

Whatever shadow properties you select, continue to apply until new ones are specified or the instructions end. So, now is a good time to remember our old friends **save()** and **restore()**, which you can call on the context before and after finishing with shadows, as a quick way to turn the shadows off again when you don't need them any longer, by placing the two lines following before and after your use of shadows (or anything else you wish to restore back to defaults quickly or easily):

context.save()

context.restore()

Editing pixels directly

This section is likely to be of less interest to you; unless you plan on learning a lot of JavaScript and have some very specific things you need to be able to achieve using the HTML5 canvas. Nevertheless, for the sake of completeness, it is necessary to detail all the features of the canvas so that you are fully equipped.

If you find this part of the book hard going, it's OK to quickly skim over it for now, as you can always come back another time if you need to learn these techniques and by skimming, you'll at least know what is possible to achieve with direct image data handling.

So, now let's proceed with looking into how it is possible to directly manipulate the data that forms a canvas using the following three new functions: **getImageData()**, **putImageData()**, and **createImageData()** which, as their names suggest, allow reading, writing, and creating image data.

To show you what's possible, *Example 10.7* loads in a photograph and displays it on the canvas, and then it iterates through all the image data, averaging out the red, green, and blue image data to convert the photo to monochrome, with the new data written back to another part of the canvas, as shown in *Figure 10.7*.

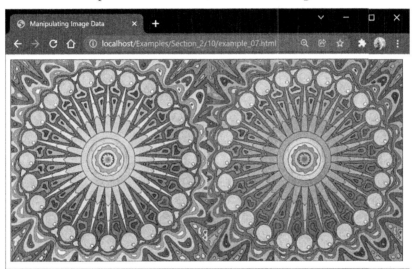

Figure 10.7: The left-hand image has been processed into a monochrome image on the right

Example 10.7:

```
1. canvas   = document.getElementById('canvas')
2. context = canvas.getContext('2d')
3.
4. // Start of example code from the book
5. image      = new Image()
6. image.src = 'painting.png'
7.
8. image.onload = function()
9. {
10.   context.drawImage(image, 0, 0)
11.   imagedata = context.getImageData(0, 0, 320, 320)
```

```
12.
13.   width  = 320
14.   height = 320
15.   ypos   = 0
16.
17.   while (ypos < height)
18.   {
19.     xpos = 0
20.
21.     while (xpos < width)
22.     {
23.       colorpos = ypos * width * 4 + xpos * 4
24.
25.       average = (imagedata.data[colorpos    ] +
26.                  imagedata.data[colorpos + 1] +
27.                  imagedata.data[colorpos + 2]) / 3
28.
29.       // This line is intentionally left empty
30.
31.       imagedata.data[colorpos    ] = average
32.       imagedata.data[colorpos + 1] = average
33.       imagedata.data[colorpos + 2] = average
34.
35.       xpos = xpos + 1
36.     }
37.
38.     ypos = ypos + 1
39.   }
40.   context.putImageData(imagedata, 320, 0)
41. }
```

Yes, this is a longer example, and it does include some new JavaScript features, but you're ready for them, and the following explanation should make complete sense if you work through it along with the example code. You can see the result of this code in *Figure 10.7*:

Lines 1 to 6 should be fairly familiar to you now. They create a new and empty image object and then specify that the file **painting.png** to be loaded into it. After that, the **onload** event of the image is attached such that the code between the braces in the following anonymous function is only executed once the image is fully loaded into memory.

The first new thing of note here is the call to the **getImageData()** function, which asks for all the data in the image starting at location **0,0** and with both a width and height of **320** pixels, to be loaded into an object called simply **imagedata**. This is the data that will be processed.

Next, three variables are assigned values. The variables **width** and **height** are assigned the width and height of the image in pixels (both 320), and a variable called **ypos** is set to have the value **0**. This variable will be used as a counter to move through the different rows of data in the image. It will increment by 1 each time a row of the data has been processed, until it reaches the value 320 (representing the row following the image bottom), where it will cease to be used and the code will end execution.

How the color data is stored

Before looking at the **while()** loop that will do this data processing, first we need to understand how the image data is laid out in memory. Don't worry, it's quite simple and obvious. Colors in a canvas image are made up of four different values, each of which can be between 0 and 255 (or 0x00 and 0xFF in the hexadecimal numbering system, which also uses the letters A through F to allow for the 16 digits of 0 through F required to manipulate numbers in base 16).

These four values represent the amount of red, green, blue, and transparency in the color. When combined, they display as a color, with whatever transparency may be set, allowing whatever colors are in any elements underneath to show through by that amount.

We are not currently interested in the transparency, but we must still skip four values at a time to find each new color. And then we take just the first three values to discover the red, green, and blue components of that color, and ignore the fourth value.

Looping through the data

Knowing this, we're now ready to go back to the example where, at line 13 a **while()** loop is entered, which allows the contents in its braces to execute only if the value in

ypos is less than in **height**. This is a check to ensure that processing has not finished because when **ypos** later gets incremented sufficiently, it will no longer be less than **height** (which is the height of 320 pixels), and so the program will end.

So far so good. We are able to iterate down through the rows of image data. Next, during each iteration of the **ypos** loop, we then need process along each of the rows by four values at a time. To do this, a new loop counter called **xpos** is created and initialized with the value **0**, ready to enter a second loop starting on line 21. In this case, the loop contents will only execute as long as **xpos** is less than the width of the image, held in **width** (and with a value of 320). As long as it is less, the core of the pair of loops is reached on line 23.

Processing the image data

Lines 23 to 33 do all the heavy data manipulation, but it's all handled quite straightforwardly by creating a variable called **colorpos**, which will point to the precise start of the three components of the current pixel color we are interested in. The value of **colorpos** is determined by multiplying the value in **ypos** by that in **width** to get a number representing the pixel at the start of the current row.

So, if you were currently at the start of row 30 (for example) and there are 320 pixels per row, then so far you have seen 9,600 pixels, and therefore **ypos** times **width** would have a value of 9,600. However, we must remember that there are four items of data that make up each pixel's color, so this value gets multiplied by 4 to find the exact position in the image data for the row start. In the example of row 30, it would be $30 \times 320 \times 4$, or 38,400.

Next, we need to know where along the current row we are so the value in xpos is then calculated and also multiplied by 4 to account for the four values per pixels color. So, if we are 42 pixels along a row, then 42×4 equals 168.

Finally, to find out the exact start of the image data representing both the row and column, the two results are added. In the case of the example of location 30,42, the entire calculation would be $20 \times 320 \times 4 + 42 \times 4$ or, as line 23 states:

```
23.    colorpos = ypos * width * 4 + xpos * 4
```

Averaging the color data

We now know precisely where the image data for the current pixel can be found in the **imagadata** object, so lines 24 to 27 extract each of the three values at **colorpos**, **colorpos + 1**, and **colorpos + 2**, add them all together and then divide by 3 to obtain the average of the red, green, and blue components of the color, and the result is placed in the variable named **average**. This is done by the use of the square brackets after the **data** keyword, which tell JavaScript to fetch the data from **imagedata** at the offsets given.

Line 29 is then left blank for something we'll do in a minute which you should find fun.

Then, lines 31 to 33 write the value in **average** right back into the **imagedata**, replacing the three different red, green, and blue component values, all with the same value in **average**, which means that the pixel color becomes a shade of grey.

Lastly, the two nested loops need closing. This is done, by incrementing the value of **xpos** by 1 for the inner loop then closing it with a curly brace, then incrementing the value of **ypos** by 1 for the outer loop, and then closing that with a curly brace.

These increments occur after all calculations have complete such that either the inner loop is ready to move onto the next pixel along (or back to the zeroth one on the line), or the outer loop is ready to move down a line, or if finished, to drop out of the loop leaving execution to the final command of the example, which draws the modified imagedata back on the canvas, over to the right of the original image.

Other effects

Well done! If you've never used JavaScript before, you've learned a great deal about how to program with it in this chapter. Hopefully, you will agree that it's not all that hard, and really there's no easier way that could have been developed to let you achieve these types of effects. Also, you may have been surprised at how quickly this code runs. The loading, manipulation, and redrawing of the new monochrome image appears to be instantaneous.

And the code in the example can be optimized in many ways, but it was kept fairly simple, and even a little verbose, in order to show exactly how everything works. So, imagine how much faster it would run if coded highly efficiently.

Having gone through all this work, let's have a little fun with what we've learned by changing the effect just a little by adding just a single line where line 29 was deliberately left empty, just for this purpose.

The first trick is to invert the monochrome image by simply subtracting the value obtained in the variable **average** from its maximum value of 255 (hexadecimal **0xFF**), with the line below.

```
29.      average = 0xFF - average // Invert colors
```

The result of this is shown in *Figure 10.8*.

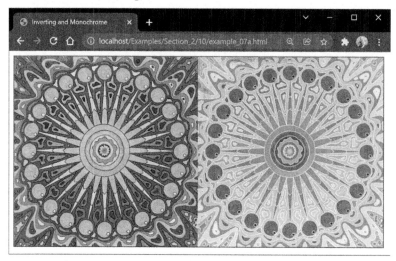

Figure 10.8: The image has been made monochrome and inverted

Let's try lightening an image, with this replacement for line 29 (this use of the **+=** operator is shorthand for **average = average + 0x50**).

```
29.          average += 0x50 // Lighten
```

The result should look like *Figure 10.9*.

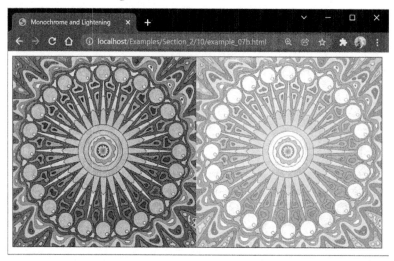

Figure 10.9: The image has been made monochrome and lightened

Or how about replacing lines 31 to 33 with the following to increase the red component and decrease the blue component of the new monochrome image, resulting in a sort of sepia tone?

```
31.      imagedata.data[colorpos    ] = average + 0x50

32.      imagedata.data[colorpos + 1] = average

33.      imagedata.data[colorpos + 2] = average - 0x50
```

The example should now display as shown in *Figure 10.10*.

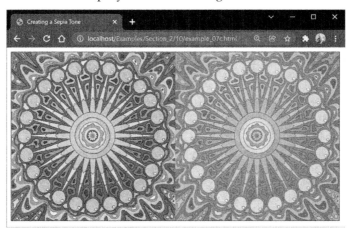

Figure 10.10: *Creating a sepia tone*

Or, for a final effect, how about adding some random noise to the image by altering those lines in the following way.

```
31.      imagedata.data[colorpos    ] = average + Math.random() * 0x80

32.      imagedata.data[colorpos + 1] = average + Math.random() * 0x80

33.      imagedata.data[colorpos + 2] = average + Math.random() * 0x80
```

The result of these changes should look like *Figure 10.11*.

Figure 10.11: *Random noise has been added to the monochrome image*

What we have done here is add a random value between **0** and **0x80** (decimal 128) to each of the red, green, and blue greyscaled color components using the **random()** function of JavaScript's **Math** library. This function returns a floating point value between 0 and 1, so multiplying it by any value returns a number between 0 and that value.

Note what happens if you reload this example several times. Each time you do so you'll get a completely different set of noise, showing that the result is truly random (well pseudo random, which is as good as a PC can get without outside assistance). Try playing with lines 29 through 33 and see if you can come up with some effects of your own.

Creating your own image data

You don't have to create an `imagedata` object directly from a canvas because you can simply create a new one with blank data by calling the **createImageData()** function, like the following, which creates a blank object with a width of 320 and height of 240 pixels, as if out of thin air:

```
imagedata = createImageData(320, 240)
```

Alternatively, you can create a new object from any existing object, as follows:

```
newimagedataobject = createImageData(imagedata)
```

It's then up to you what you do with these objects to add pixel data to them, and how you draw them on the canvas or create other objects from them. However, this may be an exercise more suited to slightly more advanced JavaScript users.

Conclusion

Well, that's it, you've almost made it to the end of the HTML5 canvas tutorial. Not only have you learned all the main skills needed to get the best out of the canvas, but if you weren't already a JavaScript programmer, you should by now be able to class yourself at the very least as a proficient beginner in the language. In the following chapter, you will move onto becoming a master of the canvas by learning advanced features such as compositing and transparency.

CHAPTER 11
Advanced Canvas Features

Introduction

In our final foray into the treasure trove of features offered by the HTML5 canvas, we will examine the remaining more advanced effects that you can achieve by applying transparency, choosing the type of compositing to use and using translations, transformations, rotations, and scaling to their best effects.

Discussion will get a little technical in places, but no more-so perhaps that learning how to use a new graphics program, except that in this case, you will learn about new functions you can call from JavaScript.

More than anything else, in this chapter, you should be able to see clearly how all the features of the canvas can be used in combination to create almost any result you desire, and that you can achieve quite fantastic results due to the precision of programmed graphics, even if you don't perceive yourself as being particularly arty.

Structure

In this chapter, you will:

- Learn about composting and transparency and how they work together
- Discover 12 different new ways of drawing on the canvas

- Become used to using a few more JavaScript features

- Understand how to manipulate images with rotations and other transformations

Objectives

By the time you finish reading this chapter, you will have completed your education in the HTML5 canvas to the point that you will have mastered most of its most common features, and be aware of what is possible with the more advanced ones. You will also have learned more about looping, data structures, and manipulating the **Document Object Model (DOM)** from JavaScript.

Compositing and transparency

We will cover a great deal of ground in this chapter; most of it making use of compositing and transparency, so these subjects are a great place to begin with. And do remember that with such major changes being made on the canvas context, using **save()** and **restore()** to quickly be able to revert back to a previous state when doing so will often come in very handy.

You may be wondering what is meant by the term compositing. Well, it's a way of describing the way you place elements of a drawing on the canvas. For example, should it go in front or behind an existing object, and so forth? To control this compositing behavior, you can use a property called **globalCompositeOperation**, which can totally change the way an object is drawn, depending on the value supplied to it.

The default value for this property is **source-over**, which simply tells JavaScript to overwrite everything already on the canvas but there are, in fact, twelve possible property values, so it's probably best to give them to you as a list, as follows:

- **source-over**: As already mentioned, this is the default. The source image is copied over the destination image, in other words, everything under the object is overwritten.

- **source-in**: Only parts of the source image that will appear within the destination are shown, and the destination image is removed. Any alpha transparency in the source image causes the destination under it to be removed.

- **source-out**: Only parts of the source image that do not appear within the destination are shown, and the destination image is removed. Any alpha transparency in the source image causes the destination under it to be removed.

- **source-atop**: The source image is displayed where it overlays the destination. The destination image is displayed where the destination image is opaque and the source image is transparent. Other regions are transparent.

- **destination-over**: The source image is drawn under the destination image.

- **destination-in**: The destination image displays where the source and destination image overlap, but not in any areas of source image transparency. The source image does not display.

- **destination-out**: Only those parts of the destination outside the source image's non transparent sections are shown. The source image does not display.

- **destination-atop**: The source image displays where the destination is not displayed. Where the destination and source overlap, the destination image is displayed. Any transparency in the source image prevents that area of the destination image being shown.

- **Lighter**: The sum of the source and destination is applied such that where they do not overlap, they display as normal, but where they overlap the sum of both images is shown, but lightened.

- **Darker**: The sum of the source and destination is applied such that where they do not overlap, they display as normal, but where they overlap, the sum of both images is shown, but darkened.

- **Copy**: The source image is copied over the destination. Any transparent area of the source causes any destination that it overlaps to not display.

- **Xor**: Where the source and destination images do not overlap, they display as normal. Where they overlap their color values are exclusive-ored.

Now, compositing can be a bit hard to get your head around, so let's create a document to test all these properties and see the results, as in *Example 11.1*, which uses the circular globe image with a transparent background shown in *Figure 11.1* as a source image, which is drawn over filled circles in twelve different ways:

Figure 11.1: *A globe image for using with compositing*

Example 11.1:

```
1.  <!DOCTYPE html>
2.  <html>
3.   <head>
4.     <title>Compositing Examples</title>
5.   </head>
6.   <body>
7.    <script>
8.       image      = new Image()
9.       image.src = 'globe.png'
10.      types     = ['source-over',        'source-in',
11.                    'source-out',         'source-atop',
12.                    'destination-over', 'destination-in',
13.                    'destination-out',  'destination-atop',
14.                    'lighter',            'darker',
15.                    'copy',               'xor']
16.
17.      image.onload = function()
18.      {
19.        for (j = 0 ; j < 12 ; ++j)
20.        {
21.          canvas                  = document.createElement('canvas')
22.          canvas.width            = 120
23.          canvas.height           = 120
24.          canvas.style.background = '#ddd'
25.          canvas.style.margin     = '5px'
26.          context                 = canvas.getContext('2d')
27.
28.          context.arc(50, 50, 50, 0, Math.PI * 2)
29.          context.fillStyle = 'orange'
30.          context.fill()
31.
32.          context.globalCompositeOperation = types[j]
```

```
33.                context.drawImage(image, 20, 20, 100, 100)
34.                document.body.appendChild(canvas)
35.            }
36.        }
37.    </script>
38.    </body>
39. </html>
```

This example is a little different from those in previous chapters because when you use the **globalCompositeOperation** attribute, it applies to the entire canvas, and therefore, in order to show all twelve different attribute values, it is necessary to create twelve independent canvases. And to keep the code short, a couple of more advanced JavaScript techniques have been employed. In this particular case, the example is shown in its entirety.

Let's break the program down, starting with lines 1 through 6 which are very standard for an HTML document. So, we only need to consider the content between the script tags in lines 8 to 36.

You will recognize lines 8 and 9 because they are familiar instructions for loading in an image. In this instance, it's **globe.png**. Next, there's something very new on lines 10 to 15. What you see there is the storing of all the possible attribute value names into what is known as an array. An array is like a stacked collection of variables, and you reference them in order by number.

So, for example, **types[0]** contains the value **source-over**, while **types[11]** contains **xor**, with all the other values in **types[1]** through to **types[10]**. We will shortly see how this array gets used.

You've also seen lines 17 and 18 earlier. They simply create an anonymous function that will only allow the code within its curly braces to be run once the image's **onload** event is triggered, which means that the image has been fully loaded into memory.

Using a loop

Lines 19 to 35 contain a new feature of this book, which is another type of loop called a **for()** loop. This is similar to the **while()** loops seen in previous chapters, but it is more concise in that it takes three arguments which enables you to set up the loop counter to use as the first argument. In this case, it's the variable **j**, which is initialized to the value **0**.

You then tell the loop the condition under which it can be executed which, in this case, is as long as **j** has a value less than **12** (since there are 12 types of attributes to apply). Finally, you tell the loop what to do after each iteration. In this case, we ask the loop to increment the variable **j** by **1**, using the shorthand **++** operator, such that **++j** and **j = j + 1** are equivalent, but the former is chosen for brevity.

Now, we are in the loop at line 21, the instructions shown will be executed a total of 12 times, with values of **j** from **0** to **11**. The first thing we do each time around the loop is create a new canvas object simply called **canvas** using the **document. createElement()** function. This is much simpler than creating twelve different canvases in the HTML document, as we can do this on-the-fly, so to speak in JavaScript.

Next, the width and height of the new canvas object are set on lines 22 and 23, then lines 24 and 25 apply CSS styling of the color represented by **#ddd** for the background of the canvas, and give it a margin of 5 pixels. Now, we are ready to create a context from the canvas on line 26, as we have done in many recent examples.

Drawing the image

Next, on lines 28 to 30, a filled orange circle is drawn on the current canvas, which will be the object over which we will draw the globe image using the current compositing setting. Speaking of which, on line 32 the current compositing attribute name is retrieved from the **types** array as described a little earlier, and applied to the **globalCompositeOperation** attribute.

On line 33, we are now ready to draw the image on the canvas using the current compositing setting, and then to finish each loop off; the new canvas just created is attached to the current document body on line 34, using a call to the **appendChild()** function.

Hopefully, this has made complete sense to you, and you have substantially increased your knowledge of JavaScript (if you didn't know these things already). Now, let's look at the result of running this code in *Figure 11.2* which shows the 12 types of compositing in action, in the order shown in the array at line 10 of the example.

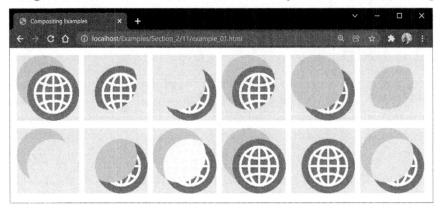

Figure 11.2: *Demonstrating the 12 possible compositing attributes in action*

As you can see, you have a wide variety of possible ways of drawing on the canvas using these attributes, offering some quite interesting effects. If you find them fascinating, try modifying the example using different types of source and destination images, especially employing different shapes and colors, to give yourself a good grasp of the types of things you can do.

Changing transparency

When drawing on the canvas, you can choose the precise amount of transparency you wish to apply by providing a value of between 0 and 1 to the **globalAlpha** property of the context. For example, let's modify the currently blank line 27 as follows:

```
27.              context.globalAlpha = 0.5
```

The value **0.0** means there will be no transparency, while a value of **1.0** specifies that full transparency should be applied. So, the value **0.5** entered above sets it to the halfway point, with the result shown in *Figure 11.3*, where you can, perhaps, more clearly understand the effects of the various compositing operations because they are only half applied, since any parts of the image that would be erased, become only half so.

Figure 11.3: The compositing effects are more clearly understood if transparency is also applied

Applying transformations

When drawing on the HTML5 canvas, there are three types of transformations you can apply to modify the way the drawing is applied. These are the use of scaling, rotation, translation, and transformation. Let's look at these in turn.

In *Example 11.2*, a diamond shape is drawn seven times using a loop, in which the only changes are the color applied and the scaling values used, resulting in *Figure 11.4.*

Example 11.2:

```
1.  colors = ['red',  'orange', 'yellow', 'green',
2.                    'blue', 'indigo', 'violet']
3.
4.  for (j = 0 ; j < 7 ; ++j)
5.  {
6.     context.save()
7.     context.beginPath()
8.
9.     context.scale(1 + j, 1 + j)
10.
11.    context.moveTo( 0, 40)
12.    context.lineTo(40,  0)
13.    context.lineTo(80, 40)
14.    context.lineTo(40, 80)
15.    context.lineTo( 0, 40)
16.    context.fillStyle = colors[j]
17.    context.fill()
18.    context.restore()
19. }
```

Here, we are back to displaying just the main JavaScript code (and not even the bit of JavaScript that creates the **context** object), with the complete HTML document available on the companion website, and the remainder of this document being the same as the examples from previous chapters.

Looking at line 1 you should be familiar with what's going on by now. An array called **colors** has been created, and given the seven color names of the rainbow, in order. Then, at line 4, a **for()** loop is entered to iterate through seven values in **j** (that is **0** through to **6**).

On line 6, the entire context of properties is saved with a call to the **save()** function, so that it can be later restored (returning any scaling back to how it was). Then, a new path is created on line 7, and on line 9, a scaling value of **1 + j** is applied to both the horizontal and vertical coordinates supplied from now on via a call to the `scale()` function.

When **j** has a value of **0,** this evaluates to just **1**, and so the scaling is set to a normal one-to-one ratio in both dimensions. But as **j** increases to **1**, then **1 + 1** has a value of **2**. Then, **1 + 2** evaluates to **3**, all the way to **1 + 6**, which is **7**. So, the loop has the effect of increasing the scaling values from 1 to 7.

Next, lines 11 to 15 create the path required to draw a diamond shape, and then line 16 applies one of the colors in the **colors** array to the **fillStyle** property, and line 17 fills the diamond. Finally, line 18 calls **restore()** to set the scaling factor back to the default. If this is not done, the current scaling would remain in place next time around the loop, and then an additional scaling factor would be added to that, and so on each iteration, increasing at an exponential rate.

When you look at *Figure 11.4*, you can see these diamonds drawn on-top of each other, all increasing in size for each iteration, even though the coordinates specified in lines 11 to 15 do not change – just the scaling factor changes.

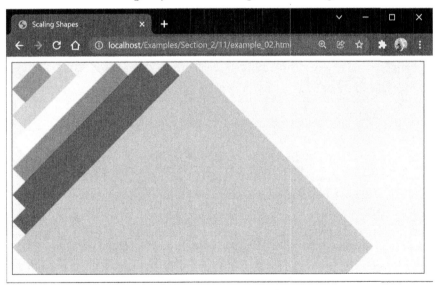

Figure 11.4: *The same sized shape scaled up several times*

This means you are able to create paths and shapes of one size, and then rescale them to any size you like when drawing them to the canvas.

Just remember that when you need to restore the previous scaling, or wish to change the scaling, use calls to **save()** and **restore()** to easily revert to the previous settings. Also remember that these two functions save and restore *all* the properties of the context from fill styles and transparency to line widths, shadows, text alignment, transformations, and more.

Using rotations

A great way to see the power of rotations is to apply it to an example we already have, so let's create *Example 11.3* by modifying line 10 of *Example 11.2* by adding in a rotation value, as follows:

Example 11.3 *(just the modified line)*:

```
10. context.rotate(j / 7)
```

This has the effect of rotating the drawing of the object by a small amount each time, as shown in *Figure 11.5*.

Figure 11.5: The object is scaled and rotated a number of times

The actual amount of rotation used here is a number between 0 and 6 radians, divided by 7 because a radian has a value of 180/PI, or about 57 degrees. Through dividing radians by 7, the rotation of each new shape ends up at just over an extra 8 degrees for each iteration of the loop.

Applying translations

One problem with *Example 11.3* is that the rotation starts to disappear off the left-hand side of the screen. So, let's add a translation to each iteration by inserting an instruction in line 8 of *Example 11.3*, to create *Example 11.4*.

Example 11.4 *(just the modified line)*:

```
8. context.translate(j * 40, 0)
```

As with scaling, translation takes two arguments, which are the amount by which to translate in both a horizontal and a vertical direction in pixels. In this instance, we only need to translate horizontally to bring the larger diamonds back into the canvas and have done so by just an additional 40 pixels each time (`j * 40`). The result of adding this instruction is shown in *Figure 11.6*.

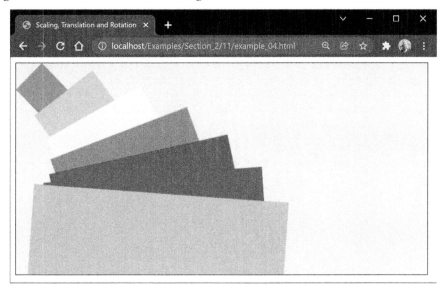

Figure 11.6: *The objects are increasingly scaled, translated, and rotated*

Applying multiple transformations

It is possible to achieve some weird and wonderful results using one or both of the `transform()` and `setTransform()` functions, but they rely on transformation matrixes which are 3 × 3 matrices containing various parameters, the explanation of which would finally start to take us beyond the scope of this book. However, if you are interested, there's a lot of further reading available at **tinyurl.com/canvastransforms**.

Conclusion

Well, you made it! You have now learned all there is to know about using the HTML5 canvas. Yes, there are some advanced ways of accessing the canvas that haven't been fully detailed, but most of what they can do can be achieved (if slightly more long-windedly) using the features you've already mastered.

Now, it's time to continue our examination of the entire HTML5 infrastructure by moving onto studying geolocation in the following chapter.

CHAPTER 12
Using Geolocation

Introduction

With the incredible rise in popularity of smartphones, the ability to determine the location of a device has become almost essential, particularly for running interactive maps and navigation software, and even for finding local Wi-Fi hotspots, or services such as restaurants or cash dispensing machines, and so on.

Geolocation is also being used more and more to try and sell you services by offering promotions in stores that are near to you, and a little more benevolently in enabling you to know whether friends or acquaintances are within your near vicinity. Thankfully, you are in control of when you allow your location information to be revealed, so you can minimize any privacy or security risks the technology could create.

In this chapter, you'll learn how to use JavaScript to determine the location of any geolocation-enabled device, as long as the user allows you, and as long as the browser supports the feature. On success, you will be given the user's longitude and latitude as a pair of coordinates, as close to where the browser can determine you actually are (usually on a mobile device via a GPS satellite chip).

Structure

In this chapter, you will:

- Understand geolocation, whether provided by GPS or through other means
- Understand how to check whether a user's browser supports geolocation
- Handle user blocking and acceptance of providing their location
- Turn a user's location into latitude and longitude for mapping

Objectives

In this chapter, you will learn everything about HTML5 geolocation, from what it is, how useful it is under different circumstances, and even how to deal with any errors you may encounter. By the time you finish reading the chapter, you will have fully mastered geolocation, and you will be able to obtain precise latitude and longitude coordinates of a user, as long as they grant access.

Explaining GPS

The **Global Positioning Satellite (GPS)** service consists of multiple satellites orbiting the earth whose positions are very precisely known. When a GPS-enabled devices tunes into these satellites, the different times at which signals from these various satellites arrive at it enable the device to know where it is to within just a few feet.

This is achieved by the fact that the speed of light (and radio waves) is a known constant, and the time it takes for a signal to get from a satellite to a GPS device precisely indicates the satellite's distance.

By making a note of all the different times at which signals arrive from different satellites, a simple calculation allows the device to derive each of the satellite's positions relative to each other, and therefore very closely triangulate the position of the device relative to the satellites.

Many mobile devices such as phones and tablets have GPS chips and can provide this information. But some don't, others have them tuned off, and others may be used indoors where they are shielded from the GPS satellites, and therefore cannot receive any signals. In these cases, additional techniques may be used to attempt to determine your location.

Alternatives to GPS

If your device has mobile phone hardware but no GPS (which is unlikely) or GPS is disabled, it may attempt to triangulate its location by checking the timings of signals received from the various mobile phone communication towers with which it can communicate (and whose positions are very precisely known). If there are a few towers, this can get almost as close to your location as GPS.

But where there's a single tower, the signal strength can be used to determine a radius around the tower, and the circle it creates represents the area in which you are likely to be located. This could place you anywhere within a mile or two of your actual location, down to within a few tens of feet.

Failing that, there may be known Wi-Fi access points within range of your device whose positions are known, and since all access points have a unique identifying address called a **Media Access Control** (**MAC**) address, a reasonably good approximation of location can be obtained, perhaps to within a street or two.

And if that fails, the **Internet Protocol** (**IP**) address used by your device can be queried and used as a rough indicator of your location. Often though, this provides only the location of a major switch belonging to your Internet provider, which could be dozens or even hundreds of miles away. But at the very least, your IP address can (usually) narrow down the country, and sometimes the region someone is in, and you may get as close as the user's service provider main hub nearest to that user, which is usually pretty good for most purposes.

Note: Your IP address is commonly used by media companies that restrict playback of their content by territory. However, some people are able to set up proxy servers that use a forwarding IP address in the country that is blocking them to fetch and pass content through the blockade directly to their browser. Therefore, you should be aware that if you locate someone by IP address it is not 100 percent definite that you do, in fact, have the right country for them.

Testing whether geolocation is available

As you have already learned in previous chapters on the canvas, HTML5 features are sometimes so advanced that they cannot be accessed by simple HTML, and therefore, some familiarization with JavaScript is necessary to use them; let alone handle them in advanced ways.

This means that if you are not currently a JavaScript programmer, you will now learn even more about the programming language via the examples in this chapter. Little by little, the cut-and-paste examples will become second nature to you, such that they'll no-longer be pre-packaged sections of code, but you will have extracted their full intent and usage and will be able to create your own routines to access the various features, in ways that suit you and your projects best.

So, let's get stuck into the job straight away in *Example 12.1*, which simply detects whether your browser supports geolocation by issuing a pop-up `alert()` message.

Example 12.1:

```
1.  <!DOCTYPE html>
2.  <html lang="en">
3.    <head>
4.      <meta charset="utf-8">
5.      <title>Testing for Geolocation</title>
6.    </head>
7.    <body>
8.     <script>
9.       // Start of example code from the book
10.      if (typeof navigator.geolocation == 'undefined')
11.      {
12.        alert("Sorry, no geolocation support.")
13.      }
14.      else
15.      {
16.        alert("Great, geolocation is supported.")
17.      }
18.      // End of example code from the book
19.     </script>
20.   </body>
21. </html>
```

Now, this example doesn't make use of the canvas, so it's a little different and shorter than those in recent chapters. Therefore, this first example is provided in full. Thereafter in this chapter, only the lines within the comment markers (in this instance on lines 9 and 18) will be shown in the examples.

Hopefully most of this is clear to you, leaving only lines 10 to 17 to explain. What is going on here is that a property called **navigator.geolocation** that all browsers must have if they support geolocation, is tested for existing. If it is found to be **undefined,** then the property doesn't exist and so neither does the geolocation feature. Nowadays, almost all browsers will support this feature, but for the sake of a couple of extra lines of code, you can alert your users that a feature on your website is not available if they are using an older browser.

Speaking of alerting, the way the user is informed about the existence or not of the geolocation feature is by means of popping up a little window with some text in it. This is achieved with a call to the **alert()** function, which will then pause all execution until the user clicks (or in the case of a mobile browser, taps) on the **OK** button.

To perform the check, an **if()** statement is employed, with a statement inside the brackets which, if it evaluates to **true**, the instructions within the curly braces are executed. So, by checking whether **navigator.geolocation** doesn't exist as a property, the answer can only be **true** or **false**. If **true,** the alert message with text about no support is displayed on line 12.

Next, comes an **else** statement which is, as you would expect, somewhere to place instructions to execute of the statement evaluates to **false**. In which case, any code within its curly braces will be executed. In *Figure 12.1*, the browser does support geolocation, so the statement did evaluate to **false**, and therefore the second alert window has popped up at line 16, indicating success.

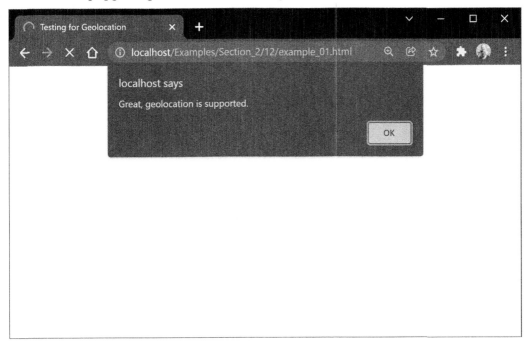

Figure 12.1: This browser does support geolocation because the success alert window has popped up

Using the developer console

A better method than using alert windows for testing your code as a developer would be to send messages to the JavaScript developer console. This way there are no distracting pop-ups and you can easily see the information in the console. So, for example, instead of the two alerts in *Example 12.1*, during developing the code could look like the following, with the console display looking like *Figure 12.2*.

```
if (typeof navigator.geolocation == 'undefined')
{
  console.log("Sorry, no geolocation support.")
}
else
{
  console.log("Great, geolocation is supported.")
}
```

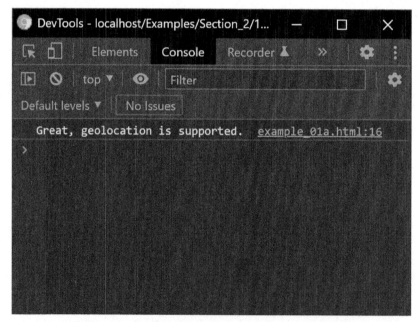

Figure 12.2: The message is displayed in the Develop Console

Details on setting up and using the Developer Console are provided in *Chapter 3, Visual Studio Code*. But now, you can see how the console is not only useful for stepping through and examining documents and their styles, but also using it to receive messages during development, without hindering the running of the code you are testing.

Redirecting users

If your code determines that the browser does not support geolocation, you would probably wish to do more than just pop-up an alert window (which isn't actually all that helpful or informative), or just send a developer message to the console.

Better, perhaps, would be to direct the user to another web page where you do have content suitable for them. This is easily achieved by giving a new URL to the browser's location setting. So, let's see how to do this with *Example 12.2*, in which only the JavaScript part of the document is shown.

Example 12.2:

```
1.  if (true == true)
2.  {
3.    window.location = 'http://google.com'
4.  }
```

To ensure that this example will work every time, the test statement has been replaced with one that will always return the value **true** because **true** is always equal to **true**. This is here because if we keep it in the geolocation existence check, you can only test the URL relocation (on line 3) on browsers without geolocation. Anyway, the result of running this example is that the user will be taken immediately to the Google website, as shown in *Figure 12.3*.

Figure 12.3: *The user has been redirected to another URL using JavaScript*

Of course, on your own website, the test statement will be the correct one for the existence of the geolocation feature in the browser, and the URL to which you send such users will be one of your choosing that you will have previously created.

Perhaps at this new URL, you would ask the user to enter their location using a web form, which you could then use with a matching database to return their location as a pair of longitude and latitude coordinates, just as geolocation would do if it had been supported by the browser:

We won't create that page here, though a skeleton page has been put in the companion archive of example files, saved as **no_geo.html**, as shown in *Figure 12.4.*

Figure 12.4: A generic skeleton page for when there's no geolocation

It's up to you (if you wish) to make a much better page as a further exercise. If you so, you'll need a web form designed to return as much location information as the user is prepared to give you.

Obtaining a user's location

In place of the **else** section of code at line 14 shown earlier in *Example 12.1*, where it has been established that geolocation *is* supported, we now need to place some more useful code than an alert window. Firstly, we need to ask the browser for the user's current location. If the user has placed restrictions, they will have to answer a Yes/No question when you do this, and decide whether or not to give you this information.

Therefore, you need to be able to respond in two different ways.

- If the user grants permission, you need to do something with the location returned, or…

- If you are denied access, perhaps you can send the user to the URL you would do if the browser didn't support geolocation.

On this page, they can then manually enter a location of their choice, or you may also give them an option to enter nothing and move onto doing something else instead that's not dependent on location information.

The geolocation service offers a very handy way for you to do this when you call it, by providing it with the names of two JavaScript functions: the first of which will be called if the user grants access, and the second is called if access is denied. The function is called **getCurrentPosition()** and a program to use it might look like *Example 12.3*, which now cleanly takes into account whether or not the browser supports geolocation in lines 1 to 5.

Example 12.3:

```
1.  if (typeof navigator.geolocation == 'undefined')
2.  {
3.      console.log('No geolocation')
4.      window.location = 'no_geo.html'
5.  }
6.  else
7.  {
8.      navigator.geolocation.getCurrentPosition(granted, denied)
9.
10.     function denied(error)
11.     {
12.         switch(error.code)
13.         {
14.           case 1: message = 'Permission Denied'; break
15.           case 2: message = 'Position Unavailable'; break
16.           case 3: message = 'Operation Timed Out'; break
17.           case 4: message = 'Unknown Error'
18.         }
19.
20.         console.log("Error with geolocation: " + message)
21.         window.location = 'no_geo.html'
22.     }
23.
24.     function granted(position)
```

```
25.  {
26.    console.log('Geolocation granted')
27.
28.    // Stuff to do goes here
29.  }
30. }
```

It does this by sending a message to the console stating what happened, and then changing the page location to the web page previously shown in *Figure 12.4*, saved as **no_geo.html**, which is simply there for illustration purposes, to provide a landing destination for the example.

In this example, line 8 is where the request is made to the browser asking for permission to know its location. For testing purposes, just in case you have previously run this example and given permission, and that permission has been retained, in *figure 12.5*, the browser has been taken into incognito mode (a mode supported by all browsers, in which all cookies and other identifying information are withheld), and you can see the request being made to know your location:

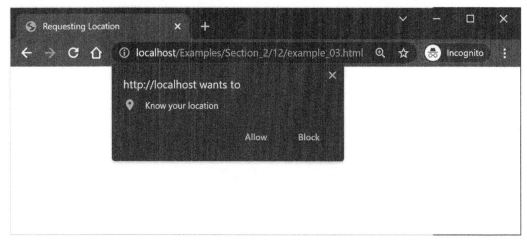

Figure 12.5: The browser is asking the user for permission to reveal its location

If the user opts to block the geolocation, then the code within the function named **denied()** is executed. You have seen functions before, in the chapters on the canvas but they were anonymous functions, that is, ones that had not been given names because we were running them immediately in place, and therefore naming them would serve no purpose.

However, line 8 needs to know the two places to which it should pass program control according to a user either blocking or accepting geolocation, so now we use functions that we give names to, so that we can supply their names within this instruction.

Named functions

Named functions have the ability to be placed virtually anywhere in your code due to the fact that they have names, and so JavaScript can always find them. But it makes sense to place them near the code likely to call them for ease of use, and also understanding the code when you come back to it at a later date. Therefore, the **denied()** function starts immediately below, online 10.

This function features a new (to this book) JavaScript construct called **switch()**. This is a concise and clean way to test a value and then do different things according to that value. In this case, the value tested is an object called **error**, which has been sent to the function by JavaScript to tell the function precisely why it has been called. The **error** object has a property named **code** that will have a value between 1 and 4, as set out on lines 14 to 17, indicating that permission was denied if the value of **code** is **1**, the position was unavailable if **code** is **2**, the operation took too long and timed out if **code** is **3**, or we haven't a clue what went wrong if **code** is **4**.

The **break** keywords are at the end of lines 14 to 16 (after the instruction separating semi-colons), to tell JavaScript that's all it needs to know, and to break out of the **switch()** and drop to the line below it. At line 17, there is no need for a **break** keyword because execution can only continue at the line below it.

Finally, in this function, line 20 sends the error to the console to help you with debugging and, as there's not much else left we can do here, line 21 sends the browser to the URL at **no_geo.html**, where hopefully the situation can be retrieved by giving the user something else to do.

When permission is granted

Finally, if execution reaches the function named **granted** on line 24, we know that permission has been given, and that the object passed with the name **position** will contain all the information we need. So, that's about it for this example, which simply ends with a message sent to the console, and a comment on line 28 reminding us to write more code!

We can do so by updating the code to *Example 12.4*, which shows only the contents of the **granted** function because the rest of the example is identical to *Example 12.3*.

Example 12.4 *(just the **granted** function)*:

```
1. function granted(position)
2. {
```

```
3.    console.log('Geolocation granted')
4.
5.    lat = position.coords.latitude
6.    lon = position.coords.longitude
7.    map = "https://www.google.com/maps/@"
8.
9.    window.location = map + lat + "," + lon + ",8z"
10. }
```

The result of running this example for someone in New Delhi will look like *Figure 12.6*.

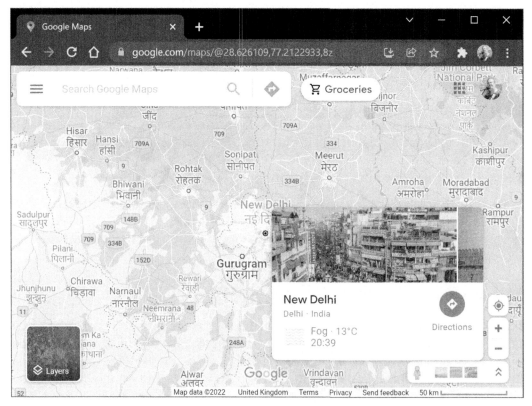

Figure 12.6: *Using geolocation a local Google Maps URL has been created*

As mentioned earlier, line 3 sends a message to the console for debugging purposes, but it's not essential or even needed in production code. Then line 5 and 6 extract data from the **position** object by reading its **coords.latitude** and **coords. logitude** properties and putting them into the variables **let** and **lon**. This isn't actually necessary because those properties can be applied directly in line 9, but keeping your code short and understandable is always a great idea, especially as a beginner. And the use of these temporary variable names makes line 9 shorter and easier to understand.

Likewise line 7 is also unnecessary because the string assigned to the variable **map** can also be passed directly on line 9. However, now that we are about to examine line 9, it will be much easier to describe exactly what's going on by using theses shortened variable names.

So, finally onto line 9, you will be familiar with assigning a value to `window.location`, as that's what we've been doing to send the user to `no_geo.html`. Well, here we're doing almost the same thing, except that we are sending them to the Google Maps website and appending the latitude and longitude for the map (separated with a comma) to the URL. The final value of `,8z` tells Google Maps the amount to zoom in by. The smaller the number the further out the zoom will be, so you can try playing with that number to get different results.

In JavaScript, the **+** operator when applied to a string concatenates strings together, such that, for example, `'geo' + 'location'` and `'geolocation'` evaluate to equivalent strings. This is how the full URL string is constructed and assigned.

Conclusion

Although when dealing with the numbers used by longitude and latitude will require the use of JavaScript, you can already see how easy it is to offer your users a map of their locality just by their agreeing to accept geolocation, and with what are, at the end of the day, very few lines of code.

In this chapter, we discussed ways of getting around the issues of the user's browser not supporting geolocation, or of them blocking access to it. In the next chapter, we'll examine the advanced form features offer by HTML5, some of which may prove handy in providing a user-driven alternative to geolocation.

CHAPTER 13

Form Handling

Introduction

By virtue of the fact, you are reading this book you presumably already know a great deal about using HTML forms, so this chapter ought to be a breeze for you because it explains all the extensions that have been added to bring form creation right up to date, based on your prior knowledge.

For example, there are now point and click date pickers, there's validation of data types to ensure the input provided from a user matches expectations, there are special data types for phone numbers and email addresses, and even the ability to pattern matching using regular expressions.

With the update to forms that HTML5 brings, they have evolved from functional but clunky input methods, to sophisticated and user-centered data acquisition features that will no-longer make your users less inclined to register and join a site, or enter other details because the process is now intuitive and easy.

Structure

In this chapter, you will:

- Learn all the new form features added to HTML5
- Know how to use date, time, and color pickers

- Understand how to support (and disable) autocompletion
- Become a master of advanced features such as overrides and ranges

Objectives

The intent of this chapter is to bring all the new HTML5 form features together into a single place. Every one of them is discussed, even if it has no apparent current use, and by the time you finish the chapter, you will have become a power form user.

HTML5 form attributes

Since 2015, when HTML5 finally started to settle down and work the same way in different browsers, what had previously been known as Web Forms 2.0, has been fully assimilated into HTML5 in all major browser versions, and on all platforms, both static and mobile.

This means you can use all the following features without concerning yourself about whether or not they may be supported by your user – something that was a constant headache in the early days of adopting HTML5.

There are numerous new form attributes and tags, and this chapter takes you through them, detailing what each one is for and how to use it. First, let's take a look at the new form attributes, beginning with **autofocus**.

The autofocus attribute

The **autofocus** attribute can be applied to any **<input>** tag to give its field automatic focus when a page loads. This has the effect of placing the cursor in an input field ready to type, or selecting any other type of field ready to change it. *Example 13.1* illustrates how it is activated. The entire example is shown here because the examples in this chapter are slightly different than those in previous ones. But after this example, only the statements within the **<body>** of the document will be displayed as shown in *Figure 13.1*.

Figure 13.1: *The second input has been autofocused*

Example 13.1:

```
1.  <!DOCTYPE html>
2.  <html lang="en">
3.    <head>
4.      <meta charset="utf-8">
5.      <title>Testing for Geolocation</title>
6.    </head>
7.    <body>
8.      <form method='post' action='myform.php'>
9.      Some text <input type='text' name='text1'><br>
10.     More text <input type='text' name='text2'
11.     autofocus='autofocus'>
12.     <input type='submit'>
13.     </form>
14.   </body>
15. </html>
```

This is a pretty standard HTML5 document in which a form has been created that has two inputs fields: **text1** and **text2**. Because the **autofocus='autofocus'** attribute is set, however, the second of the two fields has been given focus, instead of the first, which would be the default. You can see this because the input box outline is emboldened and contains the input cursor, as shown earlier in *Figure 13.1*.

For the purpose of making the example work, should you submit the form, the PHP file **myform.php**, which receives the posted values, should also be present. Although this is not a book on PHP, there are few instances when we must use it such as when we need to examine the result of the user input, like in this situation. Therefore, the PHP code for this file is shown in *Example 13.2*.

Example 13.2:

```
1.  <?php
2.    echo "text1: '" . $_POST["text1"] . "'<br>";
3.    echo "text2: '" . $_POST["text2"] . "'<br>";
4.  ?>
```

This example simply displays the values of the two fields as received by the program, with the result as shown in *Figure 13.2*.

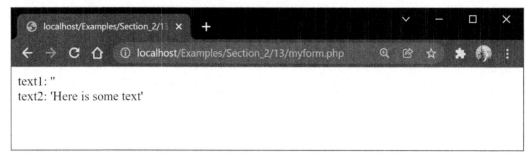

Figure 13.2: The PHP code displays the inputs received

Since only the second field was highlighted, only that one had any text entered, and so in this figure, only **text2** contains any input, but if both fields are given values, then both values will be shown.

There's also a shorthand form of setting the **autofocus** attribute, an example of which is to change line 10 of *Example 13.1* to the following, in which the **='autofocus'** part is omitted, but the result is exactly the same:

```
10.     More text <input type='text' name='text2' autofocus>
```

The autocomplete attribute

This attribute can be applied to the **<form>** tag, or any of the **color**, **date**, **email**, **password**, **range**, **search**, **tel**, **text**, or **url** types of the **<input>** tag. Valid arguments for this attribute are either **on** (the default) or **off**.

When **autocomplete** is **on**, any field with an ID that has previously had an input entered will remember its value and offer it as a suggested value, even cross different websites, as long as the field ID name is the same, it will save you from having to enter it again. However, when **autocomplete** is off, this behavior is disabled. Generally, **autocomplete** is a good feature to enable for fields such as a user's name, address, phone number or email address, but not a good idea for passwords, social security numbers, bank account details, or other sensitive information.

When applied to a **<form>** tag, the attribute affects all relevant fields within a form, but when applied to an **<input>** tag, only that particular field is affected. For this reason, when creating forms that may include sensitive information, it's best to not allow autocompletion on the entire form, and to apply it only to the inputs that request non-sensitive information. The reason for this is for cases such as when a third party may have access to someone's PC and there could be a security risk if they were to go to a page with a form that autocompleted their bank account details (for example), which would then be plainly visible and easily copied by the third party.

Example 13.3 shows how to use this feature across an entire form by replicating *Example 13.1*, but with the addition of autocompletion.

Example 13.3:

```
1. <form action='myform.php' method='post' autocomplete='on'>
2.    Some text <input type='text' name='text1'><br>
3.    More text <input type='text' name='text2'>
4. </form>
```

If you have previously submitted either of the fields, then when you run this example the result will look something like *Figure 13.3*.

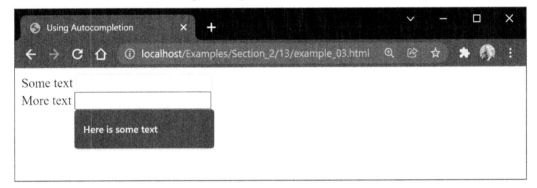

Figure 13.3*: The second field is offering an autocompletion pull down list*

In this example (as previously stated), only the lines of HTML within the document's body are shown, as the rest of the document remains the same. We are not setting autofocus in the example either, so the only important thing to note is the **autocomplete='on'** in line 1. With this enabled, both fields on lines 2 and 3 will supply drop down windows of previously entered inputs.

To disable autocompletion you could remove the attribute setting on line 1, or you could instead add **autocomplete='off'** to one or more field inputs, so let's do the latter on the second field, altering line 3 as follows:

```
3.    More text <input type='text' name='text2' autocomplete='off'>
```

The result of this is when you click the second input number, a drop-down list is displayed. Alternatively, you can choose to not enable autocompletion on the whole form, but then just enable it on specific inputs, as in *Example 13.4*, which displays exactly the same as *Figure 13.3*.

Example 13.4:

```
1. <form action='myform.php' method='post' autocomplete='off'>

2.   Some text <input type='text' name='text1'><br>

3.   More text <input type='text' name='text2' autocomplete='on'>

4. </form>
```

Remember that autocompletion being on is the default in all browsers; therefore, if you need it off, you need to take specific actions to turn it off, as shown in line 1. Then, line 3 specifically enables it, with the same result as *Figure 13.3*. There is no shorthand option available for this property like there is for **autofocus**.

The form attribute

Using this attribute, you can place your input fields anywhere you like in a document, as long as you specify the ID name of the form to which they apply. The use of this may not become apparent until you realize you can use it with the new **<fieldset>** tag (for example) to create a set (or group or collection) of fields, and then apply them to a form. This can be a way of making longer and more complicated forms easier to create, and for others to understand. But you don't have to use the form attribute in fieldsets, it's just one of the options open to you.

Example 13.5 shows three input fields; two of which are within a fieldset, and the other is on its own.

Example 13.5:

```
1. <form id='myform' action='myform2.php' method='post'>

2.   <input type='submit'>

3. </form><br>

4.

5. <fieldset form='myform'>

6.   Some text <input form='myform' type='text' name='text1'><br>

7.   More text <input form='myform' type='text' name='text2'>

8. </fieldset><br>

9.

10. Even More <input form='myform' type='text' name='text3'>
```

Also, the backgrounds of the fieldset inputs have changed color too. This shows how fieldsets are useful for placing fields together that have something in common and may belong together, such as a phone number and email address.

There are no actual input fields in the form itself (although there could be if we desired). The result of loading this example into a browser is shown in *Figure 13.4*, where you can see that one benefit of placing two inputs in a fieldset is that the browser has separated them and placed a box around them as well:

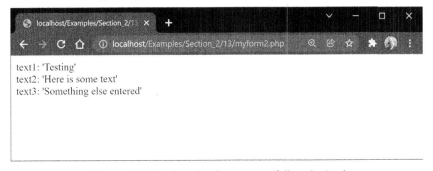

Figure 13.4: A form built using the fieldsets and solo inputs

Now, you will also immediately see that the submit button is now at the top, but this is to show you the flexibility we now have because you are able to put that button anywhere you like. If you wish, you can place the form itself below its various inputs – it's entirely up to you. This is because lines 1 to 3 of this example are now just a shell of a form with only a submit button in it. However, the form does have the addition of an ID such that its **id** property has been set to **myform**, which is how the fieldset and solo inputs can attach themselves to the form.

Remember that you need to provide the name of the from to the form attribute of both the fieldset and the inputs within it, for the form to fully understand how to use them. To accompany this example, **myform.php** has been updated to **myform2. php**, with the addition of an extra line of code to handle the **text3** input, as follows:

```
3.    echo "text3: '" . $_POST["text3"] . "'<br>";
```

The result of submitting these fields is shown in *Figure 13.5*.

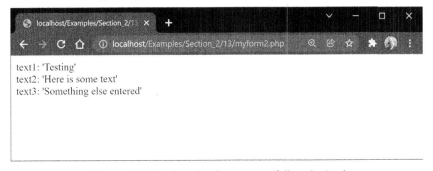

Figure 13.5: The form has been successfully submitted

The formaction attribute

Using this attribute, you can change the destination action of the **submit** and **image** types of the **<input>** tag to send the input to a URL or your choosing, overriding any destination previously specified for the form. To illustrate this, fortunately we already have **myform.php** and **myform2.php** which display two and three values, respectively. So, *Example 13.6* creates a form that submits to **myform.php**, but with an extra submit button to submit to **myform2.php** instead, if it should be clicked or pressed.

Example 13.6:

```
1.  <form action='myform.php' method='post'>
2.      Some text <input type='text' name='text1'><br>
3.      More text <input type='text' name='text2'>
4.      <input type='submit'><br>
5.
6.      Even More <input type='text' name='text3'>
7.      <input type='submit' formaction='myform2.php'>
8.  </form>
```

The result of loading this into a browser will look like *Figure 13.6*.

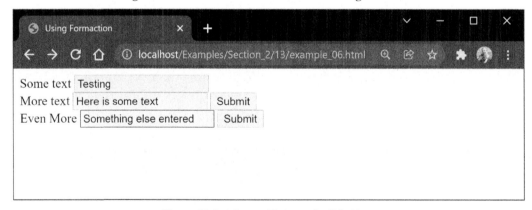

Figure 13.6: A form with two submit buttons

This form is very similar to *Example 13.1*, but with the extra **text3** input added, all enclosed within standard **<form>** tags, submitting its data to the program **myform. php** with a submit instruction on line 4. The thing that is unusual is the addition of a second submit instruction on line 7, which instead submits to **myform2.php** because that's the value assigned to the **formaction** attribute.

If you try out this example, you will indeed see that the first submit button submits to one form with a result similar to *Figure 13.2*, and the second button to the other form, with a result similar to *Figure 13.5*.

Other form overrides

Along with modifying the formation of an individual submit button, you can also change the encoding type and the method of encoding. For example, you can set up a form to post multipart data to **prog.php** with a form as follows:

```
1.  <form action='prog.php' method='post' enctype='multipart/form-data'>

2.    <input type='file'>

3.    <input type='submit'>

4.  </form>
```

This will enable the uploading of a file. But, supposing you had an additional submit button that you wanted to give a different action, such as only submitting a text field, you can send that submission to another program such as **prog2.php**, and in standard URL encoding, by modifying the preceding code to this:

```
1.  <form action='prog.php' method='post' enctype='multipart/form-data'>

2.    <input type='file'>

3.    <input type='submit'><br>

4.    <input type='text' name='filename'>

5.    <input type='submit' formaction='prog2.php'

6.      formenctype='application/x-www-form-urlencoded'>

7.  </form>
```

Now, lines 4 – 6 offer the input of providing a text input named **filename**, and with that input accepting only standard form encoding if the second input button is clicked or pressed, rather than the first. Line 6 is indented and moved down from the previous line because it would not fit without a potentially unsightly wrap. However, HTML is forgiving and allows you leeway in placing as much whitespace (including line breaks) as you like to layout your code, so it was decided to make a clean break after **'prog2.php'**.

Now, this hasn't been made into a numbered example, as we have no file to upload, and neither do we have a PHP file to process such an upload. However, you should already know about file uploading being a standard HTML feature from before HTML5, so these lines of code illustrate how you can overload both the encoding type and the form action.

But we haven't finished yet because you can also change the form method of an input if you wish using the **formmethod** attribute. For example, using line 5, you can change the default **method** of submission from **post**, as specified in the first line, to **get**, just for this input button.

```
5.   <input type='submit' formaction='prog2.php' formmethod='get'
```

Much as you can override the form method and action, with **formtarget,** you can change the target frame or page of an individual input too, in a similar way.

The multiple attribute

We just looked at uploading files. Well, as long as you have the PHP or other server-based code to process them, you can allow the upload of multiple files at a time with the **multiple** attribute. You can use it as easily as follows:

```
<input type='file' name='docs' multiple='multiple'>
```

Now, your users can upload several files at a time by holding the *Ctrl* key when selecting them.

The novalidate attribute

This attribute specifies that a form should not be validated when it is submitted (usually, you would do this only when you have your own validation in place which you feel fills your needs better). It accepts values of **true** or **false** applicable to the **<form>** tag and many of the special new types of the **<input>** tag such as **tel** and **num**. You can use it as follows:

```
<input type='text' name='field' novalidate='true'>
```

A matching **formnovalidate** attribute allows you to override the **novalidate** attribute directly to a single input.

The width and height attributes

If you are using an image type of input button in place of the default offered, then you can change its width and height with these two attributes, as shown in *Example 13.7.*

Example 13.7:

```
1.  <form method='post'>
2.    Name <input type='text' name='name'><br>
```

```
3.    <input type='image' src='submit.png' width='214' height='24'>
4.  </form>
```

This example creates a form that doesn't have any URL to which it should submit (so it will post it to itself – and nothing will seem to happen), and with a submit button image that has original dimensions of 220 **x** 66 pixels, which has been resized to 214 **x** 24 pixels, to fit the width of the input, as shown in *Figure 13.7*.

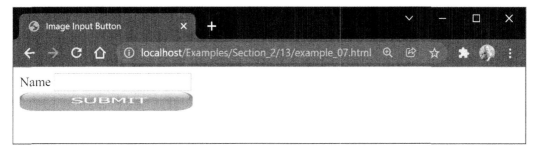

Figure 13.7: *The input button image is resized*

Of course, you will use much more interesting images and apply better styling, but this shows how you can resize them directly in the input. Alternatively, you can use CSS if you prefer:

The list attribute and <datalist> and <option> tags

Pop-down lists are a great way to make your user experience better and they are easily achieved without needing any JavaScript or CSS, simply by placing lists inside the **<datalist>** tag as a set of **<option>** tags. Then, in your input, you need to specify the **id** attribute name of the list as an argument for the **list** attribute, and it all comes together.

For example, suppose you wish to ask your users what their favorite search engine is, *Example 13.8* would be one way of doing this.

Example 13.8:

```
1.  <form method='post'>
2.    Select your favorite <input type='url' name='site' list='links'>
3.    <input type='submit'>
4.  </form>
5.
6.  <datalist id='links'>
```

```
 7.    <option label='Google' value='http://google.com'>
 8.    <option label='Yahoo!' value='http://yahoo.com' >
 9.    <option label='Bing'   value='http://bing.com'  >
10.    <option label='Ask'    value='http://ask.com'   >
11. </datalist>
```

You should note that when you submit, the same page is reloaded, as there's no need to write any PHP code to receive the submission, as we're only looking at what happens before submission, as shown in *Figure 13.8*.

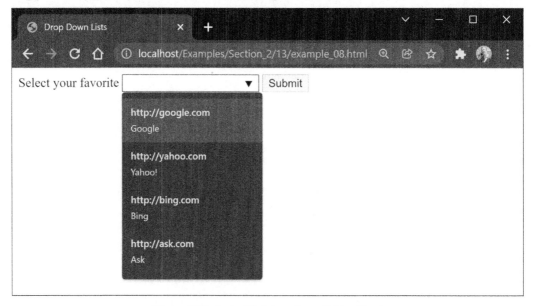

Figure 13.8: *A pre-filled drop-down list is offered*

Lines 1 to 4 create a standard form, with a submit button on line 3, and line 2 having a standard input field. What's new on line 2 is that we are asking for an input type of **url**, instead of having to ask for text, and the list attribute has been supplied the **id** given to the **<datalist>** tag below the form on line 6. Then, lines 7 to 10 include a number of **<option>** tags in which are four different search engine names assigned to the **label** attribute of each, and URL to the **value** attribute. This list has not needed to be included within the **<form>** tag because it is identified by name.

What's great about the way this list is applied is that the user can ignore all those offered and enter their own choice, perhaps **duckduckgo.com** or another alternative engine, so it offers maximum ease of use, combined with flexibility for the user. Also, you don't have to use the URL type of input here because all alphanumeric input types are accepted.

The min, max, and step attributes

Sometimes, your users may not have totally understood what is being asked of them for input so it can be helpful to guide them where you can. For example, you can specify minimum and maximum values for inputs that contain numbers or dates. Not only will only values in the range supplied be the only ones accepted, the up and down keyboard buttons can modify the values within the range, as can the mouse be used with a time picker by clicking on the clock icon shown in *Figure 13.9*.

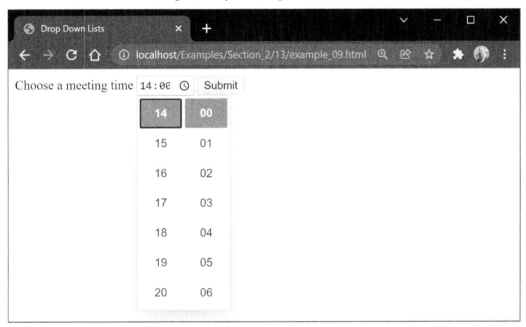

Figure 13.9: A time picker has been popped up

In *Example 13.9*, a time is requested from a user for a meeting, which needs to be between 14:00 and 17:00 hours (2pm and 5pm); this uses the new HTML5 input type of **time**.

Example 13.9:

```
1. <form method='post'>
2.    Choose a meeting time
3.    <input type='time' name='meeting' value='14:00'
4.      min='14:00' max='17:00'>
5.    <input type='submit'>
6. </form>
```

On line 3, a start time for the input is set at 14:00, and the range available follows. Using the cursor keys, you cannot scroll these numbers out of this range, but you can select hours and minutes. With a mouse, you can call up a time picker with the clock icon, and if you try to select a time that is not in bounds, you'll get a message like the one in *Figure 13.10* (which also shows that a time of 19:07 was requested).

Figure 13.10: The user is informed this time is not available

Talking about odd times, if you don't wish the user to be able to alter the minutes, you can limit that facility with the **step** attribute, specifying the number of seconds allowed for time intervals. For 15 minutes, the value would be 15 **x** 60, or 900, for 30 minutes, the value would be 1800, and so on. The following is how you can modify line 4 to only allow on-the-hour times:

```
4.        min='14:00' max='17:00' step='3600'>
```

When you do this, the user cannot alter the minutes using the keyboard. And if they try to enter a time via the mouse with the time picker that is not on-the-hour, a message as shown in *Figure 13.11* will be displayed.

Figure 13.11: The time requested is not on-the-hour and is rejected

Other date and time input types

There is also a new HTML5 input type of **date**, which will return a value in the form **YYYY-MM-DD**, and which can be used in a similar manner to **time**. Also, there's a

month input type, which returns a value of **YYYY-MM**, and a **week** input type, which returns a value of **YYYY-WNN**, where **YYYY** is the year and **WNN** is the week in the format **W23**, for example.

You can also request input of the date and time together with the **datetime** input type, which returns a value of **YYYY-MM-DDTHH:MMZ**, and which might look something like **2027-05-02T17:56Z** for May 2nd 2027 at 17:56, for example. Not only that, but you can ask for the user's local time with the **datetime-local** property, which returns a value of **YYYY-MM-DDTHH:MM**, without a trailing **Z** (which **datetime** does return).

It is up to your back-end server software how it interprets and deals with these returned values.

The pattern attribute

Nowadays, a main focus of web development is prompting users how to make the right inputs your program needs in the most convenient and easiest way for them. At the same time, the aim is to catch any unusable input and correct it even before the user submits it.

Using the **pattern** attribute, among many other possibilities you can, for example, test whether a valid email address has been entered, without resorting to JavaScript, or waiting for the server back-end software to do the checking. This attribute can be applied to any **<input>** tag that uses any of **email**, **password**, **search**, **tel**, **text,** or **url** as their **type** attribute.

In *Example 13.10*, some alphanumeric text is being requested, that is, letters, numbers, and spaces only.

Example 13.10:

```
1. <form method='post'>
2.    Enter alphanumeric text only
3.    <input type='text' name='text' pattern='[a-zA-Z0-9 ]+'
4.       title='Use letters, numbers and spaces only'>
5.    <input type='submit'>
6. </form>
```

Figure 13.12 shows what is displayed if the user's input doesn't match the pattern specified.

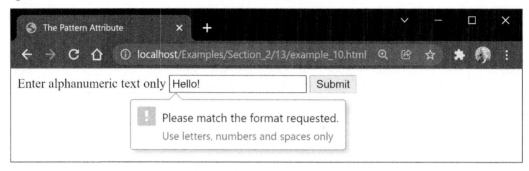

Figure 13.12: *The exclamation mark is not allowed and has cause an error message*

The pattern used on line 3 lists the letters **a-z** and **A-Z**, plus the digits **0-9** and a space character, all within square brackets, followed by a **+** sign, indicating that at least one of those types of character within the brackets must be present.

On line 4, further guidance is given to the user in the form of the text assigned to the input's title property. This text is seen either when the user passes their mouse over the input, or if an attempt is made to submit inadmissible characters, as shown previously in *Figure 13.12*.

So how does this work? Well, something called a regular expression is used, which is a concise way of representing text types. The way it works can be fairly complex and explaining regular expressions is beyond the scope of this book. But you can learn all about using them at: **tinyurl.com/reg-expr**.

Having said that, sometimes you don't need to use the `pattern` attribute; for example, the `email`, `num`, `tel,` and `url` input types will automatically validate the input for you:

The placeholder attribute

This is a fantastic user-focused feature. With it, you can place an instruction directly in an input field, slightly greyed out so that it's obviously an instruction and not pre-filled text, which disappears once the user starts typing. Just assign any text of your choice to the placeholder attribute as in *Example 13.11*, which is prompting for a 2 to 6 character username.

Example 13.11:

```
1.  <form method='post'>
2.    Choose a username
```

```
3.    <input type='text' name='u' placeholder='Any 6-16 character name'>

4.    <input type='submit'>

5.  </form>
```

The result of this example is shown in *Figure 13.13*.

Figure 13.13: Some placeholder text is advising the user what to enter

If you wish, you can also add a **pattern** attribute to check the input (given the correct regular expression), and maybe also a **title** attribute to further guide the user, but generally, this will be enough to start with. Do remember to change the **size** attribute to being large enough if your guide text is long.

The required attribute

Using the **required** attribute, you can ensure that a field has not been left uncompleted when a form is submitted, as in *Example 13.12*.

Example 13.12:

```
1.  <form method='post'>

2.    Choose a username

3.    <input type='text' name='username' required>

4.    <input type='submit'>

5.  </form>
```

Figure 13.14 shows the guidance that is given if the form is submitted while the field is blank:

Figure 13.14: The user is prompted to complete the field before submission

The syntax of this attribute is supposed to be **required='required',** but as you can see from the example, you can use the shorthand of simply **required** and it will work.

The color input type

Sometimes, you need a user to select a color, and this is now very easily done using the **color** input type, as shown in *Example 13.13*.

Example 13.13:

```
1.  <form method='post'>
2.      Choose a color
3.      <input type='color' name='color'>
4.      <input type='submit'>
5.  </form>
```

Figure 13.15 shows this example in action, with a color block used in place of textual input, and then a picker window in which various options are offered, including a dropper to pick up a color, a rainbow slider, a rectangular color selector, or simply just entering direct RGB color values.

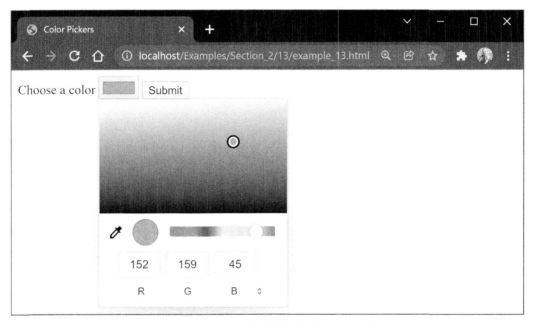

Figure 13.15: *The color picker has been popped up*

Users can even click on the up and down arrow icon at the bottom right-hand corner to change to hue, saturation, and luminance, or once again to use hexadecimal values.

The color submitted using the color picker will not be a name but rather it will be a hexadecimal CSS color string starting with a **#** symbol, like this: **#8f9b31**. Regardless of whether the user clicked on a color or chose an HSL value instead of RGB, the value returned will be in this hex format. You can verify this by changing the method type on line 1 to **get**, submitting a color, and viewing the URL that is returned back to the browser's address bar, which should end with something like: **?color=%238f9b31**. Here, because it is part of a URL, the browser has converted the preceding **#** symbol to the HTML entity **%23**, but the actual value, if submitted to a program, will start with a **#**.

Numbers and ranges

The processing of numbers has been significantly enhanced in HTML5 with the support of the **number** input type. When used, it causes a pair of up and down icons to be placed to the right of the input field when the mouse passes over the field, which can be clicked to increment or decrement the value in it. Or the user can enter their own value directly. *Example 13.14* illustrates how to use it, with an initial value of **18** provided as a default.

Example 13.14:

```
1. <form method='get'>
2.    How old are you?
3.    <input type='number' name='age' value='18'>
4.    <input type='submit'>
5. </form>
```

The result of this example is shown in *Figure 13.16*, where the up arrow has been clicked once.

Figure 13.16: The number input type in use

If you want to prevent the user from entering non-sensical values, you can also provide a **range** input type, which will then generate a slider image. You can use it in conjunction with the **min**, **max**, and **step** attributes, as shown in *Example 13.15*, where the input on line 3 has been split over two lines to make it wrap neatly – as it's a fairly long line.

Example 13.15:

```
1. <form method='post'>
2.    How old are you?
3.    <input type='range' name ='num' min ='1'
4.           max ='110'   value='18'   step='1'>
5.    <input type='submit'>
6. </form>
```

The result of loading this example into a browser can be seen in *Figure 13.17*, in which you may spot a problem:

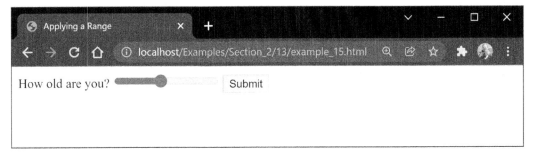

Figure 13.17: A range slider is displayed

Did you see the problem? While the slider looks great, there's no indication of the actual value selected. This can be a serious issue with the **range** input type, but fortunately there's a sneaky and simple way to rectify this omission, as demonstrated by *Example 13.16*, which has an extra JavaScript instruction inserted into the input element at line 5, and also an additional **<output>** tag in line 6.

Example 13.16:

```
1.  <form method='post'>
2.    How old are you?
3.    <input type='range' name ='num' min ='1'
4.          max ='110'   value='18'  step='1'
5.      oninput='this.nextElementSibling.value = this.value'>
6.    <output>18</output>
7.    <input type='submit'>
8.  </form>
```

What is going on here is that all HTML elements support the attaching of events, and here, the **oninput** event of the input has been attached to. A JavaScript instruction is then set to run whenever that event is triggered – which will be the case whenever the slider is moved.

The JavaScript is very clever which employs the use of a pseudo object called **this**, which represents the current element. So, by writing to the **nextElementSibling** property of **this**, it writes immediately in the **<output>** element following.

At the start, **<output>** contains an initial value of **18** to match the default supplied on line 4. Then, whenever the slider is moved, **this.value** (the value currently in the input field) is copied to the **<output>** element. This is a truly elegant solution, which you can see applied in *Figure 13.18*.

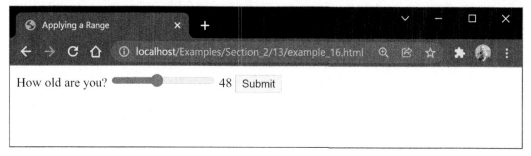

Figure 13.18: *The current value in the range is now displayed*

The search input type

This looks like it can be useful, but in all the years the **search** input type has been around, all it seems to offer is an **x** icon at the right of the field with which you can clear the input, and slightly different styling on a Mac computer. The only reason for possibly wanting to use it is to ensure your page is better understood semantically by search engines.

Even the web docs state that this input type is functionally identical to the **text** input type. Nevertheless, you now know about it for the sake of completeness.

Conclusion

This wraps up all that's new in HTML5 as far as using forms goes. The best part is that early all of these features work stand-alone without requiring additional JavaScript, and together they go a very long way towards maximizing the best experience when your users need to complete forms.

In the next chapter, we'll be getting back into a little bit of JavaScript programming by looking into the new local storage facilities of HTML5.

CHAPTER 14

Local Storage and More

Introduction

There are a number of additional HTML5 features that are sort of miscellaneous, so they have been collected together in this penultimate chapter on HTML5. They include the use of local and session storage, making your documents easier to understand by robots such as search engines using microdata, handing off intensive code to web workers, and creating offline web apps.

Many of these features require the use of JavaScript, and so the basics of how to use them are detailed, with pointers to where you can learn more if you need it.

Structure

In this chapter, you will:

- Learn how to store data on a user's local device
- Understand why it's important to make web documents robot readable
- Understand how to make code run faster with web workers
- Make your web pages into offline web apps

Objectives

In this chapter, you will tie up a lot of loose ends by learning various bits and pieces of HTML5 that are controlled using JavaScript, and you'll be able to make your web documents make complete sense to robots such as search engines. By the time you finish reading this chapter, you'll even be able to offload JavaScript routines to separate workers, and create your own web apps.

Using local storage

In the past, the only way you could store data on a user's computer was with cookies, which were limited in number and could hold only 4KB of data in each. They also have to be passed back and forth on every page reload and, unless your server uses **Secure Sockets Layer (SSL)** encryption, each time a cookie is transmitted it travels in the clear, without being ebcrypted.

But with HTML5, you have access to a much larger local storage space (typically, between 5MB and 10MB per domain depending on the browser) that remains over page loads and between website visits (and even after powering a computer down and back up again), and which is not sent to the server on each page load.

You can handle the data in pairs comprising a key and its value. The key is the name assigned for referencing the data and the value can hold any type of data, but it is saved as a string.

All data is unique to the current domain. Any local storage created by websites with different domains is separate to the current local storage for security reasons, and it is not accessible by any domain other than the one that stores the data.

> **Note: Possibly, the biggest reason that local storage has become a hit with web developers is that cookies can only be created on (and sent by) a web server. Without cookies there would be no easy way to save state. Local storage, on the other hand, is manipulated directly in the browser, making it possible to create stand-alone web apps that can work offline (to some extent or other). In addition, cookies can be up to 4KB only, while web storage can be up to 5MB on most browsers.**

Storing and retrieving local data

To access local storage, you can use methods of the **localStorage** object such as **setItem()**, **getItem()**, **removeItem()**, and **clear()**. For example, to locally store a user's username and password, you can use the following code:

```
localStorage.setItem('username', 'WHouston')
localStorage.setItem('password', 'bodyguard1992')
```

If the size of the value is larger than the disk quota remaining for the storage area, an **'Out of memory'** exception is thrown. Otherwise, when another page loads, or when the user returns to the website, these details can be retrieved to save the user entering them again, as shown in the following code:

```
username = localStorage.getItem('username')
password = localStorage.getItem('password')
```

If the key doesn't exist, then the **getItem()** function returns a value of null, as you will see later in *Figure 14.2*.

> **Note: Local storage would create security issues if all websites could see all others' saved data. Therefore, only local storage saved via a particular website can be retrieved by that site, and all other local data is invisible to it, as if it doesn't exist. Having said that, poorly written code can be subject to Cross Site Scripting attacks (XSS), in which a malicious person finds ways to fool a browser into thinking data is coming from one site when it's actually coming from another. Therefore, although the examples in this chapter are for a username and password pair, these are items you probably should avoid saving in local storage if you have any concerns about XSS being a possibility on your website. The whole subject of XSS is quite advanced, however, so if in doubt, only save non-sensitive data such as a user's layout and color preferences in local storage.**

You don't need to use these function names if you don't want to, and you can access the **localStorage** object directly because the two following statements are equivalent to each other:

```
localStorage.setItem('key', 'value')
localStorage['key'] = 'value'
```

And the two following statements are therefore also equivalent to each other:

```
value = localStorage.getItem('key')
value = localStorage['key']
```

Let's put what we've learned so far into some runnable code, as given in *Example 14.1*, which shows just the instructions from within the **<script>** section.

Example 14.1:

```
1. if (typeof localStorage == 'undefined')
2. {
3.     alert('Local storage unavailable.')
4. }
5. else
6. {
```

```
7.    localStorage.setItem('username', 'WHouston')

8.    localStorage.setItem('password', 'bodyguard1992')

9.

10.   username = localStorage.getItem('username')

11.   password = localStorage.getItem('password')

12.

13.   alert("Data retrieved: username = '" +

14.     username + "', password = '" + password + "'.")

15. }
```

In lines 1 to 4, a test is made to check whether the browser supports local storage. If local storage is not supported in the browser, the **localStorage** object will have a value of **undefined**, so this is an easy test to make.

All browsers these days should support local storage, but in the event that a user is running an older browser, a few lines of code doesn't hurt to help them. Of course, instead of this **alert()** window, you would probably place some more usable instructions ,or maybe even issue a change to the **location** property of the **window** object to call up a new page.

Lines 5 to 15 are executed if local storage is supported, with lines 7 and 8 storing some details to the user's local device, and lines 10 to 11 retrieving them again. Line 13 pops up an **alert()** window just to show you that the process has indeed worked, as shown in *Figure 14.1*.

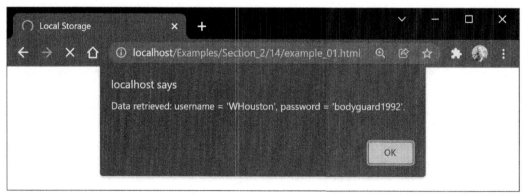

Figure 14.1: The local storage has been saved to and retrieved from

Until they are erased, once saved these values will remain in the local storage, and you can verify this by trying commenting out lines 7 and 8 as shown below, and then running the example again. The result of which should be the same as just shown in *Figure 14.1*.

```
7.   // LocalStorage.setItem('username', 'WHouston')

8.   // LocalStorage.setItem('password', 'bodyguard1992')
```

Removing and clearing local data

To remove an item of data from the local storage, all you need to do is call the **removeItem()** function as follows:

```
username = localStorage.removeItem('username')

password = localStorage.removeItem('password')
```

This serves to retrieve the item of data and place it into a variable (in this case, the variables **username** and **password**), and then deletes the data from local storage. If you don't need to first read the data you are removing, you can simply call the function on its own, as follows:

```
localStorage.removeItem('username')

localStorage.removeItem('password')
```

You can also completely clear the local storage for the current domain by calling the **clear()** function, as follows:

```
localStorage.clear()
```

So, let's now clear that saved data using *Example 14.2*.

Example 14.2:

```
1.  if (typeof localStorage == 'undefined')

2.  {

3.    alert('Local storage unavailable.')

4.  }

5.  else

6.  {

7.    localStorage.removeItem('username')

8.    localStorage.removeItem('password')

9.

10.   username = localStorage.getItem('username')

11.   password = localStorage.getItem('password')

12.

13.   alert("Data retrieved: username = '" +

14.     username + "', password = '" + password + "'.")

15. }
```

Here lines 7 and 8 remove the saved details such that *Figure 14.2* reports the retrieved values as both being **null**. The rest of the example is the same as *Example 14.1*, though, so you can easily see and test what's going on.

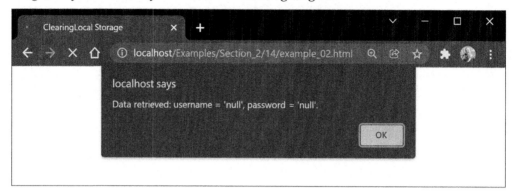

Figure 14.2: *The local data has been erased*

Of course, making good use of local storage will be down to writing accompanying JavaScript, but taking things further than already detailed is beyond the scope of this book.

Using session storage instead

Local storage has the benefit that the data stored there is saved permanently, unless the browser's cache is cleared. If you prefer to store data just during the current browsing session, then that's very easy to do. Just replace all usage of the term **localStorage** with **sessionStorage** and you'll be good to go as everything will work just the same.

The only difference is that if the user closes the current tab, or closes their browser, all the session storage data will expire. But if you're using session storage just to help support settings during the user's current session on your website (perhaps for a list of shopping cart items), then you don't care what happens to it after the user has checked out and the session is over, so you shouldn't really be trying to store it in the long-term local storage anyway.

Note: Since session storage is on a per tab setting, if a user opens up your website in more than one tab, then each tab will have its own, separate session storage. This is important to realize if some users seem to keep losing their session data during a session – perhaps they are switching between and swapping and opening up new tabs on your site. One way to keep track is to create a unique token made from some random string and save it to session storage. When you read that string back, you can then tell which storage is being accessed. Again, explaining the JavaScript required to do things such as this is outside this book's remit.

Microdata

Microdata is used to nest metadata within existing content on web pages. Search engines and web crawlers can then extract and process the microdata from a web page and use it to provide a richer browsing experience for users. What's more, the microdata clearly details to a search engine precisely the content and intent of a web document, due to the clear structure of the data. In other words, microdata is a subset of HTML designed for giving a document meaning for machines, just as it has meaning to a reader of the document.

What it does is make available the following new tag attributes: **itemscope**, **itemtype**, **itemid**, **itemref**, and **itemprop**. Using them, you can clearly define the properties of a document such as a book, providing a range of information that a computer can use to understand; for example, its authors, publishers, contents, and so on.

Example 14.3 shows how microdata is easily applied to a standard HTML document.

```
1.  <!DOCTYPE html>
2.  <html lang="en">
3.    <head>
4.      <meta charset="utf-8">
5.      <title>Incorporating Microdata</title>
6.    </head>
7.    <body>
8.      <section itemscope
9.        itemtype='http://data-vocabulary.org/Person'>
10.       <img itemprop='photo'
11.            src  ='elon_musk.jpg'
12.            alt  ='Elon Musk'
13.            align='left'
14.            style='margin-right:10px'>
15.
16.       <h2 itemprop='name'>Elon Musk</h2>
17.
18.       <p>
19.         Elon Musk is a South African-born American
20.         <span itemprop='role'>entrepreneur</span> and
```

```
21.          <span itemprop='title'>businessman</span>.
22.          He likes to call himself the
23.          <span itemprop='nickname'>Technoking</span>
24.          of Tesla, and his website is:
25.          <a itemprop='url'
26.            href='https://www.tesla.com/en_GB/elon-musk'>tesla.com</a>.
27.        </p>
28.
29.        <p>Elon's address at SpaceX is:</p>
30.
31.      <address itemscope itemtype='http://data-vocabulary.org/Address'
32.          itemprop='address'>
33.        <p>
34.          <span itemprop='street-address'>1 Rocket Road</span><br>
35.          <span itemprop='locality'     >Hawthorne    </span><br>
36.          <span itemprop='region'       >California    </span><br>
37.          <span itemprop='postal-code'  >90250         </span><br>
38.          <span itemprop='country-name' >USA           </span>
39.        </p>
40.      </address>
41.    </section>
42.  </body>
43.</html>
```

The result of loading this example into a browser is shown in *Figure 14.3*.

Figure 14.3: *The microdata on this web page is not evident in its display*

There are numerous different properties available within microdata. In fact, there are so many that you are recommended to visit **tinyurl.com/html5md** to learn all about them. Microdata is available for books, music, TV shows, events, people, places, and many more types of data.

In *Example 3.4,* the **person** microdata type is used, and if you peruse the code, you'll see such things as a **photo** type for the image **itemprop** on line 9, a **role** type of **entrepreneur** on line 20, a **url** on line 25, and a great deal more.

But all this microdata is tucked away only for search engines or other programs that need to understand the data. The web page itself is displayed identically to if there were no microdata in it at all. Which is exactly the point – now machines can quickly make as much sense of a web page as people.

However, it is only recommended that you adopt the use of microdata where it's important to the document in question that it be fully understandable by machines. In fact, search engines are already quite smart, so the use of microdata is more useful in the field of artificial intelligence, when preparing data for a program to digest and learn.

As a general web developer, it is unlikely that you will use microdata a great deal, but now you know what it is, how to use it, and where to find out all the microdata types.

Web workers

This section is of a more advanced nature in terms of the JavaScript it uses. Don't worry if it's not for you right now and feel free to skip onto the following chapter covering audio and video in HTML5. This section will be here for you to return to if/when you need it in the future.

Normally, to achieve background processing in JavaScript, you need to set up a timer that is constantly called, supplying slices of processor time to one or more functions, and these functions must then quickly do a small piece of work and return, in order to not slow down the browser and make it seem sluggish.

Web workers, however, provide a standard way for browsers to run multiple JavaScript threads in the background that can pass messages to each other, in much the same manner as the threads running in an operating system. You simply call up a new worker script which will sit there in the background waiting for messages to be sent to it, which it will then act upon.

On the whole, the aim of this is to achieve a two to three times speed increase over regular background JavaScript code, although getting to grips with programming probably requires a longer rather than shorter learning curve.

To use web workers, we need two pieces of code. The first is a web document containing some JavaScript, as given in *Example 14.4*, which in this case is the first part of a program to generate prime numbers as quickly as possible.

Example 14.4:

```
1.  <!DOCTYPE html>
2.  <html lang="en">
3.    <head>
4.      <meta charset="utf-8">
5.      <title>Running Webworkers</title>
6.    </head>
7.    <body>
8.      <p>
9.        The highest prime number discovered so far is:
10.       <output id='result'></output>
11.       <p>
12.         <button onclick='worker.terminate()'>STOP</button>
13.       </p>
```

```
14.     </p>
15.
16.     <script>
17.        if (!window.Worker)
18.        {
19.           alert("Web workers not supported")
20.        }
21.        else
22.        {
23.           worker = new Worker('worker.js')
24.
25.           worker.onmessage = function(event)
26.           {
27.              document.getElementById('result').innerHTML = event.data
28.           }
29.        }
30.     </script>
31.  </body>
32. </html>
```

This is a fairly straightforward HTML5 document. Points to note, though, are the **<output>** tag on line 10 within which the prime numbers discovered will appear, the **<button>** on line 12 with which the web worker can be halted so that it doesn't run away with itself forever, and the script section of code between lines 17 and 29.

The way the STOP button works is to simply call the **terminate()** function on the **worker** object that is created in the script section, causing it to immediately cease executing if the button is clicked.

Within the script section, lines 17 to 20 use an **if()** statement to test whether Web Workers are supported by the browser. Nowadays, they should all support them, but this code makes sure and issues an alert if not.

Then, in the **else** section, where we know that Web Workers are supported, a new **worker** object is created by calling the **Worker()** function, passing it the name of the file **worker.js** which it should load and run. We will shortly get to what **worker. js** looks like.

Finally, the **onmessage** event of the **worker** object is attached to using an anonymous function (one without a name) which is entered whenever the worker in this document receives a message from the code in the **worker.js** document. Whatever message is received arrives in the **data** property of the **event** object on line 27, where it is immediately copied into the **<output>** element we created on line 10 (so now, you see its purpose).

Now, let's get onto the **worker.js** program detailed in *Example 14.5*. This file is saved in the companion archive as both **example_05.js** and **worker.js**, so that the reference to **worker.js** on line 23 of *Example 14.4* will work.

Example 14.5:

```
1.  n = 1
2.
3.  search: while (true)
4.  {
5.    ++n
6.
7.    for (i = 2 ; i <= Math.sqrt(n) ; ++i)
8.    {
9.      if (n % i == 0) continue search
10.   }
11.
12.   postMessage(n)
13. }
```

This is a short and sweet program that begins by initializing the variable **n** to 1. Then, an endless loop is entered on line 3 (because the value **true** is always **true**), which begins a continuous search for prime numbers by incrementing **n** each time through the loop on line 5, and then performing a primality test on it in lines 7 to 10.

This is achieved by a **for()** loop on line 7 which loops through every value between 2 and the square root of **n** (as there is no need to look any higher than that), testing it for having divisors on line 9. If there *are* any divisors, then **n** is not prime, so the **continue** instruction is issued to go round the **search** loop again at line 3, testing the next value of **n**.

If there are *no* divisors of **n**, then **n** is a prime number, and so execution drops through to line 12, where a message is posted back to the main part of the web worker pair of programs with a call to **postMessage()**, containing the prime number just found.

Finally, on line 13, the code returns back to the infinite loop on line 3 to continue the search. With the result of all, as shown in *Figure 14.4*, where the purpose of the STOP button is to allow you to quickly stop the worker because it is in an endless loop and would otherwise be very hard to terminate.

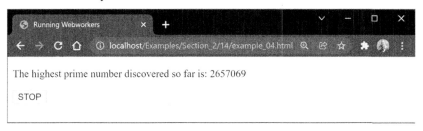

Figure 14.4: *The prime testing is running*

Offline web applications

The idea of an offline web application is that once you visit a website, it tells your browser about all the files it uses so that the browser can then download them all, and you can then run the web application locally, even without an Internet connection.

There is a slight complication with offline web applications. They may require a web server to set up with the correct **MIME** types (originally known as **Multipurpose Internet Mail Extensions**, but the word Mail has since been replaced with Media) for a browser that understands offline web applications to make use of the feature and fetch the files it needs.

If you are using a web server that is not Apache, consult your manuals for how to add the `text/cache-manifest` MIME type for `.appcache` file extensions for your server to send the manifest file using the correct type. Otherwise, for Apache users (which includes you if you're using the MAMP server set up in *Chapter 3, Visual Studio Code*), there's a neat shortcut, which is to create a file called `.htaccess` in the same folder as the files to be made available offline, with the following contents:

```
AddType text/cache-manifest .appcache
```

How offline web apps work

Here's how offline apps work. You can start with a manifest file that contains all the files you'd like to offer for offline use, like the following, which in this example is saved with the filename **clock.appcache**, as given in *Example 14.6*.

Example 14.6:

```
1. CACHE MANIFEST
2. # clock.appcache
```

```
3. clock.html
4. clock.css
5. clock.js
```

The three files detailed in the manifest are then as follows, starting with **clock.html** in *Example 14.7* (which itself links to **clock.appcache**), a script called **clock.js**, and a stylesheet called **clock.css**. Then, in the body there's an **<output>** element, in which the JavaScript will later keep the time updated.

Example 14.7:

```
1.  <!DOCTYPE html> <!-- clock.html-->
2.  <html manifest='clock.appcache'>
3.    <head>
4.      <meta charset="utf-8">
5.      <title>Offline Web Apps</title>
6.      <script src='clock.js'></script>
7.      <link rel='stylesheet' href='clock.css'>
8.    </head>
9.    <body>
10.     <p>The time is: <output id='clock'></output></p>
11.   </body>
12. </html>
```

Example 14.8 is **clock.css**, which is the CSS required to style the output. Of course, there's not a lot of styling going on in this example, but the point is that you now have all the files needed for creating most offline web apps and you can add to or alter this CSS as required.

Example 14.8:

```
1.  output { font-weight:bold; } /* clock.css */
```

And here is *Example 14.9*, the **clock.js** JavaScript code itself, which sets up a regular interval by calling the **setInterval()** function such that the code within it is called every 1,000 milliseconds (or once a second). Each time this code is called it simply copies the latest date and time into the **innerHTML** property of the **clock** element by calling **new** on the **Date()** function.

Example 14.9:

```
1.  // clock.js
```

```
2. setInterval(function ()
3. {
4.    document.getElementById('clock').innerHTML = new Date()
5. }, 1000)
```

We now have all the parts of the puzzle with which to create an offline web app, so let's do it by loading **clock.html** (*Example 14.7*) into a web browser and you should see something like *Figure 14.5*, with the full date shown and the time updating once every second.

The time is: Mon Feb 07 2022 18:22:27 GMT+0000 (Greenwich Mean Time)

Figure 14.5: *The offline web app is running*

The idea of offline web apps is that, thanks to the manifest, all these files will be downloaded and made available for use offline to use in any environment. Between them, they simply create a simple clock. It's actually all quite easy to do once you understand what is going on. For full and complete details on creating your own offline web apps, you are recommended to check out the following websites:

- **tinyurl.com/web-apps**
- **tinyurl.com/web-apps2**

Drag and drop

There are seven events associated with drag and drop in HTML5: **dragstart**, **drag**, **dragover**, **dragenter**, **dragleave**, **drop**, and **dragend**. These must all be attached to using fairly complex and in-depth JavaScript code to decide what to do depending upon each action, which is far beyond the scope of this book. However, if you are interested in pursuing this feature, there's a lot more information at: **tinyurl.com/drag-drop**.

Cross document messaging

This is another highly advanced specification designed to make it easier for documents to communicate with each other but, again, it is really beyond the scope of this book, but at least you are aware of it and can get further details at: **tinyurl.com/xdocmess**.

Conclusion

This chapter concludes almost all there is to know about the new enhancements in HTML5, with the remaining exception of HTML5 audio and video, arguably a couple of the most important new features. So, we're leaving the best till last, and you will learn more about these in the following chapter.

CHAPTER 15

Audio and Video

Introduction

Welcome to the final chapter on HTML5, detailing everything you need to know about, including audio and video media in your websites. It's possible to do this with just a few lines of HTML code, and there's no need for plug-ins or any fancy coding.

Having said that, you can if you wish enhance your users' playback of media by attaching JavaScript functions to the audio and video. But you don't have to do this unless the default options are not suited to your liking.

It really is almost a case of just dragging and dropping the required MP3 or MP4 files into their respective file locations on your web server, adding a couple of lines of code to your HTML, and you've virtually got your own *Spotify* or *YouTube* app. It just doesn't get any easier.

Structure

In this chapter, you will:

- Learn about compression codecs for both audio and video
- Select the best codecs for your media files

- Understand how to fine tune audio and video playback

- Know how to enhance media playback with JavaScript

Objectives

This chapter aims to round off your learning of HTML5 by bringing you up to date with the remaining two features: audio and video. By the time you finish reading this chapter, not only will you be a master at adding media to your web pages, but also will have completed this entire section on HTML5.

HTML5 audio

One of the biggest driving forces behind the growth of the Internet has been the need to support playing of audio and video. The high cost of bandwidth drove the development of efficient compression algorithms, such as MP3 audio and MPEG video, but even then the only way to download files in any reasonable length of time was to drastically reduce their quality.

However, it soon became possible to offer greater audio and video quality, but still only by asking the user to download and install a plug-in player such as *Flash*, which was an unwieldy solution ridden with security implications.

So, the way ahead was to come up with some web standards for supporting multimedia directly within the browser. Of course, browser developers such as *Microsoft* and *Google* had differing visions of what these standards should look like, but when the dust settled, they had agreed on a subset of file types that all browsers should play natively, and these were introduced into the HTML5 specification.

Finally, it is possible (as long as you encode your audio and video in a few different formats) to upload multimedia to a web server, place a couple of HTML tags in a web page, and play the media on any major desktop browser, smartphone, or tablet device, without the user having to download a plug-in or make any other changes.

Audio codecs

The term **codec** stands for enCOder/DECoder. It describes the functionality provided by software that encodes and decodes media such as audio and video. In HTML5, there are a number of different sets of codecs available, depending on the browser used.

Following are the codecs supported by the HTML5 `<audio>` tag (and also when audio is attached to HTML5 video):

- **AAC**: Advanced Audio Encoding is a proprietary patented technology that generally uses the **.aac** file extension (mime type: **audio/aac**).

- **FLAC**: Free Lossless Audio Codec uses the **.flac** extension (mime type: **audio/flac**).

- **MP3**: MPEG Audio Layer 3 uses the **.mp3** extension (mime type: **audio/mpeg**.

- **PCM**: Pulse Coded Modulation is a lossless codec which uses the extension **.wav** (mime type: **audio/wav** or **audio/wave**).

- **Vorbis**: Ogg Vorbis is less supported and uses the extension **.ogg** (mime type: **audio/ogg** or **audio/webm**).

These audio types are supported by most operating systems and browsers, with some Safari-related exceptions to Vorbis so, unless you really have a reason to use Vorbis, it's best to just stick with either AAC or MP3 for compressed lossy audio, FLAC for compressed lossless, or PCM for uncompressed audio. These examples use only MP3 files as they'll work fine on all modern browsers.

Playing audio

To insert audio in your web pages, you can use the new **<audio>** tag in conjunction with a **<source>** tag to tell the browser where to find the audio to be played. *Example 15.1* loads an MP3 file and adds user controls

Example 15.1:

```
1.  <!DOCTYPE html>
2.  <html lang="en">
3.    <head>
4.      <meta charset="utf-8">
5.      <title>Playing Audio</title>
6.    </head>
7.    <body>
8.      <audio controls>
9.        <source src='music.mp3' type='audio/mpeg'>
10.     </audio>
11.   </body>
12. </html>
```

The result of this example is shown in *Figure 15.1*.

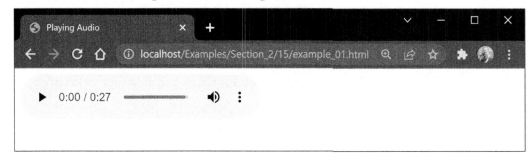

Figure 15.1: Playing an audio file

As you can see looking at line 7, an **<audio>** tag is created with visible user controls by adding the attribute **controls** to it. Within the tag it's simply a matter of telling the browser where to load the file from, which in this case is **music.mp3**. Optionally, the mime type of **audio/mpeg** is also provided, but in most cases, you can leave this out as the browser will work out the mime type for itself.

Users can start and stop the audio, move forward, and backward through it using the slider, change volume with the speaker icon, and by clicking on the three vertical dots settings icon to the right, they can choose a different playback speed of up to two times the original.

If you would like the media to start playing immediately, you can also add the **autoplay** attribute to line 8, as follows:

```
8.    <audio controls autoplay>
```

You can also cause the audio to loop over and over with the **loop** attribute, as follows:

```
8.    <audio controls loop>
```

Or you can mix and match these attributes as required. For example, you can choose to hide the controls by not supplying the **controls** attribute, in which case you may wish to give your users at least a way to stop the audio if it starts to annoy them. *Example 15.2* shows how you can add a couple of buttons to a web page, with which the audio can be played and paused.

Example 15.2:

```
1.  <!DOCTYPE html>
2.  <html lang="en">
3.    <head>
4.      <meta charset="utf-8">
5.      <title>Playing Audio with JavaScript</title>
```

```
6.    </head>
7.    <body>
8.      <audio id='music'>
9.        <source src='music.mp3' type='audio/mpeg'>
10.     </audio>
11.
12.     <p>
13.       <button onclick='playaudio()'>Play Audio</button>
14.       <button onclick='pauseaudio()'>Pause Audio</button>
15.     </p>
16.
17.     <script>
18.       function playaudio()
19.       {
20.         document.getElementById('music').play()
21.       }
22.
23.       function pauseaudio()
24.       {
25.         document.getElementById('music').pause()
26.       }
27.     </script>
28.   </body>
29. </html>
```

In this instance, the music is not set to autoplay because there is a **Play Audio** button on line 13, and a **Pause Audio** button on line 14. These attach to the **onclick** event of the button and then call either the **playaudio()** or the **pauseaudio()** function in the following JavaScript section.

These two functions start on lines 18 and 23, respectively, where they simply call either the **play()** or the **pause()** function on the audio element. The result of loading this example into a browser can be seen in *Figure 15.2*.

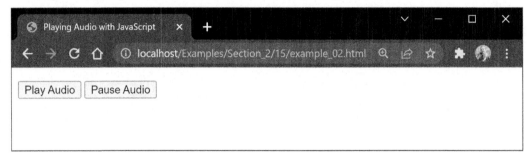

Figure 15.2: The audio is now controlled via buttons

When not displaying the controls, you can still use other attributes such as **autoplay** and **loop** if you wish. Additionally, to ensure speedy response for longer media files, you can add the **preload** attribute, which will start loading the file into memory as soon as it can, ready to be instantly played at will.

HTML5 video

As with audio, it quickly became apparent that video compression was also a major priority for growing the Internet, but doing so brings a whole new ballgame of complication compared with audio.

For example, using MP3 it's possible to reduce an audio file that consumes 10MB of data per minute down to half a megabyte or less, with almost no discernable loss in quality. For example, the **music.mp3** file used in these examples is 26 seconds long and just 457KB in size. But high definition video is an order of magnitude greater in size.

Thankfully there are many tricks that can be employed such as reducing the color information since our eyes respond more to contrast than color, and then breaking images up into chunks similar to each other. Think of a cloudy sky and how many parts will be quite similar and so compression will be effective. Also, by just noting the changes between frames a lot more data can be saved.

This means that a 1-minute 1080HD, 30 frame per second video that would normally be about 1.3GB in size, can be reduced to about 180MB, or less if the quality is allowed to be further reduced. Amazingly, as you can tell by watching subscription TV like Netflix, the result of all this compression is hardly noticeable when done well. Again, this is all achieved using codecs, the main ones for video being explained as follows.

Video codecs

As with audio, there are a number of video codecs available, with differing support across multiple browsers. These codecs come in different containers, as follows:

- **MP4**: A multimedia container format of MPEG-4 (mime type: **video/mp4**)

- **Ogg**: An open container format (mime type: **video/ogg**)

- **WebM**: An audio-video format (mime type: **video/webm**)

These may then contain one of the following video codecs:

- **H.264** or **H.265**: Proprietary video codecs – **H.265** uses half the bitrate of **H.264**

- **Theora**: A proprietary video codec

- **VP8** or **VP9**: Similar to Theora but open source – **VP9** uses half the bitrate of **VP8**

Modern browsers support all of these, with the exception that OGG is not fully supported on all versions of iOS and MacOS. Therefore, unless you have a good reason for using OGG, you should probably stick with either MP4 or WebM. These examples use only MP4 files as these are supported on all modern browsers.

Playing video

Playing video is just as easy as playing audio and works in a very similar way. *Example 15.3* illustrates the loading in playing of a video with user control support.

Example 15.3:

```
1.  <!DOCTYPE html>
2.  <html lang="en">
3.    <head>
4.      <meta charset="utf-8">
5.      <title>Playing Video</title>
6.    </head>
7.    <body>
8.      <video width='320' height='240' controls>
9.        <source src='bunny.mp4' type='video/mp4'>
10.    </video>
11.  </body>
12. </html>
```

In this example, the **<video>** tag is used in line 8, where it is given dimensions of 320 × 240 pixels, and user controls added. Then, line 9 specifies the filename of the video to play, which is **bunny.mp4**, and supplies the optional file type of **video/mp4**. Browsers will usually work out the mime type so this is generally not required. The result of loading this into a browser is shown in *Figure 15.3*. Amazingly, this entire two minute plus video is only 10MB in size thanks to the codec used.

Figure 15.3: *The video is loaded and has user controls*

The user controls for a video have more options than audio. There's a volume control, play and pause, and an icon for displaying the video in full screen mode. What's more, by clicking on the three vertical dots settings icon to the right, users can choose to download the video, change the speed of playback from a quarter to two times the original, or even pop it out to a picture-in-picture mode in the corner of the desktop (although, this latter feature is not available on mobile browsers).

If you would like the media to start playing immediately, you can also add the **autoplay** attribute to line 8, as follows:

```
8.    <video  width='320' height='240' controls autoplay>
```

You can also cause the video to loop over and over with the **loop** attribute, as follows:

```
8.    <video  width='320' height='240' controls loop>
```

Or you can mix and match these attributes as required. For example, you can choose to hide the controls by not supplying the **controls** attribute, in which case you may wish to give your users at least a way to stop the video. *Example 15.4* shows how you can add a couple of buttons to a web page, with which the video can be played and paused.

Example 15.4:

```
1.  <!DOCTYPE html>
2.  <html lang="en">
3.    <head>
4.      <meta charset="utf-8">
5.      <title>Playing Video with JavaScript</title>
6.    </head>
7.    <body>
8.      <video id='bunny' width='320' height='240'>
9.        <source src='bunny.mp4' type='video/mp4'>
10.     </video>
11.
12.     <p>
13.       <button onclick='playvideo()'>Play Video</button>
14.       <button onclick='pausevideo()'>Pause Video</button>
15.     </p>
16.
17.     <script>
18.       function playvideo()
19.       {
20.         document.getElementById('bunny').play()
21.       }
22.
23.       function pausevideo()
24.       {
25.         document.getElementById('bunny').pause()
26.       }
27.     </script>
28.   </body>
29. </html>
```

Structurally this is almost identical to *Example 15.2*, but with video instead of audio. Lines 8 to 10 load the video without user controls, lines 13 and 14 add buttons to play and pause the video, and the functions starting at lines 18 and 23 do the actual playing and pausing by calling the **play()** and **pause()** functions on the video, the result of which is shown in *Figure 15.4*.

Figure 15.4: The video is now controlled via buttons linked to JavaScript functions

When not displaying the controls, you can still use other attributes such as **autoplay** and **loop** if you wish. Additionally, to ensure speedy response for longer media files, you can add the **preload** attribute, which will start loading the file into memory as soon as it can, ready to be instantly played at will.

Plus, with video you have the additional attributes not available with audio, of **muted** to mute audio output, **poster** to choose an image to display where the video will play and, as you have already seen, the **width** and **height** to use for displaying the video.

And don't forget that you don't need to use any JavaScript to give your users a full screen experience because it's already built into the video software. As long as you provide the user controls, then users can click on the full screen icon to enter full screen mode, as shown in *Figure 15.5*.

Figure 15.5: *The video has been set to play full screen*

If you wish, you can also make a video enter full screen mode with some simple JavaScript, as given in *Example 15.5*, which is a revised version of *Example 15.4*, but with an extra button on line 15 for the user to click to enter full screen, and a matching JavaScript function starting on line 29.

Example 15.5:

```
1.  <!DOCTYPE html>
2.  <html lang="en">
3.    <head>
4.      <meta charset="utf-8">
5.      <title>JavaScript and Full Screen</title>
6.    </head>
7.    <body>
8.      <video id='bunny' width='320' height='240'>
9.        <source src='bunny.mp4' type='video/mp4'>
10.     </video>
11.
12.     <p>
13.       <button onclick='playvideo()'>Play Video</button>
```

```
14.        <button onclick='pausevideo()'>Pause Video</button>
15.        <button onclick='fullvideo()'>Full Screen</button>
16.    </p>
17.
18.    <script>
19.      function playvideo()
20.      {
21.         document.getElementById('bunny').play()
22.      }
23.
24.      function pausevideo()
25.      {
26.         document.getElementById('bunny').pause()
27.      }
28.
29.      function fullvideo()
30.      {
31.         document.getElementById('bunny').requestFullscreen()
32.      }
33.    </script>
34.  </body>
35. </html>
```

All you really need to take note of here is that on line 31, the **requestFullScreen()** function is called on the video, and that's all it takes to do the job. When you load this version of the example into a browser the result will look as shown in *Figure 15.6*.

Figure 15.6: *A full screen button has been added*

Interestingly, even if no controls were selected in the `<video>` element, if users choose to enter full screen mode, then they will also be presented with a complete set of controls while in full screen view, and there does not appear to be any way to change this behavior.

Conclusion

Well, here you are! You have now worked your way through everything new that was added to HTML in HTML5, including the powerful audio and video features that were previously sorely lacking. You should be proud at what you now know, and already see ways to apply your new knowledge to improve the projects you are working on.

Now, it's time to move onto another major part of modern web development in the next chapter and, indeed, the next section of this book, by learning everything new in CSS that was added in CSS3.

CHAPTER 16

Introduction to CSS3

Introduction

You are now about halfway through this book and have already learned a great deal of new information. By now, you should be a master at various features in HTML5, so let's match that knowledge by bringing you up to speed on everything that's new in CSS3.

It is assumed that you already have a basic knowledge of CSS2, but this section of the book takes you step by step through CSS3. We will cover one feature at a time, referring back to earlier CSS features, and even if your knowledge is only passing, you will still be able to absorb what is being taught.

You are in for an exciting learning experience because CSS3 has so many new and dynamic features, which can sometimes go beyond what you might have considered wasn't possible without employing JavaScript.

Structure

In this chapter, you will:

- Get a complete overview of all the new features added to CSS3

- Understand how and why CSS is and remains a work in progress

- Be aware of all the powerful new styling tools available to you

- Learn the basics of each of these tools prior to mastering them

Objectives

The objective of this chapter is to give you a thorough grounding in how and why CSS continues to be developed, and what the current and future states of play are and are likely to be. By the time you finish reading the chapter, you will know precisely what types of new styling options are available in CSS3, and you will be ready to learn their ins and outs in detail throughout the rest of this section of the book.

CSS3 is still in development

CSS was first conceived in around 1996, and then took a few years to come together to its first release in 1999. By the year 2001, all new browsers supported CSS, as it was a logical step forward from HTML-only web pages and offered features web developers had been crying out for.

But even that wasn't enough because the appetite of Internet users for more, better, and more dynamic content grew greater over time, so CSS2, which was already being worked on in the late 1990s before CSS itself was even released (yes that's how crazy the growth of these technologies is), became standardized in around 2007 and was again revised in 2009.

So, both CSS and CSS2 were around in the latter part of the first decade of this millennium, and even they were not enough. Thankfully, work had already begun on CSS3 by 2001, work which continued for about 10 years, and even now CSS3 has not been officially finalized, though it has matured into a set of features that all modern browsers support.

Some argue that CSS3 will never reach a final stage, and that it will always be under development because the specification has been modularized, such that new and independent modules can keep being added. However, it seems likely that at some point, some company or other will make a stand for the current capabilities of CSS3 to be committed in stone, so to speak, and the other developers will follow and agree that future extensions should become CSS4. However, that day appears to be some time away, and while there are no definite plans for a CSS4, this author expects it will come to pass, eventually, as indeed, there will likely be an HTML6 one day too – who knows what that will be, perhaps virtual reality-based browsing!

Perhaps, eventually, once the dust has settled, we'll go back to referring simply to CSS and HTML, and when we do so, we'll mean all features currently supported by the two technologies. In the meantime, however, the development of CSS3 is still in a state of flux, so during the lifetime of this book, it is possible it will gain further enhancements. But, for now this section of the book reveals the state of play during the early 2020s.

If you would like to follow the ongoing development of CSS, the following URL at *w3.org* will keep you updated:

tinyurl.com/w3orgcss

New in CSS3

In this chapter, you'll get a thorough introduction to the new features in CSS3, along with plenty of figures to illustrate what they do and how they can be used. There are also a number of example files you can try out and work with to gain a deeper understanding, all of which are available from the free companion examples archive to save you typing them in.

With this knowledge of what's coming fresh, you'll be ready to work through the following chapters until you have mastered all of CSS3.

So, let's take a quick reconnaissance of the layout of the land of CSS3 as it stands today, and see what new features are available for use right now, including enhancements to attribute selectors, backgrounds, borders, box shadows, overflow, colors and opacity, column layouts, text and fonts, box sizing, transitions, transformations and more. And not forgetting Flexbox layout and CSS Grid.

Attribute selectors

CSS3 brings three enhancements to attribute selectors through the use of the new operators: **|**, **~**, **^**, **<**, **$**, and *****. As you will know, CSS offers support of IDs and classes through the **#** (hash, or pound) and **.** (period) operators. In *Example 16.1*, the **<body>** section contains two lines of HTML at lines 13 and 14, with an **<h1>** tag and a **<p>** tag, with two IDs called **intro_1** and **first_para**, and a class called **first_line**.

Example 16.1:

```
1.  <!DOCTYPE html>
2.  <html lang="en">
3.    <head>
4.      <meta charset="utf-8">
5.      <title>Attribute Selectors</title>
6.      <style>
7.        #intro_1   { color        : red;    }
8.        #first_para { font-weight : bold;   }
```

```
9.          .first_line { font-style  : italic; }
10.     </style>
11.   </head>
12.   <body>
13.     <h1 id='intro_1'>This is a heading</h1>
14.     <p id='first_para' class='first_line'>Welcome to my website</p>
15.   </body>
16. </html>
```

The CSS used to style this HTML in lines 7 to 9 is all pretty standard stuff. But with the new attribute selectors, you can do things such as modifying the existing CSS into the following to test values for starting with a string (**intro...**), ending with a string (**...para**), or simply just containing the string (**...t_1...**), in that order:

```
7.        h1[id   ^= 'intro'] { color       : red;     }
8.        p[id    $= 'para' ] { font-weight : bold;    }
9.        p[class *= 't_1'  ] { font-style  : italic; }
```

The result in both the cases will look like *Figure 16.1.*

Figure 16.1: *Simple styling of two elements*

As discussed, there are several other operators you can also use, but these three will give you an introduction to how they work. Further details on attribute selectors are provided in *Chapter 17, CSS3 Attribute Selectors.*

Note: For readability, extra whitespace is added to the CSS to make columns and attributes line up under each other, making them easier to read. This can be a good habit to get into when developing your own websites, but the layout of the whitespace is entirely up to you, or the styling and commenting requirements of your employer.

Backgrounds

Several new ways of creating backgrounds have been added to CSS3, including being able to change the origin of the background, specifying how borders should be displayed relative to background images, clipping areas, and the use of multiple background images as with *Example 16.2*.

Example 16.2:

```
1.  <!DOCTYPE html>
2.  <html lang="en">
3.   <head>
4.     <meta charset="utf-8">
5.     <title>Backgrounds</title>
6.     <style>
7.       .border {
8.         font-family : 'Times New Roman';
9.         font-style  : italic;
10.        text-align  : center;
11.        padding     : 60px;
12.        width       : 250px;
13.        height      : 300px;
14.        background  : url('b1.gif')  top     left    no-repeat,
15.                      url('b2.gif')  top     right   no-repeat,
16.                      url('b3.gif')  bottom  left    no-repeat,
17.                      url('b4.gif')  bottom  right   no-repeat,
18.                      url('ba.gif')  top             repeat-x,
19.                      url('bb.gif')  left            repeat-y,
20.                      url('bc.gif')  right           repeat-y,
21.                      url('bd.gif')  bottom          repeat-x }
22.     </style>
23.   </head>
24.   <body>
25.    <center>
26.      <div class='border'>
```

```
27.          <h1>Certificate of<br>Attendance</h1>
28.          <h2>Awarded To:</h2>
29.          <h3>_____</h3>
30.          <h2>Date:</h2>
31.          <h3>___/___/_____</h3>
32.      </div>
33.    </center>
34.  </body>
35. </html>
```

Figure 16.2 shows an example of using several of these features at once, created using this example.

Figure 16.2: *A border created using multiple images*

As you will see from lines 14 to 21, the border comprises eight individual images that assemble together seamlessly. In *Chapter 18, Creating Backgrounds*, we'll look into how this works, as well as other background features.

Borders

In the previous section, you saw a border being created using multiple background images, but there are also several new ways of applying colors to borders, and using images as borders in CSS3, including supplying radius values to create rounded borders.

In *Example 16.3*, the same images are used for creating a background in the previous example, have been assembled into a single image (as shown in *Figure 16.3*).

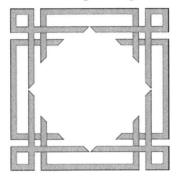

Figure 16.3: *The border.png file*

Then parts of the image have been extracted one at a time and placed into the actual border (rather than the outside part of the background as in the previous example), with the result looking like *Figure 16.4*.

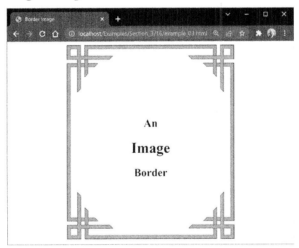

Figure 16.4: *The border.png image has been expanded into the element's border*

Here's *Example 16.3*, in which the main improvement is that only a single image is used, keeping things simpler:

Example 16.3:

```
1.  <!DOCTYPE html>
2.  <html lang="en">
3.    <head>
4.      <meta charset="utf-8">
```

```
5.      <title>Border Image</title>
6.      <style>
7.        .border {
8.           font-family  : 'Times New Roman';
9.           text-align   : center;
10.          padding      : 33px;
11.          width        : 100px;
12.          height       : 150px;
13.          border-width : 102px;
14.          border-style : dotted;
15.          border-image : url('border.png') 102; }
16.      </style>
17.   </head>
18.   <body>
19.     <center>
20.       <div class='border'>
21.         <h3>A</h3>
22.         <h2>One Image</h2>
23.         <h3>Border</h3>
24.       </div>
25.     </center>
26.   </body>
27. </html>
```

This example is quite similar to *Example 16.2*, with the main difference in the **<style>** section. *Chapter 19, Building Borders*, discusses in detail how this is achieved. Now, take a look at line 15, where the single file **border.png** is loaded and assigned the dimensions to apply for the border. The image has dimensions of 205 x 205 pixels, so the value of 102 extracts the four corners of 102 x 102 pixels each, and then the top, bottom, and sides comprise the small parts of the image that are unused by the corners.

It really is as easy as that, with the other CSS instruction there simply to style the **<div>**. Although, you should know that line 14 *is* needed to fix a *'bug'* wherein some browsers may not display border images if the **border-style** attribute is set to **none** (or if **border-width** is **0**, which in this case it is not). Anyway, should the image not load for any other reason, at least there's now a fallback border of sorts to display.

Box shadows

In CSS3, it's now possible to place shadows behind elements, using a variety of different values for color, offset, and blurring, which means you can give the finest hint of a shadow all the way up to making something look like it's in direct sunlight, all with a single instruction. *Example 16.4* creates an element with nothing in it given a border with a shadow offset behind it, down and to the right.

Example 16.4:

```
 1.  <!DOCTYPE html>
 2.  <html lang="en">
 3.    <head>
 4.      <meta charset="utf-8">
 5.      <title>Box Shadows</title>
 6.      <style>
 7.        .box {
 8.           width       : 500px;
 9.           height      : 140px;
10.           border      : 10px solid #800; }
11.        .shadow1 {
12.           box-shadow : 15px 15px 10px #888; }
13.      </style>
14.    </head>
15.    <body>
16.      <center>
17.        <div class='box shadow1'></div>
18.      </center>
19.    </body>
20. </html>
```

Line 12 does the work of applying the shadow to the **<div>** element, while the preceding instructions set up the box dimensions and apply a border. You can even make a shadow appear inside an element, as explained in *Chapter 20, Box and Text Properties*.

The result of this example is shown in *Figure 16.5*.

Figure 16.5: An element with a shadow behind it

Columns and overflow

Also, in *Chapter 20, Box and Text Properties*, we'll take a look at using multiple columns, as created in *Example 16.5*.

Example 16.5:

```
1.  <!DOCTYPE html>
2.  <html lang="en">
3.    <head>
4.      <meta charset="utf-8">
5.      <title>Multiple Columns</title>
6.      <style>
7.        .columns {
8.          text-align    : justify;
9.          font-size     : 16pt;
10.         column-count : 3;
11.         column-gap    : 1em;
12.         column-rule   : 1px solid black; }
13.      </style>
14.    </head>
15.    <body>
16.      <div class='columns'>
17.        Now is the winter of our discontent
```

```
18.        Made glorious summer by this sun of York;

19.        And all the clouds that lour'd upon our house

20.        In the deep bosom of the ocean buried.

21.        Now are our brows bound with victorious wreaths;

22.        Our bruised arms hung up for monuments;

23.        Our stern alarums changed to merry meetings,

24.        Our dreadful marches to delightful measures.

25.        Grim-visaged war hath smooth'd his wrinkled front;

26.        And now, instead of mounting barded steeds

27.        To fright the souls of fearful adversaries,

28.        He capers nimbly in a lady's chamber

29.        To the lascivious pleasing of a lute.

30.    </div>

31.    </body>

32.</html>
```

The result of loading this example is shown in *Figure 16.6*.

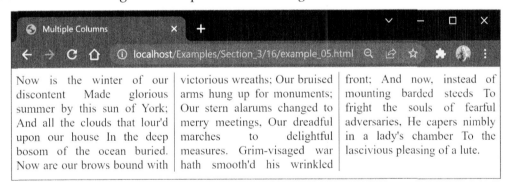

Figure 16.6: Some text from Shakespeare's Richard III flowing over columns

There are also different ways in which you can manage overflow within and outside an element; the example for which is rather long and so we'll leave discussion of that until *Chapter 20, Box and Text Properties*.

Colors and transparency

CSS3 brings with it a number of new ways of handling colors and transparency, including choosing between using the **Red, Green, Blue (RGB)** color space colors, or the **Hue, Saturation, Luminance (HSL)** color space. And knowing which you are using is important as green in HSL is not the same color as green in RGB, for example.

Example 16.6 creates an elongated color wheel in CSS using a **<div>** and conic gradients.

Example 16.6:

```
1.  <!DOCTYPE html>
2.  <html lang="en">
3.    <head>
4.      <meta charset="utf-8">
5.      <title>Color Wheel</title>
6.      <style>
7.        .color-wheel {
8.          width         : 600px;
9.          height        : 300px;
10.         border-radius : 50%;
11.         background    : conic-gradient(red, yellow, lime,
12.                             aqua, blue, magenta, red);
13.     </style>
14.   </head>
15.   <body>
16.     <center>
17.       <div class="color-wheel"></div>
18.     </center>
19.   </body>
20. </html>
```

In *Chapter 21, Colors and Opacity*, we'll look further into HSL and RGB colors and also use transparency, with different variations of this color wheel, as shown in *Figure 16.7*.

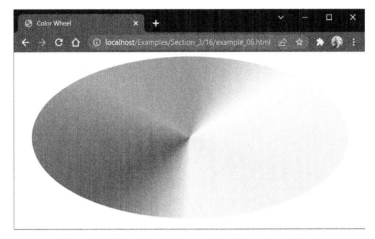

Figure 16.7: A color wheel created with conic gradients

Text effects and fonts

In *Chapter 22, Text Effects and Fonts*, we'll look into all the various effects that you can now create with text using CSS3, including applying shadows, resizing, outlining, and making use of web fonts such as those freely offered by *Google*, which now provides over 1,300 front families for you to use, as shown in *Figure 16.8*.

Figure 16.8: A tiny sample from Google's free web font collection

Example 16.7 downloads a few samples of Google fonts and then uses them to display some text.

Example 16.7:

```
1.  <!DOCTYPE html>
2.  <html lang="en">
3.    <head>
4.      <meta charset="utf-8">
5.      <title>Web Fonts</title>
6.      <style>
7.      .cantarell   { font-family : "Cantarell",          sans-serif; }
8.      .droidsans   { font-family : "Droid Sans",         sans-serif; }
9.      .inconsolata { font-family : "Inconsolata",         monospace; }
10.     .lobster     { font-family : "Lobster",       fantasy, serif; }
11.     .nobile      { font-family : "Nobile",           sans-serif; }
12.     .reenie      { font-family : "Reenie Beanie", cursive, serif; }
13.     .tangerine   { font-family : "Tangerine",     cursive, serif; }
14.     .yanone      { font-family : "Yanone Kaffeesatz", sans-serif; }
15.     html         { font-size   : 42pt; }
16.     </style>
17.    <link rel='stylesheet' type='text/css' href=
18.       'http://fonts.googleapis.com/css?family=Cantarell'>
19.    <link rel='stylesheet' type='text/css' href=
20.       'http://fonts.googleapis.com/css?family=Droid+Sans'>
21.    <link rel='stylesheet' type='text/css' href=
22.       'http://fonts.googleapis.com/css?family=Inconsolata'>
23.    <link rel='stylesheet' type='text/css' href=
24.       'http://fonts.googleapis.com/css?family=Lobster'>
25.    <link rel='stylesheet' type='text/css' href=
26.       'http://fonts.googleapis.com/css?family=Nobile'>
27.    <link rel='stylesheet' type='text/css' href=
28.       'http://fonts.googleapis.com/css?family=Reenie+Beanie'>
29.    <link rel='stylesheet' type='text/css' href=
30.       'http://fonts.googleapis.com/css?family=Tangerine'>
31.    <link rel='stylesheet' type='text/css' href=
```

```
32.          'http://fonts.googleapis.com/css?family=Yanone+Kaffeesatz'>
33.   </head>
34.   <body>
35.     <div style='float:left; margin-right:10px;'>
36.         <div class='cantarell'  >Cantarell</div>
37.         <div class='droidsans'  >Droid Sans</div>
38.         <div class='inconsolata'>Inconsolata</div>
39.         <div class='lobster'    >Lobster</div>
40.     </div>
41.     <div>
42.         <div class='nobile'     >Nobile</div>
43.         <div class='reenie'     >Reenie Beanie</div>
44.         <div class='tangerine'  >Tangerine</div>
45.         <div class='yanone'     >Yanone Kaffeesatz</div>
46.     </div>
47.   </body>
48. </html>
```

The result of loading this example into a browser will look like *Figure 16.9*. As you should be able to tell, the **<style>** section sets up the **font-family** attributes and gives class names to them, and then the **<link>** tags below actually fetch in those fonts from Google's servers. All that's then needed to use them is to apply chosen classes where you wish to use a particular font in the **<html>** section.

Figure 16.9: *A handful of Google fonts in use*

Transitions and transformations

Transformations are a tremendously powerful new addition to CSS. Not only can they be used to create almost any shape you can imagine, in conjunction with CSS3 animation, but also you can create stunning rollover and other interactive and dynamic effects.

In *Example 16.8,* a **<div>** element is created, colored, bordered, and populated with text. A 45-degree rotation is then applied to it using the instruction on line 13 of the code.

Example 16.8:

```
1.  <!DOCTYPE html>
2.  <html lang="en">
3.    <head>
4.      <meta charset="utf-8">
5.      <title>Transformations</title>
6.      <style>
7.        .box {
8.           font-size : 14pt;
9.           width     : 100px;
10.          height    : 100px;
11.          background: yellow;
12.          border    : 6px solid blue;
13.          transform : matrix(1, 1, -1, 1, 0, 0); }
14.      </style>
15.    </head>
16.    <body>
17.      <center>
18.        <br><br><br><br>
19.        <div class='box'>
20.          This box has been rotated clockwise by 45 degrees
21.        </div>
22.      </center>
23.    </body>
24. </html>
```

The result of this is shown in *Figure 16.10*.

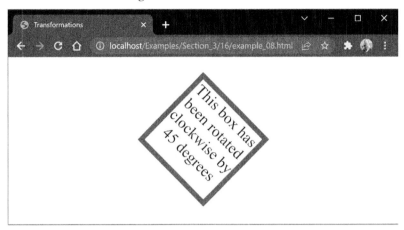

Figure 16.10: Applying a 2D rotation to an element

In *Chapter 23, 2D Transformations*, we'll look at how this works in detail. Then, in *Chapter 24, 3D and Animation*, we'll add a whole new dimension as we examine how to perform 3D transformations.

Flexbox layout

First drawn up in 2009 and while still (at the time of writing in 2022) just a candidate for including in CSS3, Flexbox is already widely implemented across all modern browsers. These days, browser developers know a good thing when they see it and are keen to ensure they provide powerful new features to their users and developers.

Interestingly, the idea for Flexbox grew out of the way when the Mozilla Firefox browser implemented its user interface, using layout primitives that are easier to design with than plain old HTML This interface was thought to be so useful and flexible that it was considered a perfect candidate for creating web pages too.

By 2012, Flexbox was felt to be stable enough that its features began to be incorporated into most browsers. However, as explained at the start of this chapter, CSS is in a constant state of development, and until Flexbox is sealed in stone and no-longer just a candidate, parts of it may still change or be enhanced. Having said that, after all these years nobody wants to break the web, so any changes made will almost certainly be backward compatible.

Flexbox is a module

Rather than being a single new attribute or feature, Flexbox is, in fact, a complete module full of a variety of properties and features. It's another way of implementing your layouts, sometimes based on the parent or container element, and sometimes on the child element.

But for just a small taste of what you can achieve with a Flexbox layout, in *Example 16.9*, Flexbox is being used to create a responsive layout *without* using the **float** or **position** attribute.

Example 16.9:

```
1.  <!DOCTYPE html>
2.  <html lang="en">
3.    <head>
4.      <meta charset="utf-8">
5.      <title>Flexbox</title>
6.      <style>
7.        .parent {
8.          border      : solid 1px black;
9.          padding     : 5px;
10.         background  : red;
11.         display     : flex;
12.         flex-wrap   : wrap;
13.       }
14.       .child {
15.         border      : solid 1px black;
16.         padding     : 10px;
17.         margin      : 2px;
18.         background  : yellow;
19.         color       : blue;
20.         font-size   : 36pt;
21.         font-weight : bold;
22.       }
23.     </style>
24.   </head>
25.   <body>
26.     <div class="parent">
27.       <div class='child'>Elem 1</div>
```

```
28.        <div class='child'>Elem 2</div>
29.        <div class='child'>Elem 3</div>
30.    </div>
31.  </body>
32. </html>
```

Lines 26 to 30 of this example feature a container **<div>** element given the class name of **parent**, and three further **<div>** elements within it, each given the class name of **child**. In the **parent** set of CSS instructions, all should be familiar until you get to lines 11 and 12, which feature a **display** property of **flex** and a **flex-wrap** property of **flex**. If these lines were not there, this example would look like *Figure 16.11*, much as you would expect.

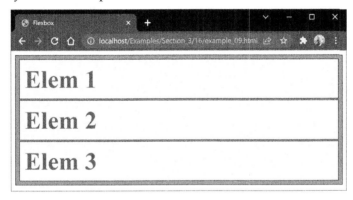

Figure 16.11: Example 16.9 but without the Flexbox features

However, as soon as you apply lines 11 and 12, things change dramatically for the **child** elements, as shown in *Figure 16.12*, where these **<div>** elements are now floating alongside each other, and also have their dimensions reduced in size to fit their contents.

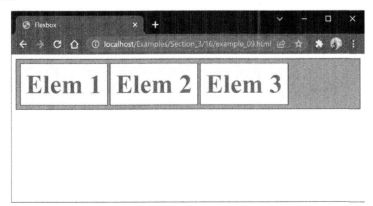

Figure 16.12: With Flexbox properties in place the elements now float

But what's the point of a Flexbox, you may ask, if there's no flexing? Well, watch what happens when you resize the browser to reduce its width as shown in *Figure 16.13*, in which the **child** element that no-longer fits has dropped to the line below. This is just one of many behaviors you can assign to Flexbox layouts, including right-alignment, no wrapping, and many more.

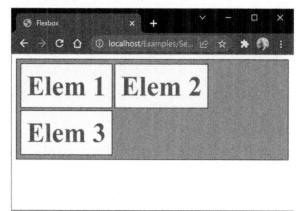

Figure 16.13: *Browser width reduction forces the final element to the next line*

As you may imagine, there is a great deal more that you can do with Flexbox layouts, which are fully detailed in *Chapter 25, Flexbox Layout*. And for further details, if you wish to keep an eye on how Flexbox continues to develop, you can refer to the following official URL:

w3.org/TR/css-flexbox-1

CSS grid

Like Flexbox, CSS Grid is another complete module for CSS, rather than just a single feature or attribute. The difference is that Flexbox is mostly about creating one-dimensional flexible layouts, whereas, as you might imagine, CSS Grid is all about working in columns and rows in a grid layout. Again, in common with Flexbox, CSS Grid replaces the need for using the **float** or **position** attribute.

CSS Grid is also a work in progress, and its first draft was created in around 2011 by developers at Microsoft who were working on Internet Explorer. Yes, something great has come out of IE – it had to happen one day! Sarcasm aside though, as of 2017 all the main browsers had fully supported this vision by implementing CSS Grid, with the exception of Opera Mini which currently does not (and apparently does not plan to) support CSS Grid.

But to give you a feel for what it can do right now, *Example 16.10* creates a grid layout of nine **child <div>** elements in lines 29 to 37 within a **parent <div>** starting at line 28.

Example 16.10:

```
1.  <!DOCTYPE html>
2.  <html lang="en">
3.    <head>
4.      <meta charset="utf-8">
5.      <title>CSS Grid</title>
6.      <style>
7.        .parent {
8.          border               : solid 1px black;
9.          padding              : 5px;
10.         background           : red;
11.         display              : grid;
12.         grid-gap             : 5px;
13.         grid-template-columns : auto auto auto;
14.         justify-content      : space-evenly;
15.       }
16.       .child {
17.         border               : solid 1px black;
18.         padding              : 10px;
19.         margin               : 2px;
20.         background           : yellow;
21.         color                : blue;
22.         font-size            : 36pt;
23.         font-weight          : bold;
24.       }
25.     </style>
26.   </head>
27.   <body>
28.     <div class="parent">
29.       <div class='child'>Elem 1</div>
30.       <div class='child'>Elem 2</div>
31.       <div class='child'>Elem 3</div>
```

```
32.        <div class='child'>Elem 4</div>
33.        <div class='child'>Elem 5</div>
34.        <div class='child'>Elem 6</div>
35.        <div class='child'>Elem 7</div>
36.        <div class='child'>Elem 8</div>
37.        <div class='child'>Elem 9</div>
38.    </div>
39.  </body>
40.</html>
```

The `child` class is styled exactly the same as in the previous example, while the `parent` class now includes grid instructions in lines 11 to 14, to create a grid with 5 pixels gaps and with automatically assigned dimensions to fit the content, all evenly spaced out, as shown in *Figure 16.14*.

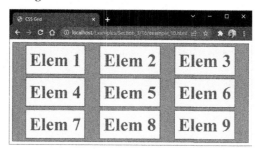

Figure 16.14: A layout created using CSS Grid

Also, as with Flexbox, a CSS Grid layout can be flexible according to the attributes you select, of which you have a variety of options. In this example, the grid will smoothly stretch and shrink as the browser width is resized, as shown in *Figure 16.15*.

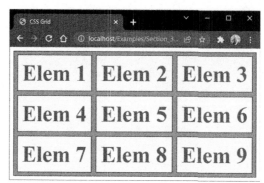

Figure 16.15: The grid layout has shrunk proportionately with the browser width

The point of this being more to cater for different screen widths and heights than for browser resizing. But it works for both, giving maximum customization to your users, whilst retaining the best visual results at all times.

Conclusion

As you will surely have realized from this chapter, a great deal of development work has been going on behind the scenes with CSS and will continue to do so. In the following chapters, we'll turn to each of these new developments and look at how to use them to make the best possible page layouts.

CHAPTER 17

CSS3 Attribute Selectors

Introduction

As you know, selectors in CSS are used to match HTML elements, and then style these matched elements in certain ways. Already in CSS2, we have the **id** and **class** selectors of **#** and **.** (period), and the universal selector *****. Then, there are descendant selectors which are placed after each other, like this: **span em**, and child selectors which are separated with a greater than symbol, like this: **span > em**.

As well as these, you can select adjacent siblings with a plus sign, like this: **span + em**, and there are pseudo classes that check for something happening, like this: **a:hover**, or which single out a specific part of an element, like this: **p:first-letter**.

Finally, there are the attribute selectors, which delve deeper into the inner content of attribute properties, like this: **a[href = 'info.htm']**, and these are the type of selectors that have been extended in CSS3.

Structure

In this chapter, you will:

- Recap the use of selectors in CSS2
- Understand the development of new CSS3 attribute selectors

- Learn how to find and match any attributes that require styling

- Know how to match either case-sensitively or insensitively

Objective

The aim of this chapter is to give you a thorough grounding in the use of CSS3 attribute selectors and to show you what they can do for you as well as how to use them. By the time you finish reading this chapter, you will be a master in the application of attribute selectors, taking your CSS styling to the next level.

CSS attribute selectors

You may be thinking what exactly could possibly be done to enhance the power of attribute selectors? Well, it turns out that the answer is a great deal, because the following operators are now available to you, where **attr** is the attribute, **value** is the value being tested, and the part between is the operator. If any of these don't yet make full sense to you, don't worry because all are explained as you proceed through this chapter:

- **[attr]**: This selects elements with the name **attr**.

- **[attr = value]**: This selects elements with the name **attr** whose value exactly matches **value**.

- **[attr ~= value]**: This selects any matching word of the string in **value** from a whitespace separated list of words.

- **[attr |= value]**: This selects values of **attr** that exactly match **value**, or that exactly match, and are immediately followed by a hyphen.

- **[attr ^= value]**: This selects values of **attr** that start with the string in **value**.

- **[attr $= value]**: This selects values of **attr** that end with the string in **value**.

- **[attr *= value]**: This selects values of **attr** that contain the string in **value**.

- **[attr operator value i]**: When **i** (or **I**) is placed before the closing bracket, the value is compared case-insensitively, ignoring differences between upper and lower case.

- **[attr operator value s]**: When **s** (or **S**) is placed before the closing bracket, the value is compared case-sensitively, such that the **value** must match the string exactly, lower for lower, and upper for upper case (currently, appears to be Firefox only).

Name selector

The first couple of selectors will be easy to follow because you will most likely already have come across, and perhaps used, them in your CSS2 projects, as in *Example 17.1*, which simply selects a named attribute; in this case, it's an **<img>** element with a **title** attribute.

Example 17.1:

```
1.  <!DOCTYPE html>
2.  <html>
3.    <head>
4.      <title>Name Attribute Selectors</title>
5.      <style>
6.        img[title] { border : 5px solid black; }
7.      </style>
8.    </head>
9.    <body>
10.     <center>
11.       <img src='cat.png' title='main'>
12.       <img src='cat.png'>
13.     </center>
14.   </body>
15. </html>
```

On lines 11 and 12, the same image of cat's eyes is displayed on both lines, but only on line 11 is the attribute **title** applied. Therefore, the CSS at line 6 only places a border around the first image that has this attribute, as shown in *Figure 17.1*.

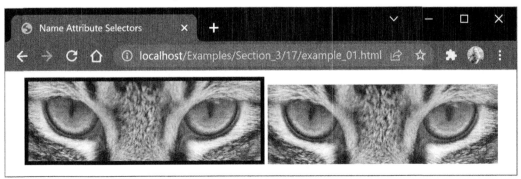

Figure 17.1: *Only the first image with a title attribute is selected*

Value selector

Let's take the example a little further by not only testing whether an attribute is present, but also for the value applied to the attribute, as given in *Example 17.2*, where only the **<img>** element that has a **title** attribute *and* that attribute's value is **main** will be selected.

Example 17.2:

```
1.  <!DOCTYPE html>
2.  <html>
3.    <head>
4.      <title>Value Attribute Selectors</title>
5.      <style>
6.        img[title = 'main'] { border : 5px solid black; }
7.      </style>
8.    </head>
9.    <body>
10.     <center>
11.       <img src='cat.png' title='main'>
12.       <img src='cat.png' title='second'>
13.       <img src='cat.png'>
14.     </center>
15.   </body>
16. </html>
```

Here, the image is displayed three times on lines 11 to 13, but only the instance on line 11 has a **title** attribute matching the word **main**. *Figure 17.2* shows the result we would expect because only the first instance has a border, even though the second one *does* have a **title** attribute because the attribute **value** doesn't match, it remains un-bordered.

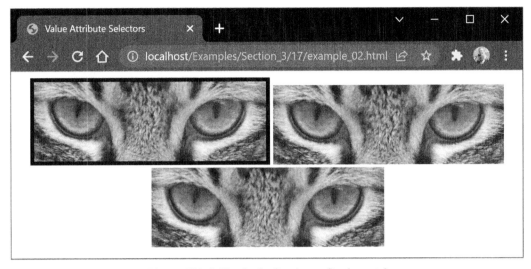

Figure 17.2: Still only the first image fits the match

Word list selector

This selector will match if the value following the selector is found as any single word in the element attribute, among a group of values separated by whitespace. One typical instance is applying of more than one class name at a time to an element, as given in *Example 17.3*, in which only the element that uses a class name of **main** is matched.

Example 17.3:

```
1.  <!DOCTYPE html>
2.  <html>
3.   <head>
4.     <title>Word List Selector</title>
5.     <style>
6.       p[class ~= 'main'] { text-decoration : underline; }
7.     </style>
8.   </head>
9.   <body>
10.    <center>
11.      <p class='article main intro'>This is the first paragraph</p>
12.      <p class='article intro'>This is the second paragraph</p>
```

```
13.        <p class='article body'>This is the article body</p>
14.     </center>
15.   </body>
16. </html>
```

On lines 12 to 13, there are three **\<p>** elements, applying various class names such as **article** and **intro**, but only the first element on line 12 uses the class name **main**. This means that the instruction on line 6 will only modify the first of these paragraphs to be underlined, as shown in *Figure 17.3*.

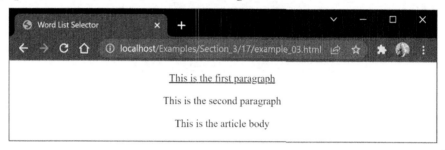

Figure 17.3: *Only the first paragraph is matched and underlined*

You can equally change line 6 to only match the element at line 14 by matching for the word **body**, or to match both elements at lines 12 and 13 by matching for the word **intro**.

Hyphen selector

The hyphen selector is similar to the value selector. It matches the entire string if found in the attribute's value. However, it will also match any string that is followed by a hyphen. The reason for this is that some property values rely on the hyphen, such as when specifying a language to use like **en-us** and **en-uk**. With this selector, you can support all values starting with **en-** to match the English language regardless of the nationality. *Example 17.4* does exactly that for a small selection of languages.

Example 17.4:

```
1. <!DOCTYPE html>
2. <html>
3.   <head>
4.     <title>Hyphen Selector</title>
5.     <style>
6.       p[lang |= 'en'] { font-weight : bold; }
7.     </style>
```

```
8.    </head>
9.    <body>
10.     <center>
11.        <p lang='en-us'>Howdy. How's your day?</p>
12.        <p lang='gr'   >Guten Tag und viel Gesundheit!</p>
13.        <p lang='en-uk'>Hello. Would you like some tea?</p>
14.        <p lang='fr'   >Bonjour. Comment allez-vous?</p>
15.     </center>
16.   </body>
17. </html>
```

In this example, only lines 11 and 13 get matched on line 6 due to being the only ones with **en-** in the value so, as shown in *Figure 17.4*, only the first and third paragraphs are displayed in bold.

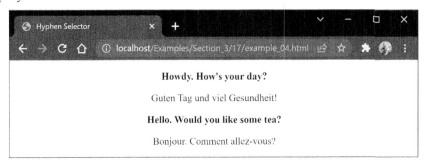

Figure 17.4: *The English language paragraphs have been matched*

Start selector

When you wish to match only a few letters that may appear at the start of a property value, you can use the start selector, as given in *Example 17.5* in which there are four hyperlinks on lines 12 to 15, with line 7 matching only those that are on the local server (commencing with **/home**).

Example 17.5:

```
1.  <!DOCTYPE html>
2.  <html>
3.    <head>
4.       <title>Start Selector</title>
5.       <style>
```

```
6.        body                   { font         : 22pt Sans-Serif; }
7.         a[href ^= '/home'] { font-weight : bold;              }
8.     </style>
9.    </head>
10.   <body>
11.    <center>
12.     <a href='https://google.com'  >Google</a><br>
13.     <a href='/home/page1'         >Page 1</a><br>
14.     <a href='https://facebook.com'>Facebook</a><br>
15.     <a href='/home/'              >Home Page</a><br>
16.    </center>
17.   </body>
18. </html>
```

Line 6 is simply there to make the text larger and clearer, and you can see the result of loading this example into a browser in *Figure 17.5*.

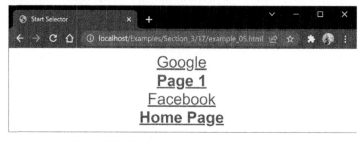

Figure 17.5: *Links to local pages are emboldened*

End selector

Sometimes, you may have a need to match at the end of an attribute's value string, which you can do using the end selector, as given in *Example 17.6*, which highlights only those links that point to **.org** domains.

Example 17.6:

```
1. <!DOCTYPE html>
2. <html>
3.   <head>
4.     <title>End Selector</title>
5.     <style>
```

```
6.      body                { font        : 22pt Sans-Serif; }
7.        a[href $= '.org' ],
8.          [href $= '.org/'] { font-weight : bold;              }
9.      </style>
10.   </head>
11.   <body>
12.     <center>
13.       <a href='https://google.com'    >Google</a><br>
14.       <a href='https://wikipedia.org' >Wikipedia</a><br>
15.       <a href='https://facebook.com'  >Facebook</a><br>
16.       <a href='https://www.icann.org/'>Icann</a><br>
17.     </center>
18.   </body>
19. </html>
```

As with the previous example, four lines at 13 to 16 are hyperlinks to various web properties, and line 6 is simply there to make the display clearer. Lines 7 and 8 are interesting because something new is happening here. On line 7, the **$=** (or end) operator is obvious by now. In this instance, it refers to any string that ends with **.org**. But then, there's a comma followed by another match expression. This is to illustrate how you can perform multiple matches at a time, by just separating the expressions with a comma, and how you can then have as many match expressions as you like.

In this case, the second expression was needed because sometimes people copy hyperlinks from their browser's address bar, which frequently results in a trailing **/** at the end of the URL, such as **.org/**. This is completely valid, but would fail matching the expression if not also accepted as a match, which is the purpose of line 8. The result of loading this example into a browser will look like *Figure 17.6*.

Figure 17.6: Only those web domains ending in .org or .org/ are highlighted

Of course, if there are subdirectories included in the URL of a **.org** domain, this selector will not match, so that's where the global selector comes in, as follows.

Global selector

When you simply need to test for a sequence of characters existing somewhere in the value string, you can use the global selector, as given in *Example 17.7*, in which lines 14 to 17 contain hyperlinks, with line 16 referring to a local folder with the name **pdfs**, and line 15 containing a link to a folder named **pdfs**.

Example 17.7:

```
 1.  <!DOCTYPE html>
 2.  <html>
 3.   <head>
 4.    <title>Global Selector</title>
 5.    <style>
 6.      body { font : 16pt Arial; }
 7.      a[href *= 'pdf'] {
 8.        background   : url('pdf-icon.png') no-repeat;
 9.        padding-left : 16px; }
10.    </style>
11.   </head>
12.   <body>
13.    <ul>
14.      <li><a href='https://google.com'   >Google</a></li>
15.      <li><a href='/home/pdfs/'          >Documents</a></li>
16.      <li><a href='https://facebook.com'>Facebook</a></li>
17.      <li><a href='/home/'               >Home Page</a></li>
18.    </ul>
19.   </body>
20. </html>
```

Line 6 is purely to enlarge the text, but lines 7 to 9 do something very powerful. First, if the sequence of letters **pdf** is found anywhere in any **href** attribute of an **<a>** element, then in lines 8 and 9 that element will be given a non-repeating background image loaded in from **pdf-icon.png**, and then the attribute value string will be given a left padding of **16** pixels, to move it to the right of the icon. The net result is that all URLs with the letter sequence **pdf** anywhere in them will have a small icon placed to their left, as shown in *Figure 17.7*.

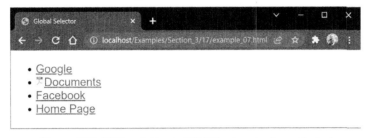

Figure 17.7: URLs relating to PDF files have an icon attached

Case-insensitive flag

The previous example is very clever but potentially flawed. It will only match the sequence **pdf**, and not **PDF** or any other combination that is not all lowercase. So, let's imagine we change line 7 of the previous example to the following, creating *Example 17.8*, in which the match being looked for is the upper-case sequence PDF.

Example 17.8 (showing only the modified line):

```
7.      a[href *= 'PDF'] {
```

If you load this example into a browser, then no match will be made and the result will look like *Figure 17.8*. But if we then alter that same line just a little more to create *Example 17.9*, any sequence of the letters PDF in either upper or lower case will match.

Example 17.9 *(showing only the re-modified line)*:

```
7.      a[href *= 'PDF' i] {
```

The result of this change will be reverting to looking like *Figure 17.8*.

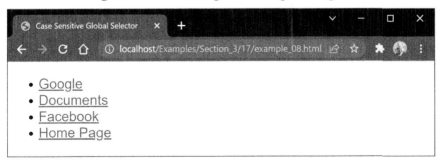

Figure 17.8: When the expression is case-sensitive there is no match

All we have done here is place the letter **i** (which could also have been an upper case **I**) just before the closing square bracket, and that's enough to make the matching case insensitive. This means your match string could go back to being **pdf**, or it could be **pDf** or **PdF** because when matching is insensitive, these are all equivalent.

Case-sensitive flag

Lastly, sometimes it's important to match using the correct upper and/or lower case, and for this, you can use the case-sensitive flag to ensure this will be the type of match. And you'll be pleased to know that by default, in English all the matching *will* usually be case-sensitive, so generally you'll be fine.

However, there are times when you may wish to ensure that a match is being made in a case-sensitive manner, and there is a specification in CSS Level 4 to support the use of the **s** (or **S**) flag, but this author's tests seem to show it is only supported (at the time of writing) by the *Firefox* browser.

Example 17.10 contains three **<div>** elements; two of which use the upper-case word **DIV** in their **title** attributes, while the middle one contains the word **divides**.

Example 17.10:

```
1.  <!DOCTYPE html>
2.  <html>
3.    <head>
4.      <title>Forced Case Sensitivity</title>
5.      <style>
6.        div[title *= "DIV" s] { background: lime; }
7.      </style>
8.    </head>
9.    <body>
10.     <div title='This is a DIV element'>
11.       First section
12.     </div>
13.     <div title='This element divides the page'>
14.       A divider
15.     </div>
16.     <div title='This is another DIV element'>
17.       Final section
```

```
18.     </div>
19.   </body>
20. </html>
```

With non-sensitive matching a match for **DIV** will style all three elements due to it accepting the sequences **DIV** and **div** as being equivalent, but (in *Firefox*, at least) only the two upper case instances get matched by the global, case-sensitive expression on line 6 (as shown in *Figure 17.9*), where those elements that match are given a lime-colored background.

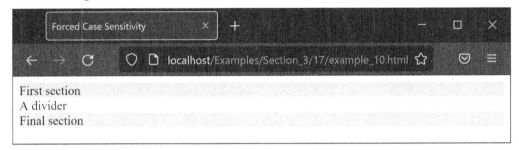

Figure 17.9: *Current Firefox appears to be the only browser supporting forced case sensitivity*

At some point, this example will likely start to work in all browsers, but if you try it and it doesn't work, then the feature has not been supported yet by your browser. As with the history of CSS development, you are now aware of another feature that is coming down the line, but perhaps you'll do best not to use it until you are certain it works on all browsers – just rely on testing with the default case sensitivity setting for the language you have selected for your web pages. You can also refer to the following website to check for browser compatibility with CSS and other features:

caniuse.com

Conclusion

You now have the full power of attribute selectors in your styling toolkit, along with the ins and outs of how to use them, as well as what currently may or may not work in certain browsers. In the following chapter, we will move on to looking at how to create great looking backgrounds for your web pages.

CHAPTER 18
Creating Backgrounds

Introduction

Creating backgrounds is an important new addition in CSS3. With the new features available, you are no longer stuck with either a single color or a single image background because now you can use multiple images and apply elements over them in a plethora of ways.

You can work with the outer edge of the border with the **border-box** attribute just to the edge of the padding area with **padding-box**, or only to the edge of the content area using **content-box**. What's more is that you can set clipping areas based on these values, or define where the origin of your content should be placed relative to these values.

Finally, you can lay out not only your content how you desire with CSS, but also define its relation to and interaction with the background. And because this is a subject that is highly suited for it, some examples use template literals, whereby you place your HTML inside JavaScript sections of a document, enabling you to insert variables directly within your HTML. As you will discover, this can take your web development to a whole new level.

Structure

In this chapter, you will:

- Learn about the different types of backgrounds available

- Understand how to use template literals for your HTML

- Change the way backgrounds display in an element

- Learn how to use gradients in place of solid backgrounds or images

Objectives

This chapter details all the new background features available to you in CSS3, including images and the use of gradients. By the time you complete it, you'll be able to style the background of any element you wish to, in a variety of interesting ways. Along the way, you'll also discover the power of templating using JavaScript.

Background clip and origin

CSS already had some support for backgrounds, but there were still areas connected with the box model that have now been addressed in CSS3 with two new properties: `background-clip` and `background-origin`.

Between them, you can specify where a background should start within an element, and also how to clip the background so that it doesn't appear in parts of the box model where you don't want it to show. Both properties support the following attributes:

`border-box`: This refers to the outer edge of the border.

`padding-box`: This refers to the outer edge of the padding area.

`content-box`: This refers to the outer edge of the content area.

Also, there's a new `background-size` property and multiple backgrounds are now supported. But let's start off by looking at the new origin and clipping properties. To do so, you must first be introduced to one of the most powerful templating tools simply because it's already built into all modern browsers called template literals.

Template literals

Although template literals are not unique to backgrounds, this is the first time in the book where they can really come into their own, so let's take this opportunity to introduce them, before continuing our exploration of backgrounds.

You are already familiar with our discussions of basic JavaScript principles such as variables, and arrays. You will recall how we can assign numeric or string values (as well as many other types) to them. In *Example 18.1*, two variables, **name** and **title**, have strings assigned to them with the values **Robin** and **Web Developer**, respectively, starting at line 11.

Example 18.1:

```
1.  <!DOCTYPE html>
2.  <html>
3.    <head>
4.      <title>String Concatenation</title>
5.    </head>
6.    <body>
7.      <h1>
8.        <output id='output'></output>
9.      </h1>
10.     <script>
11.         name    = 'Robin'
12.         title   = 'Web Developer'
13.         string  = 'My name is ' + name
14.         string += ' and I am a ' + title
15.
16.         document.getElementById('output').innerHTML = string
17.     </script>
18.   </body>
19. </html>
```

Then, on lines 13 and 14 these variable values are combined into a longer string using the **+** operator. When used with strings in JavaScript, it works to concatenate them together. Line 13 creates the first half of this string with a simple assignment combined with concatenation. Then, line 14 uses the **+=** operator as a shorthand way to append to the end of the previous string.

For example, instead of using the expression **string1 = string1 + string2**, you can use the shorter **string1 += string2**. The result is then inserted into the HTML of the **<output>** element which has an ID of **output**. This is done by the instruction on line 16, which you have seen used similarly elsewhere in this book. The result of loading this document into a browser looks like *Figure 18.1*.

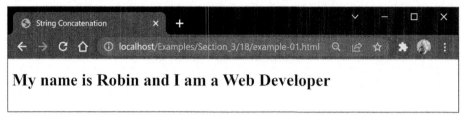

Figure 18.1: *A string is concatenated and displayed using JavaScript*

This is all plain and simple JavaScript, but you can simplify it even further with the use of template literals, which are a means of inserting variable values directly into JavaScript strings, without having to use assignments or concatenation. It works by making use of the back tick symbol, `` ` ``, instead of single or double quotes. On many keyboards, you can find this symbol to the left of the **1** key.

When you encapsulate a string using back ticks, this tells JavaScript to evaluate any content it finds inside a **${...}** expression, and relace the expression with the evaluated result. *Example 18.2* is a re-writing of the previous example.

Example 18.2:

```
1.  <!DOCTYPE html>
2.  <html>
3.    <head>
4.      <title>Template Literals</title>
5.    </head>
6.    <body>
7.      <h1>
8.        <output id='output'></output>
9.      </h1>
10.     <script>
11.        name  = 'Robin'
12.        title = 'Web Developer'
13.
14.        document.getElementById('output').innerHTML =
15.          `My name is ${name} and I am a ${title}`
16.     </script>
```

```
17.   </body>
18. </html>
```

Looking closely at line 15, you'll see the string being inserted into the HTML of the `<output>` element is contained within a single pair of back ticks, and the two variables, `name` and `title` have been placed within `${...}` expressions, such that the displayed result is identical to *Figure 18.1*. Not only is this a simple string, that is self-explanatory (once you know about template literals), lines 13 and 14 of the previous example are no-longer required. In short, you have templated the HTML to work with any values those variables may contain.

Hopefully, this simple trick impresses you with its power, which enables you to use JavaScript as a templating language as well as everything else it can do for you. Also, anyone else who has to maintain your projects will thank you for using it, by making their lives easier too.

Using the background-clip property

With that short templating tutorial completed, let's get on with looking into the wider use of backgrounds by exploring the **background-clip** and **background-origin** attributes. The former of these specifies whether the background should be ignored (not displayed) if it appears within either the border or padding area of an element. It supports the three values previously described of **border-box**, **padding-box**, and **content-box**.

For example, this rule states that the background should be displayed in all parts of an element all the way up to the outer edge of its border:

```
background-clip:border-box;
```

Or, if you wish to prevent the background from being displayed within any part of the border area of an element, you can use this rule:

```
background-clip:padding-box;
```

Finally, to prevent the background from being displayed anywhere except within the content area of an element, you can use this rule:

```
background-clip:context-box;
```

The **background-clip** attribute applies equally to background colors as it does to background images.

Using the background-origin property

Either, or combined with **background-clip**, you can also specify the offset from the top left-hand corner of an element to use when displaying a background image. You can do this with the **background-origin** attribute, which also supports the three values previously described of **border-box**, **padding-box**, and **content-box**.

For example, this rule states that the background should be displayed with its top left-hand corner exactly at the top left-hand corner of the element's border:

```
background-origin:border-box;
```

Or, if you wish the image to be displayed with its top left-hand corner exactly at the top left-hand corner of the element's padding area, you can use this rule:

```
background-origin:padding-box;
```

Or, to ensure the image is displayed with its top left-hand corner exactly at the top left-hand corner of the element's inner content area, you can use this rule:

```
background-origin:content-box;
```

The **background-origin** attribute does not affect the background colors, only images applied to backgrounds.

Background clip and origin together

Now that you know how to work with the origin and how to clip background images, let's see how these two properties work together in all different possible combinations. These are nine in total; three values supported for clipping and the same three again for the origin.

Example 18.3 brings them all together but, rather than using nine separate sets of HTML to display the different permutations, which would make for a long and overly verbose document, it uses an array (which you'll remember is simply a sequence of variables that you access by a numeric index value) and template literals to create a much shorter document.

Example 18.3:

```
1.  <!DOCTYPE html>
2.  <html>
3.    <head>
4.      <title>Background Clip and Origin</title>
5.      <style>
6.        .out { border      : 3px solid black;
7.               float       : left;
8.               margin      : 0 20px 20px 0; }
9.        .in  { font        : bold 12px monospace;
```

```
10.                    border        : 4px dotted red;
11.                    line-height   : 1.25;
12.                    text-align    : center;
13.                    width         : 132px;
14.                    height        : 132px; }
15.        .txt { margin-top    : 75% }
16.        .box { background    : url('box.jpg') lime top left no-repeat;
17.                    color         : green;
18.                    border        : 20px dashed blue;
19.                    padding       : 20px;
20.                    width         : 140px;
21.                    height        : 140px; }
22.    </style>
23.  </head>
24.  <body>
25.    <output id='output'></output>
26.    <script>
27.      attr = ['border-box', 'padding-box', 'content-box']
28.
29.      for (x = 0 ; x < 3 ; ++x) {
30.        for (y = 0 ; y < 3 ; ++y) {
31.          document.getElementById('output').innerHTML +=
32.            <div class='out'>
33.              <div class='box'
34.                style='background-clip   : ${attr[x]};
35.                       background-origin : ${attr[y]}'>
36.                <div class='in'>
37.                  <div class='txt'>
38.                      clip:${attr[x]}<br>
39.                    origin:${attr[y]}
40.                  </div>
41.                </div>
42.              </div>
```

```
43.              </div>`
44.          }
45.        }
46.    </script>
47.  </body>
48.</html>
```

The result of this example should look like *Figure 18.2*.

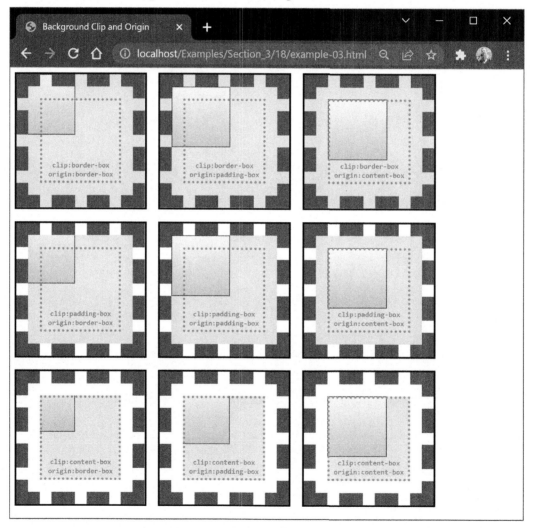

***Figure 18.2**: All nine combinations of the background clip and origin*

To explain what is going on, we need nine instances of elements that each contain an outer border, with some padding inside that and then some content within that. Then, to see how the border images (and indeed colors) are applied in each permutation, a background color is applied to the element, and an image file named **box.jpg** is loaded into the backgrounds.

Looking at the example, starting on line 6, the **out** class set of rules is created to have a solid black, 3-pixel border, for each of the nine elements to float alongside each other, and a margin is applied to separate them all.

The **in** class starting on line 9 sets up an inner element with a dotted red, 4-pixel border, sets the dimensions and styles for the text, so that each of the nine elements is clearly explained when the example is run. The **txt** class on line 15 ensures that the text will appear located in the correct place 75 percent down the content area.

Finally, for the **<style>** section, the **box** class starting on line 16 is where the background image is loaded in at the top left-hand corner of wherever the **background-origin** attribute will later place it, the background is set to lime and text color to green. At the same time, a padding area of 20 pixels is created so that we can see what happens within it and suitable dimensions are assigned.

The JavaScript section

Here, two nested loops are created on lines 29 and 30 using loop variables **x** and **y** which each iterate through values ranging between 0 and 2. Using these values, the array **attr[]** on line 27 is indexed to extract the string values it contains, according to the values in **x** and **y**.

Then, there is a block of HTML in lines 32 to 43; all contained within a pair of back ticks. The first back tick is at the end of line 31, and the matching one at the end of line 43. Inside these back ticks is standard HTML, plus four instances of template literals. If you look at **${attr[x]}** on line 34 and **${attr[y]}** on line 35, you will notice that they are simply extracting the attribute values from the **attr[]** array for the various nine possible permutations of **x** and **y**.

The values in the **y** variable serve to set the **background-clip** to **border-box** on the first row of the displayed output, to **padding-box** on the second, and to **content-box** on the third. It does this by applying the value retrieved from **attr[]** directly to the **style** attribute of the element from within the HTML.

Meanwhile, the values in **x** set the **background-origin** of each column to **border-box** for the first, **padding-box** for the second, and **content-box** for the third element, and this repeats for the following two rows. Each time around the nested loop pair, line 31 simply appends the result to the inner HTML of the **<output>** element, which is how it all gets displayed.

If you examine *Figure 18.2* carefully, you will understand what is going and will observe that for each of the rows, the lime background color starts filling all the way out to the border edge, then the padding edge, and then just fills the content area. At the same time, you can see the effect that the changes of origin make (in conjunction with the clipping), such that as you look along the columns the box image is offset from the top left-hand corner of the border in the first column, offset to the top left-hand corner of the padding in the second column, and offset to the top left-hand corner of the content in the third column, and it is also affected by the clipping rules too.

The HTML on lines 37 to 40 isn't absolutely necessary for creating the visual example, but they do display text explaining which values of the attributes have been applied for each element, so it was worth adding this slight extra level of complexity, to make the figure even more clearly understandable at a glance.

These nine permutations detail everything that can be achieved with these properties, and so *Figure 18.2* can be considered the perfect reference for when you need to remind yourself what these properties will do, and how to apply them.

What's more, you have seen the template literals put to good use, not only in a single instance, but also when applied in a more complex structure such as nested loops. Whether or not your development will use nesting structure, you will certainly find many uses for the templating that JavaScript offers, to speed up any web development that requires dynamic and variable content.

Incidentally, if you want to see exactly what HTML just created looks like, and how much we have saved in document size and replicated lines, you can insert the following instruction just before the closing **</script>** statement on line 46, and then view the output by opening up your developer console:

```
console.log(document.getElementById('output').innerHTML)
```

The result should look something like *Figure 18.3*.

Figure 18.3: Reviewing the created HTML in the console

If you are feeling especially adventurous, you can copy and paste this from the console to replace the **<output>** element, then remove the (now unneeded) **<script>** section, and you should see the same result as shown in *Figure 18.2*, but created with an unnecessarily long document of 125 lines, compared with the 48 lines in *Example 18.3*. The accompanying free archive of example files also includes such an alternative version of this example to save you the typing.

Background size

When you wish to change the dimensions of a background image, you cannot use the standard width and height properties. Instead, there is a single attribute to modify both values, the **background-size** property. You can supply one value and both dimensions will be set to that value, or you can supply two, one for width and the other for height, as follows:

```
background-size : 100px
background-size : 130px 90px
```

The first of these instructions will set the dimensions of the background to 100 **x** 100 pixels, while the second will set it to 130 **x** 90 pixels. *Example 18.4* creates two **<div>** elements: each of which loads in the same background image, but uses different **background-size** properties.

Example 18.4:

```
1.  <!DOCTYPE html>
2.  <html>
3.   <head>
4.    <title>Background Size</title>
5.    <style>
6.      .background { background      : url('painting.png')
7.                                      green center no-repeat;
8.                      color          : white;
9.                      width          : 150px;
10.                     height         : 150px;
11.                     font           : bold 16pt sans-serif;
12.                     text-align     : center;
13.                     border         : solid black 2px;
14.                     float          : left;
15.                     margin         : 20px;          }
16.       #box1       { background-size : 100px;         }
17.       #box2       { background-size : 140px 70px; }
18.       #box3       { background-size : 50%;           }
19.       #box4       { background-size : 100%;          }
20.       #box5       { background-size : 100% 100%;  }
21.    </style>
22.   </head>
23.   <body>
24.    <div class='background'  id='box1'>Box 1</div>
25.    <div class='background'  id='box2'>Box 2</div>
26.    <div class='background'  id='box3'>Box 3</div>
27.    <div class='background'
28.         style='width:300px' id='box4'>Box 4</div>
```

```
29.    <div class='background'
30.         style='width:880px' id='box5'>Box 5</div>
31.   </body>
32. </html>
```

In this example, the **background** class, starting at line 6, sets a green colored background, loads in an image to the center of the element with no repeating, gives the element a border and a margin, selects a suitable font style and color, and floats the element to the left so it will align horizontally.

The first two IDs of **box1** and **box2** on lines 16 and 17 set dimensions, respectively of 100 **x** 100 pixels and 140 **x** 70 pixels. Then, the two elements on line 24 and 25 are displayed in the **<body>** section using these IDs. The other three IDs of **box3**, **box4**, and **box5** on lines 18 to 20 use percent values of 50, 100, and then 100 x 100 percent, and are displayed using lines 26 to 30, where the fourth and fifth boxes force changes to the element's width directly in the HTML, to illustrate these effects in non-square elements.

This illustrates the, perhaps, slightly unexpected behavior of percentage values, as shown in *Figure 18.4*, where the first three boxes display as you would think.

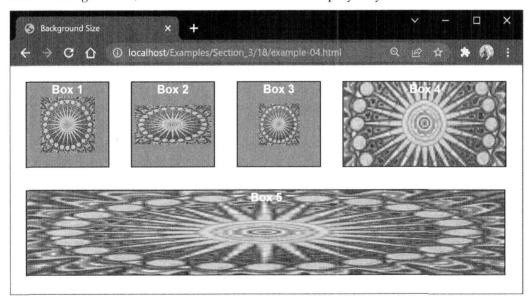

Figure 18.4: *Background images using various different background sizing values*

But look at the fourth one, where there is only one value of **100%** applied to the **background-size** property, so the image width has been set to the width of the element, and therefore the height of the image has also been set to the same as the width (due to only a single value give to the value), so both dimensions must end up the same length. In the fifth box, however, the image has been fully resized in both dimensions by supplying values of **100%** for both the width and height for them to be resized independently.

Using gradients

CSS has a wide range of color options available, as we'll discover in *Chapter 21, Colors and Opacity*, but before that let's take a look at some of the ways they can be applied to element backgrounds. In *Example 18.5*, an excerpt from Shakespeare's *As You Like It* is displayed using a background linear gradient flowing from blue at the top, down to red at the bottom.

Example 18.5:

```
1.  <!DOCTYPE html>
2.  <html>
3.    <head>
4.      <title>Background Linear Gradient</title>
5.      <style>
6.        .bground { background-image : linear-gradient(blue, red); }
7.        #quote   { color              : white;
8.                   padding            : 10px;
9.                   font               : bold 28pt sans-serif;          }
10.     </style>
11.   </head>
12.   <body>
13.     <div class='bground' id='quote'>
14.       All the world›s a stage,
15.       And all the men and women merely players.
16.       They have their exits and their entrances,
17.       And one man in his time plays many parts,
18.       His acts being seven ages.
19.     </div>
20.   </body>
21. </html>
```

Thee result of this example looks like *Figure 18.5.*

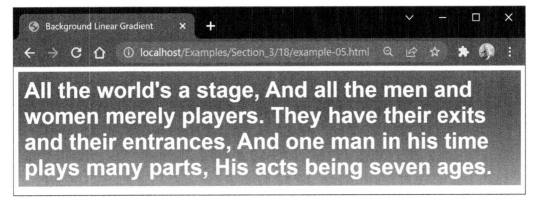

Figure 18.5: An element employing a linear gradient background

In this example, the **quote** ID in lines 7 to 9 style the element suitably for overlaying on a dark background. Line 6 creates a class called **bground** which, when applied between lines 13 and 19 causes a linear background behind the text. Simply by changing line 6 of this example, as given in *Example 18.6*, where the gradient direction is changed to flow from left to right

Example 18.6 *(just the bground rule)*:

```
.bground { background-image:linear-gradient(to right, blue, red); }
```

The result of this should look like *Figure 18.6.*

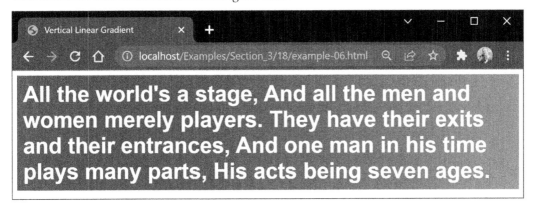

Figure 18.6: The gradient is switched to flow left to right

Using this technique, you can apply any combination of **to** with **top**, **bottom**, **left** and **right** to flow in all the main eight directions of the compass, including diagonal gradients. And if you need to be even more precise, you can specify an exact angle in degrees for the direction of gradient flow in place of the **to right** or other instruction, such as **185deg**.

Color stops

With color stops, you can use more than two colors in your gradients such as in *Example 18.7* (where only the bground rule is changed), which creates a rainbow fill diagonally at 45 degrees).

Example 18.7 (just the **bground** rule):

```
.bground { background-image:linear-gradient(45deg,
   red, orange, yellow, green, blue, indigo, violet); }
```

The result of this example is shown in Figure 18-7.

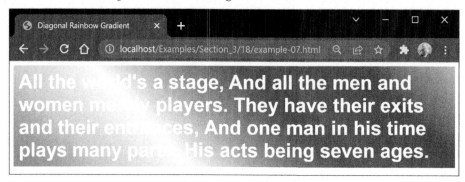

Figure 18.7: A diagonal rainbow linear gradient

Stop distances and repeating

If you wish, you can specify exactly how far along a gradient each color stop should lbe placed by following the color with a percent value. You can also decide to make a gradient repeat by replacing the **linear-gradient()** function with **repeating-linear-gradient()**. *Example 18.8* applies both of these changes.

Example 18-8 (just the **bground** rule):

```
.bground { background-image:repeating-linear-gradient(45deg,
   red   5%, orange 10%, yellow 15%, green 20%,
   blue 25%, indigo 30%, violet 35%); }
```

This example should result in *Figure 18.8*:

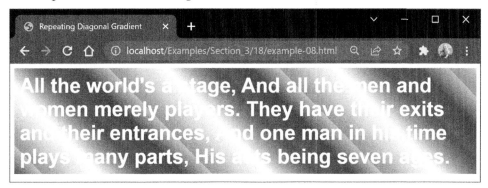

Figure 18.8: *A repeating diagonal gradient*

Radial and conic gradients

There are two remaining gradient types you can apply as a background image and they are radial and conic gradients. A radial gradient starts in the center of a circle (or oval) and works outwards, while a conic gradient flows around a circle (or oval) like a radar screen.

In *Example 18.9*, both of these types of gradients are applied in different **<div>** elements.

Example 18.9:

```
1.  <!DOCTYPE html>
2.  <html>
3.   <head>
4.     <title>Radial and Conic Gradients</title>
5.     <style>
6.       .radial { background-image:radial-gradient(
7.         red, orange, yellow, green, blue, indigo, violet); }
8.       .conic  { background-image:conic-gradient(
9.         red, orange, yellow, green, blue, indigo, violet, red); }
10.      .elem   { float   : left;
11.                margin : 10px;
12.                width  : 400px;
13.                height : 200px; }
14.    </style>
```

```
15.   </head>
16.   <body>
17.     <div class='radial elem'></div>
18.     <div class='conic  elem'></div>
19.   </body>
20. </html>
```

The result of this example is shown in *Figure 18.9*.

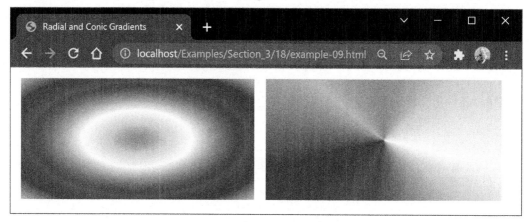

Figure 18.9: *A radial and conic gradient side-by-side*

Here, two classes are created, one called **radial** and one **conic**. Then, there's a class called **elem** which is used to style the two **<div>** elements, one of which displays a radial gradient, and the other a conic one.

If you wish, you can also set precise color stop percent values and also apply the **repeating-** prefix before the **radial-gradient()** and **conic-gradient()** function names to cause them to repeat. As discussed in *Chapter 21, Colors and Opacity*, you can also replace the English color names with RGB or HSL values, and even include transparency in those values too. But those are color-specific functions, not exclusive to backgrounds, so here is not the place to expand on them.

Conclusion

As you have discovered, background functionality has been massively enhanced in CSS3, such that you can now add a background of your choice to any element, styling it in just about any way you can imagine, including using a wide variety of gradients. In the following chapter, we'll continue this exploration by looking into using background images and gradients as borders, as part of a complete overview of CSS3 borders.

CHAPTER 19

Building Borders

Introduction

In a way this chapter is a follow-on to the previous one because there is a lot of crossover between CSS3 borders and backgrounds. But it's necessary to find a place to draw the line and make a distinction.

In this chapter, we'll start by looking at how to use background images to create borders, and then how to improve this by using only a single image, before looking into the other border types that are possible.

These other border types include various colors, which can be different for each border, and a variety of curved radius options, as well as gradients.

Structure

In this chapter, you will:

- Learn all the different border types available in CSS3

- Understand how to add a variety of rounded borders to elements

- Be able to use colors and gradients in borders

- Discover how to use single and multiple images for borders

Objectives

In this chapter, you will learn everything you need to know about creating pleasing border effects. By the time you finish reading the chapter, you will have mastered all the options, including adding a radius, changing colors in different edges, applying images, or even using colored gradients.

Border radius

One of the most fun new features for borders is modification of their radius, with which you can create all types of rounded border effects, up to having a fully circular border. The main property is called **border-radius**, but there are also a number of related properties to precisely adjust the different corners. In *Example 19.1*, a variety of different border types are created using these different properties.

Example 19.1:

```
1.  <!DOCTYPE html>
2.  <html>
3.    <head>
4.      <title>Border Radius</title>
5.      <style>
6.        .box {
7.          width                  : 100px;
8.          height                 : 100px;
9.          float                  : left;
10.         background             : lime;
11.         padding                : 10px;
12.         margin-right           : 10px;
13.         border                 : 20px solid #006;      }
14.       .border1 {
15.         border-radius          : 50px;                 }
16.       .border2 {
17.         border-radius          : 50px 50px 20px 20px;  }
18.       .border3 {
19.         border-top-left-radius : 25px;
20.         border-top-right-radius: 50px;
```

```
21.          border-bottom-left-radius   : 75px;
22.          border-bottom-right-radius  : 100px;                    }
23.      .border4 {
24.          border-top-left-radius      : 20px 80px;
25.          border-top-right-radius     : 80px 20px;
26.          border-bottom-left-radius   : 80px 20px;
27.          border-bottom-right-radius  : 20px 80px;                }
28.      .border5 {
29.          border-radius               : 100%;                     }
30.    </style>
31.  </head>
32.  <body>
33.    <div class='box border1'></div>
34.    <div class='box border2'></div>
35.    <div class='box border3'></div>
36.    <div class='box border4'></div>
37.    <div class='box border5'></div>
38.  </body>
39. </html>
```

In this example, the main class in the **<style>** section is called **box**, which is defined starting at line 7. These rules set the dimensions of each displayed element, along with the chosen background color, padding, margins, and the border width, style, and color. The elements are also floated to the left so that they can line up in a row. After this, there are five classes that apply different border styles, as employed by the **<div>** elements starting at line 33 in the **<body>** of the document. The result of loading this example into a browser looks like *Figure 19.1*.

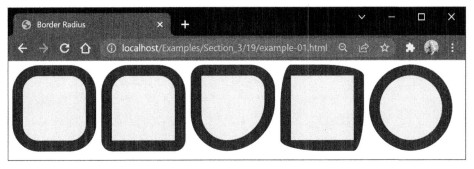

Figure 19.1: Examples of different border styles

When you apply a single value to the **border-radius** property (as in the **border1** class on line 14, the first element of *Example 19.1*), all the corners are assigned the same value, so you end up with a symmetric rectangle or square, with the borders rounded by the amount specified.

If two values are supplied to **border-radius**, the first value applies to the top left-hand and bottom right-hand corners, and the second applies to the other two corners. With three values, the first applies to the top left-hand corner, the second to the top right-hand and bottom left-hand corners, and the third to the bottom right-hand corner. When all four values are supplied (as in the **border2** class on line 16, the second element of *Example 19.1*), they apply clockwise from the top left to the top right, then bottom right and finally bottom left-hand corners.

It gets more interesting thereafter because you can also modify these corners individually with the following properties:

border-top-left-radius

border-top-right-radius

border-bottom-left-radius

border-bottom-right-radius

These properties are self-explanatory and can be seen applied in the class **border3** on line 18, resulting in the funky-looking third element in *Figure 19.1*. But that's not all. When you supply values directly to the corners, you can provide two values if you wish, in which case the first value applies to the first side given in the property name, and the second to the second named side.

For example, when you give two values to **border-bottom-right-radius**, the first value applies to the bottom edge of the corner, and the second to the right edge of the corner. This is demonstrated by class **border4** on line 23 to create the fourth element in *Figure 19.1*.

Finally, it's possible to create fully circular or oval borders by applying a maximum value to the **border-radius** property, usually **50%** or higher to be certain, as in the class **border5**, which creates the fifth element in the figure. In fact, you can apply both pixel and percentage values to any of the border properties, as you see fit.

For a complete explanation of all the various border radius functionalities, you can visit the following URL:

tinyurl.com/b-radius

Border colors

Whatever type of colored border you create, standard, or with a curved radius, you can also modify its colors in a number of ways, including a variety of gradient effects. But let's look at solid colors first.

As you know, a rule such as the following, will set a solid blue border that's 10 pixels wide:

```
border : 10px solid blue;
```

But you may not also know that you can define the color separately for each of the border edges, as shown in *Example 19.2*, in which the **box** class starting on line 6 creates a 20-pixel solid border on line 10, and then assigns four colors to it on line 11.

Example 19.2:

```
 1. <!DOCTYPE html>
 2. <html>
 3.   <head>
 4.     <title>Border Colors</title>
 5.     <style>
 6.       .box {
 7.         width        : 640px;
 8.         height       : 100px;
 9.         background   : cyan;
10.         border       : 20px solid;
11.         border-color : red yellow blue green; }
12.     </style>
13.   </head>
14.   <body>
15.     <div class='box'></div>
16.   </body>
17. </html>
```

These colors are applied in a clockwise order, starting from the top border, as shown in *Figure 19.2*.

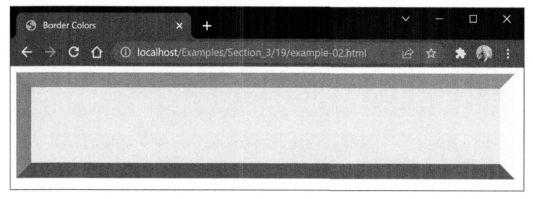

Figure 19.2: An element with four differently colored borders

If you prefer, just as you can with the **border-top-style** and so on, you can also set these colors individually using the following properties, each of which accepts a single value:

border-top-color

border-left-color

border-right-color

border-bottom-color

For a full breakdown of the border color options now available in CSS3, you can visit the following URL:

tinyurl.com/b-color

Gradient borders

If you want to create fancy borders, you can choose a gradient instead of an image, as shown in *Example 19.3*, which applies an orange to blue border on line 14.

Example 19.3:

```
1. <!DOCTYPE html>
2. <html>
3.   <head>
4.     <title>Gradient Border</title>
5.     <style>
6.       .border {
```

```
7.           font-family  : 'Times New Roman';
8.           text-align   : center;
9.           padding      : 10px;
10.          width        : 300px;
11.          height       : 200px;
12.          border-width : 10px;
13.          border-style : solid;
14.          border-image : linear-gradient(orange, blue) 27 / 35px; }
15.      </style>
16.   </head>
17.   <body>
18.     <center>
19.       <div class='border'>
20.         <h2>A</h2>
21.         <h1>Gradient</h1>
22.         <h2>Border</h2>
23.       </div>
24.     </center>
25.   </body>
26. </html>
```

The result of loading this example into a browser is shown in *Figure 19.3*.

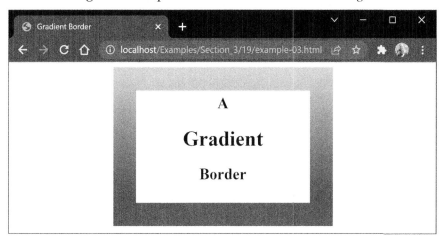

Figure 19.3: *Using a gradient for a border*

You can also use radial and repeating gradients to great effect, and you can slice border images in a variety of different ways too. The number of different effects possible would fill too many pages to fully describe, but if you'd like to get very creative with your borders, check out the official documentation, which will show you plenty of more examples, at the following URL:

tinyurl.com/css3borders

Multiple backgrounds

In *Chapter 16, Introduction to CSS3*, we briefly looked at the subject of using background images to create a border, with a document such as in *Example 19.4*.

Example 19.4:

```
1.  <!DOCTYPE html>
2.  <html>
3.    <head>
4.      <title>Multiple Border Images</title>
5.      <style>
6.        .border {
7.          font-family : 'Times New Roman';
8.          font-style  : italic;
9.          text-align  : center;
10.         padding     : 60px;
11.         width       : 250px;
12.         height      : 300px;
13.         background  : url('b1.gif') top     left  no-repeat,
14.                       url('b2.gif') top     right no-repeat,
15.                       url('b3.gif') bottom  left  no-repeat,
16.                       url('b4.gif') bottom  right no-repeat,
17.                       url('ba.gif') top           repeat-x,
18.                       url('bb.gif') left          repeat-y,
19.                       url('bc.gif') right         repeat-y,
20.                       url('bd.gif') bottom        repeat-x }
21.     </style>
22.   </head>
```

```
23.    <body>
24.      <center>
25.        <div class='border'>
26.           <h1>Certificate of<br>Attendance</h1>
27.           <h2>Awarded To:</h2>
28.           <h3>_____</h3>
29.           <h2>Date:</h2>
30.           <h3>___/___/_____</h3>
31.        </div>
32.      </center>
33.    </body>
34. </html>
```

This example should look like *Figure 19.4* when loaded into a browser.

Figure 19.4: *A border constructed from eight images*

Now that you've covered all the ground needed to understand how it all works, let's get into the details of this example, which makes use of eight individual images representing the four sides and four corners of a border. The corner images are placed in lines 13 to 16 into the correct corners at top-left, top-right, bottom-left and bottom-right of any element using this class, respectively. They are also set to not repeat.

Lines 17 to 20 place the edge images at the top, left, right and bottom edges of the element using this class, with the top and bottom images set to repeat horizontally, and the left and right ones to do so vertically. Together these images will shrink and expand to create a seamless border for any element, with the caveat that elements with dimensions of the size of the border and smaller will not display well. *Figure 19.5* shows the corner images **b1.gif**, **b2.gif**, **b3.gif,** and **b4.gif**.

Figure 19.5: *The four corner images*

The edge images can be seen in *Figure 19.6*, where they are enlarged so that you can see their individual pixels. From left to right, they are the top, left, right, and bottom border images.

Figure 19.6: *The four edge images*

One thing to note about the edge images is that while the extra white pixels are shown in the corner images due to the colored pixels extending all the way to their adjacent corners, the white pixels are not required to extend the edge images. So, these images can remain very small and fast to load in. In deployed use, you would likely set these white pixels to a transparent value using a graphics program anyway, so that they would not interfere with the color scheme you have in place.

Using a single image

Although multiple images are easy to understand and make a lot of sense, they require eight individual requests to a web server and the associated communication bandwidth and server processing increase. Especially on high traffic websites, it can make even more sense to assemble your border images together into the smallest possible border, in a single image, as shown in *Figure 19.7*.

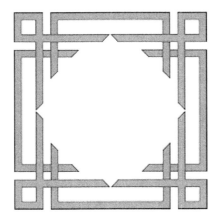

Figure 19.7: A single image created from the eight border images

Then, using this image, you can use CSS3 instructions to extract the various corners and edges and place them around the border of an element, as if they were separate. This reduces server communications by a factor of eight, leaving the browser to do the work, which it does with no noticeable hit to its performance.

You won't believe how much easier it is to work with a single image from CSS too, as shown in *Example 19.5*, in which lines 6 to 13 style the element in various ways, but line 14 is a single instruction, with just a filename and a value, that manages to split the image into the eight components required to build a seamless and expandable border.

Example 19.5:

```
1.  <!DOCTYPE html>
2.  <html>
3.    <head>
4.      <title>Single Border Image</title>
5.      <style>
6.        .border {
7.          font-family  : 'Times New Roman';
8.          text-align   : center;
9.          padding      : 33px;
10.         width        : 100px;
11.         height       : 150px;
12.         border-width : 102px;
13.         border-style : dotted;
```

```
14.              border-image : url('border.png') 102; }
15.    </style>
16.  </head>
17.  <body>
18.    <center>
19.      <div class='border'>
20.        <h2>An</h2>
21.        <h1>Image</h1>
22.        <h2>Border</h2>
23.      </div>
24.    </center>
25.  </body>
26.</html>
```

Just the **border-image** property, all on its own, will load an image and extract it into the parts required, then place them where they belong. How does it perform this, with what looks like magic, using only a single value of 102? Well, in a way, it is a little like magic because that value is all that the browser needs to be told about the image, as you can see from *Figure 19.8*.

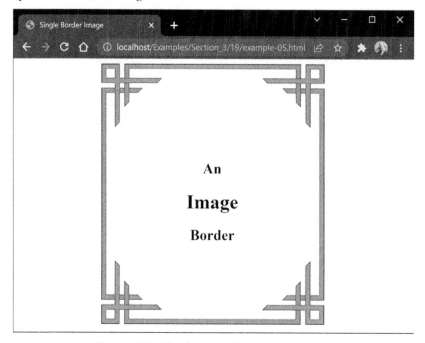

Figure 19.8: *A border created from a single image*

The web browser will have already determined that the image is 205 **x** 205 pixels, so when you provide a value of 102 pixels, it understands that each of the corners must be 102 **x** 102 pixels in dimension, and whatever is left between the corners is to be used for the edges, and that's it.

But what, if a different value were supplied instead of 102? Well, then a smaller section of each corner would be used in the element corners, while the edge sections would grow larger. For example, with a value of 75 the result would look like *Figure 19.9*, which is different but still looks fairly good.

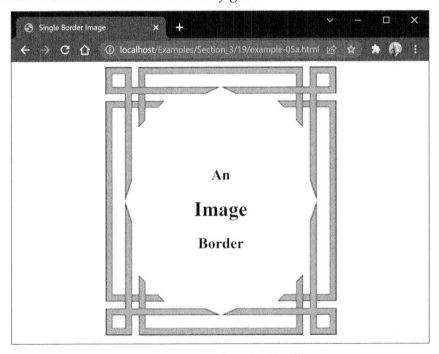

Figure 19.9: The image has been sliced in different ways

Conclusion

Following the last few chapters, this completes our investigation into backgrounds, borders, and images. In the next chapter, we'll learn how to add shadows to elements, how to specify the type of overflow to use when there's more content than will fit in an element. We will also understand how to work with columns.

CHAPTER 20

Box and Text Properties

Introduction

In this chapter, we'll take a look at some of the CSS3 effects you can apply to box-shaped elements, such as adding shadows, managing overflow when the content of an element is greater than there is room for it to fit, and flowing text across columns.

Although only three features are covered in the chapter, they are fundamental ones for good layout and styling, and therefore, it's worth spending a little time to examine them in detail.

Structure

In this chapter, you will:

- Learn how to add a variety of shadows to elements

- Understand how to control every aspect of element overflow

- Discover how to flow text across multiple columns

- Learn how to enhance the column text with automatic and manual hyphenation

Objectives

In this chapter, the objective is to provide a set of three powerful styling features to your toolkit. We will also look at the ins and outs of using them, as well as other CSS features you can combine with them for the best effect. By the time you complete reading this chapter, you will have mastered all you need to know about shadows, text overflow, and multiple columns.

Adding shadows

A simple yet effective way to emphasize content and make it stand out from the page is to apply a shadow of some sort underneath it. With CSS3, you can now do so in a variety of different ways, in any color you choose, in various directions, and inside elements too.

In *Example 20.1,* a wide selection of box shadow types are created, both outside and inside the elements.

Example 20.1:

```
1.  <!DOCTYPE html>
2.  <html>
3.    <head>
4.      <title>Box Shadows</title>
5.      <style>
6.        .boxa    { width      : 120px;
7.                   height     : 100px;                          }
8.        .boxb    { width      : 280px;
9.                   height     : 100px;                          }
10.       .all     { background : cyan;
11.                  float      : left;
12.                  margin     : 10px;
13.                  border     : 10px solid red;                 }
14.       .shadow1 { box-shadow : -6px -6px 10px #888;            }
15.       .shadow2 { box-shadow :  6px -6px 10px #888;            }
16.       .shadow3 { box-shadow : -6px  6px 10px #888;            }
17.       .shadow4 { box-shadow :  6px  6px 10px #888;            }
18.       .shadow5 { box-shadow : -6px -6px 10px #888 inset; }
19.       .shadow6 { box-shadow :  6px -6px 10px #888 inset; }
```

```
20.        .shadow7 { box-shadow :  -6px   6px 10px #888 inset; }
21.        .shadow8 { box-shadow :   6px   6px 10px #888 inset; }
22.        .shadow9 { box-shadow :   0px   0px 20px #000;       }
23.        .shadowa { box-shadow :   0px   0px 20px #000 inset; }
24.    </style>
25.   </head>
26.   <body>
27.    <div class='boxa all shadow1'></div>
28.    <div class='boxa all shadow2'></div>
29.    <div class='boxa all shadow3'></div>
30.    <div class='boxa all shadow4'></div>
31.    <div class='boxa all shadow5'></div>
32.    <div class='boxa all shadow6'></div>
33.    <div class='boxa all shadow7'></div>
34.    <div class='boxa all shadow8'></div>
35.    <div class='boxb all shadow9'></div>
36.    <div class='boxb all shadowa'></div>
37.   </body>
38. </html>
```

As shown in *Figure 20.1*, the values applied to the box-shadow property are the horizontal and vertical offset (with positive or negative values), followed by the amount of blur, the color, and then whether the shadow should be inset.

Figure 20.1: *A variety of different shadow types*

The **boxa** class creates square-shaped elements for the first eight boxes in *Figure 20.1*, while the **boxb** class creates the final two rectangular boxes. The **all** class is used by all of them to specify the color, margins, float, and border width and color.

Then, there are 10 classes for creating different types of shadows. The first four, in turn, create a shadow at the top-left, top-right, bottom-left and bottom-right corners of an element. The next four are similar except that the shadows are inset into each box. Finally, the last two classes create shadows, one outside and one inside the element. The elements in the **<body>** section are then used to display each of these classes.

One point to note here is that when offsetting a shadow, it is better to use shadow colors that are not too dark, or they can overwhelm the element they are shadowing. But, shadows that are in place with no offset may need to use darker colors, as most of their body will be obscured by the border.

Element overflow

One of the problems with making the text fit, until CSS3, was how to deal with text that is the wrong size to cleanly fit within an element. All you could do before was crudely set the overall **overflow** property to one of **hidden**, **visible**, **scroll**, or **auto**. But now you have greater control because you can apply these to just the horizontal or vertical directions if you wish, using the **overflow-x** and **overflow-y** properties.

Example 20.2 shows four combinations of these values in use by creating a class for applying each one.

Example 20.2:

```
1.  <!DOCTYPE html>
2.  <html>
3.    <head>
4.      <title>Element Overflow</title>
5.      <style>
6.        .box      { float          : left;
7.                    background      : yellow;
8.                    margin-right    : 60px;
9.                    font-size       : 20px;
10.                   border          : 1px solid #000;
11.                   width           : 100px;
12.                   height          : 100px;     }
13.        .visible-x { overflow-x    : visible; }
```

```
14.        .hidden-x  { overflow-x   : hidden;  }
15.        .scroll-x  { overflow-x   : scroll;  }
16.        .auto-x    { overflow-x   : auto;    }
17.        .visible-y { overflow-y   : visible; }
18.        .hidden-y  { overflow-y   : hidden;  }
19.        .scroll-y  { overflow-y   : scroll;  }
20.        .auto-y    { overflow-y   : auto;    }
21.     </style>
22.   </head>
23.   <body>
24.     <div class='box visible-x visible-y'>
25.        ExtraWideWord The quick brown fox jumps over
26.        the lazy sleeping dog</div>
27.     <div class='box hidden-x visible-y'>
28.        ExtraWideWord The quick brown fox jumps over
29.        the lazy sleeping dog</div>
30.     <div class='box visible-x hidden-y'>
31.        ExtraWideWord The quick brown fox jumps over
32.        the lazy sleeping dog</div>
33.     <div class='box auto-x auto-y'>
34.        ExtraWideWord The quick brown fox jumps over
35.        the lazy sleeping dog</div>
36.   </body>
37. </html>
```

The first element on line 23 has no scrolling and all the text is visible, flowing out of the element in a mess. The other elements, however, contain their contents in a variety of different ways, as shown in *Figure 20.2*.

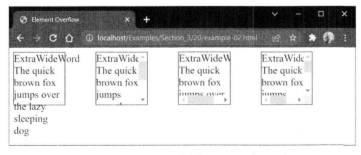

Figure 20.2: *A variety of different overflow values*

Try modifying this example yourself by switching the classes applied to the **<div>** elements to see the effects you can achieve. Sometimes, you will notice that while the **overflow-x** or **overflow-y** property is set to **visible**, the contents of the element doesn't actually display outside it. This is because according to the W3C specifications, some combinations with the **visible** argument are not possible and if one is specified as **visible**, while the other is either **scroll** or **auto**, then the **visible** value will be changed to **auto** by default.

Multi column layout

Before the advent of multi-column support, the web developers had to manually break up text into separate chunks, placing them in different elements if they wished for it to display in columns. Not only was this clumsy and inefficient, if the user's browser was not within a fairly tight sight of dimensional constraints, the layout could end up looking quite different to what the creator intended.

It's possible to flow text across as many columns as you wish, just like with newspapers, automating the whole process and also supporting browsers of widely varying dimensions.

In *Example 20.3*, a section from *Shakespeare's Richard III* is flowed over five columns, with a 1 em gap between each column and a one-pixel line divider.

Example 20.3:

```
1.  <!DOCTYPE html>
2.  <html>
3.    <head>
4.    <title>Multiple Columns</title>
5.    <style>
6.      .columns {
7.        text-align   : justify;
8.        font-size    : 16pt;
9.        column-count : 5;
10.       column-gap   : 1em;
11.       column-rule  : 1px solid black; }
12.     </style>
13.   </head>
14.   <body>
15.     <div class='columns'>
```

16.   Now is the winter of our discontent

17.   Made glorious summer by this sun of York;

18.   And all the clouds that lour'd upon our house

19.   In the deep bosom of the ocean buried.

20.   Now are our brows bound with victorious wreaths;

21.   Our bruised arms hung up for monuments;

22.   Our stern alarums changed to merry meetings,

23.   Our dreadful marches to delightful measures.

24.   Grim-visaged war hath smooth'd his wrinkled front;

25.   And now, instead of mounting barded steeds

26.   To fright the souls of fearful adversaries,

27.   He capers nimbly in a lady's chamber

28.   To the lascivious pleasing of a lute.

29.   But I, that am not shaped for sportive tricks,

30.   Nor made to court an amorous looking-glass;

31.   I, that am rudely stamp'd, and want love's majesty

32.   To strut before a wanton ambling nymph;

33.   I, that am curtail'd of this fair proportion,

34.   Cheated of feature by dissembling nature,

35.   Deformed, unfinish'd, sent before my time

36.   Into this breathing world, scarce half made up,

37.   And that so lamely and unfashionable

38.   That dogs bark at me as I halt by them;

39.   Why, I, in this weak piping time of peace,

40.   Have no delight to pass away the time,

41.   Unless to spy my shadow in the sun

42.   And descant on mine own deformity:

43.   And therefore, since I cannot prove a lover,

44.   To entertain these fair well-spoken days,

45.   I am determined to prove a villain

46.   And hate the idle pleasures of these days.

47.   Plots have I laid, inductions dangerous,

48.   By drunken prophecies, libels and dreams,

```
49.        To set my brother Clarence and the king
50.        In deadly hate the one against the other:
51.        And if King Edward be as true and just
52.        As I am subtle, false and treacherous,
53.        This day should Clarence closely be mew'd up,
54.        About a prophecy, which says that 'G'
55.        Of Edward's heirs the murderer shall be.
56.        Dive, thoughts, down to my soul: here
57.        Clarence comes.
58.     </div>
59.     </body>
60.</html>
```

The result of loading this into a browser looks as shown in *Figure 20.3*.

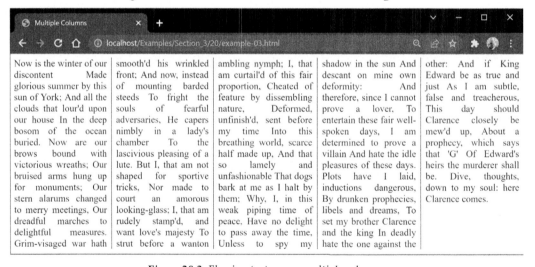

Figure 20.3: Flowing text across multiple columns

Try loading this example into a desktop browser and see how the text flows and reformats as you change the browser's dimensions. As you will see, this way of creating columns is highly fluid and responsive.

One thing you may notice, though, is that when there are a couple of longer words on a line, it may show an inordinate amount of whitespace to handle the formatting. To correct this, you can apply a couple of additional CSS rules to insert hyphens in long words, as in *Example 20.4*, which features two new rules on lines 11 and 12: **word-break** and **hyphens**.

Example 20.4 (just the start and head section):

```
1.  <!DOCTYPE html>
2.  <html lang='en'>
3.    <head>
4.    <title>Multiple Columns</title>
5.    <style>
6.      .columns {
7.        text-align   : justify;
8.        font-size    : 16pt;
9.        column-count : 5;
10.       column-gap   : 1em;
11.       word-break   : break-word;
12.       hyphens      : auto;
13.       column-rule  : 1px solid black; }
14.   </style>
15.   </head>
```

For these two rules to work correctly, it is important that the language must be specified in the **<html>** element. That has also been added on line 2 to select the English language (of any variety). The result of making these changes results in a much neater display, as shown in *Figure 20.4*.

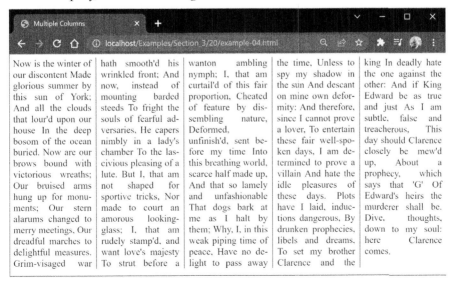

Figure 20.4: *Whitespace is reduced using auto hyphenation*

You can actually use the **word-break** and **hyphens** rules in any text, not just with columns. Though its in the creation of columns where they are generally most useful because they tend to be narrower.

The **word-break** property supports values of **normal**, **break-all**, **keep-all**, and **break-word**, which is the one used in this example. The **hyphens** property supports values of **none**, **manual**, and **auto**, which is also the one used in this example.

Even though *Figure 20.4* looks much improved than the previous one, it still suffers from some unwanted whitespace. You can correct that manually using the HTML **­** entity, which you can place at sensible potential break locations in long words. They will only be replaced with hyphens if the word needs to be broken at the line end. In *Example 20.5*, a number of these entities have been added to the text.

Example 20.5 (just the text section):

```
17. <div class='columns'>
18.    Now is the winter of our dis&shy;con&shy;tent
19.    Made glor&shy;ious sum&shy;mer by this sun of York;
20.    And all the clouds that lour'd upon our house
21.    In the deep bosom of the ocean buried.
22.    Now are our brows bound with vic&shy;tor&shy;ious wreaths;
23.    Our bruised arms hung up for monu&shy;ments;
24.    Our stern alar&shy;ums changed to merry mee&shy;tings,
25.    Our drea&shy;dful marches to delight&shy;ful mea&shy;sures.
26.    Grim-visaged war hath smooth'd his wrink&shy;led front;
27.    And now, instead of mount&shy;ing barded steeds
28.    To fright the souls of fear&shy;ful adver&shy;saries,
29.    He capers nimbly in a lady's chamber
30.    To the las&shy;civ&shy;ious plea&shy;sing of a lute.
31.    But I, that am not shaped for sport&shy;ive tricks,
32.    Nor made to court an amor&shy;ous looking-glass;
33.    I, that am rudely stamp'd, and want love's maj&shy;esty
34.    To strut before a wanton ambling nymph;
35.    I, that am cur&shy;tail'd of this fair prop&shy;ortion,
36.    Cheated of fea&shy;ture by dis&shy;semb&shy;ling nature,
37.    Defor&shy;med, unfin&shy;ish'd, sent before my time
38.    Into this brea&shy;thing world, scarce half made up,
```

39.　　And that so lamely and un­fash­ion­able

40.　　That dogs bark at me as I halt by them;

41.　　Why, I, in this weak pip­ing time of peace,

42.　　Have no de­light to pass away the time,

43.　　Unless to spy my shadow in the sun

44.　　And des­cant on mine own deform­ity:

45.　　And there­fore, since I cannot prove a lover,

46.　　To enter­tain these fair well-spoken days,

47.　　I am deter­mined to prove a villain

48.　　And hate the idle plea­sures of these days.

49.　　Plots have I laid, induc­tions danger­ous,

50.　　By drunken proph­ecies, libels and dreams,

51.　　To set my brother Clar­ence and the king

52.　　In deadly hate the one against the other:

53.　　And if King Edward be as true and just

54.　　As I am subtle, false and treach­erous,

55.　　This day should Clar­ence closely be mew'd up,

56.　　About a proph­ecy, which says that 'G'

57.　　Of Edward's heirs the murd­erer shall be.

58.　　Dive, thoughts, down to my soul: here

59.　　Clar­ence comes.

60. </div>

The result of these changes looks like *Figure 20.5.*

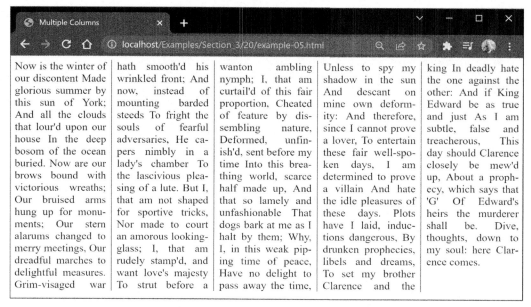

Figure 20.5: Some manual hyphen suggestions have been added

While this may seem a bit annoying to do, in cases where you are certain you want the output to look as good as possible, regardless of the dimension used by the browser, this extra effort can make all the difference. You can add as many **­** entities as you like to further hone the display until you are fully satisfied, even multiple times in a single word, because only the ones that find themselves at the end of a line will be used.

What's also great about this is that **­** works in all text, not just in columns, so if any of your web copy needs to be used elsewhere, perhaps in wider columns or not even in columns at all, the **­** entities you add will not insert the hyphens where they aren't wanted.

It is possible that you may never be able to attain the perfect whitespace for all browser dimensions, but you can ensure your text displays as well as it possibly can in the majority of cases.

Conclusion

This chapter has helped you add several new features to your styling toolkit with the appropriate application of box and text properties, including manual and automatic hyphenation within your text, reformatting text into multi-column layout, applying shadows effectively, and logical handling of text when it overflows. In the next chapter, we'll continue the process by looking into all the things you can achieve with colors and opacity.

CHAPTER 21
Colors and Opacity

Introduction

You may not realize (or even know that you needed it) but the way you can create colors has been vastly improved with CSS3, by the addition of the **rgb()**, **rgba()**, **hsl()**, and **hsla()** functions. With them, you have total control over any color, including its red, green, and blue components, its exact hue, its saturation and also the luminance to apply, as well as the amount of alpha transparency to use.

No more are you restricted to using the pre-defined color names or having to work with hexadecimal color strings. Nowadays, you can think more like you would when using a graphics program by selecting colors from color wheels, or by selecting luminance and transparency independently.

Structure

In this chapter, you will:

- Understand how to use the RGB color space
- Learn how to apply colors in the HSL color space
- Understand how to make use of alpha transparency
- Be able to combine different color types to great effect

Objectives

In this chapter, you will fully familiarize yourself with all the different ways you can now place colors in your web documents using CSS3. By the time, you finish reading this chapter, you will be a master color creator with a wide range of tools and techniques at your disposal.

RGB colors

The RGB color system is one you will likely be very familiar with due to how CSS works. It accepts color values of the form **#RGB** or **#RRGGBB**. For example, **#000** is totally black and **#FFF** is completely white, with **#F00** being red, **#0F0** being green, while **#00F** is blue, with a total of 16 **x** 16 **x** 16 (or 4,096) possible colors using the single-color digit format, such as **#FEB** for the color peach.

Or there's the double digit format supporting 256 × 256 × 256 (or over 16 million) possible colors, such as **#FFE5B4** for a particular and much more precisely defined shade of the color peach. And, as you will know, you don't have to use uppercase alpha characters in the hex names because **#feb** is also peach, as is **#ffe5b4**.

Of course, when you don't need precise color matching, you also have the option of just using one of 147 supported color names. These have the advantage of being instantly recognizable at a glance when viewing style sheets for the first time; for example, with such interesting names as **antiquewhite** or **lightseagreen**, and so on.

But now in CSS3, you can use the **rgb()** function to set the RGB values you need, and what's more you are not limited to using hexadecimal strings because you can use decimal numbers between 0 and 255, or percentage values between 0 and 100. For example, **rgb(255, 229, 180)** and **rgb(100%, 90%, 70%)** are exactly (and almost exactly for the percent values) the same color peach as **#FFe5B4**.

In *Example 21.1*, in order to make what could otherwise be a very long document much shorter, the templating feature we first encountered in *Chapter 18, Creating Backgrounds* is employed to populate the **<output>** element on line 10 with a thousand **<div>** statements, showing a range of different RGB values applied to them via the **rgb()** function.

Example 21.1:

```
1.  <!DOCTYPE html>
2.  <html>
3.    <head>
4.      <title>RGB Colors</title>
```

```
5.     <style>
6.       div { height : 1px; }
7.     </style>
8.   </head>
9.   <body>
10.    <output id='output'></output>
11.    <script>
12.      for (j = 0 ; j < 101 ; j += 10) {
13.        for (k = 0 ; k < 101 ; k += 10) {
14.          for (l = 0 ; l < 101 ; l += 10) {
15.            document.getElementById('output').innerHTML +=
16.           `<div style='background:rgb(${j}%, ${k}%, ${l}%)'></div>\n`
17.          }
18.        }
19.      }
20.    </script>
21.  </body>
22. </html>
```

The result of loading the example into a browser is shown in *Figure 21.1*. When viewing the output, you can change the zoom level of your browser to zoom in and out of the fine detail in the color bands.

In this example, three nested JavaScript loops are entered starting on line 12 in the **<script>** section. These increment the variables **j**, **k**, and **l** with values starting from 0 up to 100, in steps of 10 at a time. The result is that the **l** variable in the inner loop continuously loops through the values 0, 10, 20, and so on up to 100, then starts again, with the **k** variable in the middle loop then incremented by 10, and the inner loop re-looping, and so on, until the outer loop finally gets to increment by 10 after 100 **<div>** elements have been processed (and every 100 thereafter). In the end, the inner loop will go through a thousand iterations, the middle loop through a hundred, and the outer one by ten iterations.

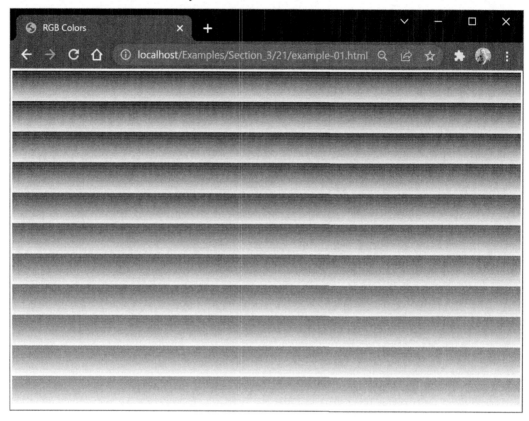

Figure 21.1: A color band chart of RGB color combinations

This results in a range of values of red, green, and blue being applied to the **rgb()** function on line 16, as percentages between 0 and 100, stepping by 10. The code *can* step through all the loops just incrementing by 1, but this would result in 100 × 100 × 100 (or a million) **<div>** elements, which would take a long time to produce and would probably crash the browser.

By reducing the overall number of **<div>** elements to a thousand, the code runs fairly fast and we still get to see a good color band chart, in which (if you zoom in using your browser and then scroll through the output) you can see the levels of blue constantly changing in the smallest bands, with green stepping through the next level up of bands, and red stepping through the outermost ten bands.

The work of inserting the required values happens on line 16, where three template values are accessed: **${j}**, **${k}**, and **${l}**. The value currently in the variables each time these template values are accessed is swapped into the string, and then each has a **%** sign appended to it, resulting in supplying percentage values to the **rgb()**

function. As you know by now, this magic works because back ticks have been employed instead of using single or double quotes for the string, thus notifying JavaScript to make template substitutions as necessary.

Following are just the first few of the 1,000 **<div>** elements created, in which you can see the incrementing process in action as described from the outer and middle loops, for the third and second values, while the first values will remain unchanged until 100 **<div>** elements have been created.

```
<div style="background:rgb(0%, 0%, 0%)"></div>
<div style="background:rgb(0%, 0%, 10%)"></div>
<div style="background:rgb(0%, 0%, 20%)"></div>
<div style="background:rgb(0%, 0%, 30%)"></div>
<div style="background:rgb(0%, 0%, 40%)"></div>
<div style="background:rgb(0%, 0%, 50%)"></div>
<div style="background:rgb(0%, 0%, 60%)"></div>
<div style="background:rgb(0%, 0%, 70%)"></div>
<div style="background:rgb(0%, 0%, 80%)"></div>
<div style="background:rgb(0%, 0%, 90%)"></div>
<div style="background:rgb(0%, 0%, 100%)"></div>
<div style="background:rgb(0%, 10%, 0%)"></div>
<div style="background:rgb(0%, 10%, 10%)"></div>
<div style="background:rgb(0%, 10%, 20%)"></div>
<div style="background:rgb(0%, 10%, 30%)"></div>
<div style="background:rgb(0%, 10%, 40%)"></div>
<div style="background:rgb(0%, 10%, 50%)"></div>
<!-- etc… -->
```

If you wish to see the full output from this code, you can insert the following line before the closing **</script>** tag to log a copy of the HTML to the developer console:

```
console.log(document.getElementById('output').innerHTML)
```

Using a color wheel

Color bands are great if you don't mind scrolling through hundreds (or thousands) of lines, but if you want a way to show as many colors as possible at a glance, with them seamlessly transitioning between each other, then a color wheel is a good way to do this.

Example 21.2 uses a conical gradient to create just such a color wheel by using the colors of the rainbow as color stops, with the first and last colors both being the same to complete a smooth color gradient all around, as shown in *Figure 21.2*.

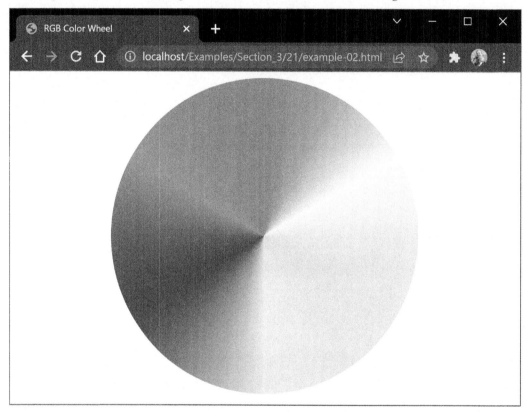

Figure 21.2: *A color wheel created with a conical gradient*

Example 21.2:

```
1. <!DOCTYPE html>
2.   <head>
3.     <title>RGB Color Wheel</title>
4.     <style>
5.       #wheel {
6.         width         : 400px;
7.         height        : 400px;
8.         border-radius : 50%;
```

```
9.          background    : conic-gradient(
10.                            red,  yellow,  lime, aqua,
11.                            blue, magenta, red); }
12.    </style>
13.  </head>
14.  <body>
15.    <center>
16.      <div id='wheel'></div>
17.    </center>
18.  </body>
19. </html>
```

This example applies rules to the **<div>** with the ID of **wheel** to give it a width and height of 400 pixels, a border radius of 50 percent to make it circular, and then applies the sequence of rainbow colors as a clockwise conical gradient, starting at the 12 O'clock position and continuing all the way around.

This color wheel will remain of interest to us throughout this chapter, especially when we start looking at how to use **hue, saturation, and luminance** (**HSL**) in place of RGB because you will note that red occupies a position at 0 degrees from the top, green is at 120 degrees, and blue is at 240 degrees from the top, with all the other colors at locations between these primary colors.

Also, the color space of **cyan, magenta, and yellow** (**CMY**) used when printing on paper (along with black, and so referred to as CMYK), is also visible in this color wheel, at 180 degrees, 300 degrees, and 60 degrees, respectively, all equidistant from the RGB colors.

As you will shortly see, by knowing this, you can uniquely select a color just by specifying a single value – the number of degrees around the color wheel at which it is located, which can be a floating point or integer value.

RGBA colors

One of the advantages of using a function to display colors is that you can use the **rgba()** function in place of **rgb()** if you wish to also make use of transparency, with the **a** standing for alpha transparency.

To see how this works, *Example 21.3* draws a yellow background and then overlays it with a gradient going from fully opaque blue on the left, to being fully transparent on the right.

Example 21.3:

```
1.  <!DOCTYPE html>
2.    <head>
3.      <title>Using RGBA</title>
4.      <style>
5.        #outer { position    : relative; }
6.         .box   { position    : absolute;
7.                  width       : 100%;
8.                  height      : 200px;     }
9.        #box1  { background  : yellow;    }
10.       #box2  { top         : 100px;
11.                background  : linear-gradient(to right,
12.                  rgba(0, 0, 255, 1), rgba(0, 0, 255, 0) ); }
13.      </style>
14.    </head>
15.    <body>
16.      <div id='outer'>
17.        <div class='box' id='box1'></div>
18.        <div class='box' id='box2'></div>
19.      </div>
20.    </body>
21. </html>
```

In *Figure 21.3* you can see how this looks when loaded into a browser.

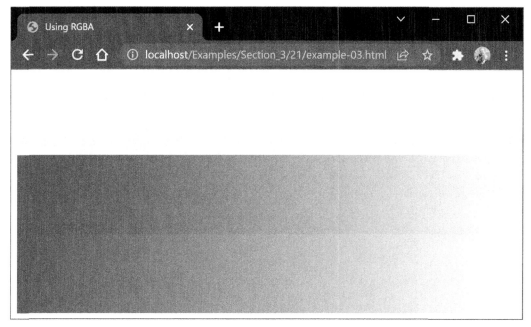

Figure 21.3: A solid and a transparent gradient color overlaid

Here, an element by the name of **outer** is created as a container for two child elements called **box1** and **box2**. A class called **box** is also created with absolute positioning so that **box1** and **box2** will both use that class and can overlay one another. The **box1** element is given a solid yellow background, while **box2** is set to solid blue using the **rgba()** function, using values of 0 red, 0 green and 255 blue. This is applied in a linear gradient with the alpha transparency slowly graduating from fully opaque (with a value of 1) to fully transparent (with a value of 2). In other words, from the first to the second set of values as follows:

```
rgba(0, 0, 255, 1)
rgba(0, 0, 255, 0)
```

The **box2** element also has its top property set to 100 pixels so this it is moved halfway down **box1**, so that the effects of both **box1** and **box2**, and also the result of overlaying the pair can be seen.

In the figure, you will notice three distinct sections. At the top is the solid color yellow, and at the bottom the solid color blue slowly graduates to fully transparent, revealing the white background under it. In the middle though, the blue color slowly graduates through green to yellow, showing the effect of the transparency as it increases, or as the opaqueness decreases (both of them being equivalent), first mixing with and finally revealing the yellow color underneath.

You can use the **rgba()** function anywhere you set a color in your CSS, not just within gradients, but a gradient is used here to show you how precisely you can set the alpha transparency of a color, by showing a wide range of values in a single image.

HSL colors

Now, let's look at the **hsl()** function for creating colors based on their hue, saturation, and luminance, as mentioned a little earlier in this chapter. Ironically though, in order to show you a color wheel with all of hue, saturation, and luminance, *Example 21.4* uses regular color names along with the **rgba()** function to create an HSL color wheel, as shown in *Figure 21.4*:

Example 21.4:

```
1.  <!DOCTYPE html>
2.    <head>
3.      <title>An HSL Color Wheel</title>
4.      <style>
5.        #outer  { position     : relative;
6.                  width        : 400px;
7.                  margin       : auto;                }
8.        .wheel  { position     : absolute;
9.                  width        : 400px;
10.                 height       : 400px;
11.                 border-radius : 50%;               }
12.       #wheel1 { background   : conic-gradient(
13.                  red,  yellow,  lime, aqua,
14.                  blue, magenta, red);               }
15.       #wheel2 { background   : radial-gradient(
16.                  rgba(255, 255, 255, 1),
17.                  rgba(255, 255, 255, 0));           }
18.     </style>
19.   </head>
20.   <body>
21.     <div id='outer'>
22.       <div class='wheel' id='wheel1'></div>
```

```
23.         <div class='wheel' id='wheel2'></div>
24.    </div>
25.  </body>
26. </html>
```

This image has a lot in common with the one created using *Example 21.2*, with the difference being that a second gradient has been overlaid upon the color wheel. This gradient, on line 15, is a radial one which graduates from the center to the outside, drawing white all the way, but starting fully opaque and then transitioning to fully transparent at the circumference.

The reason for this is that the HSL color space not only specifies the color to use (the hue), but also the saturation (the amount of this color), and the luminance (how bright it is). So, in order to get as close to an HSL color wheel as possible, the center of *Figure 21.4* is reduced in saturation and color, which then increases towards the outside.

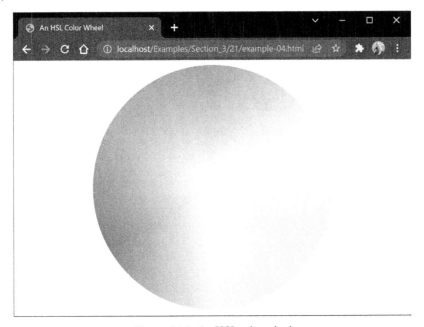

Figure 21.4: An HSL color wheel

Now, this example doesn't produce a perfect HSL color wheel, but it's close enough for us to use the figure to look deeper into how to the **hsl()** function works.

The first value supplied to the function (the hue) is the distance around the color wheel from the top at which the color can be located. This value must be specified in degrees and you may not use percentage values. The second value (the saturation) is then the distance from the center of the color wheel to the edge as a percentage.

At the center, there is little or no color, while the edge represents 100 percent of that color. The final value (luminance) is then a value (not shown on the HSL color wheel) that represents how brightly the color should appear. This value is a percent, of which 50 percent is neutral and the default.

Now that you know how the **hsl()** function works, *Example 21.5* displays a wide range of the supported values in a color band chart, as shown in *Figure 21.5*.

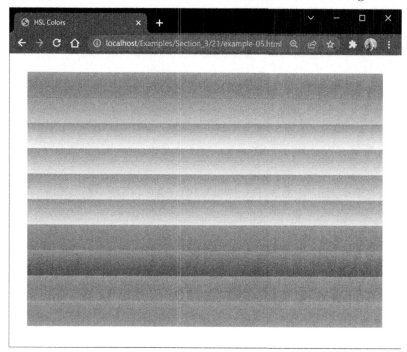

Figure 21.5: *A wide selection of hue and saturation values*

Example 21.5:

```
1.  <!DOCTYPE html>
2.  <html>
3.    <head>
4.      <title>HSL Colors</title>
5.      <style>
6.        div { height : 1px; }
7.      </style>
8.    </head>
9.    <body>
10.     <output id='output'></output>
```

```
11.    <script>
12.      for (j = 0 ; j < 360 ; j += 36) {
13.        for (k = 0 ; k < 101 ; k += 10) {
14.          document.getElementById('output').innerHTML +=
15.          `<div style='background:hsl(${j}, ${k}%, 50%)'></div>\n`
16.        }
17.      }
18.    </script>
19.  </body>
20.</html>
```

Unlike *Example 21.1*, this uses only two loops because the luminance value is pegged at 50 percent. The reason for this is that this is the standard luminance amount, and that any values below it will be much darker, down to black with a value of 0 percent, or much lighter, up to white with a value of 100 percent.

If you wish to see the HTML generated by this code, you can insert the following line just before the closing **</script>** instruction, and you can then view it in the developer console:

```
console.log(document.getElementById('output').innerHTML)
```

Applying transparency

Finally, if you wish to just apply an amount of transparency to an element without specifying any colors, you can use the **opacity** property, as in *Example 21.6*, which displays ten **<div>** elements, each with slightly less opacity.

Example 21.6:

```
1.  <!DOCTYPE html>
2.  <html>
3.    <head>
4.      <title>Opacity</title>
5.      <style>
6.        div {
7.          background : blue;
8.          font       : bold 12pt Monospace;
9.          padding    : 1px 3px; }
10.     </style>
```

```
11.  </head>
12.  <body>
13.    <div style='opacity:0.0'>Opacity:0.0</div>
14.    <div style='opacity:0.1'>Opacity:0.1</div>
15.    <div style='opacity:0.2'>Opacity:0.2</div>
16.    <div style='opacity:0.3'>Opacity:0.3</div>
17.    <div style='opacity:0.4'>Opacity:0.4</div>
18.    <div style='opacity:0.5'>Opacity:0.5</div>
19.    <div style='opacity:0.6'>Opacity:0.6</div>
20.    <div style='opacity:0.7'>Opacity:0.7</div>
21.    <div style='opacity:0.8'>Opacity:0.8</div>
22.    <div style='opacity:0.9'>Opacity:0.9</div>
23.    <div style='opacity:1.0'>Opacity:1.0</div>
24.  </body>
25. </html>
```

Looking at *Figure 21.6* you can see the result of just supplying a value between 0 for no opacity (completely transparent) and 1 for total opacity (no transparency), and that's all you need to do.

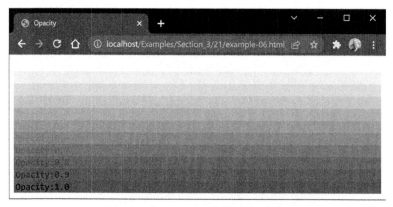

Figure 21.6: Different levels of element opacity

Conclusion

And there you have it. Your learning about the use of CSS3 colors is complete. You are now able to specify exactly the colors you need in a variety of different ways, in a way that best suits the way you think about colors. In the next chapter, it's time to turn our attention to text effects and web fonts.

CHAPTER 22

Text Effects and Fonts

Introduction

When CSS3 was drawn up, styling of text was already quite sophisticated, but there was still a lot more to be achieved if the web was to start rivalling print media in any serious fashion. So, a raft of new features and ways of styling text and fonts was introduced, including the appliance of shadows, overlapping text, types of word wrapping, and breaking out of the need to rely on a browser's or operating system's in-built set of fonts by supporting web fonts, many of which are now available for free from companies such as Google.

The box model was also revisited to add support for box sizing, where you can now decide whether the dimensions you give to an object apply to the element, including any padding and/or border, or just to the contents of an element, with padding and border considered additional to these dimensions.

And to help users manage input areas that are not large enough for their liking, it was made possible to allow them to resize elements, and to aid with seeing where focus is currently located in a document, focus outlining was improved and allowed to be styled.

Structure

In this chapter, you will:

- Discover the ins and outs of box sizing and how it relates to content

- Learn ways to manage how text overflows from an element, or not

- Be able to deal with extra-long words and support user element resizing

- Become fully familiar with applying shadows and using web fonts

Objectives

In this chapter, you will learn a variety of text-related features you will find useful for creating the best possible CSS layouts. This will include how to precisely manage the width and height of elements according to their content, padding and borders, managing overly long words, word breaks and overflow, attaching attractive shadows to text, and downloading and using any of thousands of web fonts to match whatever subject your project is about.

Box sizing

The styling of text is not purely about the text itself because where the text is on the page (or screen), how it flows, and the elements that contain it are also fundamental to the design process. So, before getting into what we can do with fonts and the text itself, let's first look at containers for fonts, in other words their elements and how they can be styled.

When you are designing CSS, do you ever make a mistake because you forgot to calculate for padding and borders? Well, now you can make that a thing of the past because you can specify right at the start how the dimension values you give will be applied.

The default **box-sizing** property value for dimensions in CSS is for the width and height of an element to refer to the content area within it with the value **content-box**, ignoring any padding or border. It is equivalent to issuing this rule:

```
box-sizing: content-box;
```

But you can also choose to give an element an excact width and height using the value **border-box**, forcing all margins and borders to fit within that space, using the following rule:

```
box-sizing: border-box;
```

When you do so, whatever width of border or padding may be specified must all squeeze inside the area you specify, reducing the content part as necessary. *Example 22.1* creates a pair of identical elements, with the only difference between them being that the **box-sizing** property of one is **content-box**, and the other is **border-box**.

Example 22.1:

```
1.  <!DOCTYPE html>
2.  <html>
3.    <head>
4.      <title>Box sizing</title>
5.      <style>
6.        .box   { font             : bold 14pt serif;
7.                 border           : 10px solid red;
8.                 width            : 200px;
9.                 height           : 100px;
10.                padding          : 20px;
11.                margin-right     : 20px;
12.                float            : left;
13.                display          : flex;
14.                justify-content  : center;
15.                align-items      : center;
16.                text-align       : center;
17.                color            : blue;
18.                background       : lime;
19.                background-clip  : content-box; }
20.       #box1 { box-sizing       : content-box; }
21.       #box2 { box-sizing       : border-box;  }
22.     </style>
23.   </head>
24.   <body>
25.     <div class='box' id='box1'>Living in a box</div>
26.     <div class='box' id='box2'>Living in a box</div>
27.   </body>
28. </html>
```

Both these elements use a class called **box** to set up the font color and styling, and to apply a 10-pixel red border, as well as 20 pixels of padding all around. The other CSS rules set the element to 200 × 100 pixels, and ensure that the elements float on a single line, and that the contents are centered. Additionally, the **background-clip** property of this class is set to just the **content-box** area so that the lime background shows exactly the bounds of the content area in each case:

As shown in *Figure 22.1*, you will see that the first element indeed has a 10-pixel red border, within which is 20 pixels of padding, and then the 200 × 100-pixel content area with some text in it.

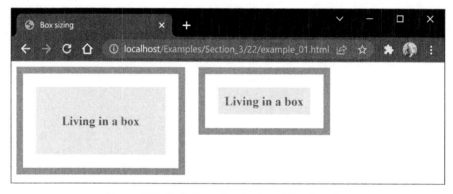

Figure 22.1: Default and border box sizing in action

On the other hand, the second element, including padding and border, is exactly the dimensions of just the content area of the first. This is because the **box-sizing** property is set to **border-box** for the second element, and therefore all the border and padding is forced to fit *within* the width and height given of 200 × 100 pixels. The result is that the content area is reduced to whatever space remains, which in this case 140 × 40 pixels, after subtracting 20 pixels padding and 10 pixels border from each side, for a total of 60 pixels reduction in each dimension.

Where this property is likely to come in most useful is conditions where the padding and/or borders of elements in a layout might change independently. If you force these parts of an element to be within the width and height your layout provides it by setting the **box-sizing** property of such elements to **border-box**, then these events can change, or even worse, break your layout design.

Text overflow

Sometimes, you may wish to truncate text short, such as in cases like the Google search engine which often quotes text from websites but then cuts it short with an ellipsis, or three dots meaning etcetera, like this …

The result can be seen in *Figure 22.2*.

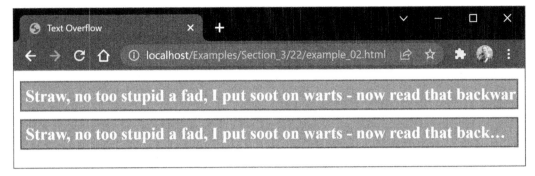

Figure 22.2: The overflow of text is truncated in two different ways

This is a neat way to create excerpts of a certain size, whilst making it clear to readers what is going on. Without this feature, excerpts may appear to end somewhat abruptly and unsatisfyingly. *Example 22.2* creates a couple of elements, each containing the same content, but with the overflow handled differently, as shown in *Figure 22.2*, where the second element neatly cuts off the text at a suitable place in the word with an ellipsis.

Example 22.2:

```
1.  <!DOCTYPE html>
2.  <html>
3.   <head>
4.    <title>Text Overflow</title>
5.    <style>
6.      .box  { font        : bold 16pt serif;
7.              border      : 2px solid blue;
8.              width       : 640px;
9.              padding     : 5px;
10.             margin      : 5px 0;
11.             float       : left;
12.             color       : yellow;
13.             background  : olive;
14.             white-space : nowrap;
15.             overflow    : hidden;    }
16.     #box1 { text-overflow : clip;     }
17.     #box2 { text-overflow : ellipsis; }
18.    </style>
19.   </head>
```

```
20.    <body>
21.      <div class='box' id='box1'>Straw, no too stupid a fad,
22.        I put soot on warts - now read that backwards.</div>
23.      <div class='box' id='box2'>Straw, no too stupid a fad,
24.        I put soot on warts - now read that backwards.</div>
25.    </body>
26. </html>
```

For the **text-overflow** property to have any effect, you will first need to set the **white-space** property to **nowrap** and **overflow** to **hidden**. Without the **white-space** property set to the **nowrap** text will just flow, wrapping down a line at a time, and without the **overflow** property set to **hidden**, it will then flow on outside the element if it needs to, resulting in a mess.

Wrapping long words

In *Chapter 20, Box and Text Properties*, we saw how to automatically make words break and wrap to the following line if they would run past the boundaries of an element. But there's an edge case it doesn't account for, which is when you have a word which itself in its entirety is wider than the element it is in. For instances such as this, you can use the **word-wrap** property with a value of **break-word** which will then force long words to always wrap, as follows:

```
word-wrap : break-word;
```

In *Example 22.3*, three elements are created, with each one displaying an example of the same very long word, namely, Antidisestablishmentarianism. This is clearly too wide for the containing element, and so its overflow is handled in different ways, as shown in *Figure 22.3*.

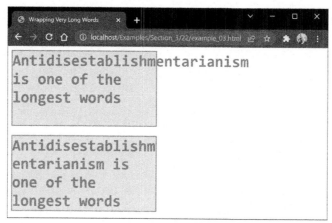

***Figure 22.3**: A very long word is handled in two different ways*

Example 22.3:

```
1.  <!DOCTYPE html>
2.  <html>
3.    <head>
4.    <title>Wrapping Very Long Words</title>
5.    <style>
6.      .wrap  { border     : 2px solid olive;
7.               font       : bold 24pt monospace;
8.               width      : 300px;
9.               height     : 150px;
10.              background  : lime;
11.              color       : purple;     }
12.      #wrap1 { word-wrap  : normal;      }
13.      #wrap2 { word-wrap  : break-word;  }
14.    </style>
15.   </head>
16.  <body>
17.    <div class='wrap' id='wrap1'>
18.      Antidisestablishmentarianism
19.      is one of the longest words
20.    </div>
21.    <br>
22.    <div class='wrap' id='wrap2'>
23.      Antidisestablishmentarianism
24.      is one of the longest words
25.    </div>
26.  </body>
27.</html>
```

In this example, element overflow is not set to hidden so that we can see what's going on more clearly. In the first element, the long word overflows its bounds because the **word-wrap** property is set to **normal** such that, if overflow were hidden, we simply wouldn't see the second half of the word as it would be invisible. But in the second element, the **word-wrap** property is set to **break-word** and thus the long word is broken in order to make it fit the element, by placing the remainder of the word on the following line.

User resizing of elements

There are times when you can help your users by allowing them to break out of the constraints of the layout you have created for them by letting them drag a corner of an element to resize it. An excellent place for doing this is in an input field where you have provided sufficient space for most purposes, but you wish to allow the user to enter more data should they wish, not just by letting them scroll (not always the best option for small elements), but by resizing an element to suit their liking.

In *Example 22.4*, there are four different elements created: two **\<div\>** elements, an **\<output\>** element, and also a **\<table\>**. The first of these doesn't support user resizing as its **resize** property is given the value **none**, while the others do as they are given various values.

Example 22.4:

```
 1.  <!DOCTYPE html>
 2.  <html>
 3.    <head>
 4.    <title>Element Resizing</title>
 5.    <style>
 6.      .box  { border       : 2px solid purple;
 7.              font          : bold 12pt Arial;
 8.              margin-right  : 10px;
 9.              width         : 100px;
10.              height        : 100px;
11.              background    : darkorange;
12.              color         : yellow;
13.              overflow      : auto;
14.              float         : left;          }
15.      #box1 { resize        : none;          }
16.      #box2 { resize        : horizontal;    }
17.      #box3 { resize        : vertical;      }
18.      #box4 { resize        : both;          }
19.    </style>
```

```
20.   </head>
21.  <body>
22.    <div class='box' id='box1'>
23.      Twas brillig, and the slithy toves did gyre
24.      and gimble in the wabe; all mimsy were the
25.      borogoves, and the mome raths outgrabe.
26.    </div>
27.    <div class='box' id='box2'>
28.      Twas brillig, and the slithy toves did gyre
29.      and gimble in the wabe; all mimsy were the
30.      borogoves, and the mome raths outgrabe.
31.    </div>
32.    <output class='box' id='box3'>
33.      Twas brillig, and the slithy toves did gyre
34.      and gimble in the wabe; all mimsy were the
35.      borogoves, and the mome raths outgrabe.
36.    </output>
37.    <table>
38.      <tr>
39.        <td class='box' id='box4'>
40.          Twas brillig, and the slithy toves did gyre
41.          and gimble in the wabe; all mimsy were the
42.          borogoves, and the mome raths outgrabe.
43.        </td>
44.      </tr>
45.    </table>
46.  </body>
47. </html>
```

In this example, the first element is not given an option for user resizing and so only scrollbars are available. The second element has been allowed to be resized only in the horizontal direction, the third one only in the vertical direction, while the last element has been given full reign to be resized in both directions. In *figure 22.4*, you can see the effect of three of the elements having been resized in this manner.

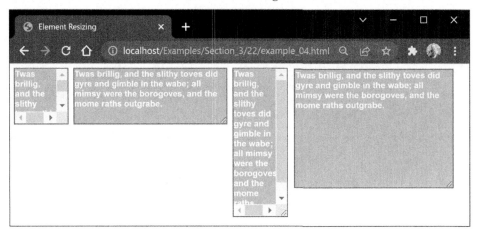

Figure 22.4: The four possible resizing settings in use

This has been achieved by supplying values to the **resize** property of **none**, **horizontal**, **vertical**, and **both**, respectively, in the IDs **box1**, **box2**, **box3**, and **box4**. If you look closely at the bottom right-hand corners of elements two to four, you'll see a small icon with two diagonal lines, which indicates to the user that the element is resizable, and with which the corner can be dragged.

Outlining focus

Since there's no other obvious place to explain the **outline-offset** property, since we've just been talking about resizing user input, here's just as good a place as any. Using this property, you can enlarge the outline that gets placed around an element when it gains focus.

Example 22.5 creates three different elements, all of which are able to gain focus, and which you can then tab through or otherwise give focus to in order to see the result.

Example 22.5:

```
1.  <!DOCTYPE html>
2.  <html>
3.    <head>
4.      <title>Outline</title>
5.      <style>
6.        html           { font          : bold 14pt Arial; }
7.        html *:focus { outline          : dashed thick;
```

```
8.                         outline-offset : 10px;                    }
9.    </style>
10.   </head>
11.   <body>
12.     <ul>
13.       <p><a href='nowhere'>A link</a></p>
14.       <p><input type='text'></p>
15.       <p><a href='alsonowhere'>Another link</a></p>
16.     </ul>
17.   </body>
18. </html>
```

The **outline-offset** property supports all CSS size values such as **10px, 0.2em,** and so forth. The result of this example can be seen in *Figure 22.5*.

Figure 22.5: The input element has been given focus and is outlined offset by 10 pixels

Text shadows

In *Chapter 20, Box and Text Properties,* we looked into giving shadows to elements. Now, let's see how that's done directly to text using the **text-shadow** property. In *Example 22.6*, this property is used four times in different classes, placing shadows to the top-left, top-right, bottom-left, and bottom-right of an element, respectively.

Example 22.6:

```
1. <!DOCTYPE html>
2. <html>
3.   <head>
4.     <title>Text Shadows</title>
5.     <style>
```

```
6.        .shadow  { color     : blue;
7.                    font      : bold 64pt Arial ;    }
8.       #shadow1 { text-shadow : -5px -5px 8px #555; }
9.       #shadow2 { text-shadow :  5px -5px 8px #555; }
10.      #shadow3 { text-shadow : -5px  5px 8px #555; }
11.      #shadow4 { text-shadow :  5px  5px 8px #555; }
12.    </style>
13.    </head>
14.    <body>
15.     <center>
16.      <span class='shadow' id='shadow1'>Me</span>    
17.      <span class='shadow' id='shadow2'>and</span>  
18.      <span class='shadow' id='shadow3'>my</span>    
19.      <span class='shadow' id='shadow4'>shadow</span>
20.     </center>
21.    </body>
22. </html>
```

The values you supply to the **text-shadow** property are the vertical and horizontal offset, which can be negative, zero, or positive, followed by the number of pixels over which to extend the blurring effect, and finally the color to use. The result of loading this example into a browser is shown in *Figure 22.6*.

Figure 22.6: A selection of differently offset shadows

The greater the offset the more the text stands out from the page, to an extent that is, because it's possible to go too far. The blurring you apply will be very sharp and strongly colored with low values, and higher values will disperse more and be fuzzier and lighter. For the color, you generally may wish to use a shade of grey or black, unless there is a tint to the page background that you'd like to match.

If you omit the color, then the text color will be used. If you also omit the blurring then an exact copy of the text will be placed underneath at the offset specified, without any blur. You must, however, supply both values for the offset.

Web fonts

Last, but absolutely not least in this chapter, it's time to examine the plethora of web fonts at your disposal. As with fonts in general, you can buy them individually, in packages or on a subscription basis, for serving from your own or another web server. Or there truly is a massive library available totally free on sites such as Google Fonts, from where we'll fetch the fonts for this section.

For example, to import the Google font called **Dancing Script,** you would place an instruction such as the following in the **<head>** of a document:

```
<link rel="stylesheet"
 href="https://fonts.googleapis.com/css2?family=Dancing+Script">
```

This informs the browser that it must import a CSS stylesheet and tells it where that stylesheet is located. Having done that, you can refer to the font from CSS, perhaps by creating a class called **dancing** to apply it, as follows:

```
.dancing { font-family : "Dancing Script", cursive, serif; }
```

Now, you can simply use the class in any element to have its content displayed using that font, as follows:

```
<span class='dancing'>This is Dancing Script</span>
```

In *Example 22.7*, these instructions have been combined into a single document featuring an excerpt from a poem by *Lewis Carroll*.

Example 22.7:

```
1.  <!DOCTYPE html>
2.  <html>
3.   <head>
4.    <title>Web Fonts</title>
5.    <style>
6.       #poem     { font-size   : 24pt;                              }
7.       .dancing { font-family : "Dancing Script", cursive, serif; }
8.    </style>
9.     <link rel="stylesheet"
10.    href="https://fonts.googleapis.com/css2?family=Dancing+Script">
11.   </head>
12.   <body>
```

```
13.     <div class='dancing' id='poem'>
14.        Twas brillig, and the slithy toves did gyre and gimble
15.        in the wabe; all mimsy were the borogoves, and the mome
16.        raths outgrabe. "Beware the Jabberwock, my son! The jaws
17.        that bite, the claws that catch! Beware the Jubjub bird,
18.        and shun the frumious Bandersnatch!.
19.     </div>
20.  </body>
21.</html>
```

Here, the text to display is in a **<div>** element with the ID of **poem**, and employing the class **dancing**. The **poem** rule simply sets the **font-size** property to a value of **24pt**, while the **dancing** rule applies Dancing Script in the normal way to which a font family is referred, and just in case, the font is unavailable for some reason, sensible alternative font families of **cursive** and **serif** are also given. The font itself is downloaded on lines 9 and 10 via the stylesheet at that URL. The result of this example is shown in *Figure 22.7*.

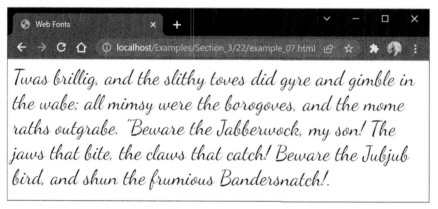

Figure 22.7: *A poem displayed in Google's Dancing Script font*

If you already have access to a font and you simply wish to load it in, you can use the **@font-face** rule, providing a name and the URL where it is located, and from which it should be downloaded by the browser. Both **TrueType** (**.ttf**) and **OpenType** (**.otf**) fonts are accepted, as well as web font format **.woff** and **.woff2** files, like this (assuming you have a font already saved as **Sacramento-Regular. ttf**):

```
1. @font-face {
2.    font-family : "Sacramento Regular";
3.    src         : url('Sacramento-Regular.ttf'); }
```

Then, you can, if you wish, create a class to make accessing the font easier, perhaps looking something like this:

```
.sacramento { font-family : "Sacramento Regular"; }
```

And that's all you need to do before you can use the font in your HTML, as follows:

```
<span class='sacramento'>This is Sacramento Regular</span>
```

Example 22.8 is a revised version of the previous example, modified to load in the font locally in just this manner.

Example 22.8:

```
1.  <!DOCTYPE html>
2.  <html>
3.    <head>
4.      <title>Local Fonts</title>
5.      <style>
6.          #poem       { font-size    : 24pt;                               }
7.          @font-face  { font-family : "Sacramento Regular";
8.                        src           : url('Sacramento-Regular.ttf'); }
9.          .sacramento { font-family : "Sacramento Regular";              }
10.     </style>
11.   </head>
12.   <body>
13.     <div class='sacramento' id='poem'>
14.       Twas brillig, and the slithy toves did gyre and gimble
15.       in the wabe; all mimsy were the borogoves, and the mome
16.       raths outgrabe. "Beware the Jabberwock, my son! The jaws
17.       that bite, the claws that catch! Beware the Jubjub bird,
18.       and shun the frumious Bandersnatch!.
19.     </div>
20.   </body>
21. </html>
```

The result of this example looks like *Figure 22.8*.

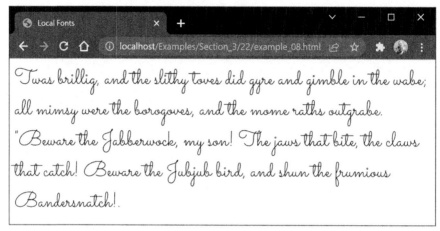

Figure 22.8: A local font has been applied

For a full description of how to import fonts using the **@font-face** rule (either locally as demonstrated here, or from elsewhere on the web) you can visit the following URL, where you will also discover a number of associated properties for fine-tuning font display:

tinyurl.com/cssfont-face

To browse and access the (currently) 1,300+ free fonts provided by Google, check out the following URL, where you can download them to use locally, or if you click on a font you like to select its style, and then click on the icon looking like three squares and a + sign, at the top right-hand corner of the web page (to pop up the Selected Families dialog), you'll be given CSS rules you can copy and paste to use them:

fonts.google.com

However, you don't need to copy and paste that code if you wish to just follow the simple instructions on this page, as long as you copy just the URL of where the stylesheet for the font is located on Google's server and use it in the manner of the examples here, then you should be good to go.

Conclusion

This concludes our examination of a variety of new text, box model, shadow, and font effects available in CSS3. At this point, you should now be a font master capable of building web projects to match the best the print world has to offer. In the next chapter, it's now time to delve into some more advanced and fun features of CSS3, such as playing with transformations to create stunning effects.

CHAPTER 23

2D Transformations

This author was fortunate enough to write on the subject of CSS3 during its development. At the time, the new features were being implemented in a somewhat haphazard function by different browsers. Sometimes, one browser would not support a feature, while a rival would, but not using the standard recommended property names and values. And other times, a browser would go off and implement a feature in a totally different way, and not even end up displaying results in the same way either.

For web developers hankering to use these features it was a bit of a minefield, requiring a lot of conditional code depending on the browser make and operating system detected. But the browser wars are done, with the majority settling on the open-source Chromium source code, as used by *Google Chrome*, *Microsoft Edge,* and the *Opera* browser. And then there's Apple's *Safari*, but it is highly compatible with the others except in a small number of instances.

Introduction

This chapter is much more pleasant and straightforward than it would have been some years ago, both for the author and (hopefully) for you as the reader because there is now a standard set of transformation properties and values that you can apply across all browsers and platforms. In this chapter, therefore, you will discover how easy and logical the handling of two-dimensional transformations has become.

You will also be able to quickly and easily scale and rotate objects as necessary and even skew them for special effects. And should you need them, you'll learn how to use matrixes to create your own transformations and transitions.

Structure

In this chapter, you will:

- Learn about all the 2D transformations possible in CSS3
- Discover how you can combine transitions with transformations
- Be able to scale, rotate, and skew objects at will
- Understand how to use matrixes for combined effects

Objectives

In this chapter, you will learn all there is to know about changing the shape and location of objects. By the end of the chapter, you will be a master at rotation, translation, skewing, scaling, and also transitioning between these effects smoothly using animation effects. You will also learn how to use them with all other relevant properties.

Transformations

CSS3 provides over 20 different transformation types that you can apply to HTML elements all handled using the **transform** property. There are translations, which are changes of position on a plane, scaling to shrink or enlarge objects in one or more dimensions, rotation, skewing and, if that's not enough for you, transformations of your choice using matrixes.

Furthermore, not only can you access transformations, but there is also a **transition** property with which you can animate them too. These two properties together makes for highly interactive and dynamic web pages.

In *Example 23.1*, an orange box is created with a red border and then positioned at an absolute location. Three buttons are placed above it with CSS hover rules applied to them, with which the box can be made to move in various directions.

Example 23.1:

```
1.  <!DOCTYPE html>
2.  <html>
3.    <head>
```

```
4.        <title>Translation and Transition</title>
5.      <style>
6.        #box                { position   : absolute;
7.                               top        : 50px;
8.                               left       : 50px;
9.                               width      : 100px;
10.                              height     : 100px;
11.                              background : orange;
12.                              border     : 5px solid red;
13.                              transition : all 1s ease-in-out;        }
14.       #x:hover ~ #box { transform   : translateX(100px          ); }
15.       #y:hover ~ #box { transform   : translateY(100px          ); }
16.       #b:hover ~ #box { transform   : translate( 100px, 100px); }
17.      </style>
18.    </head>
19.    <body>
20.      <button id='x'>Right</button>
21.      <button id='y'>Down </button>
22.      <button id='b'>Both </button>
23.      <div id='box'></div>
24.    </body>
25. </html>
```

The **box** rules start at line 6 where the **position** property is set to **absolute** and the **top** and **left** offsets from the containing element are provided, along with the box **width**, **height**, **background**, and **border** property values. These all apply to the element at line 23.

There's also a new rule in this example at line 13, which uses the **transition** property. The values provided to it state that **all** properties that may change from now on should do so over a period of **1** second, and should start slowly, speed up, and then slow down, known as **ease-in-out**. This has no immediate effect, but sets up the element such that, should any property be changed in future, it will transition (or animate) in the manner prescribed.

Now, we get to the magic part. On lines 14 to 16, there are three **hover** rules applied to the **x**, **y**, and **b** elements, which are the three buttons on lines 20 to 22. By use of the ~ operator, these rules are made to apply to the sibling element with the ID of **box**. This has the effect such that passing the mouse over any of the buttons will cause one of the three **transform** rules to be triggered, each passing slightly different horizontal and vertical values in the **translate()** function, resulting in a translation of the object (a movement in its 2D plane), which will be animated because of the previously established **transition** rule. When you load this example into a browser, the result will look like *Figure 23.1*.

***Figure 23.1**: The object can be translated by passing the mouse over the buttons*

And when you pass your mouse over any of the three buttons, you will see the box animate gracefully in the direction given. When you move the mouse away from a button, the transition will automatically return to the start position, unless the mouse happens to pass over another button.

All that, and not a hint of JavaScript in sight. If you applied this technique using JavaScript instead of CSS, you would need functions to access, and then to translate the object, and also to reset it back to the start, all attached to mouse events of the buttons. This is all straightforward for a JavaScript programmer, but is totally unnecessary if you use CSS3 rules correctly!

Transitions

Before exploring transformations any further, let's first discover exactly what is possible using transitions, in which you can specify a type of animation effect you want to occur when one or more element properties are transformed. The browser will then automatically take care of all the in-between frames for you.

There are three properties you should set in order to set up a transition, which are as follows:

```
transition-property        : property;
transition-duration        : time;
```

```
transition-delay                : time;
transition-timing-function : type;
```

For the **transition-property** value, you should assign at least one property that you wish to animate (or transition) should its value change. You can use the value **all** as a catch-all for any properties that may change. You can provide a value of **width** or **height** or **color**, or any other changeable property value, or a list of comma separated values to transition more than one property selectively.

The **transition-duration** property should be a time, generally of just a few seconds or less for user interaction animations (floating point values are allowed), such as **3s**, **1.5s** or **.75s**, and so on. Similarly, you can specify a delay period during which the transition will wait before starting. Again, values for this can look like **3s**, **1.5s** or **.75s**, and so on.

Lastly and, perhaps, most interestingly, you can decide what the animation should look like, out of the following values, applied to the **transition-timing-function** property:

ease: This starts slowly, gets faster, then ends slowly.

linear: This transitions at constant speed.

ease-in: This starts slowly, then goes quickly until finished.

ease-out: This starts quickly, stays fast, and then ends slowly.

ease-in-out: This starts slowly, goes fast, and then ends slowly.

Using any of the values with the word **ease** in them ensures that the transition looks extra fluid and natural, unlike the linear transition, which somehow seems more mechanical. And if these aren't sufficiently varied for you, you can also create your own transitions using the **cubic-bezier()** function, which creates a unique curve that the timing property can use to vary speed as the transition progresses.

For example, following are the function values you would use to re-create the preceding five transition types (ease, linear, ease-in, ease-out, and ease-in-out), in the same order:

```
transition-timing-function : cubic-bezier(0.25, 0.1, 0.25, 1);
transition-timing-function : cubic-bezier(0,    0,   1,    1);
transition-timing-function : cubic-bezier(0.42, 0,   1,    1);
transition-timing-function : cubic-bezier(0,    0,   0.58, 1);
transition-timing-function : cubic-bezier(0.42, 0,   0.58, 1);
```

As you might expect, CSS offers a shortcut to assign all these property values using different property names, and that's the simple **transition** property. Using it, you can pass values of the property name to be transitioned, followed by the length of the transition, the transition smoothing type, and finally any delay required, as follows:

```
transition : all .3s linear .2s;
```

Just for another reference, let's transition another value such as the background of an object, in *Example 23.2*, which is similar to the previous example, but adjusted just to change the color.

Example 23.2:

```
1.  <!DOCTYPE html>
2.  <html>
3.    <head>
4.      <title>Translation and Transition</title>
5.      <style>
6.        #box              { position   : absolute;
7.                            border      : 5px solid red;
8.                            transition  : background 1s ease-in-out;
9.                            top         : 50px;
10.                           left        : 50px;
11.                           width       : 100px;
12.                           height      : 100px;
13.                           background  : orange; }
14.       #b:hover ~ #box { background  : blue;   }
15.       #g:hover ~ #box { background  : grey;   }
16.       #c:hover ~ #box { background  : cyan;   }
17.     </style>
18.   </head>
19.   <body>
20.     <button id='b'>Blue</button>
21.     <button id='g'>Grey</button>
22.     <button id='c'>Cyan</button>
23.     <div id='box'></div>
```

```
24.    </body>
25. </html>
```

With this example, passing the mouse over the buttons causes the background color of the box to change, as specified on lines 14 to 16, and as shown in *Figure 23.2*.

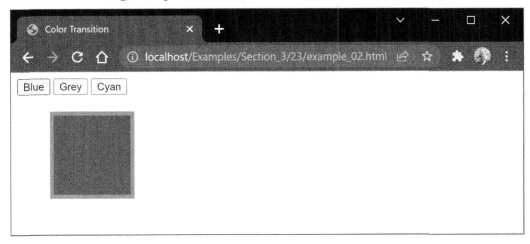

Figure 23.2: *The box changes color as the mouse passes over the buttons*

You may also notice that on line 8, instead of the catch-all value **all**, only the **background** property is referenced.

As an exercise, you might like to try combining *Examples 23.1* and *23.2* to see how the combined transition and translation would look like. For full description on transition timing and easing functions, please visit the following URLs:

tinyurl.com/trans-timing

tinyurl.com/beziereasing

Translation

So far, you have seen translation in use, combined with transitioning to create an animation. Now, let's look at precisely how to use the **translate()** function. The function accepts a pair of values, which are the horizontal and vertical amounts by which to move the object. These can be negative, zero, or positive values in any measurement type, including percentages, but more likely to be pixels.

For example, the following two rules translate to the right by 50 pixels and down by 50 pixels, respectively:

```
transform:translate(50px,  0px);
transform:translate( 0px, 50px);
```

If you just wish to translate in one dimension, you have these alternative functions available to achieve the same results:

```
transform : translateX(50px);
transform : translateY(50px);
```

Coming soon – A translate property

Also, potentially available to you, but only supported (at the time of writing) by Firefox and Safari browsers, is a regular **translate** property, which you will be able to use as follows:

```
translate : 50px  0px;
translate :  0px 50px;
```

Or you can use a single value to translate in both dimensions by the same amount, as follows:

```
translate : 50px;
```

And you can even use three values to translate in three dimensions, as follows:

```
translate : 50px 0px 150px;
```

However, the **translate** property does *not* cause other elements to flow around it, which is different from using the **transform** property with the **translate()** function, and it does not (at the time of writing) work in Chromium-based browsers. This section serves to alert you of what's coming, but is not recommended for widespread use at this point. Remember that you can always search for whether a feature is widely accessible yet at the **caniuse.com** website.

Scaling

With scaling, you can modify an element's horizontal and/or vertical dimensions using the **scale()** function with two values, or you can just modify one or the other with either **scaleX()** or **scaleY()** providing a single value. *Example 23.3* uses all three of these types of scaling.

Example 23.3:

```
1.  <!DOCTYPE html>
2.  <html>
3.    <head>
4.      <title>Scaling</title>
5.      <style>
6.        #box              { position   : absolute;
```

```
7.                              border      : 5px solid red;
8.                              transition  : all 1s ease-in-out;
9.                              top         : 50px;
10.                             left        : 50px;
11.                             width       : 100px;
12.                             height      : 100px;
13.                             background  : orange;            }
14.        #b:hover ~ #box { transform    : scaleX(1.5     ); }
15.        #g:hover ~ #box { transform    : scaleY(1.5     ); }
16.        #c:hover ~ #box { transform    : scale( 1.5, 1.5); }
17.      </style>
18.    </head>
19.    <body>
20.      <button id='b'>Stretch X</button>
21.      <button id='g'>Stretch Y</button>
22.      <button id='c'>Stretch Both</button>
23.      <div id='box'></div>
24.    </body>
25. </html>
```

Lines 14 to 16 use the scaling functions, while line 8 is reset to transition **all** properties. Just pass your mouse over the different buttons to see the results in action. Whatever condition the box is in, when a mouse passes over a different button, the CSS will intelligently transition from that condition to the new property setting(s). The result of this example is shown in *Figure 23.3*.

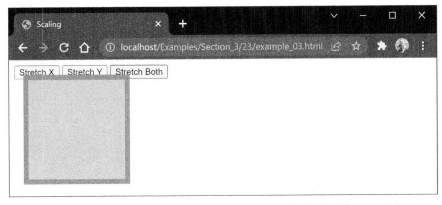

Figure 23.3: *The mouse is over the third button so the box is fully stretched*

Rotation

Not only can you stretch and shrink objects, but they can also be rotated either clockwise or counter clockwise, by as many degrees as you like, even spinning several times in a circle if you choose.

Example 23.4 performs three different types of rotation on the box we've been using in this chapter.

Example 23.4:

```
1.  <!DOCTYPE html>
2.  <html>
3.    <head>
4.      <title>Rotation</title>
5.      <style>
6.        #box          { position   : absolute;
7.                        border      : 5px solid red;
8.                        transition  : all 1s ease-in-out;
9.                        text-align  : center;
10.                       color       : blue;
11.                       font        : bold 16pt Arial;
12.                       top         : 50px;
13.                       left        : 50px;
14.                       width       : 100px;
15.                       height      : 100px;
16.                       background  : orange;          }
17.        #b:hover ~ #box { transform   : rotate(  90deg); }
18.        #g:hover ~ #box { transform   : rotate(-180deg); }
19.        #c:hover ~ #box { transform   : rotate(1080deg); }
20.      </style>
21.    </head>
22.    <body>
23.      <button id='b'>Clockwise 90</button>
24.      <button id='g'>Reverse 180 </button>
25.      <button id='c'>Three loops </button>
```

```
26.      <div id='box'>I'm Spinning Around</div>
27.   </body>
28. </html>
```

This example places some colored bold text in the box, so that you can clearly see the rotations in action. Lines 17 to 19 perform a 90 degree clockwise, 180 degree counter clockwise, and a full three times rotation, respectively, whenever the mouse passes over the buttons above it, as shown in *Figure 23.4*.

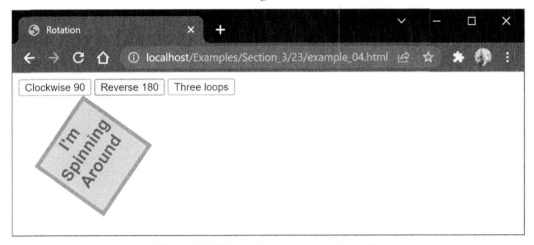

Figure 23.4: *The box is in the process of rotating*

If you prefer to work in radians, you can. You may recall that there is 2 **x PI** (which is 3.14159…) or 6.28 radians in 360 degrees, so you would really be working with values relating to **PI**. For example, **PI** equates to half a circle in radians, equivalent to 180 degrees, so a value of **3.14rad** causes a 180-degree turn, and **1.57rad** would cause a quarter turn, and so on.

Skewing

The last of the named transformations is the **skew()** function, with which you can skew in either a horizontal or a vertical plane, clockwise or counter clockwise. The function takes two arguments, the vertical and horizontal skew, in that order. Alternatively, you can use either of the **skewX()** or **skewY()** functions to skew in a single dimension.

Example 23.5 calls all three of these skew types, each according to the button over which the mouse is passed.

Example 23.5:

```
1.  <!DOCTYPE html>
2.  <html>
3.    <head>
4.      <title>Skew</title>
5.      <style>
6.        #box              { position   : absolute;
7.                            border      : 5px solid red;
8.                            transition  : all 1s ease-in-out;
9.                            top         : 50px;
10.                           left        : 50px;
11.                           width       : 100px;
12.                           height      : 100px;
13.                           background  : orange;                    }
14.      #x:hover ~ #box { transform    : skewX( 30deg           ); }
15.      #y:hover ~ #box { transform    : skewY(-30deg           ); }
16.      #b:hover ~ #box { transform    : skew(  30deg, -30deg); }
17.    </style>
18.  </head>
19.  <body>
20.    <button id='x'>SkewX 30 </button>
21.    <button id='y'>SkewY -30</button>
22.    <button id='b'>Skew Both</button>
23.    <div id='box'></div>
24.  </body>
25.</html>
```

When skewing a rectangular element, one edge moves in the direction desired causing the adjacent sides to stretch in length creating a parallelogram. If you skew clockwise in one direction and counter clockwise in the other (both by the same amounts), the relative dimensions will remain the same, but the element will get larger due to the stretched edges. So, this kind of skew is not appropriate for creating rotations unless the accompanying enlargement is what you intended. The result of this example is shown in *Figure 23.5*.

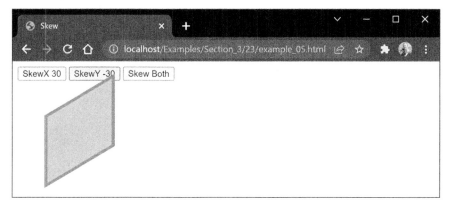

Figure 23.5: *The box has been skewed counter clockwise*

Using matrixes

All these transformation functions are powerful, but there are more ways to transform objects and so a **matrix()** function is also provided, with which you can brew your own transformations. However, as a beginner you may wish to stick with the pre-made functions wherever possible because this function uses matrix multiplication and requires six values to work.

Having said that, if you wish to create your own transformations the values you must pass to the **matrix()** function are four values describing the transformation, and two for translation. Let's call them **a**, **b**, **c**, **d**, **x**, and **y**.

Now, the intention here is not to teach you about matrix multiplication, for which a URL with more information is provided at the end of this section, but to just show you the results of modifying some of these values and seeing how they work in practice. Therefore, *Example 23.6* provides six buttons for playing with the function.

Example 23.6:

```
1.  <!DOCTYPE html>
2.  <html>
3.    <head>
4.      <title>Matrix Transformations</title>
5.      <style>
6.        #box            { position    : absolute;
7.                          border      : 5px solid red;
8.                          transition  : all 1s ease-in-out;
9.                          top         : 50px;
10.                         left        : 50px;
```

```
11.                              width      : 100px;
12.                              height     : 100px;
13.                              background : orange;                        }
14.      #a:hover ~ #box { transform : matrix(2, 0, 0, 1,  0,  0); }
15.      #b:hover ~ #box { transform : matrix(1, 1, 0, 1,  0,  0); }
16.      #c:hover ~ #box { transform : matrix(1, 0, 1, 1,  0,  0); }
17.      #d:hover ~ #box { transform : matrix(1, 0, 0, 2,  0,  0); }
18.      #x:hover ~ #box { transform : matrix(1, 0, 0, 1, 50,  0); }
19.      #y:hover ~ #box { transform : matrix(1, 0, 0, 1,  0, 50); }
20.      </style>
21.    </head>
22.    <body>
23.      <button id='a'>A</button>
24.      <button id='b'>B</button>
25.      <button id='c'>C</button>
26.      <button id='d'>D</button>
27.      <button id='x'>X</button>
28.      <button id='y'>Y</button>
29.      <div id='box'></div>
30.    </body>
31. </html>
```

In lines 14 to 19, default values of 1 are provided for arguments 1 and 4 of the **matrix()** function because the first is the horizontal scaling factor, while the fourth is the vertical scaling factor. The result of this example is shown in *Figure 23.6*.

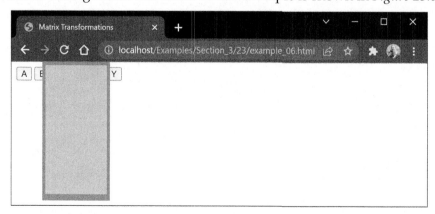

Figure 23.6: *Button D is moused over causing vertical scaling by changing value four*

Therefore, a value of 1 for each keeps the element correctly scaled, except when the mouse passes over their associated buttons, and the value of each of these is then set to 2 to double the scale in that dimension. Effectively, the six values represent the following combined actions:

```
matrix(scaleX, skewY, skewX, scaleY, translateX, translateY);
```

If you pass the mouse over buttons A or D, you will, indeed, see the box scale horizontally or vertically by a factor of two. Buttons B and C are associated with values 2 and 3 and, in turn, they perform a vertical and a horizontal skew. While, the final two buttons translate the box horizontally and vertically. Try passing your mouse over these various buttons and watch the resulting effects.

Therefore, you should see that by combining these values in different ways, you can achieve any combination of scaling, skewing, rotation, and translation you require. If you find this fascinating and would like more details, please refer to the following URL:

tinyurl.com/css-matrix

Conclusion

This concludes your discovery of using CSS3 to transform, translate, and transition objects in every way that is possible. Don't forget that other properties such as width, height, color, font-size, and many more will also respond to transitioning smoothly, so you can use these various effects subtly to make any UI experience more interactive and compelling. In the next chapter, we'll take what you've learned in this chapter into the next dimension – literally! That's right, we will move up a dimension into the world of 3D transformations and transitions to make your elements appear to pop off the web page.

CHAPTER 24

3D and Animation

Introduction

If you like 3D, you will particularly enjoy this chapter because the 3D tools provided with CSS3 are powerful, fast, and very easy to use. With the tools, you can set the depth of your 3D world and see how far away it is from the viewer. You can choose the offset at which transformations occur, and then perform a multitude of transformations, scaling, rotation, and a lot more.

In this chapter, we'll use one main example which we will keep referring back to, and a few other examples to fill in the bits and pieces that remain. What's more this example is fun and something that before CSS3 you would need to spend a lot of time coding using 3D trigonometry.

Structure

In this chapter, you will:

- Learn everything about 3D transformations
- Learn popping element off the 2D plane
- Learn how to play with the perspective to get great effects
- Understand how to manipulate 3D objects as if you were holding them

Objectives

The aim of this chapter is to teach you all about the 3D capabilities of CSS3 in such a way that you'll find it easy and exciting. By the time you complete reading the chapter, you'll be a true 3D master, ready to create anything from simple 3D effects up to pages with virtual reality effects.

3D transformations

The power that CSS provides you with 3D transformations is truly astonishing. Without a single line of JavaScript code, it is possible to fully animate 3D objects and move and rotate them in any way you can imagine.

To provide a beautiful illustration of this, we'll need a longer example than we've seen so far. *Example 24.1* combines HTML elements with pure CSS3 to animate a three-dimensional cube in a variety of ways, smoothly, and seamlessly, with results that would astonish early web developers.

Before continuing with this chapter, you should try this example for yourself and have a good play with the buttons above the 3D cube by passing your mouse over them.

Example 24.1:

```
1.  <!DOCTYPE html>
2.  <html>
3.    <head>
4.      <title>3D Transformations</title>
5.      <style>
6.        #outer  { perspective        : 500px;
7.                  width              : 200px;
8.                  margin             : 10px auto;           }
9.        #cube   { transform-style    : preserve-3d;
10.                 width              : 100%;
11.                 height             : 200px;
12.                 color              : white;
13.                 text-align         : center;
14.                 font               : bold 18pt Arial;
15.                 transition         : all 1s linear;       }
16.       .face    { position           : absolute;
```

```
17.                     width          : 100%;
18.                     height         : 100%;                    }
19.     #left   { background    : green;
20.             transform      : rotateY(  -90deg)
21.                                translateZ(100px); }
22.     #right  { background    : orange;
23.             transform      : rotateY(   90deg)
24.                                translateZ(100px); }
25.     #up     { background    : red;
26.             transform      : rotateX(   90deg)
27.                                translateZ(100px); }
28.     #down   { background    : magenta;
29.             transform      : rotateX(  -90deg)
30.                                translateZ(100px); }
31.     #back   { background    : indigo;
32.             transform      : rotateX( -180deg)
33.                                translateZ(100px); }
34.     #front  { background    : blue;
35.             transform      : rotateX(    0deg)
36.                                translateZ(100px); }
37.     @keyframes spin
38.     {
39.       to    { transform      : rotateX(   1turn)
40.                                rotateY(   1turn); }
41.     }
42.     #l:hover ~ #cube { transform : rotateY(   90deg); }
43.     #r:hover ~ #cube { transform : rotateY(  -90deg); }
44.     #u:hover ~ #cube { transform : rotateX(  -90deg); }
45.     #d:hover ~ #cube { transform : rotateX(   90deg); }
46.     #b:hover ~ #cube { transform : rotateX(  180deg); }
47.     #s:hover ~ #cube { animation : spin 6s linear 10; }
48.   </style>
49. </head>
```

```
50.  <body>
51.    <div id='outer'> 
52.       <button id='l'> L  </button>
53.       <button id='r'> R  </button>
54.       <button id='u'> U  </button>
55.       <button id='d'> D  </button>
56.       <button id='b'> B  </button>
57.       <button id='s'>Spin</button>
58.       <br><br><br><br>
59.       <div id='cube'>
60.          <div class='face' id='left'> <br><br><br>LEFT </div>
61.          <div class='face' id='right'><br><br><br>RIGHT</div>
62.          <div class='face' id='up'>   <br><br><br>UP   </div>
63.          <div class='face' id='down'> <br><br><br>DOWN </div>
64.          <div class='face' id='back'> <br><br><br>BACK </div>
65.          <div class='face' id='front'><br><br><br>FRONT</div>
66.       </div>
67.    </div>
68.  </body>
69. </html>
```

The **L**, **R**, **U**, **D**, **B**, and **Spin** buttons created on lines 52 – 57 of this example stand for Left, Right, Up, Down, Back, and Spin. Passing the mouse over any of the first five buttons results in the chosen face rotating into the view. Doing this with the final button sets the cube to spin around for 10 complete sets of revolutions. Removing the mouse from over the buttons restores the front face. The result of loading this example can be seen in *Figure 24.1*.

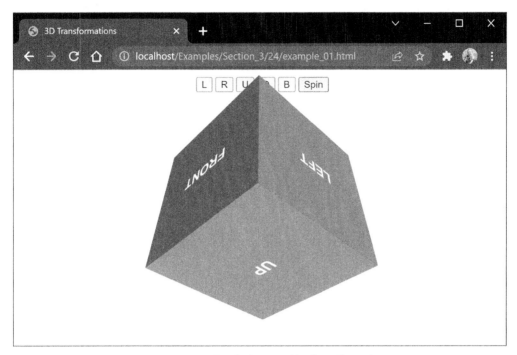

Figure 24.1: *A 3D cube is rotated in three dimensions*

Let's now look into how this example was put together by examining the way 3D transformations work in CSS.

Setting a perspective

When you wish to raise an element out of 2D CSS space into the third dimension, you use the **perspective** property. This enables the use of 3D transformations and transitions on that element.

The value you supply represents the distance between the viewer and the center of the object. Therefore, a low value means the viewer is close and there will be a very high 3D effect that will at first look far too deformed, rather than being effective 3D. A rule of thumb to start with is to take the largest dimension of an object in 3D and set a perspective value of around two to three times that. Once you see the effect, you can then tweak the value according to your taste and the effect you wish the viewer to see.

In *Example 24.1*, the cube has edge lengths of 200 pixels which, by means of Pythagoras' equation, means the diagonals will be around 283 pixels, so the example has set a value of **500px** for the perspective, in fact a little less than twice the diagonal width, but that was after tweaking – an original value of 850 was tested and then reduced in steps until 500 seemed to be the optimal amount.

As an exercise for the reader, you may wish to adjust just this value on line 6, trying values lower and higher than **500px** and see what results you get. This will help you gain a quick feel for how the property works.

To illustrate this, *Example 24.2* uses a value of **50px**, creating a highly forced 3D view from inside the object. Since the buttons are no-longer visible, to rotate the object automatically, the following code is appended to the document end to create *Example 24.2*. The object will now spin for 10 cycles on its own.

Example 24.2 (just the modified lines):

```
6.        #outer  { perspective        : 50px;
```

```
70. <script>
71.   document.getElementById('cube').style.animation =
72.       'spin 6s linear 10'
73. </script>
```

It is true that lines 70 to 73 have been added *after* the closing **</html>** tag, but browsers are forgiving, and this is just a quick fix to set the object spinning without changing the line numbering of the example(s). Also, it shows how you can issue a JavaScript animation (or other transformation) instruction on an object, as shown in *Figure 24.2*.

Figure 24.2: *The view from inside the cube*

This shows how it is possible to rotate or translate CSS elements behind the viewer as well as in front, and open up a whole new possibility of creating **virtual reality (VR)** type scenarios, if you wish to be so adventurous in your web development. However, if you choose to do this, you will probably work with much larger dimensions so that they can appear farther away from the viewer and less 3D distorted.

To rotate an object through the three dimensions, you can use the **rotate3d()** function, or the **rotateX()**, **rotateY()**, and **rotateZ()** functions. Similarly, other functions such as **skew()** and **translate()** have their own 3D versions.

Two ways to change perspective

There is also a **perspective()** function available, which creates a 3D-space for the current element by applying it to the **transform** property as follows:

```
transform: perspective(500);
```

When you need a group of child elements to have its own 3D space, then you should raise a parent object this way, rather than using the **perspective** property, which applies a single shared 3D space to an element and all its child objects. *Example 24.3* creates two sets of child elements: the first with their parent using the **perspective** property and the second without it.

Example 24.3:

```
1.  <!DOCTYPE html>
2.  <html>
3.    <head>
4.      <title>Perspective Types</title>
5.      <style>
6.
7.          .outer       { width      : 640px;
8.                         height     : 120px;
9.                         background : cyan;
10.                        border     : 1px solid black;      }
11.         .perspective { perspective : 200px;               }
12.         .box         { width      : 100px;
13.                        height     : 100px;
14.                        margin     : 0 55px;
15.                        float      : left;
16.                        background : red;
17.                        border     : 1px solid black;
```

```
18.                          transform   : perspective(200px)
19.                                         rotateX(45deg); }
20.      </style>
21.    </head>
22.    <body>
23.      <div class='outer perspective'>
24.        <div class='box'></div>
25.        <div class='box'></div>
26.        <div class='box'></div>
27.      </div><br>
28.      <div class='outer'>
29.        <div class='box'></div>
30.        <div class='box'></div>
31.        <div class='box'></div>
32.      </div>
33.    </body>
34. </html>
```

Each of these sets of three boxes share the same parent styling in **outer**. But, the upper set also uses the style in the **perspective** class. The **outer** class simply sets a width, height, and border, while the **perspective** class sets the **perspective** property to **200px**. The result of loading this into a browser will look like *Figure 24.3*.

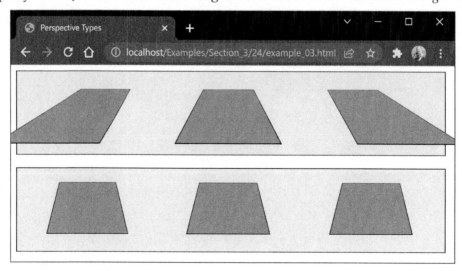

Figure 24.3: *The upper boxes share a parent's perspective*

The **box** class creates red boxes of 100 **x** 100 pixels, gives them a wide margin, and floats them on the same line alongside each other. Then, lines 18 and 19 use the **transform** property, calling the **perspective()** function on it with a value of **200px**, and calling the **rotateX()** function with a value of **45deg**.

The result of this is to rotate each of the boxes along the horizontal axis such that the top of each appears to move towards the browser, while the bottom appears to move towards the viewer, equaling a rotation of 45 degrees.

Note how the top three boxes share the same 3D space due to their parent element applying the **perspective** property, while the bottom three each rotates individually in its own 3D space. This happens even though the **box** class rules are identical for all of the boxes, even including a call to the **perspective()** function, assigning a value of **200px**.

Setting the transform style

There is an issue with *Example 24.3* that you may not have spotted, i.e., the 3D effect isn't quite right. This is because it's necessary to tell the browser that the **transform-style** property used should not be the default of **flat** because we are working in 3D. Instead, its value should be set to **preserve-3d**, by adding the following rule to the **outer** class:

```
transform-style : preserve-3d;
```

There's no need to show it here, but the accompanying free archive of examples includes this modified file as **example_03a.html**. The result should look like *Figure 24.4*.

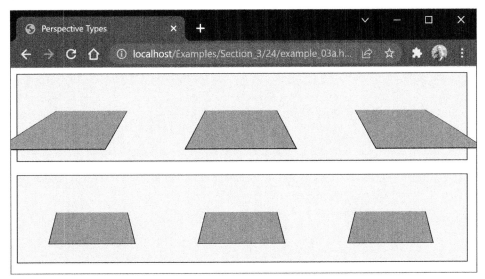

Figure 24.4*: The rotation now preservers the 3D space*

Changing the transform origin

By default, the origin of a transformation will be right at the center of the parent element, or the current element if the parent has no **perspective** property set. This includes horizontally and vertically in the X and Y directions, and halfway towards the viewer in the Z direction.

But you can change any of these values if you like using the **transform-origin** property, as used in *Example 24.4*, in which the second set of boxes has this property set to the value pair for X and Y of **0% 10%**:

Example 24.4:

```
1.  <!DOCTYPE html>
2.  <html>
3.    <head>
4.      <title>Changing Origin</title>
5.      <style>
6.        .outer  { perspective      : 200px;
7.                  width            : 640px;
8.                  height           : 120px;
9.                  background       : cyan;
10.                 transform-style  : preserve-3d;
11.                 border           : 1px solid black;     }
12.       .box     { width           : 100px;
13.                  height          : 100px;
14.                  margin          : 0 55px;
15.                  float           : left;
16.                  background      : red;
17.                  border          : 1px solid black;
18.                  transform       : perspective(200px)
19.                                      rotateX(45deg); }
20.        .origin { transform-origin : 50% 10%; }
21.      </style>
22.    </head>
23.    <body>
24.      <div class='outer'>
```

```
25.         <div class='box'></div>

26.         <div class='box'></div>

27.         <div class='box'></div>

28.      </div><br>

29.      <div class='outer'>

30.         <div class='box origin'></div>

31.         <div class='box origin'></div>

32.         <div class='box origin'></div>

33.      </div>

34.   </body>

35. </html>
```

This example works in a similar manner to *Example 24.3*. In that, the **box** class is identical in all cases, but in this example, both sets of boxes use the same parent **perspective** and **preserve-3d** properties; the difference is that the second set of boxes uses a different **transform-origin** property setting to the first. *Figure 24.5* shows the result of this example.

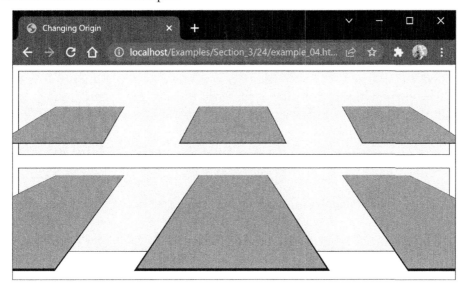

Figure 24.5: *A different origin is applied in the bottom row*

Working in 3D space

It's time now to return to *Example 24.1* and our spinning cube. Now that you have a better understanding of CSS in 3D, let's see how the cube was constructed. Referring back to *Example 24.1*, on line 51, you'll note that there is an element with the ID of **outer** enclosing everything. This is a container for holding the buttons and cube.

Inside the **outer** container is a set of six buttons, under which (after a few **
** tags for separation) is another container called **cube**. Finally, within the cube are its six faces, each in its own **<div>** element.

From the HTML, it's not immediately clear how the cube is constructed so let's go and look at the **face** class on line 16. This sets the **position** property of any element that uses it (which all the faces do) to **absolute**, and applies a full 100 percent to its width and height, as follows:

```
16.        .face   { position          : absolute;

17.                  width             : 100%;

18.                  height            : 100%;                }
```

These values are based on the parent element called **cube**, which has a width of **200px** set by its parent **outer** on line 7, and its height is set to **200px** in the rule for the **cube** element on line 11. Thus, each face of the cube has its **position**, **width**, and **height** properties assigned.

Now, let's look at each of the cube's faces in turn, starting with the one called **left** on line 19. What we need to do is place this face to the left of the cube as we look at it, and make sure it is also correctly rotated and colored. First, the color green is applied, then the face is rotated counter clockwise through the Y dimension on line 20, such that its left edge goes in towards the browser, and its right edge out towards the viewer. The element is now invisible as it is sideways on to us, and having no depth, it has nothing to display. Now, we move it into position by applying a translation of **100px** in the Z dimension on line 21, as follows:

```
19.        #left   { background        : green;

20.                  transform         : rotateY(  -90deg)

21.                                      translateZ(100px); }
```

Because the **left** face is now facing towards the left, when it is raised by 100 pixels in the Z dimension, this occurs in an upward direction relatively, as far as the element in its current position and rotation is concerned. Therefore, the face moves 100 pixels to the left and is now in place.

Similarly, the **right** face is colored and then rotated accordingly starting on line 22, also around the Y dimension but this time clockwise (from its point of view), and then translated by 100 pixels in its Z dimension, so placing it on the right-hand side of the cube.

Now, the top face which is called **up** is set to red and rotated in the X dimension starting on line 25. Then, a Z translation of 100 pixels using its current rotation places it at the top of the cube. The bottom edge (named **down**) is set to magenta and rotated counter clockwise starting on line 28, and then translated down in Z to make the cube's bottom edge.

Starting on line 31 the back of the cube (called **back**) is set to indigo and rotated around in the X dimension by 180 degrees to flip it, and then translated in Z to the back of the cube. And finally, the front (called **front**) is set to blue and rotated by 0 degrees in the X dimension (which could have been omitted as it does nothing, but appears in the example simply to match the other face rules), and then translated in Z to move 100 pixels towards the viewer – and we have our cube!

Controlling the cube

Having constructed a cube in the 3D space that was set up in the **outer** element on line 6, we can start manipulating it. In this example, it was decided to use the CSS **hover** selector applied to some buttons, starting on line 42. By use of the ~ operator, the action of the rule is applied to the sibling element called **cube**, which is our 3D cube.

The actions set a **transform** property with calls to either the **rotateX()** or **rotateY()** function, using *opposite* values to those that were assigned when the various faces were put in place. For example, the face called **left** was rotated *counter clockwise* by 90 degrees in the Y dimension on line 20. Therefore, on line 42, if the L button is hovered over, a transform *clockwise* of 90 degrees is applied to the whole cube. This results in placing the left face of the cube towards the viewer, as follows:

```
42.          #l:hover ~ #cube { transform : rotateY(   90deg); }
```

Likewise, the transformations applied on lines 43 to 46 are the opposite (or inverse) transforms to those that were applied to each of the other faces. In this instance, they are applied to the whole cube in order to rotate it in its entirety, which moves the face selected to the front as seen by the viewer. There is no transform to reveal the front face since moving the mouse away from the buttons will make that appear anyway, due to the cube returning to its default position as a result of the standard CSS hover rules.

The cube doesn't instantly switch to these new rotations, however, because a **transition** property is applied to the cube on line 15, which means it animates smoothly at a **linear** pace over a period of one second.

Line 47 is quite interesting because when the mouse hovers over the **Spin** button it applies a value to the **animation** property of the cube telling it to use the animation rules defined in **spin** at line 37 over a period of 6 seconds, and for the animation to be linear and happen 10 times.

This is a property we have not yet investigated, so to explain, the **@keyframes** rule on lines 37 to 41, assign a name of **spin** that can be used, and its rules state that this animation should rotate the chosen object all the way through the X and Y dimensions for one entire turn (from **0deg** to **360deg** each). The value **1turn** here is applied to show how you can use it as a unit of measurement equivalent to 360 degrees. Therefore, a half turn (or **0.5turn**) is equivalent to **180deg**, and so on.

In place of the value **linear,** you could use any of the easing or other transition types detailed in *Chapter 23, 2D Transformations*, and in place of the value **10,** you could set any value you like here for the number of repeats, or **infinite** for it to never stop. Now, the **animation** property can be assigned this animation rule, which will be affected when the muse is hovered over the activating button, as per this instruction:

```
47.          #s:hover ~ #cube { animation : spin 6s linear 10; }
```

3D translation

By now, you should have fully understood how *Example 24.1* works. You are encouraged to play with the code to make it do different things. There's a lot of fun and much more that you can learn from doing this. When you're done, it's time to summarize these 3D functions in detail, starting with **translate3d()**.

We've looked at translating in the Z dimension using the **translateX()** function when building the cube in *Example 24.1*. But you can also translate in the X and Y dimensions with **translateX()** and **translateY()**, and you can do so in all three dimensions at once using the **translate3d()** function as well, which takes three values, and might be used as follows:

```
transform : perspective(200) translate3d(-30px, 0px, 0px);
```

Here, the **perspective()** and **translation()** functions are applied to the **transform** property, with the X dimension translation being an example of a negative value, which is also allowed.

3D scaling

Scaling is also fully supported in three dimensions and is made possible by the **scaleX()**, **scaleY()**, **scaleZ()**, and **scale3d()** functions. The first three take a single value, while the third requires three values. A value of 1 indicates no scaling, 2 is a doubling in size, 5 is a halving, and so forth. Values may be negative as well as positive.

One example of using the **scale3d()** function could be to use it as follows to stretch the X dimension, shrink Y, and keep Z the same. The values should be integer or floating point values only, with no measurement values such as **px** or **em**:

```
transform : perspective(200) scale3d(1.2, .5, 1);
```

3D rotation

Rotation in three dimensions as also available in CSS3 using the **rotateX()**, **rotateY()**, **rotateZ()**, and **rotate3d()** functions. For the first three of these functions, that value needs to be a rotational angle value such as **45deg**, **.5turn**, or **-10grad**, or you can use radians such as **6.28rad**, and so on. To rotate in all three directions at once, you must specify three numbers and an angle value. The numbers represent a vector of the X, Y, and Z dimensions, in turn, and should be a value between 0 and 1 for each.

One way you can perform a multiple rotation would be with a rule such as the following to rotate 60 degrees clockwise in the Y dimension only in this case:

```
transform : perspective(200) rotate3d(0, 1, 0, 60deg);
```

To illustrate this, let's modify just the **face** class in *Example 24.1* to create *Example 24.5*, such that the **opacity** property of all the faces is set to just 60%, allowing whatever is behind the cube to show through. The result will look something like the *Figure 24.6*.

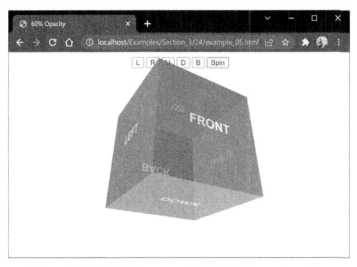

Figure 24.6: The back faces are visible due to the opacity setting

Example 24.5 (just the **face** class):

```
.face { position : absolute;
        opacity  : .6;
        width    : 100%;
        height   : 100%; }
```

Back face visibility

There remains a final piece to assemble into the CSS 3D transformation puzzle, and that's what to do with the reverse faces of elements when they are rotated. For example, as with the previous section, if you write some text on a 2D element and then rotate it in the X dimension by 180 degrees, you will see that the text still displays but is now upside down because it is showing through from the other face. Similarly, if rotated 180 degrees in Y, it would now be mirror reversed.

But let's suppose that now that we can see through them, we don't like seeing the backs of these hidden faces. We can hide them if we wish by changing the **backface-visibility** property setting to **hidden**, by adding one more line to the **face** class to create *Example 24.6*.

Example 24.6 (just the face class):

```
.face { position          : absolute;
        opacity           : .6;
        backface-visibility : hidden;
        width             : 100%;
        height            : 100%; }
```

The result is that all the back faces are now made invisible, as shown in *Figure 24.7*.

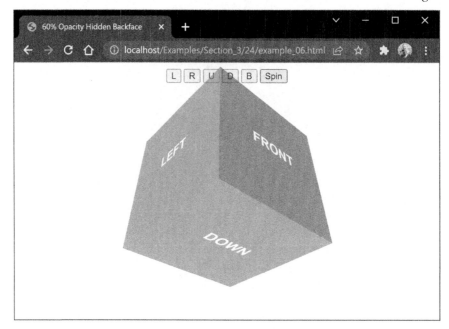

Figure 24.7: *The cube resembles that in Figure 24.1 but lighter in hue due to lower opacity*

You might think that the cube looks rather fetching when you can see the back faces, but in cases where you don't wish to see them, well, now you have the solution.

Incidentally, lowering the opacity gives the opportunity to see what the cube would look like if the faces were rotated *without* being translated in the Z dimension, as shown in *Figure 24.8*.

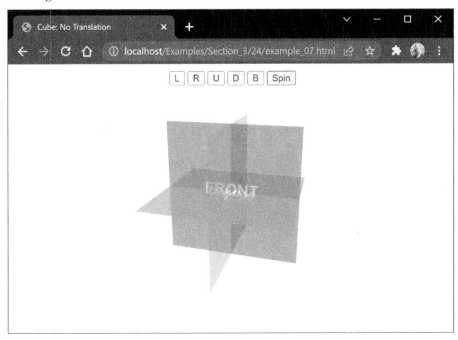

Figure 24.8: What would happen if we 'forgot' to translate the cube's faces

The code for this is too long to put here for such a frivolous (but fun) exercise, but you can find it in the companion free archive of examples saved as **Example_07. html**. Essentially, it's a modification of *Example 24.1* combined with *Example 24.5*.

Conclusion

As you will have discovered, the 3D effects you can create in CSS3 are stunning. When you combine them with transitions and animations, you can really take your web development up to a whole new level. Now, you have all you need to know about both 2D and 3D handling. In the next chapter, we'll look at a fantastic new way to make dynamically self-configurable layouts using Flexbox.

CHAPTER 25

Flexbox Layout

Introduction

Flexbox was developed in response to the need to create flexible and dynamic web layouts that align well and also distribute elements and space logically and neatly, even when the size of these elements is unknown.

For example, a website for photography portfolios in which collections of images need to sidle up to each other like multi-sized bricks in a masonry wall. It is hard to create this with standard CSS and generally would need some JavaScript. But a Flexbox is the perfect solution for such a project.

When you have a layout that looks good on a wide monitor, what do you do when you want the various elements to also line up well on a device that's taller than wide such as a mobile phone? Flexbox is definitely the perfect solution.

Structure

In this chapter, you will:

- Learn the concepts behind the Flexbox layout model
- Understand how the main axis and cross axis work together
- Work with a Flexbox playground example to test numerous features

- Become an expert at wrapping, justification, and alignment with Flexbox

Objectives

This chapter provides a complete and self-contained introduction to the Flexbox layout model. By the time you finish reading the chapter, you will have mastered this powerful set of features and be able to create stunning, dynamic, and flexible layouts.

About Flexbox

The intent behind the development of Flexbox, which occurred over a number of years, was to be able to create a container element and give it the ability to alter its child element dimensions and even their order and direction of flow in order to best fit available space.

The big driver behind this was the growing range of differently sized and dimensioned mobile devices such as phones, tablets, and laptops. Having said that, Flexbox is probably a solution best used for smaller layouts. Larger and more complex layouts will probably benefit from using a Grid layout, as described in the following chapter. But let's learn Flexbox first as it introduces the concepts needed to understand the direction-agnostic flow, as opposed to regular layouts that mostly flow either horizontally or vertically.

Flexbox is an entire module of features and not a single property or function. Some of these are applied to a container element, while others are used for its child elements. The term given for the container is *flex container,* and the term used for the child elements is *flex items.* The way Flexbox works is to control the element flow in a flexible manner (hence, the name *Flex*box).

Making a Flexbox playground

To explain how this all comes together, we need a longer example to work with. But because we've reached a part of the book where by now you have amassed a great number of skills, the complexity of the examples can increase even further, and you will be able to fully comprehend them.

A number of features have been pulled together in *Example 25.1,* which serves to replace numerous smaller examples because it allows you to alter any and all Flexbox properties, in any combination, and instantly view the effects they have.

Example 25.1:

```
1. <!DOCTYPE html>
2. <html>
```

```
 3.    <head>
 4.      <title>Flexbox Playground</title>
 5.      <style>
 6.        body   { background      : #def; }
 7.        .label { width           : 110px;
 8.                 text-align      : right;
 9.                 float           : left; }
10.        .link  { color           : blue;
11.                 text-decoration : underline;
12.                 cursor          : pointer; }
13.        #outer { display         : flex;
14.                 border          : 1px solid black;
15.                 border-radius   : 5px;
16.                 background      : linear-gradient(cyan,deepskyblue);
17.                 padding         : 5px;
18.                 box-sizing      : border-box;
19.                 width           : 100%;
20.                 height          : 400px;
21.                 resize          : both;
22.                 overflow        : hidden; }
23.        .box   { display         : flex;
24.                 background      : linear-gradient(yellow,red);
25.                 align-items     : center;
26.                 justify-content : center;
27.                 border          : 1px solid black;
28.                 border-radius   : 5px;
29.                 font            : bold 20pt Arial;
30.                 resize          : both;
31.                 overflow        : auto;
32.                 color           : white; }
33.        #Box_A { width : 100px; height : 100px; }
34.        #Box_B { width :  30px; height :  80px; }
```

```
35.        #Box_C { width : 150px; height : 130px; }
36.        #Box_D { width :  50px; height :  50px; }
37.        #Box_E { width :  70px; height : 150px; }
38.        #Box_F { width : 100px; height :  90px; }
39.        #Box_G { width : 160px; height : 180px; }
40.        #Box_H { width :  40px; height :  50px; }
41.        #Box_I { width : 120px; height : 150px; }
42.      </style>
43.    </head>
44.    <body>
45.      <output id='output'></output><br>
46.      <div id='outer'>
47.        <div class='box' id='Box_A'>A</div>
48.        <div class='box' id='Box_B'>B</div>
49.        <div class='box' id='Box_C'>C</div>
50.        <div class='box' id='Box_D'>D</div>
51.        <div class='box' id='Box_E'>E</div>
52.        <div class='box' id='Box_F'>F</div>
53.        <div class='box' id='Box_G'>G</div>
54.        <div class='box' id='Box_H'>H</div>
55.        <div class='box' id='Box_I'>I</div>
56.      </div>
57.      <script>
58.        settings = ['flex-direction', 'flex-wrap', 'justify-content',
59.                    'align-items', 'align-content', 'gap']
60.        values   = [['row', 'row-reverse', 'column',
61.                     'column-reverse'],
62.                    ['nowrap', 'wrap', 'wrap-reverse'],
63.                    ['normal', 'flex-start', 'flex-end', 'start',
64.                     'end', 'center', 'stretch', 'left', 'right',
65.                     'space-between', 'space-around',
66.                     'space-evenly'],
67.                    ['normal', 'flex-start', 'flex-end', 'start',
```

```
68.                         'end', 'center', 'stretch', 'baseline',
69.                         'self-start', 'self-end'],
70.                     ['normal', 'flex-start', 'flex-end', 'start',
71.                         'end', 'center', 'stretch', 'baseline',
72.                         'space-between', 'space-around', 'space-evenly'],
73.                     ['0px',  '10px', '20px', '30px', '40px',
74.                         '50px', '60px', '70px', '80px', '90px']]
75.
76.       for (j = 0 ; j < settings.length ; ++j) {
77.         id('output').innerHTML +=
78.           `<div class='label'>${settings[j]} : </div>`
79.         for (k = 0 ; k < values[j].length ; ++k) {
80.           id('output').innerHTML +=
81.             `<span class='link' id='${settings[j]}${values[j][k]}'
82.               onclick=›set(${j},${k})'>${values[j][k]}</span> `
83.         }
84.         id('output').innerHTML += '<br>\n'
85.       }
86.       function set(j, k) {
87.         for (x = 0 ; x < values[j].length ; ++x) {
88.         style(settings[j] + values[j][x], 'font-weight', 'normal')
89.         style(settings[j] + values[j][x], 'color', 'blue')
90.         }
91.         style(settings[j] + values[j][k], 'font-weight', 'bold')
92.         style(settings[j] + values[j][k], 'color', 'red')
93.         style('outer', settings[j], values[j][k])
94.       }
95.       function id(val) { return document.getElementById(val) }
96.       function style(obj, prop, val) { id(obj).style[prop] = val }
97.     </script>
98.   </body>
99. </html>
```

When you load this into a browser it, should look like *Figure 25.1*.

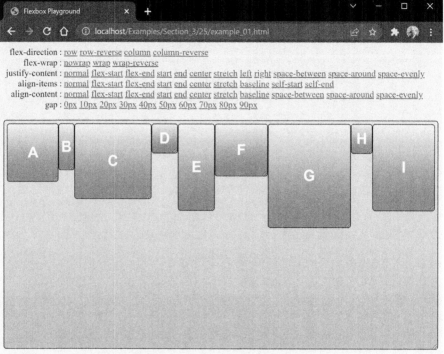

Figure 25.1: This example allows you to test the 158,400 Flexbox property combinations

Before moving on to use this example to explain the various Flexbox features, let's take a quick look at how the example works, which will also help explain a little about Flexbox.

How the example works

The example is divided into three main sections. Firstly, the `<style>` section sets up all the CSS we will be using. Then, there's some HTML which creates a blank `<output>` element, into which a number of clickable controls will be added. And lastly, there's some JavaScript used to populate the `<output>` element, and also process the mouse clicks.

Flexbox doesn't require the use of JavaScript. It is only used here as a means of either replacing a large amount of HTML with a few lines of code that generate that HTML on the fly, or as a means of altering various CSS property values behind the scenes.

Lines 6 to 12 in the `<style>` section set the gradient fill backgrounds, the clickable links, and all the various parts that display above the main Flexbox display.

The large **<div>** element underneath is the flex container, and the child **<div>** elements within it are the flex items, as discussed in the *About Flexbox* section. The parent container with the ID of **outer** is styled on line 13 with a **display** property of **flex** to set the module up for its child elements. This could also have used the value **inline-flex** to make the parent inline with any sibling elements, but not affecting the child elements.

Starting on line 23, each of the nine flexbox items is styled, also making use of a **display** property of **flex** themselves, for the sole and simple reason of centering the A-G text identifiers both horizontally and vertically – a neat and powerful additional use for Flexboxes.

The flex item boxes are created in lines 47 to 55 in the **<body>** section, where they are given ID names so that the CSS in lines 33 to 41 can give each a different width and height, and we can simulate working with a variety of flex items of different dimensions.

As shown in *Figure 25.1*, you can see these elements labelled as A through I, all stacked along the top of the flex container by default – since no flex properties have been set, other than line 13 specifying that the **outer <div>** element is a Flexbox, using the rule **display : flex;**.

Lines 58 and 59 in the **<script>** section create an array called **settings[]** which holds the six different property names to work with, while lines 60 to 74 create a matching two-dimensional array called **values[][]**, which contains the values available to apply to each of the properties. The **[]** or **[][]** after these array names indicates how many dimensions are in the array.

Lines 76 to 85 comprise a pair of nested loops to iterate through these two arrays, and from them, build up the HTML with which the top part of the example is displayed. The outer loop starting at line 76 iterates through the six property names using an index variable named **j**, while the inner loop starting at line 79 uses an index variable named **k** to iterate through, however, many property values are associated with the property indexed by **j**. (The variable names **j**, **k**, and **i** are very popular among programmers to use as temporary indexes for iterating through arrays).

The HTML created by this pair of loops builds a number of **<div>** elements to list the property names, each followed by a number of **<div>** elements for the possible property values. The resulting HTML is then stored in the **innerHTML** property of the **<div>** named **output**, appearing to the browser as if that HTML was already there. The HTML is created using template literals within back tick quoted strings.

Finally, the HTML thus created has **onclick** events attached to the links which trigger the function called **set()** at line 86. This takes the values passed to it, which are an index into the property name, and another into the property value to apply, and it then changes the style of the **outer <div>** (the Flexbox **<div>**) accordingly.

At the same time, that value is highlighted in bold red, while the previous value for that property is restyled back to plain blue. This allows us to see at-a-glance which properties and associated values are currently in use in the Flexbox area.

The two functions on lines 95 and 96, **id()** and **style()**, in turn, return an object to JavaScript based on its ID, and apply a value to an object's property.

If you would like to see the HTML created by all of this, you can add the following line of code after the **}** on line 85:

```
; console.log(id('output').innerHTML)
```

The **;** ends the previous statement, and the rest of the line outputs the HTML to the developer console where you can view it, as shown in *Figure 25.2*.

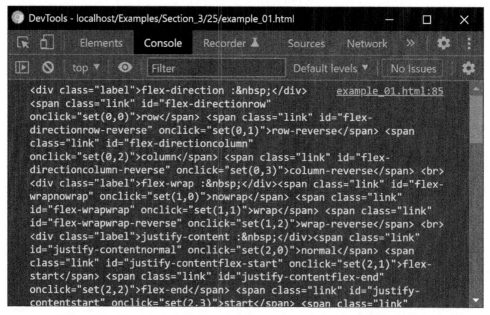

Figure 25.2: Viewing the HTML created by this example in the developer console

Using the example

It is not necessary for you to deeply understand how this example works. In fact, all you really need to know is that by clicking on any of the property values above the Flexbox, any change that value creates will be displayed in the Flexbox area below.

In addition, all the flex items in the Flexbox have been made user-resizable, so you don't have to accept the default widths and heights set by the example, and you can resize them all at will. You can also resize the Flexbox itself to see what result(s) that has. To do so, grab the bottom right-hand corner of an element with the mouse and drag it about.

To reset all values to their defaults at any time, simply reload the document into the browser, and it will re-initialize all settings. In the free accompanying archive of example files, there is also a document saved as **example_01a.html**, which is identical with the exception that it has all the flex items initialized to the same horizontal rectangular dimensions (200 **x** 50 pixels), which is useful when you want to test how same-sized flex items interact with each other. When you load this document, it will look something like *Figure 25.3*.

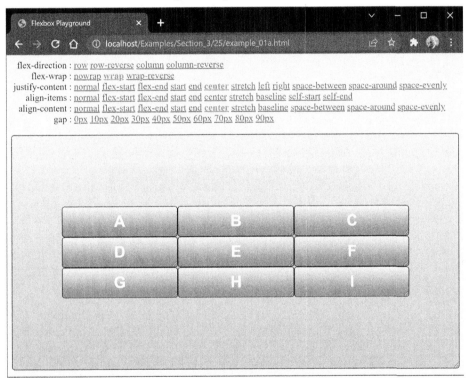

Figure 25.3: *All flex items are identical, wrapped, and centered*

Flex direction

Let's now look at these Flexbox properties individually, starting with the main axis property, **flex-direction**. It can be given four possible values, as follows:

- **row**: Flows flex items from left to right

- **row-reverse**: Flows flex items from right to left

- **column**: Flows flex items from top to bottom

- **column-reverse**: Flows flex items from bottom to top

Figures 25.1 and *25.3* have no **flow-direction** property set, so both apply the default of **row**. In *Figure 25.4*, there are three screen grabs showing the other possible values in action.

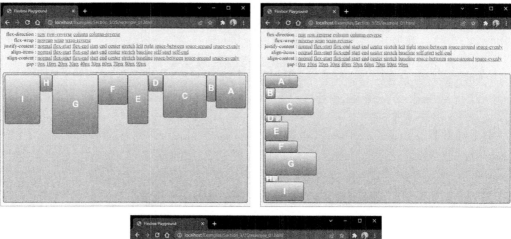

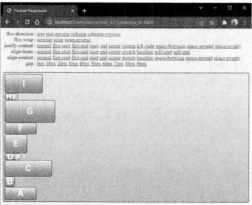

Figure 25.4: *The flex directions of row-reverse, column. and column-reverse*

As you can see, the flex items are ordered right to left in the first screen grab, then top to bottom, and finally bottom to top. Try these settings yourself, combined with changing the flex items' dimensions and perhaps their gap sizes too.

Combined with these property values are what is called the **cross axis**. This is not a user modifiable setting, but is a consequence of the **flow-direction** value. If the main axis is one of the row values, then the cross axis runs up and down the columns. If the main axis is one of the column values, then the cross axis runs left or right along the rows.

Think of this as if you are reading a book. In English, your main axis is along rows from left-to-right, and the cross axis is down columns from top to bottom. For right-to-left languages, the cross axis is the same, but for languages that read top-to-bottom, then their cross axis is left to right rows, and so on.

Wrapping flex items

There are only three ways in which you can handle flex items in terms of how they wrap using the **flex-wrap** property, as follows. If you don't set a value for **flex-wrap**, the Flexbox will behave in an unwrapped manner:

- **nowrap**: This is the default value in which all items remain in a line.

- **wrap**: With this settings, items will wrap top to bottom.

- **wrap-reverse**: Similar to **wrap** but wraps from bottom to top.

Figures 25.1 and *25.3* show the default value of **nowrap**, while *Figure 25.5* illustrates the action of using values of **wrap** and **wrap-reverse**, where the I object has wrapped to the next location allowing all flex items to assume their original unstretched or squashed values:

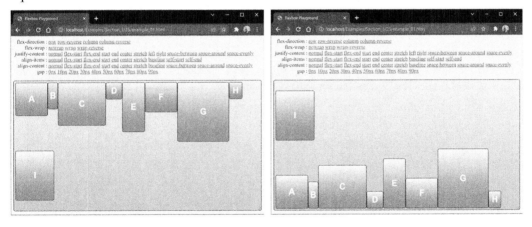

Figure 25.5: *Using wrap and wrap-reverse values*

Content justification

The **justify-content** property supports the following values, many of which are very similar to others with similar names, but have subtly different effects. This is one good reason for writing this example – so that you can try them all for yourself and watch the changes as they occur.

- **normal**: This is the default, as if no justification is set – defaults to start edge

- **flex-start**: Items are flush to each other at the start edge of the container

- **flex-end**: Items are flush to each other at the end edge of the container

- **start**: Items are flush to each other at the start edge of the container main axis

- **end**: Items are flush to each other at the end edge of the container main axis

- **center**: Items are flush to each other centered on the main axis

- **left**: Items are flush to each other at the start edge of the container

- **right**: Items are flush to each other at the end edge of the container

- **space-between**: Items are evenly distributed along the main axis flush to edges

- **space-around**: Items are evenly distributed along the main axis – small edge gap

- **space-evenly**: Items are evenly distributed along the main axis – full edge gap

Figure 25.6 shows a selection of start, end, and center values. You can try the others for yourself and may see some differences, but sometimes only when you change other property values too – so try experimenting.

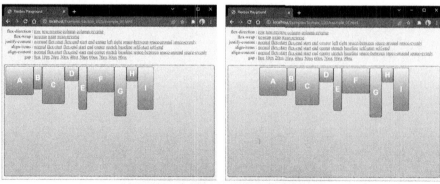

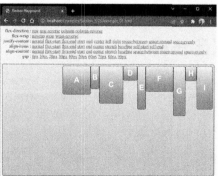

Figure 25.6: *A selection of start, end. and center justification values*

The values that define space for each flex item are subtle in their different ways of displaying, but look carefully at the screen grabs in *Figure 25.7* and you'll see the three values in action. The main difference between them is how space is applied to the outside of the items at each edge.

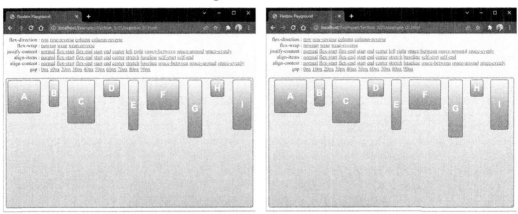

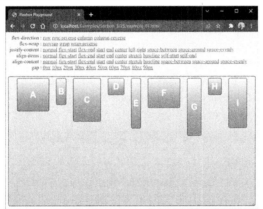

Figure 25.7: Using space values of between, around. and evenly

Aligning items

The **align-items** property supports the following values. As with the **justify-content** property, some of these values are only subtly different from others in how they work. Often, you need to change other property values to see the effect they may have. Here are the supported values:

- **normal**: The default – behaves like **stretch** for flex items

- **flex-start**: Margin edges of flex items are flush with the cross-start edge of the line

- **flex-end**: Margin edges of flex items are flush with the cross-end edge of the line

- **start**: Items are flush to each other at start edge of the container in the appropriate axis

- **end**: Items are flush to each other at end edge of the container in the appropriate axis

- **center**: Items are centered within the line on the cross-axis

- **stretch**: Items are stretched so that the cross-size of their margin box is same as the line

- **baseline**: Items are aligned such that their flex container baselines align

- **self-start**: Items are flush to the start edge of the container in the appropriate axis

- **self-end**: Items are flush to the end edge of the container in the appropriate axis

In *Figure 25.8*, a selection of end, center, and baseline values have been applied to the flex elements. To see variations of these values in action, try changing the **flex-direction** to **column-reverse**, **flex-wrap** to **wrap-reverse,** and **align-content** to **end**, and you should notice some interesting differences in how the different **align-items** values now get applied.

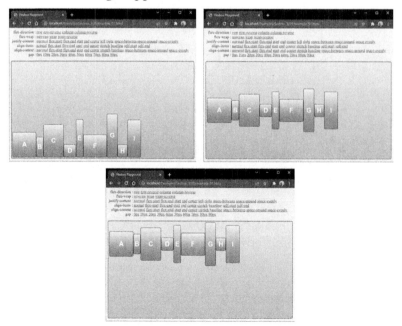

Figure 25.8: The items are aligned to the end, center, and baseline

Aligning the content

We've seen how the **align-items** property works, but there's also a property called **align-content** which sets the distribution of space between and around flex items along a Flexbox's cross-axis. Consider this as the version of **align-items** used in the opposite axis. The values supported are as follows:

- **normal**: Items are packed in their default position as if this property is not set

- **flex-start**: Items are flush against container start with the cross-start edge of the line

- **flex-end**: Items are flush against container end with the cross-start edge of the line

- **start**: Items are flush against container start with the cross axis

- **end**: Items are flush against container end with the cross axis

- **center**: Items are flush to each other in the center of the container along the cross axis

- **stretch**: If necessary, any auto-sized items have their size increased equally

- **baseline**: Items are aligned such that their flex container baselines align

- **space-between**: Items are evenly distributed along the cross-axis flush to edges

- **space-around**: Items are evenly distributed along the cross axis – small edge gap

- **space-evenly**: Items are evenly distributed along the cross axis – full edge gap

Figure 25.9 shows a selection of start, center, and end values. To experiment with **align-content,** you may wish to change the gap settings and the **align-items** values and see what results you can obtain.

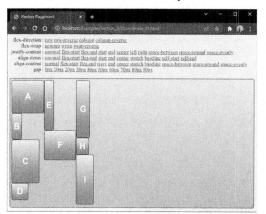
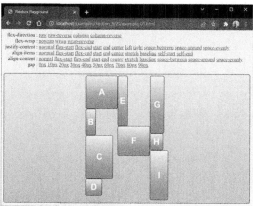

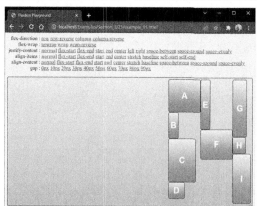

Figure 25.9: *A selection of start, center, and end aligned content*

For example, *Figure 25.10* shows the **align-content** value set to **end**, with various start, center, and end **align-items** values. Note how these alignments occur in place, without moving the items' group alignment.

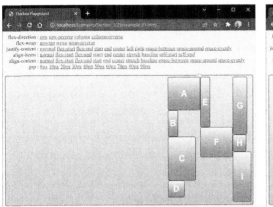 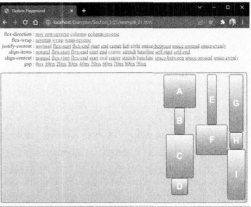

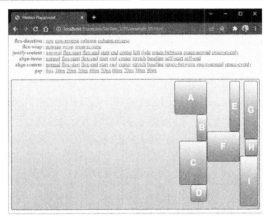

Figure 25.10*: Tweaking the item alignment to the left, center and right*

Other properties

As you have seen, there is also a **gap** property with which you can change the gap around each item. This is sort of like a margin and it takes any measurement value. For example, if you issue the rule **gap : 20px,** there will be a 20 pixel gap around the affected element. You can try a variety of values between **0px** and **90px** for yourself in the example, but those are just there for you to play with and you can use any values you like.

There are also a few properties remaining that are not used in the example. First of all, there's the **order** property. With it, you can define a priority to each flex item if you wish. By default, their order is 0, which is the highest precedence, but if some items should appear on a second level, you could give them an **order** value of 1, and if others have even less priority, you could assign them a value of 2, and so on to create as complex a set of ordering as you like.

Then, there are **flex-shrink** and **flex-grow**. When these properties are assigned values, you give permission to the browser to modify their dimensions by the amounts specified, in order to make them fit the layout better.

The values you supply are proportions. The **flex-grow** property has a default value of 0, which you can increase with integer or floating point numbers to indicate how much of the remaining space in a flex container should be assigned to an item.

The **flex-grow** property has a default value of 1, which you can change to any positive integer or floating point number to indicate how much the item can be shrunk in order to accommodate other items in the available space.

Both of these properties work in conjunction with the **flex-basis** property, which defines the size of an item in terms of the space it leaves as available space. Its default value is **auto,** but you can change it to any width measurement value such as **flex-basis : 120px**, and so on. Or you can use a value string of **fill**, **max-content**, **min-content**, **fit-content,** or just **content** (to auto size based on the item's content) as **flex-basis** values.

For a complete explanation of how Flexbox works from its designers, please visit the following URL:

tinyurl.com/flexbasics

Following is a link to a website that shows you how to create what is called the Holy Grail of layouts using Flexbox:

tinyurl.com/hgflex

Conclusion

By now, you will becoming aware of all the amazing possibilities of things you can achieve with Flexbox. The facility gives you the ability, should you so choose, to create entire layouts using it, although some larger and more complex layouts could become tricky to control due to its one-dimensionality. Therefore, the next chapter covers an alternative two-dimensional layout technology called CSS Grid.

CHAPTER 26
CSS Grid

Introduction

Powerful as it is, Flexbox was not the be-all and end-all its developers may have initially hoped it would become. Yes, it's easy, flexible, and works beautifully, but sometimes there is no substitute for a grid layout, and tables simply don't cut the cloth anymore.

Therefore, CSS Grid was developed in such a way that it could almost be considered an extension of Flexbox into another dimension because it supports many of the Flexbox attributes too – at least where their application makes logical sense.

Now, it's time to learn what extras CSS Grid offers you above and beyond the features available in Flexbox.

Structure

In this chapter, you will:

- Understand what CSS Grid does and why it was created as well as Flexbox
- Be able to use the CSS Grid playground featured in this chapter
- Learn all the main properties and features of CSS Grid

- Become a master of placing grid items exactly where you need them

Objectives

In this chapter, you will learn all the main features of CSS Grid, including what they do, why they were created, and how to use them. By the time you finish reading this chapter, you will be a master of grid layouts and be ready to apply them in your own projects to maximum effect.

About CSS Grid

Like the previous chapter on Flexbox, this chapter contains only one long example, but it's worth working through because you'll be able to test an almost unlimited number of CSS grid layouts without having to write sample documents yourself.

All the main properties are available at a single mouse click, while the properties that define where an element belongs in a grid and how many cell spaces it should cover can be entered as simple input strings.

Of course, it is only an example and not a full-blown product, so you are restricted to working with nine child elements and a maximum grid of 9 by 9 cells. Still, this is ample for learning everything necessary about using the CSS Grid module.

To keep the document length under 100 lines, a number of lines that would otherwise be left blank have been omitted in *Example 26.1*. But if you choose to play with the code after reading through its explanation, you can always take a look at the **example_01a.html** file in the free accompanying archive of example files, which is identical but includes more whitespace, and also outputs the created HTML to the developer console for you to examine, if you wish.

Example 26.1:

```
1.  <!DOCTYPE html>
2.  <html>
3.    <head>
4.      <title>CSS Grid Playground</title>
5.      <style>
6.        body    { background     : #def; }
7.        input   { width          : 33px;
8.                  margin         : 0 0 5px;
9.                  font           : 6pt monospace; }
10.       .label { width           : 110px;
```

```
11.                    text-align      : right;
12.                    float           : left; }
13.      .link   { color              : blue;
14.                    text-decoration : underline;
15.                    cursor          : pointer; }
16.      #outer { display             : grid;
17.                    border          : 1px solid black;
18.                    border-radius   : 5px;
19.                    background      : linear-gradient(cyan,deepskyblue);
20.                    padding         : 5px;
21.                    box-sizing      : border-box;
22.                    width           : 100%;
23.                    height          : 350px;
24.                    resize          : both;
25.                    overflow        : hidden; }
26.      .box    { display             : flex;
27.                    background      : linear-gradient(yellow,red);
28.                    align-items     : center;
29.                    justify-content : center;
30.                    width           : 100%;
31.                    height          : 100%;
32.                    border          : 1px solid black;
33.                    border-radius   : 5px;
34.                    font            : bold 20pt Arial;
35.                    resize          : both;
36.                    overflow        : auto;
37.                    color           : white; }
38.      </style>
39.   </head>
40.   <body>
41.      <output id='output'></output>
42.      <script>
43.        settings = ['grid-auto-flow', 'justify-content',
```

```
44.                      'align-items', 'align-content', 'column-gap',
45.                      'row-gap', 'columns', 'rows']
46.      values   = [['row', 'column', 'dense', 'row dense',
47.                      'column dense'],
48.                   ['normal', 'start', 'end', 'center', 'left',
49.                      'right', 'space-between', 'space-around',
50.                      'space-evenly'],
51.                   ['normal', 'start', 'end', 'center', 'stretch',
52.                      'baseline', 'self-start', 'self-end'],
53.                   ['normal', 'start', 'end', 'center', 'stretch',
54.                      'baseline', 'space-between', 'space-around',
55.                      'space-evenly'],
56.                   ['0px',  '10px', '20px', '30px', '40px',
57.                      '50px', '60px', '70px', '80px', '90px'],
58.                   ['0px',  '10px', '20px', '30px', '40px',
59.                      '50px', '60px', '70px', '80px', '90px'],
60.                   ['1','2','3','4','5','6','7','8','9'],
61.                   ['1','2','3','4','5','6','7','8','9']]
62.      counts   = []; out1 = ''; out2 = "<br><div id='outer'>\n"
63.
64.      for (j = 0 ; j < settings.length ; ++j)
65.      {
66.        s     = settings[j]
67.        out1 += `<div class='label'>${s} : </div>\n`
68.        for (k = 0 ; k < values[j].length ; ++k) {
69.          v     = values[j][k]
70.          out1 += `<span class='link' id='${s}${v}' ` +
71.                   `onclick='set(${j},${k})'>${v}</span>\n`
72.        }
73.        out1 += '<br>'
74.      }
75.      out1 += "<div class='label'>grid-area : </div>\n"
76.      for ( j = 0 ; j < 9 ; ++j) {
```

```
77.          l          = String.fromCharCode(65 + j)
78.        counts[j] = 'auto '.repeat(j + 1)
79.        out1     += l + ` <input onchange="ch('Box_${l}', this)">\n`
80.        out2     += `<div class='box' id='Box_${l}'>${l}</div>\n`
81.      }
82.      id('output').innerHTML = out1 + out2 + '</div>';
83.      function set(j, k) {
84.        s = settings[j]; v = values[j][k]
85.        for (x = 0 ; x < values[j].length ; ++x) {
86.          style(s + values[j][x], 'font-weight', 'normal')
87.          style(s + values[j][x], 'color',       'blue')
88.        }
89.        style(s + v, 'font-weight', 'bold')
90.        style(s + v, 'color',       'red')
91.        if (v > 0) style('outer', 'grid-template-' + s, counts[v - 1])
92.        else style('outer', s, v)
93.      }
94.    function ch(obj1, obj2) { style(obj1,'grid-area',obj2.value) }
95.     function id(val) { return document.getElementById(val) }
96.     function style(obj, prop, val) { id(obj).style[prop] = val }
97.    </script>
98.  </body>
99.</html>
```

One of the ways the length of this document was kept under 100 lines was by using JavaScript to create the entire control section above the grid area, reducing the document length by up to 100 lines, which would otherwise have filled many pages in this book.

Let's take a look at the example to understand how it works and what it does. But all that is necessary for you to know is how to use the example, which is detailed in the following section, if you wish to skip the remainder of this one.

Looking at the example, you will see that it is fairly similar to Example 25.1 in the previous chapter. Similar, but enhanced, and with Flexbox-only options removed, and Grid-only options added.

The body is given a colored background on line 6, so all **<input>** tags are suitably styled starting on line 7. These will be used later to apply settings to the **grid-area** property. After this, the clickable property names and their possible values are styled on lines 10 to 15. The **outer <div>**, the container of the child elements, is styled starting at line 16, beginning with setting the **display** property to **grid**. This is what sets the whole Grid module in action on that element. You can also use a value of **inline-grid**, which would place the container itself in line with any siblings, but not affect its child elements. This parent element can be user-resized.

The class used by each of the nine child elements is styled starting at line 26. Note that these boxes are all set to a **display** property of **flex** for one single reason – as a simple way to center text in the grid's content area both horizontally and vertically. The boxes are also allowed to be user resizable.

How the example works

The **<script>** section starting on line 43 begins with populating a couple of arrays. The **settings[]** array contains all the property names we'll be accessing, and the **values[][]** (two-dimensional array) contains all the possible values for each of the properties. After this, there's an empty array called **counts[]** which will be populated later, and two variables used to output the HTML that the JavaScript will create. The variable **out1** starts off as the empty string, while **out2** begins with a **
** tag and starts a new **<div>** element. This variable will also be appended to, before it itself is appended to **out1** later on.

A loop is then entered on line 64 which achieves a couple of things. Firstly, it extracts all the array information into the HTML as you can see in the first eight lines in the section at the top of the browser. This HTML:

- Lists the various properties.

- It details the possible property values, which can be clicked to applied their values to the **outer** parent **<div>**.

The created HTML is then appended to the variable **out1**. Then, **out1** has more HTML added on line 75 to begin the final line in the top section that supports the input of **grid-area** values, by displaying the property name.

Starting on line 76, there's another loop section in which the **counts[]** array is populated with the string **auto** in its first element, **auto auto** in the second, all the way up to nine instances of the word in its ninth element. These nine values support the settings between 1 and 9 columns and/or rows later on (if the user clicks) by assigning one of the values to either the **grid-template-columns** or **grid-template-rows** attributes. Each instance of the word **auto** adds another column or row.

The variables **out1** and **out2** are also appended with HTML to react to an **<input>** tag's value being changed and call the **ch()** function in response. Additionally, the child grid elements are given ID values and each assigned a letter from A to I for display in their center.

All the HTML so far appended to these two variables is then copied into the innerHTML property of the outer element and closed off with a **</div>** tag. If you would like to see the HTML that was assembled, you can add the following before line 83 (which is already done for you in the file **example_01a.html** in the free accompanying archive of examples):

```
console.log(id('output').innerHTML)
```

Now, we get to the **set()** function which is very similar to the same function in *Example 25.1* in the previous chapter. It responds to clicks on the property values by assigning them instantly to the properties referenced. It also changes the font to bold red for property values currently in use, and ones that are taken out of use are displayed normally again.

The three functions on line 94 to 96, in turn, apply a value entered into one of the **<input>** tags into the **grid-area** property, return an object by looking up its ID name, and apply a style to an object.

Using the example

If you skipped the previous explanation, that's fine – it's there for those who program using JavaScript and want to know how it all works.

This section is where you get to play with the various grid features as a web designer or developer, by loading the example into a browser, which should look like *Figure 26.1*.

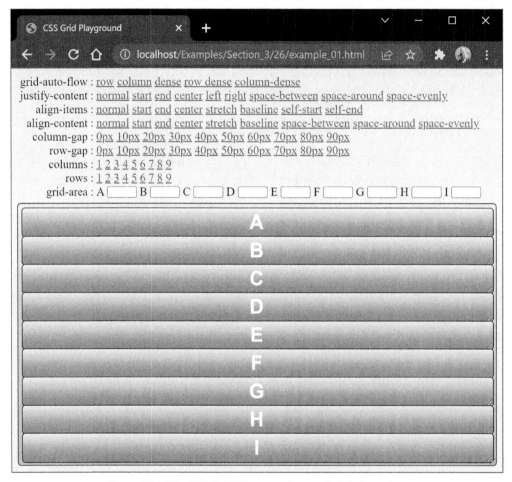

Figure 26.1: The CSS Grid Playground example default settings

In the CSS Grid module, there are nine basic properties (some of which are also used by Flexbox and other modules), along with a number of associated helper properties. These are **grid-auto-flow**, **justify-content**, **align-items**, **align-content**, **column-gap**, **row-gap**, **grid-template-columns**, **grid-template-rows**, and **grid-area**.

Some of these properties apply in different ways according to the settings of other properties. For example, if **grid-auto-flow** is set to **column** instead of **row**, then relevant properties will apply vertically rather than horizontally, and so on. Let's now look at some of these properties in detail.

Grid flow

The flow direction of a grid is specified by the **grid-auto-flow** property, which supports the following values:

- **row**: Items are placed filling each row in turn as necessary – the default

- **column**: Items are placed filling each column in turn as necessary

- **dense**: Attempts to fill in holes earlier in the grid, if smaller items come up later

- **row dense**: Items are placed filling each row, also filling any earlier holes

- **column dense**: Items are placed filling each column, also filling any earlier holes

With no value supplied to this property, the default is **row** with sparse filling of holes. To investigate dense packing, you should leave holes in a grid and see how they get filled. *Figure 26.2* shows the nine grid items set to a **grid-auto-flow** of **column**.

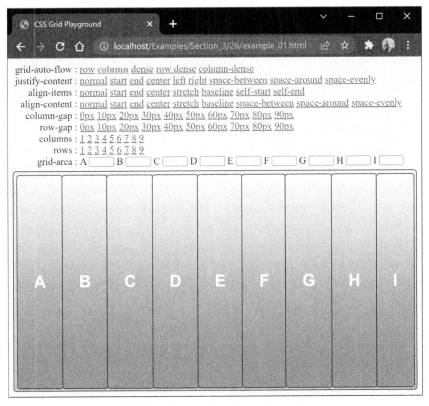

Figure 26.2: The flow has been changed to column mode

Justifying content

To justify content in a variety of ways, you can use the **justify-content** property, in a similar way as you do it with Flexbox. The values supported by this property are:

- **normal**: This is the default, as if no justification is set – defaults to start edge

- **start**: Items are flush to each other at the start edge of the container inline axis

- **end**: Items are flush to each other at the end edge of the container inline axis

- **center**: Items are flush to each other centered on the inline axis

- **left**: Items are flush to each other at the start edge of the container

- **right**: Items are flush to each other at the end edge of the container

- **space-between**: Items are evenly distributed along the inline axis flush to edges

- **space-around**: Items are evenly distributed along the inline axis – small edge gap

- **space-evenly**: Items are evenly distributed along the inline axis – full edge gap

Figure 26.3 shows three screen grabs illustrating the effects of left, center, and right justification applied to grid elements of varying dimensions (varied by using the resize icons at each one's bottom right-hand corner):

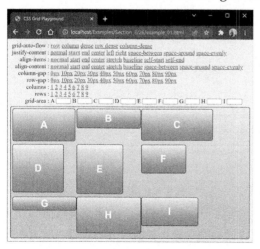
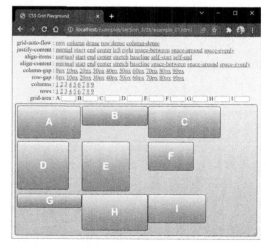

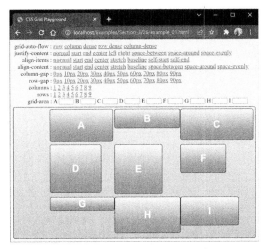

Figure 26.3: *Left, center, and right justification of grid content*

Also, as with Flexbox, you can change the spacing between and around grid elements. Once again, as shown in *Figure 26.4*, three screen grabs have been taken using different spacings, with a variety of differently sized grid elements in a 3 **x** 3 formation.

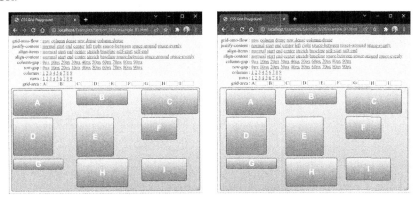

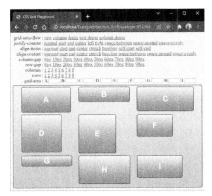

Figure 26.4: *The effects of space between, around, and evenly spaced*

Grid elements that are not given any dimensions will often be auto sized down by shrinking, or stretching to fit. When you apply this example, you will see that when applied, this is not a desired effect. You will also learn when to use absolute sizing to fit your layout, and/or relative sizing such as with percentage or **em** values, and so on.

Aligning items

In grid layout, the **align-items** property controls the alignment of items on the block axis within their grid area. The supported values for this property are as follows:

- **normal**: The default – behaves like either **stretch** or **start** for grid items

- **start**: Items are flush to each other at start edge of the container in the appropriate axis

- **end**: Items are flush to each other at end edge of the container in the appropriate axis

- **center**: Items are centered within the layout

- **stretch**: Items are stretched to fit as and when necessary

- **baseline**: Items are aligned such that their baselines align

- **self-start**: Items are flush to the start edge of the container in the appropriate axis

- **self-end**: Items are flush to the end edge of the container in the appropriate axis

Figure 26.5 shows three more screen grabs in which the **align-items** property is set to **start**, **center,** and **end**.

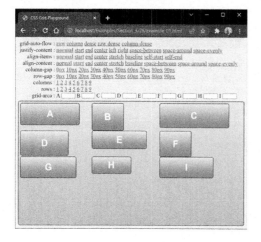
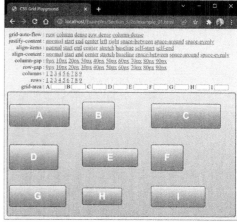

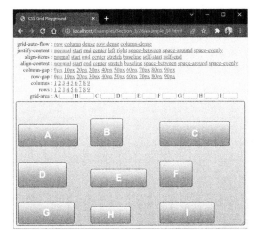

Figure 26.5: *Alignment of start, center, and end displays at the top, middle, and bottom*

In *Figure 26.6*, you can see three screen grabs in which the grid items are more closely grouped as the start, center, and end positions in the grid.

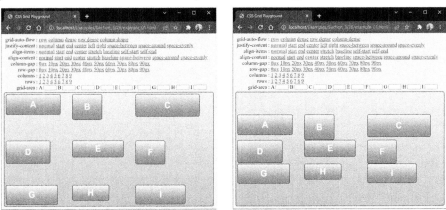

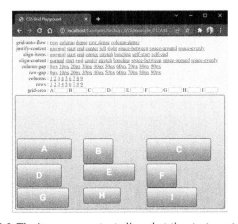

Figure 26.6: *The items are content aligned at the start, center, and end*

This property also supports spacing values, as shown in *Figure 26.7*, in which the grid items are spaced between, around, and evenly.

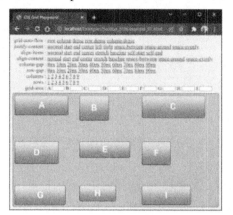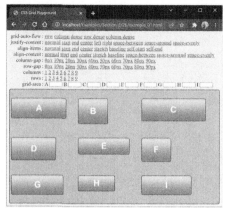

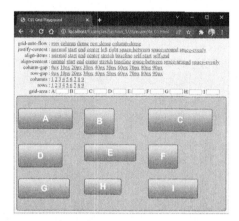

Figure 26.7: The grid items are spaced between, around, and evenly

Setting gaps

You can also specify the gap to use between grid items for both columns and rows using the column-gap and row-gap properties. You can use any standard CSS measurement values, although for simplicity just pixels are applied in the example.

Figure 26.8 shows the effect of no gap, 30 pixels gap between columns, and 30 pixels gap between both columns and rows. To best illustrate these values, the content and alignment are all centered too.

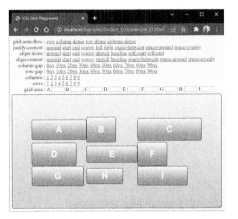
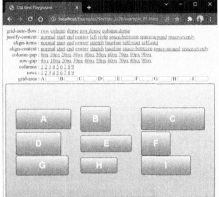
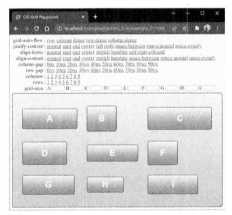

Figure 26.8: Various gap sizes in operation

Changing locations and dimensions

Now, we get to a very interesting part of CSS Grid, in which we can specify exactly where in a grid layout each grid item should be located, and also the amount of space (or number of grid locations) it should occupy.

There are four main properties you can adjust to specify these conditions, which are **grid-row-start**, **grid-row-end**, **grid-column-start**, and **grid-column-end**. As you would think, with them, you can specify exactly where each grid items should go and where its width and/or height should end.

But there's also a shorthand property called **grid-area**, as used in the example. With it, you can specify one or more of these arguments in a single rule, each separated with a forward slash. For example, to make an item begin on the second row down and the second column in, and for it to extend to the fourth row down and fifth column across, you can use a rule as follows:

```
grid-area : 2 / 2 / 5 / 6;
```

If you're scratching your head right now that this rule uses the values 5 and 6 for the final two arguments, it's not surprising because we only wanted to extend to the 4th and 5th row and column. However, the two values for how far to extend an item need to be the location immediately *following* the last one to use. In other words, while the first two values specify the exact location to start with, the second state that the extend of the item must end *before* the value supplied. Once you get that in your head and remember it, you should have no further issues.

To illustrate this in action, *Figure 26.9* uses a grid of 6 by 5 cells where the locations create a layout with a header, footer, and two sidebars. In the main area inside the grid, there's one wide plus four less wide items.

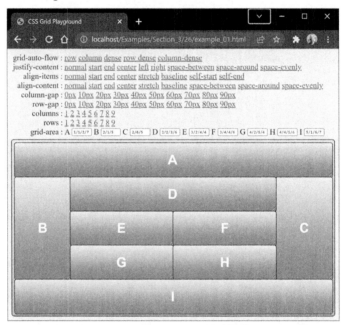

Figure 26.9: *All 9 items have been placed in chosen locations*

This has been achieved with the equivalent of the following rules, resulting in *Figure 26.9*.

```
#boxa { grid-area : 1/1/2/7; }
#boxb { grid-area : 2/1/5;   }
#boxc { grid-area : 2/6/5;   }
#boxd { grid-area : 2/2/3/6; }
#boxe { grid-area : 3/2/4/4; }
#boxf { grid-area : 3/4/4/6; }
#boxg { grid-area : 4/2/5/4; }
#boxh { grid-area : 4/4/5/6; }
```

```
#boxi { grid-area : 5/1/6/7; }
```

Note that for items 2 and 3, being sidebars with no additional horizontal extent, the fourth value has been omitted. If you wanted to add the correct value, for **#boxb** it would be **2/1/5/2** because the width of the column should not extend into the 2nd column, and for **#boxc**, it would be **2/6/5/7** because the width of the column should not extend into the 7th column.

More often than not, you might wish to work with a smaller number of grid items – perhaps just a header, footer, two sidebars, and the main content area. In which case, for testing purposes with this example, you can simply add some lines of JavaScript at line 97, before the closing **</script>** statement as follows, to remove the unwanted elements for the time being. You can always remove these lines later, or add more to hide additional items from the grid – whatever you need to do.

```
style('Box_F', 'display', 'none')
style('Box_G', 'display', 'none')
style('Box_H', 'display', 'none')
style('Box_I', 'display', 'none')
```

Now, when you load the example into a browser, you will have only five elements to work with, as shown in *Figure 26.10*, in which the previously discussed layout (often called the *'Holy Grail'* layout as it is so popular, but can be hard to implement) is applied.

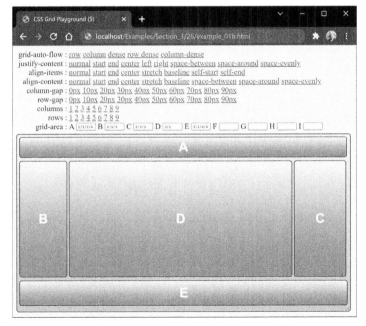

Figure 26.10*: A 'Holy Grail' layout using 5 grid elements*

For your convenience, the free accompanying archive of examples, includes such a modified version as **example_01b.html**.

Of course, this example is just a playground for you to test ideas with. By using it, you can see what is likely to work before creating your own CSS Grid layouts. For example, to create *Figure 26.10*, it was necessary to drag the grid items to the required dimensions, but in an actual website, you might be more likely to use values for the grid container's **grid-template-columns** or **grid-template-rows** attributes similar to this, for a *'Holy Grail'* layout:

```
grid-template-columns : 10% auto 10%;
grid-template-rows    : 50px auto 100px;
```

This would give you a 3 **x** 3 grid layout with a 50-pixel high header and a 100-pixel high footer, sidebars between them of 10% of the available space each, and an auto-sized content area in whatever space remains. After that, it would then be up to you to decide on column and row gaps, the direction of flow, justification, alignment, and so forth.

To take your journey even further and see how CSS Grid works according to its developers, you can check out the following URL, which covers the subject in immense detail:

tinyurl.com/css3-grid

Conclusion

You did it! You've made it to the end of this section of the book on CSS3 and all the fantastic goodies it has to offer. But your CSS journey is not yet complete because in the following section, you will learn the amazingly powerful Sass preprocessor scripting language, or Syntactically Awesome Style Sheets, which is well-named because it is, truly, awesome!

CHAPTER 27
Introducing Sass

Introduction

By now, especially after learning all the new CSS3 capabilities, you may have realized that CSS is extremely powerful and almost like a computer language. Almost is the key word here. To classify it as a useable programming language, a minimum set of features is required, which CSS lacks.

For a start, languages need to store temporary (and final) results somewhere, in the way of variables or arrays (which, as you know, are collections of variables that can be addressed by an index rather than single named variables).

Then, you need decision making structures that can perform *if ... then ... else* type operations. Loops are also considered essential for iterating through data or arrays, and so forth. Up until now in this book, we have used JavaScript to provide this programming functionality to CSS, but there is a better way, and that's something called pre-processing.

A good preprocessor for CSS allows you to use program language type syntax to describe how you want your web document to be styled in CSS, and then it takes the instructions you provide, preprocesses them into pure CSS, and then inserts that CSS into your project. As you can imagine, this opens up a whole new world of what is possible using CSS.

Structure

In this chapter, you will:

- Understand what Sass is, why it was developed, and what it can do

- Be able to install and use Sass on a variety of platforms

- Learn about how file paths work and why they are used

- Know how to pre-process Sass files into self-contained CSS

Objectives

In this chapter, you will learn all about what Sass is, why it was developed, and why it will make your web styling so much easier. By the time you finish reading this chapter, you will understand the basics and be ready to move on to examining how to use variables, nesting, mixins, and more in the following chapters.

Sass is the answer

Developed initially in 2006 using the Ruby programming language, **Syntactically Awesome Style Sheets** (**Sass**) has undergone constant development, leading to it becoming the de-facto pre-processing system in use today, and it remains fully supported by its development team.

There are a number of reasons for its popularity other than a dedicated core team. For example:

- It has always been fully compatible with all versions of CSS.

- It has more features and abilities that any other CSS extension language.

- Many of the world's top web developers have adopted its use, leading to Sass growing into an industry standard. So much so, that your chances of landing a top web development job increase substantially with a good knowledge of Sass under your belt.

Furthermore, Sass in itself is now the basis for a growing number of frameworks built on top of its technology, including Compass, Bourbon, and Susy. So, let's delve deeper into how Sass works, what it does, and how to use it.

About Sass

The Sass system actually comprises two different syntaxes. There's an original syntax called *Indented* (similar to the Haml templating system), and there's a newer syntax called SCSS (also known as *Sassy* CSS), which uses block formatting just like CSS itself. Indented Sass uses the filename extension of **.sass**, while Sassy CSS uses the extension **.scss**.

Sass is used to extend CSS by supplying a number of features normally found in traditional programming languages. To do this, you need to write in *SassScript*, which is then interpreted into blocks of CSS rules, and it provides features such as variables, nesting, mixins, and inheritance, all of which are detailed in this and the remaining chapters.

In order to use Sass, you have to first set it up for your projects by installing the software. The basic program is operated using command line instructions, but you can get applications (both paid and free) to provide a more point and click interface if you prefer, which you can find more information about at the following URL:

sass-lang.com/install

Different versions of Sass

There are three versions of Sass so far, including Ruby Sass, which was the original, LibSass, a version rewritten in C/C++, and now the primary implantation, DartSass, which is the one recommended for use. Following is a breakdown of these versions:

- **Ruby Sass** was the original implementation of Sass, but it reached its end of life and is no longer supported. Having said that, it is still in fairly common use.

- **LibSass** is an implementation of Sass in C/C++, which was designed to be easy to integrate into many different languages. However, as time has passed, it has ended up lagging behind Dart Sass in features and CSS compatibility and is therefore now deprecated, so new projects should use Dart Sass instead.

- **Dart Sass** is now the primary implementation of Sass, which means it gets new features before any other implementation. It's fast, easy to install, and it compiles to pure JavaScript which makes it easy to integrate into modern web development workflows.

Installing on Windows

The most basic way to download and install Sass on Windows is to visit its GitHub repository at the following URL:

tinyurl.com/getsass

Under the list of *Assets*, you will see a set of files, as shown in *Figure 27.1.*

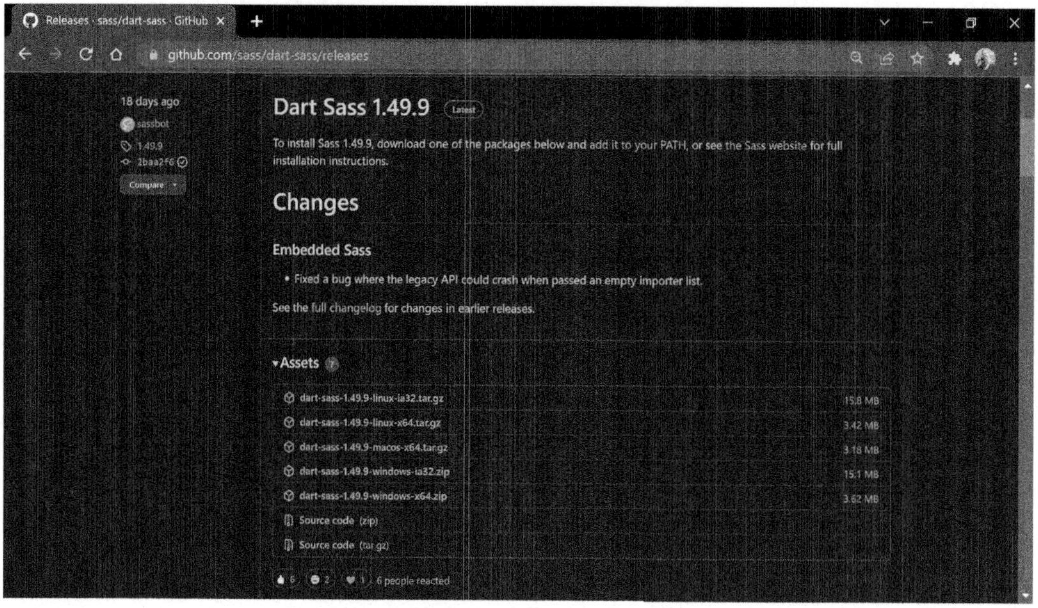

Figure 27.1: *The Sass GitHub repository*

Of these files only the Windows ones are shown below (and the filenames may vary depending on the version number):

```
dart-sass-1.49.9-windows-ia32.zip
dart-sass-1.49.9-windows-x64.zip
```

You should now download the appropriate file and use the standard facilities on your operating system to decompress its contents. Lastly, you must add the sub-folder **dart-sass** (or whatever you name the extracted folder) to your system path.

As you may know, a path is a set of folder names saved as a setting on your computer. When you type in the name of a program that is not contained in the current folder, your computer can then follow this path, searching through it to find the location of the file that you desire to run. This means the program does not have to exist in the current folder you are using, and gives you the benefit of keeping your system programs apart from your project documents.

One way to add to a Windows path is:

1. Type *advanced* in the Start Menu search field..

2. From the choices that appear, select **View Advanced System Settings**.

3. Ensure that the **Advanced** tab is selected in the window that pops up.

4. Click on the **Environment Variables** button.

This section highlights *Path* in the *User variables for…* section and click on the **Edit** button. *Figure 27.2* shows both the System Properties window featuring the **Environment Variables** button, and the environment variables window showing the current path and other environment variables.

Figure 27.2: *The System Properties and Environment Variables windows*

Now, you can add to the path by clicking on the **Edit** button, then click on the **New** button and enter a new addition to the path. For example, if you have placed the decompressed **dart-sass** folder in the root of drive **C**, you can enter **c:\dart-sass**, as shown in *Figure 27.3*, then click on the **OK** button.

Figure 27.3: The new path is being added

The reason you amended the path in the *User variables for...* section is to make the change apply only to you and your account. You could have added the path to the main system path so that all users could benefit from it, but if you make a mistake doing this, you can stop your PC from working. In that case, it can no longer find required system files.

Anyway, to ensure the path amendment is activated, you now need to restart your computer (or at least log out and back in again). Once done, call up a Command Prompt or the Windows PowerShell and type the following:

```
sass --version
```

All being well you will get a simple reply such as the following (for version 1.49.9):

```
1.49.9
```

Other Windows installers

If you use Node.js, you can also install Sass with **npm** by typing the following at a command prompt:

```
npm install -g sass
```

However, this installs a pure JavaScript implementation of Sass, which will run more slowly than the other versions, but it has the same interface, so it is easy to change to another implementation later if you so choose. Or, if you use the Chocolatey package manager for Windows, you can install Dart Sass by running the following instruction:

```
choco install sass
```

Installing on MacOS

On a MacOS computer, the easiest way to get Sass is to first install the Homebrew package manager to handle everything for you.

If you don't already have Homebrew, you need to open a Terminal window. One way to do this is by clicking on the Launchpad icon in the Dock and type **Terminal** in the search field. Then, carefully enter the following command as a *single line*, typing a space after **fsSL** in place of the line break:

```
ruby -e "$(curl -fsSL
  https://raw.githubusercontent.com/Homebrew/install/master/install)"
```

This process is shown in *Figure 27.4* (in which a password is being requested to allow the **sudo** operation to continue).

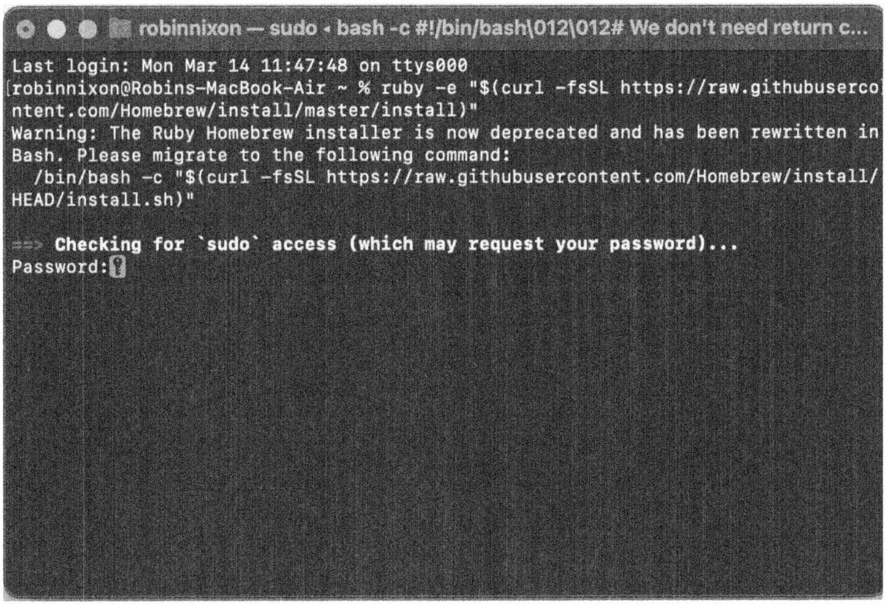

Figure 27.4: The MacOS Homebrew installation is waiting for a password

If prompted for your computer password at any time, type it in and press *Enter*. The installation of Homebrew is undertaken by Ruby, which should already be on your Mac, and depending on your Internet connection, could take a few minutes to complete. During installation, you will see a number of programs being run, and various tools installed for use with XCode, as shown in *Figure 27.5*:

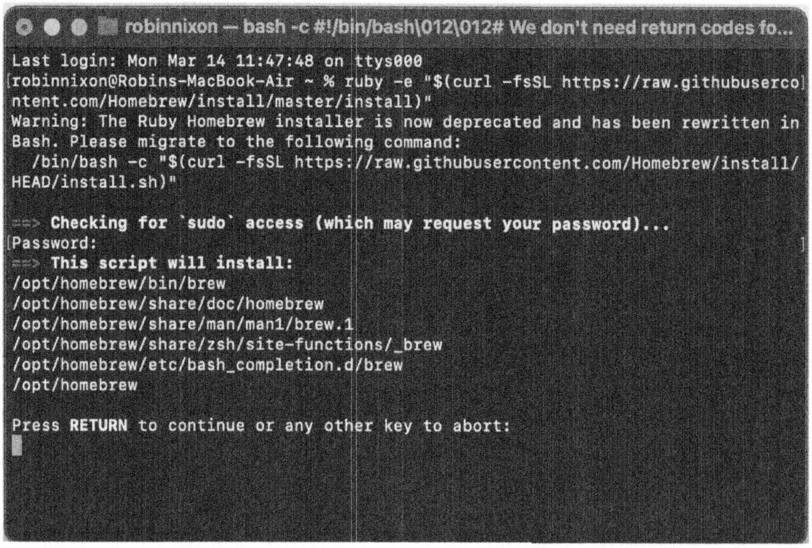

Figure 27.5: *Homebrew installation is ready to begin*

After you complete all you need to do, enter the following command in Terminal to perform the Sass installation:

```
brew install sass/sass/sass
```

The process is shown in *Figure 27.6* (in this case, it is already installed but Homebrew has updated some formulae).

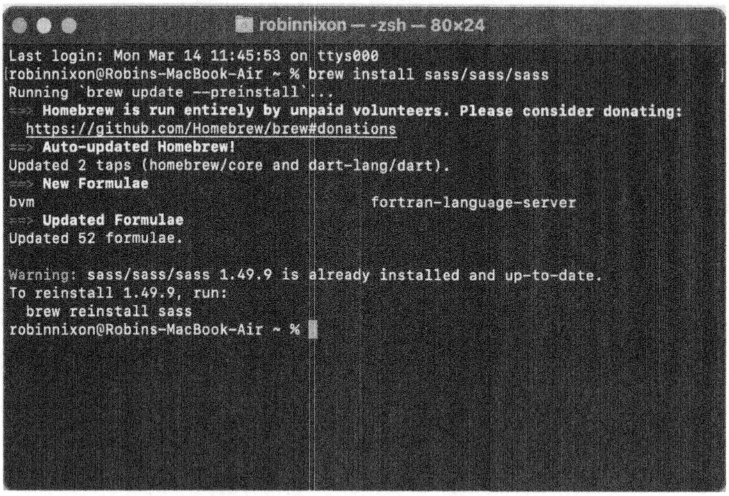

Figure 27.6: *Sass is installed and/or updated*

Your Mac will then report that it is downloading various files and, once installed, you can confirm its success by typing the following command:

```
sass --version
```

All being well! You will get a simple reply such as the following (for version 1.49.9):

```
1.49.9
```

Using this method for MacOS installation means that the system path will be updated automatically for you, so that whichever folder you are currently in, the Sass program can be run just by typing its name at the command line.

Installing on Linux

On a Linux operating system, visit the Sass GitHub repository at the following URL:

tinyurl.com/getsass

Under the list of *Assets,* you will see a set of files (as shown earlier in *Figure 27.1*), of which only the Linux ones are shown here (and the filenames may vary depending on the version number):

```
dart-sass-1.49.9-linux-ia32.tar.gz
```

```
dart-sass-1.49.9-linux-x64.tar.gz
```

You should now download the appropriate file and use the standard facilities on your operating system to decompress its contents. Once done, you should modify the path used by your command line program (such as Bash) to include the folder **dart-sass** (or whatever you have named the decompressed folder).

As you may know, a path is a set of folders saved in a location on your computer that will search through for the names of any programs you type in. This means the program does not have to exist in the current folder you happen to be using and gives you the benefit of keeping your system programs apart from your project documents.

You can do this temporarily each time you plan on running Sass by issuing the **setenv** command, as follows:

```
setenv PATH "$PATH\:path_to_dart-sass"
```

Replace **path_to_dart-sass** with the correct location of where you unpacked the Sass files to. This change will apply during your current command line session. For permanent modifications to your system path, you should refer to your Linux distribution's documentation.

To ensure the path has been correctly modified, type the following at the command line:

```
sass --version
```

All being well! You will get a simple reply such as the following (for version 1.49.9):

```
1.49.9
```

Alternative Linux installations

An alternative way to install Sass on Linux (albeit an older version) is with an app manager. For example, on Ubuntu, you can first issue the following command to ensure everything is up to date:

```
sudo apt-get update -y
```

Then, you can install Ruby Sass (which is slightly different to Dart Sass) by entering the following command:

```
sudo apt-get install -y sass
```

Figure 27.7 shows these two instructions applied in an Ubuntu shell within a Windows operating system, as supported by the **Windows Subsystem for Linux** (**WSL**). But it will work equally well in a stand-alone instance.

Figure 27.7: *Install Sass in Ubuntu Linux using apt-get*

To ensure it has worked, just type the following:

```
sass --version
```

If you prefer, you can install using Node.js. To do this, if you don't have it installed already on your Linux system, you should issue the following command:

```
sudo apt-get install -y npm
```

Once installed, you should then be able to install Sass with it, as follows:

```
sudo npm install -g sass
```

Should you experience any issues with either the Ruby implementation of Sass, or using Node.js to install Dart Sass, you are recommended to do the manual installation from the **tar.gz** file on GitHub, as described a little earlier, to ensure everything works as expected and that you are fully up-to-date.

Pre-processing to CSS

On all three major operating systems, at the command line you can now process your Sass files into finalized CSS files by issuing a command such as the following to take the file **styles.scss** from one location, process it, and then save the result to **styles.css** in another location:

```
sass source/stylesheets/styles.scss build/stylesheets/styles.css
```

Specifying the source and destination files is essential, and it's recommended that you store your folders containing them in different places so that it is clear to you which are your source files, and which are your finished build files.

When you do this, you can then set Sass to watch a source file and automatically process it every time it changes – which is a real-time saver and works in the background as if by magic, as follows:

```
sass --watch source/stylesheets/styles.scss build/stylesheets/styles.css
```

Now, every time you save a new version of the source file, you can just assume that the build version is almost immediately available for testing (assuming the file processes quickly, which is normally the case with all except the largest and most complex Sass files).

You can also watch entire folders and keep their matching builder folders updated through the use of a colon as a separator, as with the following command:

```
sass --watch source/stylesheets:build/stylesheets
```

Now, whenever any file in the source folder is updated, it will be processed and saved as a matching file of the same name but with the extension **.css** in the build folder.

Conclusion

You now have a basic understanding of Sass, its various implementations, what it does, and how to use it on a variety of different platforms. You are now ready to start using Sass yourself, and take a deep dive into using it with variables, nesting, mixins, and more in this book's remaining chapters.

CHAPTER 28
Sass Variables and Flow

Introduction

There are no two ways about it, CSS is hardly a programming language and creating great layouts with it can be quite time-consuming. However, Sass is there to the rescue, but you will need to learn some programming techniques to use it to its fullest.

But don't worry, it definitely is easier than it may seem, mostly because it's like giving CSS plain English instructions combined with just a bit of mathematics. If you can write a shopping list with if/else substitutions, then you can write Sass code.

Structure

In this chapter, you will:

- Learn about the difference between CSS and Sass variables

- Understand what variable scope is and how it works

- Be able to use Sass operators with precision

- Become an expert at using the Sass flow control features

Objectives

By the time you complete reading this chapter, you will have become fully acquainted with the advanced techniques that the Sass pre-processor offers. You will be comfortable using variables and looping structures and be able to create expressions to control the flow of the code exactly how you need it.

Variables in CSS

To recap, recent versions of browsers support the limited use of variables in CSS3 by accepting the double hyphen (`--`) as a variable prefix, as follows:

```
#element { --main-bg-color: cyan; }
```

In this instance, the variable is named **--main-bg-color** and it has been given the value **cyan**. Thereafter, any use of this variable within the element with the ID of **element** (and its child elements) will apply. But outside this scope, the variable is ignored, so inherited values are used instead. To make variables have the global scope and thus apply everywhere in your CSS, the pseudo class of **:root** can be used, as follows:

```
:root { --main-bg-color: cyan; }
```

To then assign a variable's value to a property, you must use the **var()** function, as follows:

```
#mydiv { background-color: var(--main-bg-color); }
```

There is no in-built language syntax for processing variables using operators, but you can use the CSS **calc()** function to achieve a similar result. You can, for example, create a couple of variables containing pixel values, as follows:

```
:root {
  --default-width  : 100px;
  --default-height : 80px;
}
```

These can then be used in a **calc()** function and applied using **var()**, as follows:

```
#mydiv { width : calc(var(--default-width) + 20px); }
```

Let's put these ideas together in *Example 28.1* and see them in action.

Example 28.1:

```
1.  <!DOCTYPE html>
2.  <html>
```

```
3.    <head>
4.      <title>CSS Variables</title>
5.      <style>
6.        :root {
7.          --default-width  : 100px;
8.          --default-height :  80px;                              }
9.        #div1 {
10.         width            : var(--default-width );
11.         height           : var(--default-height);             }
12.        #div2 {
13.         width            : calc(var(--default-width ) + 20px);
14.         height           : calc(var(--default-height) + 20px); }
15.        div {
16.         background-color : lime;
17.         float            : left;
18.         margin           : 10px;
19.         border           : 1px solid black;                   }
20.      </style>
21.    </head>
22.    <body>
23.      <div id='div1'>This is div1</div>
24.      <div id='div2'>This is div2</div>
25.    </body>
26. </html>
```

As shown in line 16 of this example, by default, all **<div>** elements are given a black border, a lime background, and a ten-pixel margin, are set to float on a line. Earlier in the document, the variables are assigned their values on lines 7 and 8, while the two **<div>** elements named **div1** and **div2** are assigned their rules from line 9 to line 14. Finally, in the **<body>** section of the document, starting at line 22, the two elements are displayed.

The result looks like *Figure 28.1*, in which you can clearly see that the second element is both 20 pixels wider and deeper than the first, as a result of adding that amount to each of the variables, and then applying the results of these calculations to the elements' dimensions.

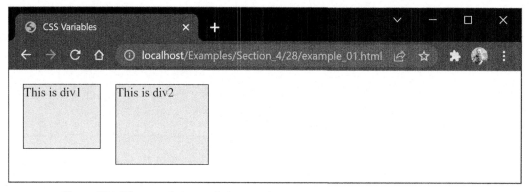

Figure 28.1: The second element is increased in size using CSS variables and functions

Using some rather long-winded function names, you can also read and set these variable values from within JavaScript. For example, to obtain a CSS variable's value, you can call the **getComputedStyle()** function to return the relevant element, and once you have that element, you can then call the **getPropertyValue()** function on it, with an instruction as follows:

```
getComputedStyle(document.body).getPropertyValue('--default-width')
```

To change the value, you can call the **setProperty()** function on the **style** property of the relevant element, with an instruction as follows:

```
document.body.style.setProperty('--default-width', '50px')
```

In fact, if you open your browser's development console and enter the latter of these two instructions into it, the new value will be instantly applied, with the result looking like *Figure 28.2* (which shows the console window floating over the browser):

Figure 28.2: A CSS variable has been updated in JavaScript

Variables in Sass

One of the main reasons for the rapid uptake of Sass was that CSS didn't support the use of variables for the longest time. Thankfully, though, all major browsers now do, with the notable exceptions of *Opera Mini* and most pre-2022 *Android* browsers – so beware! But as along with all the other reasons for using Sass, the CSS implementation of variables remains quite basic and unwieldy to use. Therefore, Sass users don't often make use of the in-built CSS variable features, relying instead on the greater power of Sass itself.

You see, in Sass you can create a variable at any point by prefacing it with a dollar sign and assigning it a value. In the previous example, *Example 28.1*, we created a variable called **--default-width** and had to apply it to the pseudo class of **:root** in order to give it global scope. If it is not given global scope, a variable applies only to a chosen element and its child elements. This means that a CSS variable can have different values depending on where and how it is used!

With Sass, on the other hand, once a variable is set, it has that single value everywhere it is used unless changed, and if so, that new value applies thereafter. This means you can start off with a variable called **$default-width** having a value of **100px**, and then later change it to **150px**, and only subsequent uses will be given the new value. Earlier uses will retain its previous value of **100px**.

CSS variables, however, if updated, change all instances of where they have been used within their scope. This means that when you change a CSS variable's value from **100px** to **150px**, all uses within that scope are set to the new value of **150px**. This behavior is useful for animation and mouse-over events or other dynamic interactions, for example, and you can always use CSS variables as well as Sass ones.

The main thing to bear in mind with Sass variables is that they go away once the preprocessing is complete and are all replaced with fixed values in the newly generated CSS. This is known as being *imperative* in that only the current value of a variable is used at the time it is applied. CSS variables, however, are called *declarative*, which means that when their values are changed; all previous uses are also updated.

Both CSS and Sass variables are case sensitive, which means that the exact use of upper and/or lower case is important. In other words, the CSS variables **--Text-Color** and **--text-color** are different because they have differently capitalized initial letters. Likewise, the Sass variables **$Text-Color** and **$text-color** are also different to each other.

However, Sass has one peculiarity, it treats underscores (_) and hyphens (-) equally. You can interchange them if you wish and your Sass will still work just fine. This is because Sass originally used the underscore character as the separator of choice, and only later also adopted the hyphen to become more compatible with CSS. The result is that in CSS, the hyphen and underline are different characters, but in Sass, they are considered the same as each other.

Default variable values

When you assign a value to a variable, it takes on that value regardless of whether or not it already had been given a value. In other words, if it had no value, the value is assigned and, if it already had a value, that value is overwritten.

Sometimes, however, you need greater control over when to overwrite an existing value and so the **!default** flag is provided to help you protect previously assigned values. Variables that are created using the **!default** flag cannot be modified unless they are not already assigned a value, or their value is **null**. But you *can* make use of the **@use** rule with Sass libraries to modify a variable that has the **!default** flag set.

Let's suppose you have a library file called **library.scss** (assuming you are using SCSS formatting, rather than SASS which, as you will remember, uses indentation in place of the parentheses of SCSS).

Since this library is going to be imported, the recommended convention is to preface the file name with an underscore, like this: **_library.scss**. The idea is to keep all imported libraries together because they will sort starting with the underscore, and usually appear first in directory listings. This is entirely optional, and up to you whether or not to apply this convention. Therefore, that style is not used in this book.

Example 28.2 shows the sort of contents you can place in such a library file, including the use of the **!default** flag.

Example 28.2:

```
1.  // library.scss

2.  $black          : #000 !default;

3.  $border-radius  : 0.25rem !default;

4.  $box-shadow     : 0 0.5rem 1rem rgba($black, 0.15) !default;

5.

6.  code {

7.    border-radius : $border-radius;

8.    box-shadow    : $box-shadow;

9.  }
```

Now, we will create *Example 28.3*, **style.scss**, which will import this library:

Example 28.3:

```
1.  // style.scss
2.  @use 'library' with (
3.    $black          : #222,
4.    $border-radius : 0.1rem
5.  );
```

So, what is going on between these two files? Well, **library.scss** creates a few variables such as **$black** on line 2, which is given the color **#000** and also the **!default** flag. Likewise, the other two variables are also set to **!default** values for the **$border-radius** and **$box-shadow** variables. After this, the default HTML code element is styled to apply the **$border-radius** and **$box-shadow** variable values to their respective properties.

In **style.scss**, the **library.scss** library file is imported with the **@use** rule, but with overrides for the **$black** and **$border-radius** variables, which are assigned new values. Do remember, though, that variables declared within a built-in module cannot be modified. For example, if you try to redefine the value of PI to be 3, as follows, it will fail:

```
@use "sass:math" as math;
math.$pi : 3;
```

Variable scope

As with almost any programming language that uses variables, there is the matter of scope to consider. The scope of a variable is the part of a program within which its value applies. For example, at the top of a stylesheet, a variable will have global scope by default because it is outside any subsections. This is called the top level.

However, variables declared within a block that has braces (or in an indented section in SASS formatting) are considered to be local. This means their scope applies only within that section of code. What's more, a local variable can have the exact same name as a global one, without either interfering with the other.

In *Example 28.4*, there is a top level and two local rule blocks.

Example 28.4:

```
1.  $global-bg    : #000;
2.
3.  .content {
4.    $local-fs  : italic;
```

```
5.      background : $global-bg;
6.      font-style : $local-fs;
7.  }
8.
9.  .sidebar {
10.   background : $global-bg;
11.   font-style : $local-fs;
12. }
```

Here, on line 1, a global variable is declared with the name **$global-bg** (it doesn't have to begin with the word **global-**, this is just a handy convention you can use to remind yourself what is going on). This stores the color **#000** intended for use as a background (hence, the **bg** in the variable name).

Below it are two sections of code providing rules for a content and sidebar portion of a webpage. In the **.content** section, a local variable called **$local-fs** is created on line 4 with the value **italic**. Clearly, the **fs** in the variable name indicates it is being used to apply a **font-style** attribute, but remember that you can use any variable naming convention of your choosing (or that of your employer), and keeping this convention consistent will be really helpful to you and everyone else who accesses your code.

Next, on line 5, the **background** property is assigned the value in **$global-bg**. This works because the variable has global scope. After this, on line 6, the **font-style** property is assigned the value in **$local-fs**, which also works because that variable is in local scope.

However, take a look at the **.sidebar** section, in which the **background** property on line 10 is correctly assigned the global variable value in **$global-bg**. What do you think will happen on line 11? The answer is that **$local-fs** is not in the local scope because it has not been defined in that section, and neither is it in global scope because the only other instance of this variable name is within a different section that has its own local scope. Therefore, the assignment on line 11 will fail.

Forcing global scope

Sometimes, you may wish to update a global variable from within a subsection of a stylesheet and you can do this with the **!global** flag. Simply put, adding **!global** after a variable assignment that allows you to update a previously existing global variable from within a section of code that would normally disallow this. Note that you cannot create a new global variable in this manner; however, you can use the **!global** flag as follows to update a global variable:

```
.content {
  $global-bg : #246 !global;
  background : $global-bg;
}
```

Remember that when you change a global variable's value, no matter where you do so, the new value is used from that point on wherever the variable is accessed.

Flow control

One of the most important aspects of a programming language is that you can control the flow of instructions that are executed according to various flow control rules, combined with a number of different operators.

In Sass, there are four main flow rules, which are as follows:

- `@if … @else … if`
- `@each … in`
- `@for … from … through/to`
- `@while`

To explain how these work, either alone, or in various combinations, it's necessary to understand the use of operators in Sass. These are symbols such as **+**, **-**, *****, and **/** that you know well, and also more interesting operators like **==**, **!=**, **>**, **<**, and more.

With operators, you can compare values as well and make them interact with each other in a variety of different ways. So, let's take a deeper look.

Sass operators

There are six types of operators supported by Sass, which are as follows:

- **Equality**: == and !=
- **Arithmetic**: +, -, *, /, = and %
- **Comparison**: <, <=, > and >=
- **Boolean**: **and**, **or** and **not**
- **Concatenation**: +, - and /
- **Precedence**: (and)

Although this may look a little daunting if you've never programmed, it's all quite straightforward really. For example, the == operator (double equals) compares two values to see whether they are *equal* to each other. Two equals symbols are used to differentiate from a single equals symbol, which is used to assign values. The != symbol simply tests for two values being different or *not equal*.

The arithmetic operators should be clear to you, with the possible exception of the **%** operator, which is used to calculate a remainder after a division. For example, **15pt % 6pt** is **2pt** with a remainder of **3pt**, so it results in the value **3pt** (**15 / 6** equals **2** remainder **3**). And yes, you can use any allowable CSS measurement values, not just numbers, and of varying types too.

Comparison operators should make immediate sense too. For example, **2 < 3** is **true** because **<** is the *less than* operator. You also have **<=** for *less than or equal to*, and the opposites of **>** for *greater than*, and **>=** for *greater than or equal to*. Since you can mix and match CSS measurement types, these operators really come into their own because when the result of a mixed calculation between mixed measurement types is not clearly obvious at a glance (otherwise, you could just enter that result value), you can instead use an expression such as **1in < 73pt**, which evaluates to **true** because there are 72 points in an inch.

Let's now turn to the, perhaps, lesser obvious operators, starting with the Boolean operators **and**, **or**, and **not**. With these, you can create compound expressions of the type *if this **and** that*, or maybe *if **not** this*, or *if this **or** that*. Think of their use as exactly how you would say them in English because that's how they work. They are called Boolean after the chap who invented them (*George Boole*), and they represent truth values in logical expressions.

That leaves us with just a few more, concatenation and precedence operators. Concatenation simply means attaching two items together, which are generally string values, but in the process, numeric values can attach to string values to make a new string. But you have to be careful because the **+** operator is also used for addition. Therefore, **1 + 2** is equal to the number **3**, but **Light + Blue** is equal to the CSS color string value of **LightBlue**.

The **-** operator when used for concatenation works in an unusual way as a shorthand for expressions such as **sans- + serif**, which evaluates to **sans-serif**. Instead, you can use **sans - serif** to arrive at the same string value. Likewise, the **/** operator can be used for concatenation when placed before a non-entirely numeric value like this: **/ 24pt**, which concatenates to **/24pt** as, in fact, will the **-** operator when used like this: **- moz**, which concatenates to **-moz**. However, these latter uses are for reasons of historical compatibility and are not really recommended for use. But you need to know about them so that you will understand existing code you encounter that may utilize these operators in this way.

Sass expressions (Sass Script)

An expression in Sass is anything that goes on the right-hand side of a property or variable declaration. Each expression produces a value and any valid CSS property value is also a Sass expression. Sass expressions are passed as arguments to mixins and functions and are used for control flow and manipulated using arithmetic. The Sass's expression syntax is called **SassScript**.

We've already looked at the operators used by Sass and also briefly seen the flow control types supported, so now let's examine each of these four types in turn.

@if ... @else

As you might expect, the **@if** flow control type takes an expression which, if it evaluates to **true**, then executes the instruction, declaration, or assignment following. If the optional **@else** keyword is also used and then if the expression does *not* evaluate to **true**, whatever follows the **@else** will be executed. Let's see this in action in *Example 28.5*.

Example 28.5:

```
1. $bord-rad : false;

2.

3. @if $bord-rad {

4.    border-radius : 10px;

5. }

6. @else {

7.    border-radius : 0;

8. }
```

On line 1, a variable called **$bord-rad** is created and given the value **false**. The **@ if** instruction on line 3 then tests this value and if it evaluates to **true**, the following **border-radius** property is set to **10px**. On the other hand, if **$bord-rad** does not evaluate to **true**, the **@else** instruction on line 6 is executed ensuring that borders will not have a radius. By default, this example will not display rounded border corners due to **$bord-rad** having a value of **false**.

This is a very simple example of an expression where just the value of a single variable is evaluated. Any value that is null or zero is considered *falsey* by Sass and so evaluates to **false**. Every other value is considered *truthy*, and will evaluate to **true**. This even extends to empty strings, empty lists, and even the number **0**. All these are considered *truthy*. And yes, *falsey* and *truthy* are words used in the Sass documents!

So, what does this mean in practice? Well, as well as being able to assign the values **true** or **false** to variables, you can also work with any values they may have (or not), and they will still evaluate to either true of false. For example, a value of **24pt** is true, so is **""**, as is **"Arial Bold"**. The only single values of a variable that will evaluate to **false** are false and **null**.

Complex expressions are a different matter, though, because the entire expression is evaluated to arrive at a Boolean result of either **true** of **false**, as shown in *Example 28.6*.

Example 28.6:

```
1. $margin   : 10px;
2. $padding : 10px;
3.
4. @if $margin + $padding >= 20px {
5.    border-color : green;
6. }
7. @else {
8.    border-color : black;
9. }
```

In this example, there are two variables called **$margin** and **$padding**, each of which is given a value of **10px**. On line 4, these two values are added and the result is tested for being equal to or greater than **20px**. If so, then the **border-color** property is set to **green** on line 5, otherwise it is set to **black** on line 8. Obviously, any other comparison could be made, such as **<=** or **==** and so on, all depending on what you need to evaluate.

Alternatively, you might want to test more than one expression such as with *Example 28.7*, in which the two variables are independently examined.

Example 28.7:

```
1. $margin   : 10px;
2. $padding : 10px;
3.
4. @if ($margin == 10px) and ($padding >= 10px) {
5.    border-color : green;
6. }
7. @else {
8.    border-color : black;
9. }
```

Here, a test is made to determine whether **$margin** has a value exactly equal to **10px** and also whether **$padding** is greater than or equal to **10px**. If, and only if, both of these evaluate to **true** (due to the use of the **and** keyword), then the **border-color** property will be set to **green** on line 5.

The power of parentheses

Notice how parentheses have been used in *Example 28.7* to encapsulate each expression and make it clear both to you and Sass exactly what is intended.

Using parentheses, you can ensure the contents within them is evaluated before items outside. For example, you can use parentheses to override the natural precedence of operators. You see, by convention ***** and **/** have a higher precedence than **+** and **-**, because they have far more reaching effects.

So, the sum **2 + 3 * 5 - 4** actually evaluates to **13** and not **21** (which would be the answer if Sass only evaluated from left to right). But by convention, Sass will multiply **3** by **5** first, and only then add the **2** and subtract the **4**. However, should you wish to force Sass to evaluate from left to right you can do so with parentheses like this: **(2 + 3) * 5 - 4**, and you will indeed get a result of **21**. Note that **(2 + 3) * (5 – 4)** would be an entirely different calculation resulting in the answer **5** because the two outside expressions would be evaluated first, and then multiplied together.

@else if

You can actually do more than just **@if … @else** because you can extend this type of flow control as far as you like by further adding **if** after any **@else**. *Example 28.8* shows this in action.

Example 28.8:

```
1.    $margin : 10px;

2.

3.    @if $margin == 10px {

4.       border-color : green;

5.    }

6.    @else if $margin == 15px {

7.       border-color : blue;

8.    }

9.    @else {

10.      border-color : black;

11.   }
```

In this example, line 6 shows the use of **@else if** to test for a different value in **$margin** to the test on line 3. In this case, if **$margin** has a value of **15px**, then the **border-color** property is set to **blue** on line 7. Finally, there is a stand-alone **@else** on line 9 to finish off the sequence – and there could be more **@else if** statements in-between if needed.

@each … in

Now that you have got the hang of **@if** … **@else** expressions, let's move on to something a little more complex with **@each**. To understand the power of this feature, imagine that you want to create a number of different sizes of icons, but don't want to write several separate sets of rules. Using Sass this is easy to do, as shown in *Example 28.9*.

Example 28.9:

```
1. $sizes : 40px, 60px, 80px, 100px;

2.

3. @each $size in $sizes {
4.    .icon-#{$size} {
5.       font-size : $size;
6.       height    : $size;
7.       width     : $size;
8.    }
9. }
```

"*Woah*", you may be thinking, "*what on earth is that?*". Relax, because you're going to like this. These 9 lines of Sass will actually result in many more lines of CSS for you. On line 1, a variable called **$sizes** is created. But it's a special type of variable called a list. You create it in the normal way, but add extra values separated with commas to turn a variable into a list. In this case, it's a set of four values ranging from **40px** to **100px**.

The power of the list is demonstrated starting on line 3 with the **@each** keyword. What this statement does is pull out each of the values in **$sizes** one at a time going around in a loop. Each time around the loop, the value extracted from **$sizes** is placed in **$size**, (note that this is the singular of **$sizes**, but could be any name of your choice), and then on line 4, that value is accessed using **#{$size}**, which gets replaced with the actual value, and then appended to the string **.icon-**. So, for example, the first list item value is **40px**, that gets appended to **.icon-**, resulting in **.icon-40px**.

The **@each** command then continues through the remaining three values in the list, ending up creating the CSS shown in *Example 28.10*.

Example 28.10:

```
1.  .icon-40px {
2.     font-size : 40px;
3.     height    : 40px;
4.     width     : 40px;
5.  }
6.
7.  .icon-60px {
8.     font-size : 60px;
9.     height    : 60px;
10.    width     : 60px;
11. }
12.
13. .icon-80px {
14.    font-size : 80px;
15.    height    : 80px;
16.    width     : 80px;
17. }
18.
19. .icon-100px {
20.    font-size : 100px;
21.    height    : 100px;
22.    width     : 100px;
23. }
```

Now, you have four CSS classes all ready to use. See how using **@each** can save you from a lot of tedious CSS scripting. Any set of values that can be stored in a list and then iterated out into multiple rule sets can be optimized with this technique.

@for ... from ... through

The power of the **@each** keyword should be clear to you now, but there are even more powerful things you can do with looping structures in Sass, such as with the

@for command. With it, you can count up (or down) from one number to another, evaluating a block of rules for every step between. As with @each, each value is assigned to a variable each time around the loop.

Let's take the case of wanting to assign values to the **font-size** property of the various **h1** through **h5** elements, to replace their default values, ranging from **24pt** for **h1** down to **8pt** for **h2**. *Example 28.11* shows one way you can do this with Sass:

Example 28.11:

```
1. $heading-size: 28pt;

2.

3. @for $i from 1 through 5 {

4.    h#{$i} {

5.       font-size : $heading-size - ($i * 4);

6.    }

7. }
```

What is happening here is that a variable called **$heading-size** is created on line 1, with a value of **28pt**. Then, on line 3, the **@for** keyword is used with the **from** and **through** keywords to iterate through the values 1 through 5, and on line 4, the letter **h** is then appended with each of these numbers to build the element names of **h1** through **h5**.

Line 5 then sets the **font-size** property for each of these elements by subtracting the value in **$i** multiplied by **4** from the value in **$heading-size**. The result is that **h1** will have a **font-size** property value of **24pt**, **h2** will be **20pt**, all the way to **h5**, which will be as small as **8pt**. The resulting CSS will look like *Example 28.12*:

Example 28.12:

```
1. h1 {

2.    font-size : 24pt;

3. }

4.

5. h2 {

6.    font-size : 20pt;

7. }

8.

9. h3 {

10.    font-size : 16pt;
```

```
11. }
12.
13. h4 {
14.     font-size : 12pt;
15. }
16.
17. h5 {
18.     font-size : 8pt;
19. }
```

@for ... from ... to

Example 28.11 is all well and good, but there was a bit of a workaround required in the Sass because the first line had to start with a **font-size** property **4pt** larger than was required, in order to account for the subtractions of multiple amounts of **4pt** in the loop.

A better way is to utilize **@for ... from ... to** instead, which will iterate from the **from** value up to but *not* including the **to** value. This is different from the previous example, which used the **through** keyword and iterated up to *and* including the **through** value. *Example 28.13* shows how to do this in a slightly better way.

Example 28.13:

```
1. $heading-size : 24pt;
2.
3. @for $i from 5 to 0 {
4.     h#{$i} {
5.         font-size      : $heading-size;
6.         $heading-size : $heading-size - 4pt;
7.     }
8. }
```

In this example, the correct initial **$heading-size** value is assigned on line 1, then the **@for** loop on line 3 counts down from **5** to **1**, but not to **0** because the **to** keyword is used in place of **through**. Each time around the loop this value is assigned to the **font-size** property of elements **h5** to **h1**, then line 6 subtracts **4pt** from the variable's value, so that the next time around its value will be that much smaller. The end result is similar to *Example 28.12*, except that the **h5** through **h1** elements appear in reverse order.

Of course, you can also turn *Example 28.13* into *Example 28.14* using **through** instead of **to**, showing that how you choose to pick between the **to** and **through** keywords will generally be just a matter of personal preference, as you can normally find ways to make either keyword work for you.

Example 28.14:

```
1. $heading-size : 24pt;

2.

3. @for $i from 5 through 1 {

4.   h#{$i} {

5.     font-size     : $heading-size;

6.     $heading-size : $heading-size - 4pt;

7.   }

8. }
```

@while

The final way you can manage flow control and looping is with **@while**. Beware with this one because you can create an infinite loop that never stops. Well, **@while** goes round and round the loop as long as the expression it evaluates results in the value **true**. If it never evaluates to **false**, it will repeat forever. On the whole, you are better off using **@each** or **@for** because they are easier to use and for others to understand your code. Also, the risk of infinite looping is not there. However, there can be times when **@while** is preferable, but they are so complex that they are beyond the scope of this book.

Nevertheless, let's change *Example 28.14* to make it use **@while** as an exercise in understanding how this keyword works, as shown in *Example 28.15*.

Example 28.15:

```
1. $heading-size : 24pt;

2.

3. @while $heading-size >= 8pt {

4.   h#{$i} {

5.     font-size     : $heading-size;

6.     $heading-size : $heading-size – 4pt;

7.   }

8. }
```

See how only line 3 is changed in this example. What's now happening is that only one simple test is made each time around the loop. As long as the value in **$heading-size** is greater than or equal to **8pt**, the looping continues. But when the value drops below **8pt**, the loop is exited. In some ways, this can be seen as simpler than **@ for**, but if you were to forget or incorrectly decrement the value in **$heading-size** to less than **8pt**, the loop would never end. So, be careful if you use this keyword.

Conclusion

This concludes a fairly comprehensive introduction to using variables and managing flow control in Sass. With this grounding, you are now ready to move on to looking into nesting and inheritance in the next chapter.

CHAPTER 29
Advanced Sass

Introduction

With Sass, you can write cleaner, better self-contained CSS than CSS itself supports. For example, creating a list in CSS requires separate sets of rules, but in Sass, you can nest all the relevant rules within a single section. In this chapter, we will examine the features that provide all this power to you.

For example, Sass offers superior support for sharing the CSS properties of one selector with other selectors by means of inheritance. This obviates the requirement to replicate sets of rules over and over because once you have a set of rules, you would like to use elsewhere; you can simply extend them with minimal typing.

What's more; you can also use a feature called mixins with which you can copy styles into a current style rule. As you will see, mixins are used to group CSS code that has to be reused, and they can accept parameters too.

Between these features, Sass takes CSS more in the direction of a programming language than ever. They allow simple and logical constructs that make understanding and debugging your CSS as easy as possible, as well as making your job faster and more enjoyable.

Structure

In this chapter, you will:

- Learn about how Sass allows you to nest sections of rules

- Understand the difference between inheritance and using mixins

- Be able to load in and use extensive additional features in Sass modules

- Learn more and keep up with Sass development

Objectives

The intention of this chapter is to fill the remaining gaps in your knowledge of Sass, such that by the time you have finished it, you will have assimilated all the main features and benefits of Sass. After reading this chapter, you will know where to get more information when you need it. On top of that, by completing reading this book, you will complete your HTML5 and CSS3 Masterclass.

Nesting in Sass

In the *Introduction,* the concept of nesting with lists was discussed. Let's now look into how that works by considering *Example 29.1*, a simple HTML5 document with some CSS and some HTML.

Example 29.1:

```
1.  <!DOCTYPE html>
2.  <html>
3.    <head>
4.      <title>Navigation List</title>
5.      <style>
6.        nav ul {
7.          margin        : 0;
8.          padding       : 0;
9.          list-style    : none;
10.       }
11.       nav li {
12.         display       : inline-block;
13.       }
```

```
14.      nav a {
15.        display        : block;
16.        padding        : 3px 8px;
17.        font-weight    : bold;
18.        text-decoration : none;
19.      }
20.      nav a:hover {
21.        text-decoration : underline;
22.      }
23.    </style>
24.  </head>
25.  <body>
26.    <nav>
27.      <ul>
28.        <li><a href='https://google.com'>Google</a></li>
29.        <li><a href='https://microsoft.com'>Microsoft</a></li>
30.        <li><a href='https://apple.com'>Apple</a></li>
31.        <li><a href='https://amazon.com'>Amazon</a></li>
32.      </ul>
33.    </nav>
34.  </body>
35. </html>
```

This example simply displays a navigation list of four items in a line, and when the mouse hovers over one, it becomes underlined to show that it's clickable. The CSS for this is between lines 7 and 22, and the HTML between lines 26 and 33.

As shown in *Figure 29.1*, the link to Apple is underlined due to the mouse hovering over it. (the browser has also displayed the link destination at the bottom-left for the user's convenience):

Figure 29.1: *A navigation list with one link highlighted by underlining*

But let's now see how much more self-contained we can make the CSS section using the Sass code in *Example 29.2*.

Example 29.2:

```
1.  nav {
2.    ul {
3.      margin           : 0;
4.      padding          : 0;
5.      list-style       : none;
6.      li {
7.        display          : inline-block;
8.        a {
9.          display          : block;
10.         padding          : 3px 8px;
11.         font-weight      : bold;
12.         text-decoration  : none;
13.       }
14.       a:hover {
15.         text-decoration  : underline;
16.       }
17.     }
18.   }
19. }
```

See how there is now just a single mention of the <nav> element right at the start, while all the elements within it in the HTML are now also within the Sass. This makes a lot of sense as it mirrors the way HTML is laid out in lines 26 to 33 of *Example 29.1*. In fact, even the nesting of the <a> elements within the <li> elements, all within a <nav> element is replicated here.

Of course, if you wanted to allow the sub elements within the <nav> element to be able to appear in any order at all (not just in the nesting order currently shown in *Example 29.1*), then you can just place them all a single nesting level down. The beauty of this approach is that it's entirely up to you, according to the result you desire.

Nested properties

Although this amount of nesting is very useful and easy to understand, Sass is even more powerful because it also takes nesting a stage further with nested properties. For example, consider all the **font-** and **text-** rules supported by CSS using different rule names. Well, take a look at the Sass in *Example 29.3*, and see how these rules can now all be nested, resulting in a clearly easier to follow layout than plain CSS.

Example 29.3:

```
1.  font: {
2.    family     : Courier New, monospace;
3.    size       : 16px;
4.    weight     : bold;
5.  }
6.
7.  text: {
8.    align      : justify;
9.    transform  : capitalize;
10.   indent     : 7px;
11.   overflow   : hidden;
12. }
```

Here, there are just two main sections: one for the **font** and one for the **text**, within each are the rule parts that would normally appear after a hyphen, but are just on their own.

Wherever there is a CSS rule type that is hyphenated, you can use nesting to lay your Sass out much more clearly and logically. And remember that with shorthand property names, when all the property values are of different kinds, this is easier than having to recollect the right order in which to place multiple values, such as the rule you may have learned of, *"When in doubt go clockwise."*

Inheritance in Sass

Do you find it irritating when writing CSS rules to keep going back and forth copying and pasting sets of rules that apply in more than one section? If so, then Sass has a great solution for you, which is the use of inheritance to allow classes to inherit properties from each other.

It works by means of the Sass **@extend** directive and is a powerful way to add clarity and simplicity to your CSS as shown in *Example 29.4*, in which a message display set of rules is being applied.

Example 29.4:

```
1.  .messagebox {
2.     border        : 2px dashed #000;
3.     border-radius : 10px;
4.     background    : #222;
5.     padding       : 10px;
6.     color         : #ddd;
7.  }
8.  .loggedin {
9.     @extend .messagebox;
10.    background    : darkgreen;
11.    color         : #dfd;
12. }
13. .notloggedin {
14.    @extend .messagebox;
15.    background    : dimgrey;
16.    color         : #dad;
17. }
18. .badlogin {
19.    @extend .messagebox;
20.    background    : darkred;
21.    color         : #fdd;
22. }
```

Firstly, a **messagebox** class was created starting at line 1. It has a two-pixel dashed border in black, curved corners, a background of very dark grey, and off-white color and some padding. Following this are three more classes (**loggedin**, **notloggedin**, and **badlogin**) that extend **messagebox** by changing the **background** and **color** properties, but keeping all other attributes as necessary.

Now let's see how this might be achieved in plain CSS, as shown in *Example 29.5*, in which multiple classes are given rules at the same time.

Example 29.5:

```
1.  .messagebox, .loggedin, .notloggedin, .badlogin {
2.    border         : 2px dashed #000;
3.    border-radius  : 10px;
4.    background     : #222;
5.    padding        : 10px;
6.    color          : #ddd;
7.  }
8.  .loggedin {
9.    background     : darkgreen;
10.   color          : #dfd;
11. }
12. .notloggedin {
13.   background     : dimgrey;
14.   color          : #dad;
15. }
16. .badlogin {
17.   background     : darkred;
18.   color          : #fdd;
19. }
```

See how on line 1, all the class names are supplied separated with commas. This makes all the rules within the curly braces apply to all the listed classes. Then, underneath the last three classes named are given their unique property values.

A problem with the CSS example is that it does not explicitly state within these classes that they have inherited values. This illustrates how Sass can be a better solution than CSS from the point of view of clarity because it uses a more logical approach by ensuring that each of the latter classes clearly tells you where they have inherited their other properties from.

From a programmer's point of view, CSS can be unclear, especially if the **messagebox** class is separated by some distance from the other classes. But the Sass is completely understandable at a glance, and is thus less prone to picking up styling errors, either by you, or by someone else who is tasked with maintaining your code.

This is where good styling and good programming practices converge to make life easier for everyone involved.

Using mixins

Having covered inheritance, we now need to examine mixins, which are similar, but have their own unique features. In programming terms, as we have seen, the use of **@extend** is to support inheritance, which means you extend the reference to get the exact same body.

On the other hand, using **@include** is like calling a function (whether with or without parameters), in a similar way to calling a JavaScript function.

In *Example 29.6*, a mixin named **fullres** is created to set the **width** and **height** properties of any object using it to **100%**. Underneath this, the **body** and **p** elements of the document are assigned these values by using **@include** to call the **fullres** mixin.

Example 29.6:

```
1. @mixin fullres {
2.    width  : 100%;
3.    height : 100%;
4. }
5. body {
6.    @include fullres;
7. }
8. p {
9.    @include fullres;
10.}
```

At this point, you may be asking how this is any better than using **@extend** to inherit property values. This is a good question which is best answered with *Example 29.7*, which also passes parameters.

Example 29.7:

```
1. @mixin fullres($w: 100%, $h: 100%) {
2.    width  : $w;
3.    height : $h;
4. }
5. body {
6.    @include fullres(960px);
7. }
```

```
8. p {
9.    @include fullres;
10. }
```

Now, the full power of mixins should become evident by examining line 1 of *Example 29.7*, where two variables called **$w** and **$h** (for width and height) are each given a value of **100%**. Then, below, on lines 2 and 3, these variable values are applied to the **width** and **height** properties.

The fun, though, is on line 6, where the mixin is called *and* passed a value of **960px**. This value is now passed to the **fullres** mixin where it overrides the default value given in its definition of **100%**. Therefore, the **$w** variable now has a value of **960px**, so the mixin returns a value of **960px** for the **width** property, and (because no second value was passed to the mixin) the default value of **100%** is returned for the **height** property. On line 9, **fullres** is called without any arguments, and so the default **100%** values are returned for that element's **width** and **height** properties.

Therefore, the general rule to follow is to use **@extend** to inherit a set group of properties from another function, and **@include** to call a mixin function that can be passed arguments, and which will return values to apply to properties.

Sass modules

As you might expect, Sass comes with a number of pre-built modules (seven to be precise) that you can call like mixins to achieve various results, covering areas from mathematics to color handling, and a great deal more.

Before using these modules, you need to know that before the module system was introduced all functions were globally available at all times, and any functions still have global aliases. For example, you can access **sass:math.$pi** globally.

However, the Sass team discourages such use because it is planning to deprecate this means of access in the future. Therefore, the recommended usage is to first apply the **@use** command to load in any modules you require, as follows:

```
@use "sass:math";
```

Now, you can access the features within **@use** modules as follows:

```
$twopi : calc(math.$pi * 2);
```

With that in mind, here's a list of available modules:

- **sass:math**: These are functions that operate on numbers.

- **sass:string**: These are functions to combine, search, or split apart strings.

- **sass:color**: This generates new colors based on existing ones.

- **sass:list**: This allows you to access and modify values in lists.

- **sass:map**: This looks up the values associated with a key in a map.

- **sass:selector**: This provides access to Sass's selector engine.

- **sass:meta**: This exposes the details of Sass's inner workings.

Detailing every single module and all the features available in each can fill up an entire book in itself, so at this point, it's time to refer you to the comprehensive documentation available from Sass at the following URL, where all the information you need is clearly explained:

tinyurl.com/sassmodules

Future versions

New versions of Sass are designed to be as backwards-compatible as possible, but sometimes a breaking change is necessary because of the need to keep up with the evolving CSS specification, plus old language design mistakes occasionally need to be fixed.

Before any breaking change is released, Sass implementations will produce deprecation warnings for stylesheets whose behavior will change. Whenever possible, these warnings include suggestions for how to update the deprecated styles to make them forward-compatible.

You should note that different implementations have different policies for breaking changes and deprecations. For example, Dart Sass will emit deprecation warnings for at least three months before releasing a breaking change and will release the breaking change with a new major version number unless that change is necessary for CSS compatibility.

CSS compatibility changes are generally both non-disruptive and time-sensitive, so they may be released with new minor version numbers instead.

What all this means is that because CSS is ever evolving, so is Sass, so once you start using it you are recommended to keep up to date with developments by following Sass on social media, checking their GitHub page, and regularly visiting the *sasslang.com* website to stay updated.

Conclusion

Well, that's it! You've made it to the end of a comprehensive and in-depth guide to using both HTML5 and CSS3 to their absolute best effect, and have now mastered all you need to put this new knowledge into any and all projects you are involved with.

Though you may not realize it, in this book, you have actually covered a great deal of ground, and well done to you for getting through it because now you know all about installing web servers and programming tools such as Visual Studio Code. You are fully acquainted with the developer console built into all modern browsers. You also now understand all the ins and outs of accessing, drawing on and writing to the HTML5 canvas, handling geolocation, advanced form handling, local storage, and other HTML5 goodies like audio and video.

On top of that, you have a thorough understanding of what CSS3 can do to help you make the best possible web sites, from background building techniques, using colors and opacity, adding text and font effects and more, all the way up to adding 2D and even 3D transformations and transitions. The latest enhancements to CSS3 such as Flexbox and CSS Grid will now be totally familiar tools to you as well. And to take your CSS even further, you are now able to access the extremely powerful Sass set of tools and features to improve the speed and accuracy of your layout designs.

You are now a master of all these tools and ready to put them into practice. Thanks so much for reading this book. If it has helped you on your web development and design journey, please leave an online review so others can learn of this book. Now, go out and build fantastic things!

Index

Symbols

2D transformations 342-344

  matrixes, using 353-355

  rotation 350-352

  scaling 348, 349

  skewing 351

  transitions 344-347

  translation 347

3D transformations 358-361

  3D space, working in 367-369

  back face visibility 372, 373

  cube, controlling 369, 370

  perspective, changing 363-365

  perspective, setting 361-363

  rotations 371

  scaling 370

  transform origin, changing 366, 367

  transform style, setting 365

  translation 370

@else if 435

@else...in 436, 437

@for...from...through 437, 438

@for...from...to 439, 440

@if...@else 433-435

@while 440, 441

A

advanced Sass

  future versions 452

  inheritance 447-449

  mixins, using 450, 451

  modules 451, 452

  nested properties 447

nesting 444-446

align-content property 389

align-items property 387, 404

Amazon Web Services (AWS) 2

Asynchronous JavaScript And XML
(AJAX) 1, 13

audio

using 60

B

backface-visibility property 372

background-clip property 268

using 271

background-origin property 268

JavaScript 275-277

using 271, 272

working, with background-clip
property 272-275

backgrounds

creating 267

background-size property 277-279

border-radius property 286

borders

building 285

colors 289, 290

gradient borders 290-292

multiple backgrounds, using 292-294

radius 286-288

single image, using for multiple
backgrounds 294-297

border types

creating 286-288

box shadow types

creating 300-302

box sizing 326-328

C

canvas

text displays, changing 96-98

text, writing 96

using, as source image 138, 139

canvas areas

clipping 115-118

canvas element 2

canvas examples 76-78

canvas manipulation 133

Cascading Style Sheet (CSS) 2, 6

class attribute 7

div element 7

id attribute 7

span element 6

stylesheets, using 8-10

codec 216, 217

CODECs 59

compositing 152, 153

containers 78

cross axis 384

cross document messaging 213

CSS

development 230

features 231

CSS2 2

CSS3 2

attribute selectors 231, 232

backgrounds 233, 234

borders 234-236

box shadows 237, 238

columns 238

CSS Grid 248-251

Flexbox layout 245-248

fonts 241-243

need for 10, 11

overflow 239, 240

text effects 241-243

transformations 244, 245

transitions 244, 245

CSS3 attribute selectors 253, 254

case-insensitive flag 263, 264

case-sensitive flag 264, 265

end selector 260, 261

global selector 262, 263

hyphen selector 258, 259

name selector 255

start selector 259, 260

value selector 256

word list selector 257, 258

CSS Grid 393-398

content justification 402-404

dimensions, changing 407-410

example 398, 399

example, using 399, 400

flow direction 401

gaps, setting 406

items, aligning 404-406

locations, changing 407-410

CSS variables 424-426

curved lines

arc, drawing to location 123, 124

attractors, using 125-127

capping 127-131

direction, selecting 119-122

drawing 118, 119

joining 127-131

custom image data

creating 150

cyan, magenta, and yellow (CMY) 317

D

Dancing Script 337

Dart Sass 413

DECoder 216

developer console 37

accessing 38-42

autocompletion 43-46

elements, inspecting 46, 47

features 43

using 168

Document Object Model (DOM) 152

drag and drop 213

E

element overflow 302-304

elements

resizing 332-334

enCOder 216

F

fills

applying 115

flex-basis property 392

Flexbox 375, 376

   content, aligning 389, 390

   content justification 385-387

   direction 383, 384

   example 380-382

   example, using 382, 383

   items, aligning 387, 388

   playground, creating 376-380

flex-direction property 383

flex-grow property 392

flex items

   wrapping 385

flex-shrink property 392

focus

   outlining 334, 335

G

gap property 391

geolocation 163

   availability, testing 165-167

   developer console, using 167, 168

   users, redirecting 169, 170

globalCompositeOperation property
     152

Global Positioning Satellite (GPS) 164

   alternatives 164, 165

gradient borders 290-292

gradients

   color stops 282

   conic gradient 283, 284

   diagonal gradient 282

   radial gradient 283

   repeating gradient 282, 283

   using 280, 281

grid-area property 407

H

HSL colors 320-323

HTML 3

HTML5 49, 50

   applications 58, 59

   audio 216

   audio, playing 217-220

   canvas 63

   canvas, converting, to image 71-73

   <canvas> element 50, 51

   forms 55, 56

   geolocation 52-55

   local storage 57

   microdata 58

   need for 10, 11

   semantic tags 58

   session storage 57

   web applications 59

   web workers 58, 59

HTML5 form attributes 178

   autocomplete attribute 180-182

   autofocus attribute 178-180

   color input type 194, 195

   <datalist> tag 187, 188

   date and time input types 190, 191

   formaction attribute 184

   form attribute 182, 183

   form overrides 185, 186

   list attribute 187

   max attribute 189, 190

min attribute 189, 190

multiple attribute 186

novalidate attribute 186

numbers 195-198

<option> tag 187, 188

pattern attribute 191, 192

placeholder attribute 192, 193

ranges 195-198

required attribute 193, 194

search input type 198

step attribute 189, 190

width and height attributes 186, 187

HTML5 video 220

codecs 221

playing 221-227

HTML tags 3-5

style attribute 5

tag attributes 5

hue, saturation, and luminance (HSL)
    317

Hyper Text Transfer Protocol (HTTP) 3

I

image

drawing with 134-136

parts, extracting 136, 137

shadows, attaching 139-141

IndexedDB 58

inheritance, in Sass 447-449

Internet Protocol (IP) address 165

J

JavaScript

code, in separate file 67-70

code, within <script> tags 64-67

crash course 64

getElementByID() function 70, 71

justify-content property 385, 402

L

LAMP 14

LibSass 413

lines

drawing with paths 110-115

Linux

MAMP installation, performing 24, 25

Sass, installing 419, 420

VS Code, installing 33, 34

local storage

accessing 200-202

local data, clearing 203, 204

local data, removing 203, 204

local data, retrieving 200-202

local data, storing 200-202

using 200

loop

using 155, 156

M

MacOS

MAMP installation, performing 20-22

Sass, installing 417-419

VS Code, installing 31-33

MAMP 14

MAMP, on Linux

document root, working with 25

installing 24, 25

MAMP, on MacOS
  document root, working with 22-24
  installing 20-22
MAMP, on Windows
  document root, working with 18, 19
  installing 14-17
MathML 62
Media Access Control (MAC)
      address 165
microdata 205-207
MIME types 211
mixins
  using, in Sass 450, 451
modules, in Sass 451, 452
multi column layout 304-310

N
named functions 173
nested properties, Sass 447
nesting in Sass 444-446

O
offline web apps
  working 211-213
opacity property 323
order property 391
outline-offset property 334, 335

P
paths
  lines, drawing with 110-115
perspective() function 363
perspective property 361
pixels, editing 142-145

color data, averaging 146, 147
color data, storing 145
data, looping through 145, 146
image data, processing 146
other effects 147-150
property values 152, 153

R
rectangles 78
  clearing 81, 82
  drawing 78
  drawing styles, applying 79, 80
  gradient fills, applying 82-84
  line width, changing 80, 81
  multicolored gradient fills 85-88
  pattern fills, using 88, 89
  radial gradient, applying 85
  translation, using 90-93
  variables, using 78, 79
RGBA colors 317-320
rgba() function 317
RGB color system 312, 313
  color band chart 314, 315
  color wheel, using 315-317
  HSL colors 320-323
rotate3d() function 371
Ruby Sass 413

S
Sass expressions 432
  @each...in 436, 437
  @else if 435, 436
  @for...from...through 437, 438

@for...from...to 439, 440

@if...@else 433-435

@while 440, 441

Sass Script 432

Sass variables 427

  default variable values 428, 429

  flow control 431

  global scope 430, 431

  scope 429, 430

Scalable Vector Graphics (SVG) 62

scale3d() function 370

scale() function 348

Search Engine Optimization (SEO) 58

Secure Sockets Layer (SSL) 200

session storage

  using 204

shadow

  adding 300

  attaching, to images 139-141

  attaching, to text and lines 141, 142

  box shadow types, creating 300-302

skew() function 351

source-in property 152

source-out property 152

source-over property 152

Syntactically Awesome Style Sheets
    (Sass) 412, 413. *See also* advanced
    Sass

  Dart Sass 413

  expressions 432

  installing, on Linux 419

  installing, on MacOS 417-419

  installing, on Windows 413-416

  LibSass 413

  Linux installers 420, 421

  operators 431, 432

  pre-processing, to CSS 421

  Ruby Sass 413

  Windows installers 416, 417

T

template literals 268-271

text

  aligning 98, 99

  filled text, writing 103-105

  pattern, for text fill 105, 106

  stroke width, changing 100-103

  writing 96

text overflow 328-330

text shadows 335, 336

transformations

  applying 157-159

  multiple transformations, applying
    161

  rotations, applying 160

  translations, applying 160, 161

translate3d() 370

translate property 348

transparency

  applying 323, 324

  using 157

U

user location

  named functions 173

  obtaining 170-172

permission, granting 173-175

V

variables
  in CSS 424-426
  in Sass 427
video
  using 60, 61
Visual Studio Code 27
  installing, on Linux 33, 34
  installing, on MacOS 31-33
  installing, on Windows 29-31
  significance 28
  working with 34-36

W

WAMP 14
Web Apps Working Group
  (WAWG) 58

web fonts 337-340
Web Logs (Blogs) 2
Web Platform Working Group
  (WPWG) 58
web workers 208
  offline web application 211
  using 208-211
Windows
  MAMP installation,
    performing 14-17
  Sass, installing 413-416
  VS Code, installing 29-31
words
  wrapping 330, 331
word-wrap property 330

X

XML 4